Preaching the Gospel of Mark

D0885790

Also available from Westminster John Knox Press

Keith F. Nickle, *Preaching the Gospel of Luke: Proclaiming God's Royal Rule*
Lamar Williamson Jr., *Preaching the Gospel of John: Proclaiming the Living Word*

Preaching the Gospel of Mark

Proclaiming the Power of God

Dawn Ottoni Wilhelm

Westminster John Knox Press
LOUISVILLE • LONDON

© 2008 Dawn Ottoni Wilhelm

All rights reserved. No part of this book may be reproduced or transmitted in any form or by any means, electronic or mechanical, including photocopying, recording, or by any information storage or retrieval system, without permission in writing from the publisher. For information, address Westminster John Knox Press, 100 Witherspoon Street, Louisville, Kentucky 40202-1396.

Scripture quotations, unless otherwise indicated, are from the New Revised Standard Version of the Bible, copyright © 1989 by the Division of Christian Education of the National Council of the Churches of Christ in the U.S.A., and used by permission.

Book design by Sharon Adams
Cover design by Kevin Darst & Jennifer K. Cox

First edition
Published by Westminster John Knox Press
Louisville, Kentucky

This book is printed on acid-free paper that meets the American National Standards Institute Z39.48 standard. ♾

PRINTED IN THE UNITED STATES OF AMERICA
08 09 10 11 12 13 14 15 16 17 — 10 9 8 7 6 5 4 3 2 1

Library of Congress Cataloging-in-Publication Data

Wilhelm, Dawn Ottoni.
    Preaching the Gospel of Mark : proclaiming the power of God / Dawn Ottoni Wilhelm. — 1st ed.
        p. cm.
    Includes bibliographical references.
    ISBN 978-0-664-22921-4 (alk. paper)
    1. Bible. N.T. Mark–Homiletical use.   2. Bible. N.T. Mark–Commentaries.   I. Title.

    BS2585.55.W55 2008
    226.3'07–dc22

                                                           2008001278

In memory of Donald H. Juel—
with thanks for his preaching and teaching
about the surprising power of God's grace

CONTENTS

INTRODUCTION

The power of God is on the loose in the world, and the Gospel of Mark proclaims this startling reality as the good news of Jesus Christ. Both history and current events teach us that power is exercised through any number of means. Economic resources, military might, political movements, and the dynamics of social change all exert their force and pressure in ways that call forth the best and worst of human intention and response. But the power of which Mark speaks is of another kind, from another source. Stripped of economic security and political clout, the power of Jesus Christ invades this world with the good news of God's gracious, just, and loving reign. From the dynamic opening chapter to the controversial closing chapter, Mark will not let us sit at ease as the Gospel urges our way to the cross—and beyond.

This is good news for all people. It is also difficult news for those of us who recognize the complexities of interpreting, discerning, relating, proclaiming, and engaging Scripture with the life of faith and the world at large. The goal of this commentary is to help preachers, teachers, pastors, and students of Scripture to faithfully interpret and engage Mark's Gospel as it proclaims the power of God's reign and urges the participation of all God's people in the witness of the gospel. Mark occupies a prominent place in the preaching cycle of the lectionary (Year B) and has gained widespread interest among biblical scholars over the past several decades. With power and purpose, the Gospel of Mark moves us through the events of Jesus' life, death, and resurrection, commanding our attention and provoking our response.

However, most of us read or hear the Gospel in brief fragments, a few verses at a time, with little appreciation for its larger narrative purposes, rhetorical ingenuity, plot development, myriad characters, layers of conflict, and the theological concerns that run throughout its account. Reading or hearing the entire Gospel in one sitting can help widen our perspective and enrich our encounter. Although most services of public worship today do not include lengthy Scripture readings, preachers and worship leaders may choose to follow lectionary readings that include a sequence of texts from Mark's Gospel over a period of several weeks, or they may preach through the Gospel of Mark over several months, offer a sermon series based on various themes or stories from the Gospel, or prepare dramatic readings and enactments of selected portions. In whatever way we encounter the Gospel of Mark, there are several theological, literary, and rhetorical emphases that should claim our attention.

THEOLOGICAL THEMES IN THE GOSPEL OF MARK

First and foremost, Mark's Gospel proclaims the power of God as the good news of Jesus Christ alive among us, intervening in human lives and events. More than personal morality or communal ethics, spiritual disciplines or best practices, the good news is that God has entered and transformed human reality through Jesus Christ. This transformation affects personal as well as social aspects of life. Jesus confronts poverty, illness, social boundaries, demons, individual sin, and institutional evil. As we read the Gospel of Mark, Jesus is the main character to whom all of the Gospel's key events and multiple characters relate. As we preach the Gospel of Mark, Jesus is the one whose words and deeds persuade us of God's just and loving purposes, calling forth a convictional response from all who have ears to hear.

At least three features dominate Mark's portrayal of Jesus Christ. First, the identity of Jesus is of great interest. He is introduced as "Jesus Christ, the Son of God" at the beginning of the Gospel (1:1), he discusses his identity with his closest followers in the very middle of the Gospel (8:27–9:1), and he admits to being the Messiah during his trial near the end of the Gospel (14:61–62). Ironically, it is demons and strangers who correctly identify him (e.g., 1:27; 1:38–39; 2:10; 3:23–27) while his closest followers do not understand or refuse to accept his ministry and messianic role (e.g., 8:31–33; 9:32; 10:35–40). Many ascriptions and titles reveal his role and relationship to God: Holy One of God, Son of David, Son of Man, teacher, and prophet (see **messianic titles and other designations for Jesus**). By the end of the Gospel, there is no doubt that Jesus is more than God's messenger: he is the Messiah who is authorized and empowered to transform illness to health, sin to forgiveness, death to life.

The second dominating feature in Mark's portrayal of Jesus is his encounter with the cross. Over one-half of the Gospel turns our attention to the cross as Jesus repeatedly foretells his rejection, suffering, crucifixion, and resurrection in chapters 8–10 and as the geography of Mark's account moves from Galilee to Jerusalem in chapters 11–16. Throughout these chapters, God's power moves decisively to subvert the powers of injustice, domination, terror, and death. The failure of the cross to pronounce the last word in the Gospel assures us that there is no cosmic, demonic, institutional, or personal source of evil that cannot be overcome by the power of God in Jesus Christ. After his resurrection Jesus does not seek retribution or revenge but sends word for his disciples to meet him in Galilee. The dramatic ending of Mark's Gospel urges us to follow him anew in his resurrected power.

His proclamation of God's reign is the third feature to dominate Mark's portrayal of Jesus. From the opening verses and Jesus' first "sermon" in 1:15, the good news is proclaimed as the nearness of God's kingdom. In all that he says and does, Jesus proclaims God's will to transform human reality, shatter false boundaries, exorcize demons, and heal the diseased.[1] All of his words and deeds are manifestations of God's intervention in human reality and call for our active participation in God's reign. The reign of God inaugurated by Jesus confronts both individual and social sins and ministers to both personal needs and institutional corruption. Throughout his kingdom proclamation, Jesus engages us in the power of God at work in the world: a power that refuses to control or crush others but is willing to risk rejection and suffering for the sake of drawing all people into God's just and loving reign.

In addition to Jesus' identity, cross, and proclamation of God's reign, the Gospel of Mark develops other themes that are of great interest to preachers and teachers. Discipleship is a major concern as the initial enthusiasm of Jesus' disciples turns to incomprehension and faithlessness. The invitation to discipleship, the empowerment of Jesus' followers, the risk of crossing boundaries and serving others, the certainty of suffering, and the promise of new life are all part of Mark's vision of discipleship. Related to discipleship is the new community of faith inaugurated by Jesus. Intended for Israel but extended to Gentiles, Jesus' vision of God's reign includes tax collectors and sinners (e.g., 2:16), the infirm and impure (e.g., 1:40–45; 5:25–34) and those who are less than fastidious in following various religious laws (e.g., 2:23–28; 7:1–23). Jesus' companionship with these persons bears testimony to the complex nature of life in Christian community according to Mark's Gospel.

Mark's account is also permeated with a sense of apocalyptic fervor, as the realities of Roman imperialism and religious provincialism conflict with God's reign. There is no doubt that Jesus' ministry challenged the values and practices of the most powerful institutions of his time. Conflicts with his family (3:20–22, 31–35), disciples (8:31–10:45) and various religious figures (2:1–3:6; 11:18–33) feature prominently in Mark's account, and Jesus' ultimate confrontations with the Sanhedrin and Roman officials culminate in his crucifixion (14:43–15:20). As religious interests play an ever increasing role in U.S. politics and international relations, Mark's Gospel calls us to consider anew Jesus' way of actively engaging others in God's just and loving reign. Mark challenges us to relate the gospel to movements of militarism, terrorism, religious fundamentalism, economic injustice, and racial prejudices and ethnic rivalries that threaten individual lives and social well-being today.

BACKGROUND TO THE GOSPEL OF MARK

Little is known about the author(s) of the second Gospel. Although the church through the centuries has identified Mark as the secretary or interpreter of Peter, this tradition has been widely questioned by recent scholarship. Any references to "Mark" must admit that we are speaking of the *implied author* of Mark—that is, "the sum total of the judgments and outlook that result from literary analysis rather than historical reconstruction."[2] Whoever this faithful and thoughtful writer may have been, there is no doubt that the Gospel of Mark was crafted with theological integrity, rhetorical purpose, and literary care as the author sought to address those who would continue the gospel's witness amid circumstances of great difficulty.

It is very likely that the Gospel of Mark was composed around the time of the Jewish-Roman war in 66–70 CE, making it the earliest of the canonical Gospels. In 66, the Jews led an insurrection against Roman rule in Jerusalem that spread to the surrounding regions. The Romans launched a counterattack but were initially repelled. They retaliated with a vicious, scorched-earth campaign that extended until the spring of 70 with the final assault on Jerusalem and the destruction of the Temple (reflected in Mark 13). Mark's interest in the crucifixion and resurrection of Jesus would be of particular interest to a community of faith struggling with persecution, disillusionment, and uncertainty as it endured great political and religious turmoil. The intra- and intercommunal tensions produced by the upheaval of the Jewish-Roman war were most keenly felt in Palestine, and it is likely that Mark's context was somewhere in the region of southern Syria or just north of Palestine. Also, the Gospel's many explanations of Jewish practices suggest that Mark wrote for a largely Gentile Christian community while drawing on Hebrew Scripture and interpretive traditions.

One of the outstanding features of Mark's Gospel is its distinct literary and rhetorical style. The church's ancient symbol for Mark, the lion, characterizes many of the Gospel's inherent qualities: it is powerful and imposing, a voice that heralds God's reign, a guardian of what is sacred, commanding and authoritative, swiftly moving yet purposeful, and surprisingly elegant in its design. With remarkable brevity and momentum, Mark addresses the ultimate realities of life in just sixteen chapters. The riveting pace and dramatic structure of the Gospel of Mark claim our attention and propel us ever onward. Mark's rhetorical strategy includes the frequent use of the words "immediately" (41 times) and "again" (25 times), which urge us to look forward and backward and draw us into extended and repeated reflection on the Gospel account. The dramatic ending of Mark (16:1–8) calls us to go in search of the resurrected Jesus Christ and to proclaim his power among us.

PREACHING AND TEACHING
THE GOSPEL OF MARK TODAY

In accordance with the Hebrew tradition to which it is indebted, the Gospel of Mark is intended for public presentation in worship, personal and corporate study, and interpretation by the community of faith. Although it includes biographical information, its purposes reach beyond the historical to inspire faith, provoke our response, and empower us to proclaim the good news to others in word and deed.

The commentary that follows lends itself to preaching and teaching about distinct portions of the text while honoring the larger narrative framework of Mark's account. Following a treatment of the announcement of the good news of God's power on the loose in the world (1:1–13), the following three sections reflect three major movements in the Gospel of Mark. Part 1 (1:14–8:21) focuses on God's power in Jesus Christ to preach, heal, and intervene in human lives for the well-being of all people. Part 2 (8:22–10:52) explores servanthood, discipleship, and Jesus' predictions of suffering, death, and resurrection while his followers continue to misunderstand his teaching. Part 3 (11:1–15:47) recounts God's power to confront and transform the powers of evil and death through the cross of Jesus Christ. Finally, Mark's ending opens the way for us to continue the proclamation of the gospel (16:1–8). Texts included in the Revised Common Lectionary (RCL) are noted throughout, and quotations are from the New Revised Standard Version. A glossary is provided to expand on key words and concepts found in Mark's Gospel (cited in bold throughout this volume). Finally, a select bibliography suggests additional resources for the reader to consult.

However, it must be noted that textual resources are never enough to help us understand, interpret, and proclaim Scripture anew. Having been nurtured within the Anabaptist-Pietist tradition (Church of the Brethren), my own life of faith has taught me the joyful necessity of listening and attending to the Spirit's leading among the gathered community of faith. After twelve years of pastoral ministry and eight years of teaching homiletics, I have come to believe that preaching opens the way for individuals and communities to hear the transforming power of the gospel and to engage one another in following Christ's way. The goal of preaching is not the interpretation of right beliefs or right behaviors but a transformed people with whom the Spirit effects the transformation of the world.[3] For this reason, I happily confess my indebtedness to many people who have accompanied me in faith and without whose help this volume would not have been possible. In addition to the resources noted in the bibliography and many teachers of Scripture and homiletics who have inspired and instructed me along the way, I am particularly thankful to Barbara K. Lundblad and the members of a small-group Bible study who met with me during the preparation of this book and whose voices are noted throughout: Carrie Eikler, Torin Eikler, Nan Erbaugh, Amy Gall Ritchie, Isaac Ottoni Wilhelm, Mark Ottoni Wilhelm, and Richard Gardner, biblical studies professor emeritus at Bethany Theological Seminary. Their faithful insights, thoughtful exchanges, searching questions, and playful wisdom permeate this commentary. I trust they will forgive any errors they discover in these pages, since I claim these as my own. A sabbatical leave from Bethany Theological Seminary and several weeks' sojourn as scholar-in-residence at the Cathedral College of Washington National Cathedral enabled me to complete this project. As always, I am grateful for insightful conversations and endless encouragement from my spouse, Mark, and our three children, Isaac, Sophie, and Aidan.

May this resource help you to preach the Gospel of Mark anew as you participate in God's transforming power for the church and world.

Opening the Gospel

The Power of God
on the Loose in the World

Mark 1:1–13

The opening verses of Mark's Gospel waste no time telling us who Jesus is and what he is about. The long-awaited Messiah, the beloved Son of God, is empowered to overcome the forces of evil and proclaim the reign of God. There is no lengthy genealogy as we find in Matthew's first chapter, no extensive birth narratives or angelic announcements such as Luke provides, and none of John's theopoetics. Instead, Mark sets us on a path into the wilderness alongside John the Baptist and Jesus. From the outset, Mark reveals the dangers involved in gospel living and the Spirit's presence to empower us along the way.

Several key themes emerge in the first thirteen verses of the opening chapter: Jesus is clearly named as "**Christ,** the **Son of God,**" and John's announcement of one coming who is more powerful than he anticipates Jesus' messianic activities and ministry in subsequent chapters. Mark mentions the Spirit of God three times in thirteen verses, and when the heavens are torn asunder and the Spirit enters at Jesus' baptism, we know that God's presence and **power** are on the loose in the world as never before. Finally, the vitality of **proclamation** is underscored in the opening of Mark's Gospel as prophetic voices witness to God's way among us and John's prophetic utterance heralds the beginning of Jesus' own preaching ministry.

The importance of these opening verses is further underscored by their recurring presence in the lectionary. In particular, on three separate occasions the opening verses of the Gospel of Mark are divided in three different ways: the second Sunday of Advent features verses 1–8, the First Sunday of Epiphany includes verses 4–11 and encompasses both John's baptismal ministry and Jesus' baptism, and the First Sunday of Lent draws on verses 9–15. To be sure, there are credible reasons to divide the text in these different ways. However, preachers and teachers must be aware of what is omitted as well as what is offered by each Gospel reading so that

3

the fullness of the message is appreciated in each context and occasion. For example, it is entirely fitting during services of baptism that John's call to baptism and Jesus' experience of baptism are recounted in worship (vv. 4–11). However, the relationship of Jesus' baptism to the Spirit's urging him into the wilderness (vv. 12–13) is also profoundly important as it relates to John's wilderness proclamation and the wilderness experiences of subsequent believers.

There are several reasons to consider 1:1–13 as a coherent unit.[1] First, these verses take place entirely in the wilderness, conjuring up images of the exodus and diaspora. We may associate the wilderness with experiences of welcome solitude (as Jesus sought in v. 35 and monastics have practiced throughout history) or hostile testing (as Jesus experienced in his encounter with Satan and the wild beasts in vv. 12–13 and as homeless teens face on the streets of our cities every day). Whether divine or demonic forces pull us into strange places where faith is forged anew, verses 1–13 certainly portray events that are concentrated in the wilderness, whereas verse 14 turns our attention to Galilee as Jesus begins his movement into public ministry.

Second, the Holy Spirit serves as a significant character whose presence is singled out and named three times in verses 1–13. Although the Spirit is surely active throughout Jesus' ministry, attention is given at the beginning of Mark's Gospel to the Spirit of God, whose presence and power is formative for the whole of Jesus' ministry. John tells us that Jesus will baptize with the Holy Spirit (v. 8), and the Spirit formally enters the Gospel at the time of Jesus' baptism (v. 10) and then drives Jesus into the wilderness, where he is tempted by Satan and cared for by angels (v. 12). As divine agent, the Spirit also represents divine presence and divine empowerment for Jesus and his followers.

Finally, a dramatic shift takes place in verse 14 when Jesus begins his public ministry of proclaiming the reign of God. Following his experiences of baptism and testing, these words mark the beginning of Jesus' ministry with and for others.

ANNOUNCEMENT OF THE GOOD NEWS AND THE MINISTRY OF JOHN (1:1–8)

Exploring the text

The Gospel of Mark begins as abruptly as it ends. With just nine words (five in Greek) the brief superscript in verse 1 announces the beginning of the gospel, names Jesus as Christ, and provides us with the title and heading of Mark's book. Mark privileges the hearers and readers of this text with "insider information" so that, unlike the disciples and other contemporaries of Jesus, we may understand from the outset that Jesus is the **Messiah**.

Nevertheless, several questions arise in light of this dramatic opening verse. First, what kind of beginning is Mark offering to us, and to what does the word "beginning" refer? Is Mark offering us the beginning of a new book, the beginning of Jesus' ministry, or the beginning of a movement that extends beyond the written page and into human history? The latter possibility points us beyond Mark's narrative and the fearful silence of the disciples at the empty tomb to participate in the church's ongoing proclamation of the gospel.

Second, "**gospel**" is an ancient term associated with the announcement of military victory on the battlefield or the ascension of a new political ruler. Why would Mark use a military and political term to begin the story of Jesus Christ, who neither wields the sword nor imposes imperial control? Is he being ironic? Or is Mark somehow suggesting that our understanding of power, success, and political authority is in need of radical transformation as we consider the good news of Jesus Christ and the reign of God he inaugurates? Further tension arises when we ask ourselves what is "good" about Jesus' tragic death on the cross. It is only in light of his suffering and death that we may recognize God's resurrection **power** alive in the world, a power that cannot be overcome by death or the forces of evil that threaten all of creation. Further ambiguity arises since we do not know if the good news is *about Jesus Christ* (objective genitive) or if it is the good news that *Jesus Christ himself announces* (subjective genitive). It is entirely possible that Mark intends both meanings, as the gospel seeks to proclaim the fullness of God in Jesus Christ as well as the good news of God's reign enacted and proclaimed by him. Since Mark is the only Gospel to refer to itself as such, there can be no doubt that the reference is both intentional and ripe with meaning.

Finally, it is important to note that Mark chooses to disclose Jesus' messianic identity from the very first verse. This is all the more remarkable because later in the Gospel Jesus silences those who would proclaim his identity to others. Hearers and readers of Mark's account are privileged to know Jesus is the Messiah (or anointed one) and **Son of God**.[1] The title "Messiah" is given at two other crucial points in the Gospel: when Peter responds to Jesus' question in 8:29 and when the high priest questions Jesus in 14:61. As the unfolding drama of the Gospel reveals, to know something is not necessarily to understand it; we need more than a little time to understand what Jesus' messianic mission means and where it leads. Mark gives us sixteen chapters to begin our encounter with Jesus Christ and to guide us along the journey of discipleship and faith.

In verses 2–3, Mark proclaims God's voice through Hebrew prophets. We hear allusions to three ancient sources as the Gospel offers new hope and guidance to God's people: Malachi 3:1 refers to God's messenger and issues a warning of God's imminent judgment against evildoers in the Temple; Exodus 23:20 recalls the divine messenger who guides and guards Israel through the wilderness; and Isaiah 40:3 is heard as the divine messenger cries out in the wilderness to prepare the way of God. Weaving the three texts together, Mark provides subtle references to both Temple and wilderness settings, locations that are in constant tension throughout Mark's account.

Mark also underscores the importance of God's messenger who comes to prepare the way of God among us. John abruptly appears on the page just as he does in the wilderness and with as much dramatic presence as these few verses can muster. Although we will hear more of him later (1:14; 6:14–29), John's role at this point is to proclaim "a baptism of repentance for the forgiveness of sins" and, in the spirit of Elijah, to call God's people to readiness. Like the prophets before him, John wears a rough garment of camel's hair (Zech. 13:4) and a leather belt (2 Kgs. 1:8), and his diet includes items found in the wilderness (locusts and wild honey). John's prophetic mandate demands turning away from sin even as he points to the imminent arrival of one more powerful than he. In contrast to the other Gospels, Mark does not portray John as announcing judgment or condemnation. Instead, he focuses our attention on Jesus Christ.

To be sure, John and Jesus share much in common: both men proclaim God's words to others, both are accused of sedition, and both suffer death as a consequence of their faithful witness. However, these verses announce that Jesus is superior to John for three reasons: he is more powerful than John, more worthy of honor, and his baptism includes the Holy Spirit (1:7–8). Although both John and Jesus bear witness to God's intervention in the world and convey a sense of apocalyptic passion in their preaching,[2] John's ministry focuses on a verbal call to repentance (or "turning around"), baptism, and confession of sins, whereas Jesus' proclamation includes not only the announcement of God's reign but acts of healing, exorcism, confrontation, and teaching moments that reveal the power of God's reign at work among us (see overview of 1:14–45). John's strength is his charismatic preaching, to which people from Jerusalem and all of Judea are powerfully attracted, but Jesus' power is that of God's own Spirit, who moves with him throughout his ministry, blessing and engaging others in God's just and gracious rule.

In contrast to the cultic center of Jerusalem with its system of ritual purification and sacrifices overseen by priestly authorities, the wilderness is where both men begin their ministries, a place of divine support as well as satanic testing. According to Mark, John draws people from the Judean countryside and the city of Jerusalem and offers God's forgiveness without the need for Temple sacrifices or the religious hierarchy of Jerusalem.[3] Whereas Luke focuses on Jerusalem as the holy city to which the disciples return following Jesus' resurrection, according to Mark, Jerusalem is the place where Jesus is tried and crucified. The Gospel of Mark ends with a call to Galilee (16:7), where Jesus has promised to meet his disciples after the resurrection (14:28). The fact that people come in droves to the wilderness suggests that John has continued Elijah's work of announcing Christ's coming. Much is wild and untamed in these verses: not only is the wilderness referred to four times in 1:2–13, but John himself is a wild man who refuses to be domesticated by religious rules or cultic practices, and the beasts Jesus encounters are wild animals who threaten his well-being. In other words, all that is wild in these verses is not necessarily evil but is certainly threatening. The powers of both life and death are at work among those who risk the journey of faith that leads to unknown territory.

Preaching and teaching the Word

There are many ways to approach the preaching and teaching of this multifaceted text.

1. Metaphorical. References to the wilderness abound in these verses. For ancient Israel, the wilderness was a place of freedom as well as political exile, preparation as well as temptation, transformation as well as testing. John's call to the wilderness represents a call to the margins, to places of exile and strange landscapes we would otherwise refuse to inhabit. It is a call to more honestly encounter ourselves in relationship to God and to confess the ways we have sinned and violated God's just and loving intentions for humanity.

At times, the wilderness is a chosen place of rest and reflection, a welcome respite from the clamor of all that claims our allegiance and attention. At other times, the wilderness may come upon us as an unexpected experience that arises when we move through transitional and life-changing events such as leaving home, giving birth, or committing ourselves to some new form of ministry. At yet other times, the wilderness is forced upon us as we flee danger and face the trauma of displacement as refugees. Indeed, for many people the wilderness is experienced as a cruel reality imposed from the outside when racial prejudices, ethnic rivalries, natural disasters, or political, economic, or religious forces displace people from their homes or prevent them from earning their livelihood. The prophetic voice crying out in the wilderness compels us to remember that the journey of faith often takes us beyond the careful and comfortable boundaries we have created for ourselves, our neighborhoods, and our nation so that we may participate in God's transforming work among us.

2. *Seasonal.* These verses arise at two key points in Year B of the RCL, and the context of each Sunday suggests vital ways of highlighting John's preaching and baptismal ministry. During the season of Advent, this passage speaks powerfully of John's role in preparing the way of God among us, calling us to remember God's past words and deeds recounted in the prophets and to look forward to the Messiah's coming. This season "in between" is a time of recollection and anticipation as we remember our lives in light of the prophetic witness of God's activity among us and anticipate the fullness of God's reign yet to come. John's call to repentance challenges us to live our lives according to God's larger purposes. During the First Sunday of Epiphany, this reading is combined with the story of Jesus' baptism (1:9–11). For John, baptism is associated with repentance, forgiveness, and cleansing from sin, and it is important to note that Jewish religious practices during his lifetime included immersion as a means of ritual purification.[4] For Jesus, baptism is associated with the Holy Spirit, whose coming was promised through the prophets (Isa. 44:3; Ezek. 39:29; Joel 3:1–2). It becomes an occasion for marking his identity (his epiphany/manifestation) as God's beloved son.

3. *Liturgical/sacramental.* This text not only lends itself well to occasions of baptism, but it also challenges our ideas about this vital practice. For example, although repentance, forgiveness, and confession are all associated with the baptism John proclaims, it is not altogether clear whether confession is a condition or consequence of water baptism in the context of Mark 1 (see v. 5 in particular). However, the reality of human sin and divine forgiveness dominates these verses as John urges all people to turn anew and seek God's way. Mark's Gospel offers compelling reasons to consider our faith ever anew. Whether our baptism as infants is entrusted to the memory of others, or we remember our adult baptism ourselves, or we hear John calling us to baptism at some future time, the way of the Lord that John proclaims urges us to move forward in faith.

4. *Theological/topical.* What is the "good news" spoken of in 1:1, and how does this relate to John's prophetic ministry? Verses 2–8 present John as a prophet who acts as a catalyst for change, but it also highlights his role in pointing people toward Christ. John's prophetic ministry is more than a call to repentance and something other than righteous indignation: the prophet speaks *for* God's reign as surely as the prophet speaks *against* sin and all that violates God's just and loving intentions among us. As preachers and teachers of the gospel, what do we speak against and what do we point toward in the prophetic witness of our faith today?

Related to questions about prophetic ministry, what kind of power is John speaking of in verse 7, and in what ways is Jesus stronger than John? According to Mark, Jesus' power is connected with the Spirit, who is visibly present at the time of his baptism, drives him into the wilderness, and enables him to battle demonic forces (3:22–30). The prophet Isaiah also speaks of the Spirit of God, who empowers the people of Israel and speaks with God's own authority (48:16; 61:1; 63:11). Consistent with God's Spirit, Jesus does not use power to coerce, manipulate, or control other people. Instead, divine power is given across religious and national boundaries to restore people to health and to renew life in community. The "principalities and powers" against which Jesus battles include economic, physical, spiritual, political, social, and institutional forces in need of God's transformation.[5] Beyond our own goodwill and hard work, the Spirit of God is the source of both individual and institutional transformation—and the power of the Holy Spirit is available to us through the baptism we share in Jesus Christ.

THE BAPTISM OF JESUS AND THE SPIRIT'S POWER (1:9–11)

Exploring the text

The baptism of Jesus follows closely after the baptism of countless others by John in the Jordan River. Jesus travels to the wilderness from his hometown in Galilee, and just as others are baptized in expectation of God's saving intervention and in preparation for the Holy Spirit, Jesus also participates in the ritual of baptism, as it opens the way for God's blessing and the Spirit's empowerment. However, Jesus' baptism is different from that of others; most notably, he makes no confession of sin. Also Mark does not mention John's message of repentance in the description of Jesus' baptism. His experience is cast in more intimate terms, as Mark relates the event from Jesus' perspective: the heavens are torn apart, the Spirit descends in the form of a dove, and a heavenly voice declares that he is the Son of God—events that parallel Jesus' death when he breathes out his spirit, the curtain of the Temple is torn apart, and the centurion declares that Jesus is God's Son (15:37–39). We do not know if John or any other witnesses were privy to these revelations, but Jesus and the hearers of Mark's Gospel certainly are.

If Jesus did not need to submit to a baptism of repentance for the forgiveness of sins as others do, what does his baptism represent? At least two meanings are suggested by Mark's account. First, on the occasion of his baptism Jesus is named the **Son of God** and is identified with the Spirit of God. The heavens are torn apart, the Spirit descends, and God's voice is heard speaking directly to Jesus: "You are my Son, the Beloved; with you I am well pleased." These last words are drawn from Isaiah 42:1, which anticipates the coming Messiah who will enact God's justice for all people. The dramatic tearing of the heavens in Mark 1:10 also recalls Isaiah's longing for the coming of the Holy Spirit (63:11) as the prophet prays that God will tear open the heavens to make known God's name and power among all people (64:1). Matthew and Luke report the heavens being *opened* at the time of Jesus' baptism, but Mark uses the word *schizō* (to tear or rip apart) to suggest that something much more dramatic is taking place. According to Juel, "the image may suggest that the protecting barriers are gone and that God, unwilling to be confined to sacred spaces, is on the loose in our realm."[1] A new dynamic is at work: "What is opened may be closed; what is torn apart cannot easily return to its former state."[2] Jesus' baptism not only identifies him as God's beloved Son but also associates his person and identity with the Spirit's unstoppable power. We now have access to God, but this is a God we cannot tame or control. The intrusion of God's Spirit at the time of Jesus' baptism alerts us to the wonderful and fearful prospect of God's **power** alive among us.

Second, Jesus' baptism reveals not only his divinity but also his humanity and identifies him alongside sinners and all others who are on the margins and outskirts of society. Without explanation, he submits to a baptism of repentance for the forgiveness of sins and demonstrates his radical identification with all people who struggle and yearn for the fullness of God's just and loving reign. Although John announced the coming of one more powerful than he who would baptize with the Holy Spirit, Jesus does not arrive on the scene as a conquering hero, mighty warrior, or member of the religious elite who baptizes others with ritual ceremony. His first appearance in the Gospel is not in Jerusalem, the great city of David, but in the wilderness where sinners and outcasts have come to confess their sins and receive divine forgiveness. Jesus' baptism represents a scandal of the greatest possible magnitude. God crosses the impenetrable boundary between divine and human realms and acts as one who identifies fully with human sin, life, and longing. Jesus' coming shatters our assumptions and confounds our sense of what is expected. His baptism not only identifies him as God's Son but also empowers him for ministry to all people.

This passage also reveals God as divine parent, beloved son, and active spirit. Although Mark in no way outlines a formulaic understanding of God's nature (and does not name God as Father, Son, and Holy Spirit), the opening of the Gospel intimates a full expression of God's being that draws on feminine (divine voice and dove), masculine (son) and neuter (spirit) expressions of God's presence and power. Other details and images draw

our attention. With the tearing of the heavens, the Spirit appears as a dove–
a familiar apocalyptic symbol that recalls the Spirit's brooding over the
waters of chaos (Gen. 1), its peaceful mission in the aftermath of the flood
(Gen. 8), and the newness of life promised by these events.[3] God's voice
speaks directly to Jesus (see also 9:7) even as it echoes words from Hebrew
Scripture to bless and name him (Ps. 2:7; Isa. 42:1).

Preaching and teaching the Word

Mark's rich and detailed description of Jesus' baptism highlights important facets of Christian baptism for his followers today.

Christian identity and the scandal of baptism. Jesus' baptism identifies him
as God's Son and each of us as God's children. All who come in search of
forgiveness and a new way of life gather at the water's edge, where we are
named as God's beloved children. Although identity thieves may steal our
credit cards and damage our financial ratings, no one can remove the name
given to us at baptism. As a sign of grace, we share this rite with others and
happily join them in following his way and will. But there is something
strange here also, something terrifying and scandalous. The tearing of the
heavens and the coming of God's Spirit at Jesus' baptism also mean that
God's power is on the loose in the world as never before. As we rise from
the baptismal waters, we not only hear God's blessing but also the Spirit's
urging us into the wilderness and other dangerous places just as Jesus himself was called out of the water to confront the powers of Satan (see comments on 1:12–13). We belong to a strange family whose members are
willing to go to difficult and demanding places. By the power of Christ's
Spirit, we participate in God's just and loving reign, wherever it may lead.

Baptism and newness of life. One member of our Markan Bible study
noted that birthing images abound in these few verses, as the heavens are
torn open and new life arrives in the presence and power of God's Spirit.[4]
As a woman giving birth experiences the power of her contractions and
labor, the Spirit moves intentionally among us to guide our way; as water
breaks and the final stages of birth commence, newly baptized members
of the body of Christ arise from the baptismal waters in newness of life;
as danger threatens to overwhelm a mother with pain, the tearing of her
body, and the possibility of death during delivery, heaven itself is torn
open, and the Spirit urges us forward to unknown places. Most poignant
of all, once the journey of new birth begins, there is no turning back; the
unstoppable power of God insists on its way, surprising us with beauty,
confounding our expectations, and confronting our worst enemies with
the good news of God's love for all people. Birth is never easy. But the
power of new life and the possibility of participating in God's new creation propel us to whatever wild calling God would have us pursue.

The blessing of baptism. Baptism offers us the grace of Christian blessing: we receive God's blessing and the blessings of others as we participate in the mystery of God's mercy and grace. In a world that too often ignores the power of blessing and the need for words and gestures that convey the grace of God for all humanity, baptism offers the opportunity for God's people to participate in divine blessing and the mystery of new life. In my own Anabaptist tradition, it is common for members of a congregation to name aloud the gifts of a newly baptized member, to express their support, and to share stories of their own baptism and the surprising ways God has guided their lives. In Marilynne Robinson's Pulitzer Prize–winning novel, *Gilead*, the Reverend John Ames describes his childhood experience of baptizing cats and wonders what was meant by this tender gesture: "For years we would wonder what, from a cosmic viewpoint, we had done to them. It still seems to me to be a real question. There is a reality in blessing, which I take baptism to be, primarily. It doesn't enhance sacredness, but it acknowledges it, and there is a power in that. I have felt it pass through me, so to speak."[5] One of baptism's greatest gifts to us can be this opportunity for blessing one another as God in Christ blesses us.

Baptism and the ongoing experience of Christian discipleship. In the RCL, the story of Jesus' baptism is presented in two ways, both of which press us to consider something more than a private experience of divine grace. During the First Sunday of Epiphany, 1:4–11 includes both John's baptismal ministry and Jesus' decision to be baptized by John so that Jesus is seen to identify himself and his ministry with sinners who seek forgiveness and reconciliation with God. During the First Sunday of Lent, 1:9–15 places Jesus' baptism as the prelude to his testing in the wilderness and subsequent public ministry. In this context, Jesus' baptism points us beyond the safety of private experience to the dangerous consequences and vitality of our public witness of faith. Either way, these verses urge us to consider baptism not as the culmination of religious experience but as an initiation into Christian discipleship, or in imitation of Jesus' life, undertaken with faith and hope.

JESUS' TEMPTATION AND CONFRONTATION WITH THE POWER OF SATAN (1:12–13)

Exploring the text

With barely a moment to catch his breath, Jesus emerges from the baptismal waters and is swept into the wilderness by the Spirit of God. Mark links this episode as closely as possible to Jesus' baptismal experience by the use of the word "and" at the beginning of verse 12, through continued references to the wilderness and God's Spirit, and in telling us that Jesus is driven "immediately" from the Jordan to a confrontation with Satan. Jesus' wilderness experience is empowered by his baptism and is also the necessary prelude to his public witness of God's reign.

Several details are worth noting. First, Mark speaks of the Spirit driving (*ekballei*) Jesus into the wilderness, and the same verb is used repeatedly in the Gospel to describe Jesus' expulsion of demons throughout his ministry. Although his enemies accuse Jesus of demon possession in 3:22, Mark is clear from the outset that Jesus is not possessed by Satan but by the Holy Spirit, who compels him into the wilderness and empowers him to overcome the forces of evil and destruction. Second, the whole of Mark's opening (1:1–13) underscores the importance of the wilderness. Jesus' forty days recalls Israel's period of wandering in the wilderness as well as Moses' forty days at Sinai (Exod. 34:28) and Elijah's travels to Horeb over a forty-day period (1 Kgs. 19:8). During this time, Jesus encounters curious creatures reminiscent of Israel's earlier experiences (Isa. 13:21–22; Ps. 22:12–21; Ezek. 34:5, 8; Dan. 7:1–8). In contrast, the angels serve (*diēkonoun*) Jesus and offer him sustenance and support (cf. 1:31 when Peter's mother-in-law serves Jesus, *diēkonei*).

Finally, in contrast to Matthew and Luke, Mark does not tell us the details of Jesus' wilderness experience. Instead, this brief account alerts us to the dramatic and cosmic nature of his ordeal as Christ overcomes the power of Satan. According to Mark, Jesus' role as blessed Son of God does not exempt him from the battle against demonic powers but pushes him toward a confrontation with evil. He emerges from the wilderness to begin his public ministry and drive out the forces of evil as he extends God's reign to all people and places. This event, like the whole of Mark's opening, declares Jesus' sovereignty and proclaims his power.

Preaching and teaching the Word

The story of his encounter with Satan tells us something of vital importance about Jesus and our own journey of baptismal faith.

Jesus Christ is empowered by God's Spirit to overcome the forces of death and destruction. Ours is a God who knows and understands the trials of humanity, who engages and resists evil in its many guises, and who persists and overcomes the **power** of death with the power of life. This strange and dramatic story of Jesus' confrontation with Satan in the wilderness assures us of God's ultimate sovereignty and power.

In fact, the first thirteen verses of Mark's Gospel cast the whole of Jesus' life and ministry in an **apocalyptic** framework, with verses 12 and

13 focusing on the cosmic struggle between God's rule and that of Satan. Before politely dismissing such apocalyptic imagery, we would do well to remember that our North American culture thrives on images of cosmic battles such as those waged in *Star Wars* and *The Lord of the Rings*. The difference between these epic dramas and Jesus' own confrontation with evil is that Jesus never wields the sword or advocates violence; instead, he proclaims the reign of God in word and deed and effects the transformation of the world through the Spirit's power to heal, forgive sins, confront evil, and overcome the forces of death. Jesus' battle with Satan in the wilderness is the first of many encounters with evil and shows us that the Son of God is empowered by the Holy Spirit to move into the most difficult and demanding situations in order to overcome evil. From the wilderness to the seashore and every town he inhabits, Jesus refuses to control or coerce others to obey God's commands but issues a call to participate in God's reign.

Baptismal faith urges us to unexpected and difficult places. Jesus' wilderness experience reminds us that times of trial are inextricably related to the life of faith as the Spirit of God guides us to unforeseen places. The call to the wilderness may be experienced as a sharp push or a gentle leading; it may come through the Spirit's whisper or a neighbor's need. Wilderness places are also somewhat surprising in terms of their landscape: they may be as near as our local neighborhood and downtown district, or as far as natural disasters and international crises that call for humanitarian response. An example of witnessing in the wilderness is the ministry of Christian Peacemaker Teams, who travel to volatile areas of the world in order to intercede in situations of severe conflict and work for peace and reconciliation between enemies.[1] In witnessing to Christ's way of nonviolent response in contexts of heightened tension and violence, Christian Peacemakers practice their motto of "Getting in the Way" as they engage others in nonviolent ministries of reconciliation, often at great personal risk to themselves. Their example can inspire others to follow the Spirit's urging to enter any number of wilderness settings in need of Christ's presence and the Spirit's power.

PART ONE

Jesus Christ Proclaims the Power of God

1:14–8:21

Preliminary Remarks

J esus Christ has come to proclaim the fullness of **God's reign**, and the **power** of God is suddenly alive among us as never before. Although the cross looms large in Mark's account, so does Jesus' extraordinary embodiment of God's presence and power in the world. In the first half of the Gospel, he preaches and teaches, drives out demons, heals various diseases, confounds religious authorities, feeds multitudes, and commands the forces of nature. These first eight chapters recount his witness first among Jews but also Gentiles, men and women, leaders and followers, and many who are attracted and others who are appalled by his ministry. God is actively engaged in combating evil through Jesus Christ. All that Jesus says and does urges us to recognize and respond to God's impending reign.

But what does it mean for us to proclaim God's power and participate in God's reign today? Each of the first eight chapters of Mark's Gospel relates something of the purpose and power of God in Jesus Christ, and through his ministry we can begin to understand what God's reign means for our lives and the world we love.

Proclaiming the Powerful
Reign of God

Mark 1:14–45

Following his baptism and encounter with Satan in the wilderness, Jesus begins his public ministry in Galilee by proclaiming God's reign and enacting God's **power**. These verses not only introduce us to his ministry but also offer a preview of upcoming events. Jesus proclaims the **good news** through preaching, teaching, exorcism, healing, and interacting with persons who are considered unclean and outside the realm of religious acceptability–activities that characterize Jesus' mission throughout Mark's narrative. During the Third through Sixth Sundays of Epiphany in Year B, these verses appear in sequence as they communicate the new manifestation of God's reign in Jesus Christ.

However, in the first chapter of Mark's Gospel, Jesus does more than enact God's loving intentions for humanity: Jesus' words and deeds **proclaim** his role as Messiah. According to Mark, Jesus Christ is empowered by God to overcome evil, and he alone has authority to establish **God's reign**. A sense of **apocalyptic** urgency begins with the inauguration of his public ministry in verses 14–15 when Jesus announces the fullness of time and the arrival of God's reign. As the Gospel of Mark unfolds, all of Jesus' words and deeds reveal his identity as **Messiah**, proclaiming God's power in the world and opening the way for others to participate in God's reign.

But let preachers and teachers beware: words are not enough to proclaim the reign of God revealed in Jesus Christ. If his witness is normative for our own lives and ministries, then we need to consider carefully how Jesus proclaims God's way in the world through both words and deeds so that the gospel we proclaim is more than good advice, churchly admonition, or clever biblical exegesis. The dominance of the word *kērussō* (translated as both "preach" and "proclaim") in this chapter serves as a reference point for all that Jesus says and does, with various forms of the verb appearing six times in the first chapter of Mark and twelve throughout the entire Gospel.[1] The Gospel affirms a larger understanding of Jesus' proclamation. It encompasses all of his ministry while giving priority to his preaching (1:38). According to Mark, Jesus' preaching and teaching as well as his exorcisms and healings reveal God's intervention in human reality and proclaim God's kingdom come. Preaching is central to Mark's opening narrative. In the words of Brian Blount, "the proclamation not only declares the intervention, it also effects it. Transformation follows immediately."[2] Thus, it is significant that this section is framed by two decisive preaching moments: in the beginning Jesus speaks forth the good news of God's reign, and at the end an unnamed leper freely preaches the good news he has experienced through the healing ministry of Jesus Christ. In between, Mark insists that God is at work to intervene in human events for the well-being of others. Words alone will not suffice. Our preaching and teaching about Jesus Christ must necessarily be accompanied by deeds that call others to join in his ministry of compassion to a blessed but broken world.

JESUS PREACHES AND CALLS DISCIPLES (1:14–20)

Exploring the text

In his first act of public ministry, Jesus proclaims the gospel and calls others to follow him in ministry. Most translations divide these verses in two parts, with verses 14–15 offering Jesus' first recorded "sermon" and verses 16–20 focusing on his call to the first disciples. Thematically there is a clear relationship between the two: both represent public events urging people to respond to God's impending reign. Also, both events are characterized by the radical initiative of Jesus Christ, who is determined that we know the grace and power of God's claim on our lives. Nevertheless, it is wise to recognize that 1:14–15 functions transitionally in the text so that, as noted in the exploration of 1:9–13, Jesus' inaugural sermon may be considered in the context of his baptism and subsequent time of testing in the wilderness (as it is presented in the lectionary reading for the First Sunday of Lent, Year B). However, if taken alongside Jesus' call to the disciples (as suggested for the Third Sunday after Epiphany, Year B), these verses mark Jesus' purposeful and decisive movement into the public sphere.

Proclaiming the Good News (1:14–15)

This brief passage signals the beginning of Jesus' public ministry and offers us a summary of his message: the **good news** of God's impending reign. The brevity and general setting of this passage (somewhere in

Galilee, at the very beginning of his ministry) underscore its importance. These two verses tell us the essential purpose and nature of Jesus' mission but, like the summary offered in verses 38–39, do not elaborate on it. We must listen to the whole of Mark's narrative to hear more about God's reign and to encounter for ourselves the fullness of the gospel that Jesus proclaims. For now, we are swept into the commencement of a new and startling era.

There are a few details worth noting in verse 14. In contrast to John's Gospel, Mark chooses to announce the beginning of Jesus' public ministry after John's arrest (cf. John 3:22–30). There are at least two reasons for this: to underscore that John's role as forerunner to Jesus Christ is now complete and to alert us to John's fate, which foreshadows that of Jesus. Although further description of John's execution is given in 6:17–29, the mention of his imprisonment at the outset of Jesus' public ministry alerts us to the terrible reality of political maneuverings against God's prophet. From the beginning of Jesus' ministry, the forces of evil are ready to exert themselves against those who proclaim God's way.

Another important detail arises in connection with the reference to Galilee as the locus of Jesus' ministry in the first half of Mark's Gospel. In contrast to the region of Judea and the holy city of Jerusalem within it, Galilee is a place where both Jews and Gentiles live in close proximity and regular commerce with one another. It also represents more of an ethnically diverse environment than other locations in the region. With the announcement of Jesus' entry into Galilee, Mark clarifies that Jesus neither withdraws into the wilderness as John did nor focuses his ministry among the religious elite in Jerusalem and the Temple complex, the rallying place for those who seek to destroy him. Jesus' ministry flourishes in Galilee, and he later calls his disciples to join him there after the resurrection (1:14, 28, 39; 3:7; 15:41).

Finally, verse 14 uses the term "good news," or "**gospel**," a noun that neither Luke nor John uses and that occurs only four times in Matthew. In Mark's account it refers to "the gospel of God," that is, the good news related to God's reign among us and the new and radical change that is about to take place (v. 15). But it is not only the content of his message that grabs our attention—it is the person who announces this good news that compels us to listen. Jesus is heir to God's throne and the living embodiment of God's authority and power. He battled the forces of Satan and was named God's Son in baptism. What he proclaims is good news because he is the one to proclaim it. We can turn around (repent) and believe his message because in him God's kingdom has drawn near.

When Jesus speaks in verse 15, the gospel is proclaimed and the **reign**

of God draws near. Although the fullness of God's reign is yet to be realized, Jesus' brief words and their apocalyptic nature urge us to recognize that a new era has arrived. The kingdom he proclaims is not only a spiritual hope but a present reality. The term "kingdom of God" in ancient Hebrew literature is not so much a *place* where God rules as the *fact* that God rules or the *power* by which God's sovereignty is manifest among us.[1] It is a political term and, like the word "gospel," recalls the reality of a public and prominent event that affects all who hear it. Jesus' preaching calls for a dual response that includes both repentance (turning away from former ways) and belief (turning toward God's reign). Like John, Jesus urges people to repent and reorient their lives according to God's way. Unlike John, Jesus does not offer baptism of repentance for the forgiveness of sins. Instead, his preaching calls hearers to repent and believe in the good news of God's reign present now as never before. All that follows in Mark's Gospel is intended to help us recognize, understand, and respond to the reign of God proclaimed by Jesus Christ.

Calling Disciples (1:16–20)

The dynamic force of Jesus' message does not end with the announcement of God's reign. In Mark's narrative, Jesus' message continues with a call to the first **disciples**, who hear his words and immediately follow him.

Jesus sees something in these men they do not see in themselves. More than their professional identity as fishermen or their role as breadwinners, Jesus sees disciples who are able to serve as divine witnesses. Although it was certainly common for rabbis to have disciples, in rabbinic literature teachers do not solicit prospective disciples in the way Jesus models for us in Mark 1. His initiative in this passage is indeed amazing. Thus, what is most remarkable is not that the disciples immediately left everything to follow Jesus but that without any evident relationship with them or demonstration of their faithfulness, Jesus calls them to be his closest companions and future witnesses of the gospel.

In quick succession two sets of brothers are called to follow Jesus, and they do so without question or hesitation. In the first call to Simon (Peter) and Andrew, Jesus issues a command, then offers a promise: "Come after me and I will make you fish for people." The Greek phrase reflects the spirit of calling someone to "come after" rather than to simply follow; it suggests that these disciples are in a successive line of prophets and other witnesses who testify to God's intervention in human events and bear witness to God's reign.[1] They are not asked to repent and believe (as Jesus commanded in vv. 14–15) but to leave their nets and come after Jesus.

This proves to be a costly venture, since their middle-class occupations afforded them a more secure income and stable home environment. For James and John, the stakes are even higher: they not only leave their work but abandon their father (see 3:21, 31–35 and 7:9–13). The presence of hired men in the family business suggests the success of Zebedee's enterprise and the financial loss these brothers face as they leave home to follow Jesus.

The promise Jesus offers his first disciples is more of a challenge than an enticement. To be "fishers of people" is not a call out of the world of social activity (as if being disciples is "otherworldly") but into a new order of responsibilities and relationships that include missionary activity, teaching, preaching, and exorcism (see 1:21–28; 3:14–19b). The phrase recalls the prophet Jeremiah, who speaks of God's calling forth fishers of people to regather Israel and teach sinful humanity about God's power (Jer. 16:16–21). It also recalls other prophets who announce God's efforts to rescue those who are imperiled and would otherwise face divine judgment against their unjust deeds (Ezek. 29:4–6; 38:4; Amos 4:2; Hab. 1:14–17). Jesus' first disciples realize that the time has come to fish for what God asks and to pursue what God commands.

Preaching and teaching the Word

There are weeks in the life of every preacher when he or she would like to deliver a two-line sermon and sit down. Although the recitation of 1:14–15 would not qualify as a sermon for most preaching contexts, Mark offers Jesus' opening words as a summary of the gospel. With his announcement of God's impending reign we cannot help but to sit up, take notice, and open our ears to all that follows.

The need to proclaim the gospel. Jesus' dramatic proclamation of God's reign reminds us what an amazing and audacious task we are called to undertake. It is humbling to think that we who are just as faulty and faithless as the first disciples are entrusted with the gospel. God in Christ announces the good news and continues to call forth saints and sinners as witnesses to God's reign. It takes preachers and teachers, prophets and poets to proclaim God's power and grace, to recognize the fullness of time and the potential of those around us, to risk calling forth others who do not yet see the goodness and beauty of God within them or their own potential to love and serve others. In the words of Gardner Taylor, "To seek and find God's movement in human affairs and to cry out, passionately pointing to where that stirring is discernible though scarcely ever disputable, is the preacher's task. To hear and to suffer deeply with 'the still sad music of humanity' and then to offer to it the wonderful Gospel of healing and wholeness is the preacher's privilege."[2]

God's initiative and our response. The reign of God comes at God's initiative, not ours; it is realized according to God's gracious will and not our own effort. Jesus does not ask us to "build" the kingdom of God but to turn our lives around and believe the good news of God's reign that comes to us because of God's gracious activity. The opening chapter of Mark's Gospel portrays the **power** of God on the loose in the world, and Christ's call in verses 14–15 urges us to join God's reign and engage the transforming power of God on behalf of others. We cannot calculate God's goodness, and we cannot control the coming of God's reign; however, we can participate in God's power, and we can anticipate God's mercy and goodness as it emerges among us. Most of us work as though our lives depend on it, and we forget that God desires our company more than our work. If the response of the first disciples to Jesus' call teaches us anything about faithfulness, it is that our longing to be near Christ is our greatest hope and the best possible reason to forgo all other priorities or alliances.

Repentance and belief are essential to the life of faith for baptized members of the body of Christ. Jesus' announcement of the good news includes the dual call to repent and believe, to reject evil and embrace God's just and loving reign. Jesus proclaims the need to recognize and turn away from all that is contrary to God's will and is emphatic that we must also turn toward God's reign as the primary reference point for our lives. Baptismal vows also reflect this call to turn away from sin and toward Jesus Christ as Lord and Savior. In fact, this text parallels other New Testament passages that have been identified as baptismal formulas and that encourage us to remember what is essential to the life of faith as we seek to live faithfully as followers of Jesus Christ (see Rom. 3:12; 1 Thess. 5:5–6; Col. 1:13; Acts 26:18).[3]

The formation of a visible community of faith. These verses mark the beginning of the church's ministry as a visible, public, and active presence in the world. Jesus did not simply offer ideas for people to ponder in private meditation; he called persons to join with him in public ministry. There is something very personal about his address to specific individuals, but the context and consequences of his call were not private or removed from the shared activities of life in the public arena. At a time when many churches tend to emphasize the personal and private nature of faith, it is important to remember that Jesus calls a spiritual community that is very much a visible community, active in the public sphere. Disciples of Jesus Christ are not called out of the world; they are called to follow a new way in it, a way that, as the following verses reveal, includes ministry to the needs of strangers and those who are rejected by others.

JESUS TEACHES AND HEALS WITH AUTHORITY AND POWER (1:21–31)

Through teaching, preaching, exorcism, and healing, Jesus confronts the powers that threaten well-being and crosses various religious and social boundaries to extend God's compassion to others. Verses 21–31 encompass activities that take place on the Sabbath, and verses 32–39 describe events of the following day. Taken in sequence, the incidents described here include an impressive succession of events and two summary statements of Jesus' ministry and mission (vv. 34 and 38).

Exploring the text

The first two stories of exorcism and healing in Mark's Gospel not only assert Jesus' power and authority but also provide key examples of what typifies his ministry of word and deed in upcoming chapters. The RCL lists 1:21–28 among the readings of the Fourth Sunday after Epiphany and on the Fifth Sunday includes 1:29–31 with 1:32–39, tying together three brief segments in the first chapter of Mark's Gospel (1:21–31, 32–34, and 35–39). However, if 1:21–28 and 29–31 are considered alongside one another and apart from subsequent units (just as Mark's Gospel presents them as the events of a single day), these two episodes complement and contrast with one another in noteworthy ways.

Preaching and Healing in the Synagogue (1:21–28)

Jesus begins his public ministry in a sacred place, at a sacred time. With Simon, Andrew, James, and John beside him, Jesus enters the synagogue at Capernaum on the Sabbath to teach. In contrast to Luke's account (4:16–30), Mark's story of Jesus' first teaching in Capernaum describes his initial acceptance by others who recognize his authority. It is a promising beginning that inspires hope and confidence in the future of his ministry in Galilee.

Most importantly, this story focuses our attention on Jesus' authority. The Greek word for authority used here (*exousian*) may also be translated as **"power."** Jesus is authorized as divine Messiah in the apocalyptic battle to overcome evil and exorcise demons. The people first comment on the remarkable manner in which he speaks (v. 22) and later on the way in which his exorcism represents the authority of a "new teaching" (v. 27). Mark does not record the content of Jesus' message but focuses on the people's response and their astonishment. How he speaks reveals who he is: Jesus is inspired and empowered by God, more like a prophet who speaks on God's behalf than a scribe who depends on training or knowledge for his authority. Jesus impresses the crowd and attracts the attention of demons, who recognize his power and step forward to challenge his authority.

Although Jesus' intention at the synagogue is to teach, he is ready to respond to the unclean spirit who interrupts worship and claims the attention of everyone present. Jesus' exorcism of the possessed man is significant for several reasons. First, it demonstrates Jesus' power to act decisively and nonviolently against the forces of evil that forge their way among us. The demon uses violence to control the possessed man, convulsing and literally "tearing" or "rending" the man as it departs. Jesus uses neither sword nor magic but through divine command overpowers the unclean spirit and opens the way for healing and newness of life. Jesus' successful exorcism of the demon in the synagogue at Capernaum assures us of God's ultimate success in the **apocalyptic** showdown between the powers of God and the destructive forces of evil.

Second, the demon is the first in Mark's Gospel to identify Jesus as the Holy One of God (see also 3:11 and 5:7). The phrase "unclean spirit" is a common Hebrew expression that denotes demon possession and is understood to contrast with God's clean or holy nature. The spirit is also aware that Jesus' presence threatens the powers of evil (note the use of the plural, "us," in v. 24). The demon calls him by his common name, Jesus of Nazareth, then by his **title,** God's Holy One. It is likely that Jesus silences (literally, "muzzles") the unclean spirit because he does not want an unholy witness to testify to his divine nature and because he recognizes the demon's attempt to overpower him by naming him.

Third, this event takes place on the Sabbath, when Jesus' exorcism is sure to offend religious leaders. With this healing, Jesus introduces a new understanding of Sabbath priorities. In Mark's eschatological framework, the Sabbath represents more than a day of rest; it is also the promised day of God's dominion. Jesus' exorcism of the possessed man offers a foretaste of joy and newness of life as creation is released from the powers of death and destruction and anticipates the fullness of health, peace, and salvation in the time to come.

Finally, we hear the people's reaction. Just as they are astounded at Jesus' teaching, the people also respond with amazement at his exorcism and wonder at the authority of this "new teaching." We must be careful, however, not to confuse amazement with faith. According to Ched Myers, the words that describe the crowd's reaction to Jesus at the beginning and end of this episode are strong and "connote not just incredulity but a kind of panic associated with the disruption of the assumed order of things."[1] Astonishment and wonder do not provide a sturdy basis for faith, but they may open our eyes to the possibility of faith.

Healing Simon's Mother-in-Law (1:29–31)

Jesus moves quickly from the synagogue to the family home where Simon's mother-in-law lies sick with a fever. The mention of family relationships prompts our awareness that Simon left more than his fishing gear when he followed Jesus in ministry. Similarly, Jesus' care for Simon's mother-in-law helps us understand that his redefinition of familial relationships in no way ignores the needs of family members and kin (see also 7:9–13; cf. 3:31–35).

Like the preceding episode, this healing event takes place on the Sabbath. It also includes four disciples as witnesses and demonstrates Jesus' authority over the powers of death and destruction. Just as Jesus commanded the unclean spirit with words (v. 25), he commands the fever to leave the woman with his touch, demonstrating that his **power** extends not only to the spiritual realm but to the physical as well. When Jesus takes her by the hand and raises her up, Simon's mother-in-law takes her place among those who experience newness of life through the grace and power of Jesus Christ.

There are, however, several differences between this episode and the previous story of exorcism. Whereas the exorcism takes place in a public setting, the healing of Simon's mother-in-law takes place in private. Also, in contrast to the unclean spirit who interrupts Jesus' teaching in the synagogue, Jesus is the one who makes a house call to the bedridden woman in response to a call for help. Most importantly, the main character in this story is a woman. In touching her, Jesus reaches across the religious and social barriers of his day so that he may aid her healing. If religious authorities were offended by Jesus' exorcism of the unclean spirit on the Sabbath, they had even more reason to be angry at him for healing Simon's mother-in-law the same day: Jesus not only touched a woman who was not a member of his family but one who was ill and therefore considered ritually unclean. In just three verses, Jesus manages to cross religious, social, and sexual boundaries. The power of God moves in unexpected directions.

When Jesus "lifts her up" (a phrase that recalls resurrection from the dead and other healing miracles; see 2:11; 3:3; 5:41; 9:27; 12:26; 14:28; and 16:16), she rises to serve others. Using the same verb here (*diēkonei*) as in the description of other women disciples who follow Jesus to the cross in 15:41 and 16:7, Mark's Gospel is framed by stories of women who serve others as disciples of Jesus Christ.[1] In this larger framework, her gesture is not an act of subservience or a return to culturally prescribed expectations but an expression of servant discipleship just as

Jesus Christ himself came to serve others (10:32). She becomes a model of Christian discipleship for generations of men and women who follow Jesus Christ.

Preaching and teaching the Word

These two stories of teaching, exorcism, and healing raise more questions than we can ever address in one sermon or lesson, but they also point us toward the horizon of hope promised to us in Jesus Christ. Some questions to ponder include:

Who is Jesus and what kind of authority and power does he demonstrate? There is more here than a story about Jesus' welcome reception at a local synagogue or the account of a good deed accomplished by healing Simon's mother-in-law. These stories reveal an apocalyptic showdown between the Messiah of God and the forces of evil. The stories of exorcism and healing declare that Jesus is not only an authoritative teacher but the Holy One of God empowered to defeat the forces of evil and sickness among us. Both stories are well suited to the season of Epiphany when the church considers anew how Christ is revealed among us.

The question of miracles. Jesus' exorcism and healing miracles anticipate the day when all creation will celebrate God's Sabbath rest and peaceful dominion, when death and diseases of all kinds will finally be defeated. Until that time, how does Christian faith relate to miracles? Is human faith a necessary prerequisite for divine intervention? Rather than focusing on human faith, the opening stories in Mark focus on God's power in Jesus Christ. They offer assurance that amid all that ails us, God's loving intention is for our well-being. For those who battle cancer, AIDS, and spiritual, mental, and physical maladies of all kinds, the good news is that God in Christ works on our behalf to confront whatever threatens our well-being. His ultimate victory over death on the cross assures us of our own well-being as we move through death to newness of life. These stories raise the possibility of resurrection hope amid life's worst challenges.

What boundaries are we willing to cross as we continue the ministry of Jesus Christ? Jesus repeatedly offends religious and social convention as he reaches beyond standard definitions of what is right or appropriate, reaching out to those who were considered unclean and untouchable. Are there unacceptable persons with whom we will not share the table or from whose hands we will not receive Christ's bread and cup? Mark jolts us into realizing that God redefines these lines or erases them altogether. In doing so, the man released from the unclean spirit is free to join with others in worship, and the woman healed from fever is empowered to serve as a disciple of Jesus Christ. Who is it that awaits freedom and power to join us in Christian worship and service to others?

JESUS' REPUTATION SPREADS (1:32–39)

Exploring the text

Jesus' reputation as a healer and exorcist spreads throughout the city of Capernaum. As part of the continued manifestation of Jesus Christ and his proclamation of God's reign, these verses are well suited to the season of Epiphany and are included along with 1:29–31 in the RCL for the Fifth Sunday.

Jesus' healing of many people in 1:32–34 is followed by a recounting in verses 35–39 of Jesus' effort to find prayerful solitude while the crowd pursues him. Both episodes include summary statements outlining the scope and purpose of Jesus' mission (vv. 34 and 38–39). Themes introduced earlier in Mark 1 are continued here: verses 32–34 relate Jesus' will to overthrow the powers that bring illness and demon possession, and verses 35–39 relate Jesus' decision to give priority to **proclaim** the good news of God's reign far and wide. These sections also continue the dialectic between silence and speaking that runs throughout Mark's Gospel.

Healing People and Silencing Demons (1:32–34)

As the Sabbath draws to a close, a crowd gathers around the doorway of Simon and Andrew's home to be healed of disease, exorcised of demons, to help neighbors and loved ones, or to simply witness Jesus' healing power. As Joel Marcus points out, the post-Sabbath setting is important for at least two reasons.[1] First, it signifies that religious piety is not incompatible with reverence for Jesus. The people show positive regard for the observance of Sabbath rules and wait for the sun to set before bringing him persons in need of healing–even after Mark has related two stories of Jesus' reinterpretation of Sabbath priorities in verses 21–31. Second, Jews in the first century marked the end of the Sabbath with the service of Havdalah, celebrating God's creation of the world and anticipating the full re-creation of life in the time to come. Similarly, Mark's eschatological vision of Jesus' actions emphasizes the re-creation of all who are healed and exorcised of demons.

The image of the doorway in verse 33 is also worth noting. Simon and Andrew's home has quickly become something of a house church, with people hovering about the entryway and pressing near to Jesus. But they have not yet crossed the threshold of faith. They come to Jesus for healing and he readily responds to their needs, but at this point in the narrative no one comes to hear Jesus proclaim the good news of God's reign which, according to verses 15 and 38, is the heart of his message and reason for coming. In other words, the Gospel is telling us that the people of Capernaum do not come to Jesus because of who he is but because of what he can do for them. Those who crowd the doorway of Simon and Andrew's home have only begun to glimpse the extent of Jesus' divine power and sovereignty.

The Gospel also reports that Jesus **silences** the demons. They know who he is, and Jesus appears to have very definite ideas about who may proclaim his identity and when and how his identity is to be disclosed. Unlike his earlier command to silence the demon who sought power over him (vv. 24–25), this instance reflects other tensions in the text, as Jesus is not yet ready to be named God's promised Messiah. Perhaps he silences the unclean spirits because he does not want demons to testify on his behalf, or perhaps he does not yet want people to hear of his divine nature when all they have seen is his miraculous healing power, or perhaps he wants only those who accompany him throughout his ministry to proclaim God's presence and reign. Despite his command, word spreads throughout the entire city. God's power is on the loose as never before, and even Jesus is not able to control what people hear of him and his ministry.

Praying and Proclaiming the Gospel (1:35–39)

After an intense day of ministering to the sick and demon possessed, Jesus sets out alone to pray. We sense his weariness and frustration in the aftermath of his first two days of public ministry when Jesus leaves well before dawn, under cover of darkness and without telling his disciples where he is going. When the people awaken, they zealously pursue Jesus and enlist the help of his disciples to find him. The verb used to describe the desperation of their search (*katedioxen*) suggests that they hunted him down like an animal, recalling his earlier encounter with wild beasts in the desert (v. 13).

Jesus' experience of private prayer reflects several facets of his ministry. First and foremost, prayer reflects his reliance on God. Although Jesus engaged in corporate prayer during synagogue services and taught his followers about the purposes and power of prayer (11:15–25), Mark's Gospel relates three pivotal junctures when Jesus turns to God in private prayer: here at the outset of his ministry amid increasing demands for help, in the midst of his ministry after feeding the multitudes (6:46), and finally at Gethsemane when he asks for God's help during a time of crisis (14:32–42). These moments of prayerful solitude suggest that Jesus' ministry is directed, sustained, and inspired by God, who is the source of divine blessing and power for his life and ministry. Second, the reference to prayer near the beginning of his ministry as he exorcises demons and heals the diseased reminds us that Jesus is not a magician but relies on the **power** of God to perform miracles of healing on behalf of others. He does as God wills him to do, seeking God's direction and power in his battle against the forces of evil. Finally, Jesus' time of private prayer speaks to us of the importance of solitude in the life and practice of faith. More than a refuge from the pressures of life or an opportunity for divine intimacy, Jesus' encounter with God in prayer also enlarges his sense of divine vision and mission in the world. When Jesus emerges from private prayer, he arises with new energy and clarity that includes a wider vision of God's reign and mission to others.

This is quickly evident in the announcement he makes to his disciples when they find him after his time of prayer: "Let us go on to the neighboring towns, so that I may proclaim the message there also; for that is what I came out to do" (v. 38). Moving from the city of Capernaum to the region of Galilee, Jesus asserts a larger sense of mission and outreach to the surrounding towns. Just as important as his expanded sense of mission, however, is Jesus' insistence that the central focus of his ministry is to "proclaim the message." His ministries of healing and exorcism are manifestations of God's power to overthrow the forces of evil, and the message he has come to proclaim is the imminent arrival of **God's reign** (v. 15). Preaching is central to his mission, as Jesus goes throughout the region preaching the message of God's kingdom and casting out demons (v. 39).

Preaching and teaching the Word

It is sometimes tempting to skim summary accounts in the Gospel because they appear to lack some of the grit and gristle of stories and other descriptive episodes. But these transitional verses in the first chapter of Mark are worthy of more careful examination: their brevity serves to highlight a few carefully selected details and to emphasize specific themes that will be developed throughout the Gospel account. In verses 32–34 and 35–39, the Gospel focuses our attention on key emphases of Jesus' ministry through two summary statements and a pronouncement regarding the purpose of his mission. In particular, these verses highlight Jesus' overthrowing the power of evil that afflicts countless individuals (v. 34) and, after a time of prayer, tell us that he is determined to proclaim the message of God's reign far and wide (vv. 38–39). These verses challenge our own practice of faith and ministry at two important levels.

What is the role of private prayer in our lives and ministries? Jesus' example of prayer challenges us to reconsider the ways in which personal encounters with God in prayer may inspire, empower, and guide our faith and ministry. Do we expect prayer to provide moments of quiet refuge, or are we open to being moved by God to pursue ministries or ideas we would not otherwise imagine? When Jesus sought a place and time apart from the crowd, he was not simply seeking to escape others but to find the company of God who brings a renewed and expanded vision of life. Danger arises when we ignore the vitality, grace, humility, and power that are offered to us by God in solitary encounters with the divine. For Jesus, there is no surer sign of faithful communion with God than emerging from prayer with a renewed sense of proclaiming to others the good news of God's reign.

During my early years of pastoral ministry, a colleague and mentor of mine was as comfortable closing his office door for moments of softly spoken prayer as he was giving up his overcoat to a homeless person or stopping along the road to help a stranded trucker while we were on our way to visit shut-ins. In the words of Thomas Merton, "Prayer must penetrate and enliven every department of our life, including that which is most temporal and transient. Prayer does not despise even the seemingly lowliest aspects of man's [and woman's] temporal existence. It spiritualizes all of them and gives them a divine orientation."[1] There is a seamless movement between prayer and service that needs to be fiercely guarded when the burden of work threatens to pull us under. There are many people who experience loneliness and many more whose lives are cluttered with work, noise, and the shallow companionship of ceaseless activity. Few people cultivate the rich soil of solitude and prayer out of which, paradoxically, our greatest energy and loving service to others arises.

How does our faith in Jesus Christ clarify our sense of mission and challenge us to serve others? Arising out of his experience of prayer, Jesus had a renewed sense of focus and a larger sense of mission to others. These two points are inextricably related to one another.

With regard to a sense of clarity and focus for mission, these verses challenge us to discern and pursue what is central to our calling. Although many things are important, what is essential? What is the very heart of our calling, and what must we do to be faithful to God's claim on our lives individually and corporately? Just as Jesus experienced an endless stream of cries for help, we are barraged with pleas wherever we turn: our mailboxes overflow with unsolicited requests for money, community meetings and school board gatherings urge us to commit time and energy to an array of complex problems, and countless church-related programs vie for our attention. But what does God in Christ call us to do now, at this particular place and this particular time? Like Jesus, we must prayerfully listen to God and ask ourselves whether our sense of mission and ministry is compatible with Jesus' vision of proclaiming God's just and loving reign.

With regard to Jesus' larger sense of mission and the widening scope of his ministry, in what ways do our vision and calling compel us ever outward in service to others? How much of our time, energy, money, and attention are given to self-preservation rather than outreach to neighbors? Do we see the vision of God's reign as it extends beyond boundaries of our own making and ministries of our own choosing, or are we willing to look beyond ourselves toward the wider horizons of God's reign? The crowd that gathered around the doorway of Simon and Andrew's home did not yet understand that God's power and authority extend beyond physical ailments and demon possession to encompass the social, political, economic, and religious arenas of life. These verses point us toward the way of Jesus Christ moving beyond familiar circles to ever widening areas of outreach and service.

CLEANSING THE LEPER (1:40–45)

Exploring the text

Who is this unnamed leper hurling himself at Jesus' feet? Like many others in the first chapter of Mark, he has heard of Jesus' miraculous power and he begs for help. But this man is not just another face in the crowd; in fact, he is forbidden a place in the crowd because leprosy (from the Greek word *leprein*, meaning "to scale or peel off") renders him unclean and a source of contamination to others. Levitical law prevents him from human contact, and he must shout, "Unclean, unclean," as he passes by others or solicits alms (Lev. 13:45). On this occasion, as he presses closer to Jesus, everyone nearby steps back a few paces, stunned at his bravado and fearful of being contaminated. No longer interested in begging for loose change, the diseased man has come to Jesus for healing, desperate to reclaim a place in community and enjoy normal human relations.

Whether moved by pity or anger, Jesus' response to the leper is every bit as bold as the actions of the diseased man: he stretches out his hand to touch and heal him through physical contact and verbal command. Urging the man to say nothing to anyone, Jesus then instructs him to go to the priest, who can declare him clean. However, the healed man is overcome with enthusiasm and tells everyone what has happened. Once again, word of Jesus' healing power precedes him (see vv. 32–33). Ironically, the cleansed man's message is far more infectious than any disease. The crowds gather around Jesus in ever growing numbers, and he is no longer able to enter the towns of Galilee.

Two themes introduced earlier in Mark's Gospel arise again. First, Jesus' ministry of healing demonstrates the **power** of God to prevail over disease and overcome human notions of what is right and acceptable. Like the stories of Jesus' exorcising the demon in the synagogue (vv. 25–26) and healing countless others in Capernaum (v. 34), this story reveals that in the eschatological battle between divine and demonic forces, God in Christ overcomes the powers of destruction, illness, and alienation that threaten humankind. When Jesus reached out to the leper, the power of illness did not infect him, but the power of God effected wholeness in the man who suffered from disease and rejection by others. In contrast to the priests who can declare the man clean but are not able to effect his healing, Jesus is able to do what no other earthly power can accomplish: he brings healing and crosses seemingly impenetrable boundaries because of his divine compassion for others.

Second, the tension between **silence** and speaking emerges with new urgency in this story. Jesus silenced the demons in verses 25 and 34 just as he commanded the cleansed leper not to speak to anyone but to show himself to the priest for readmission to the community of faith. When the cleansed man instead freely proclaims the good news of his healing, Jesus is besieged by crowds. Ironically, he is no longer able to walk around openly but, like the leper, is forced to the outskirts of town. After Jesus' announcement that the first priority of his ministry is to proclaim the gospel throughout Galilee (1:38–39), it is ironic that this unnamed leper spreads the good news far and wide. Perhaps the greatest irony of all is that the man healed of leprosy and several other unnamed witnesses in Mark's account are among the most ardent evangelists of the gospel (5:18–20; 7:36) while Jesus' closest followers often fail to recognize him or to tell others about him (6:49; 14:66–72; 16:6–8). The first chapter of Mark's Gospel opens and closes with the good news of Jesus Christ, whose power cannot be contained and whose story will continue to be told by surprising and unexpected witnesses.

Preaching and teaching the Word

In the RCL for the sixth week following Epiphany, the story of the cleansed leper is presented alongside the story of the Hebrew commander Naaman, who is also healed of leprosy (2 Kgs. 5:1–14). Both stories reveal God's power to heal the afflicted, albeit under very different circumstances. When Jesus heals the leper and proclaims the gospel far and wide, we witness the power of God moving among us in dangerous and surprising ways.

Jesus' cleansing of the leper challenges the boundaries we have drawn between those who are acceptable and those who are not. When Jesus touched the infected man, he not only risked contamination but also rejection by those who judged his actions unacceptable and unclean. His words and deeds reveal God's longing to do more than be aware of strangers or to help others from a safe distance: Jesus bears witness to the active love of God that moves beyond places of comfort and safety to respond to the needs of others. Jesus' outreach to the diseased man does not justify reckless behavior or promote unwanted intimacy. He makes available the resources of God to one who has been rejected by others.

Thankfully, there are many ways to extend God's compassion to others. A friend of mine always keeps extra money in his pockets so that he never passes a person in need without sharing financial help. Another person taught me that there is nothing so dehumanizing as being ignored by others and that whether or not we have money to share, we can always stop, look in the eyes of those who call out to us, and speak to them. Recently I was walking through Baltimore with my family. We were deeply engaged in conversation when we passed a man in a wheelchair calling for our attention. We scarcely noticed him as we continued on our way. I suddenly realized our eight-year-old daughter was no longer beside me. When I turned to look for her I saw that she was standing beside the man, asking him his name, sharing her own name, and asking him how he was doing. Before we knew it, all of us were part of the conversation, unexpectedly drawn into a wonderful exchange. There are many ways to step beyond our fears and respond to others.

The power of the gospel awaits our participation in God's healing intentions for the world. The gospel cannot be controlled or contained. We may choose to spread the good news of Christ's healing, restoration, and wholeness for all people, or we may choose to infect others with our mean-spiritedness, alienation, and prejudice. This occurs both individually and corporately. During the summer of 1763, General Jeffrey Amherst urged the distribution of smallpox-infested blankets among the Ottawa Indians as an early form of biological warfare against opponents of English expansion. Within weeks, hundreds of the Ottawa died.[1] Sin and evil are ever present among us, infecting our spirits and hardening our hearts. But evil does not have the last word. The power of God is on the loose in the world, awaiting our participation and proclamation.

Opposition to Jesus' Authority
and Power

Mark 2:1–3:6

The gospel is not only good news but dangerous news. Following the initial success of his ministry, in the second chapter Jesus draws the attention of **Jewish religious leaders** who question his actions and resist his authority. In swift succession, five episodes in 2:1–3:6 recount mounting opposition to Jesus from scribes, Pharisees, and Herodians. In the RCL this cycle of stories is divided between two different seasons (Epiphany and Pentecost), and the break in sequence can disrupt the growing sense of urgency they convey. Nevertheless, each episode relates distinct features of God's reign proclaimed by Jesus Christ. As the fifth controversy draws to a close, we not only hear of the plot to destroy Jesus but have no doubt that preaching the good news, eating with sinners, and healing the diseased are more than benign acts of kindness: they demonstrate the radical power of God at work in the world to break boundaries and overturn human relationships that defy God's compassion and life-giving intentions for all people.

Each of the five episodes includes a precipitating question from a religious leader (explicit in the first four but implicit in the fifth) followed by Jesus' counterquestion and/or enacted response. The arrangement of these stories is also significant. For example, the first and fifth episodes relate instances of healing, whereas the second, third, and fourth episodes share the motif of eating; the first two stories mention sin, and the last two have the Sabbath as their setting; the third and central story in this cycle speaks of offering "new wine" (the eschatological in-breaking of God's reign) that cannot be contained by the old wineskins of Jesus' critics. What is most impressive about this sequence of events is the mounting opposition to Jesus that culminates in the plot to destroy him. According to Marcus, "The opponents move from questioning Jesus silently (2:7) to interrogating the disciples about him (2:16) to interrogating him about them (2:18, 24) to seeking legal grounds for condemning him (3:2) to plotting his murder (3:6)."[1]

35

These observant Jews do not approach Jesus as enemies but as religious colleagues who raise questions that engage him in vital issues of faith and practice. The scribes and Pharisees were among the most devoted and well-informed Jews in Jesus' time, and their initial questioning of him and the ensuing debate about Jewish law is in keeping with their concern for the right interpretation of religious faith and practice, including dietary rules and Sabbath observance.[2] We offend both the gospel and Jewish tradition if we trivialize their concerns or accuse them of hypocrisy.[3] Their sense of religious identity is different from that of Jesus. But like the twelve disciples, the scribes and Pharisees do not fully comprehend his mission and identity.

FORGIVING AND HEALING THE PARALYTIC (2:1–12)

Exploring the text

The first in a sequence of five controversies is perhaps the most complicated and provocative. Jesus not only forgives and heals a man suffering from paralysis, but the religious leaders who witness this amazing event suspect him of committing blasphemy against God. It is possible that Mark has chosen to combine two separate and remarkable stories about healing and forgiving sins. The likely insertion of one story into another allows us to view this text in three segments, each of which reveals key theological concerns.

In the first section, 2:1–5, Jesus returns to Capernaum (cf. 1:21–28). The home he is visiting is likely the family residence of Andrew and Simon, whose mother-in-law Jesus earlier healed of fever (1:29–31). Jesus' growing popularity is evident by the multitudes who gather to hear him speak. They are drawn to Jesus, who is "speaking the word" to them, which is Mark's way of alluding to the whole of Jesus' message and the good news of God's impending reign (see 1:15, 38–39; 4:10, 34). The authoritative power of Jesus' words is evident in his announcing forgiveness (2:5), confronting those who quietly accuse him of blasphemy (2:8–10), and conveying God's healing power (2:11).

Because of his remarkable message crowds press near, and soon there is no room remaining, not even in the doorway. The paralytic and his friends must not only overcome the limitations of severe disability but must make a way through the crowd. Digging their way through the roof and lowering their friend on his pallet, the four companions make a way where there was no way. They not only demonstrate faith in Jesus but persistent love for their friend. Jesus witnesses their extraordinary behavior, commends their faithful determination, and heals the paralytic because of their faith. It is not just faith that is approved, however, but faith acting on behalf of another's well-being. Brushing the debris from his head, Jesus issues his own surprising response and announces to the man that his sins are forgiven.

In the second section, 2:6–10a, the scribes are alarmed by Jesus' pronouncement of forgiveness. He has caught everyone by surprise: the paralytic and his friends also must have wondered why Jesus did not first address the man's physical condition, since that was the obvious reason for their coming. Even if one views sin as the origin or cause of the man's disability (as was often the case in ancient culture), it is striking that Jesus did not address the paralytic's physical ailment in his first words to him. Similarly, we cannot blame the scribes for their initial confusion and concern. As interpreters of the law and guardians of its traditions, the scribes would be the first to recognize the radical nature of Jesus' announcement as he claimed the right to speak for God. Their silent questions indicate that Jesus has done more than claim priestly prerogative in declaring God's forgiveness: they suspect he is guilty of blasphemy for asserting God's authority as his own.

The severity of their charge reflects their perceived violation of the first commandment. To confront the scribes and their indictment of him, Jesus proves his divine power and prophetic gifts by reading the thoughts of their hearts. He challenges their questions and raises his own: Why do you raise such questions in your hearts? Is it easier to forgive sins or heal disease? Jesus' questions not only serve to underscore his claim to authority but open the way for him to demonstrate God's **power** in their midst by healing the paralytic. Through words and deeds, Jesus demonstrates both divine authority to forgive and divine power to heal.

One of the most challenging aspects of this story is the suggestion of a relationship between sin and sickness.[1] Hebrew Scripture testifies to the ways sin can lead to sickness (see Deut. 28:15–68; Ps. 107:17–18), and New Testament texts can be found to support this idea as well (see John 5:14). However, other passages of Scripture challenge this understanding and refute a causal relationship between human sin and illness (see Job 1–2:10; John 9:1–3). In the story of the paralytic's healing, Jesus does not explicitly state that the man's disability has been caused by sin. The story does not focus on sin and its consequences but turns our attention to faith (particularly the community of faithful friends who surround the paralytic man) and Jesus' authority and power to bring divine healing, both spiritual and physical. Jesus takes a holistic approach to the man's well-being and does not offer healing apart from God's will to forgive.

The third section, 2:10b–12, draws our attention to healing and the glad response of all who witness the man's recovery. It also records the first of several instances when Jesus refers to himself as the Son of Man (see 2:28; 8:38; 13:26; 14:62; see **messianic titles** in the glossary). Jesus commands the man to rise, a term that is repeated three times in this episode and recurs throughout Mark's Gospel with overtones of God's resurrection power (see 3:3; 5:41; 6:14, 16; 12:26; 14:28; 16:6). The power of Jesus' words is immediately felt. When the man stands and follows Jesus' command to take his mat and go home, the crowd is amazed and gives glory to God for this new and astonishing event. The charge of blasphemy is utterly refuted by those who give praise and glory to God. The scribes slip quietly away. However, their concerns do not disappear but repeatedly arise to the very end of Mark's Gospel.

Preaching and teaching the Word

There are many good reasons to be attracted to this story and at least one reason to be repelled by it. It attracts our attention because of its dramatic portrayal of the paralytic's compassionate friends and Jesus' response to their active, persistent faith. We may also be impressed by the holistic approach to healing that Jesus takes in addressing the man's spiritual and physical needs. But given that Christians sometimes wrongly assume that illness is due to individual sin or insufficient faith, we may also feel ambivalence or even resentment toward this and other healing stories. When interpreting the paralytic's story it is important to remember that Jesus calls all people (not only those afflicted with mental and physical ailments) to repent and believe the good news of God's impending reign. Of course, theological insight and pastoral sensitivity are always welcome companions in the work of biblical interpretation and never more so than when we consider matters of human suffering.

One way of approaching this multifaceted story is to consider the many characters who inhabit the text and interact with Jesus. Because human and divine involvement interact in dynamic ways, it is possible to preach or teach about the paralytic's forgiveness and healing from three perspectives.

From the perspective of human involvement, we may focus on the role of individual and corporate responsibility. For example, despite his disability the paralytic is an active participant in this healing event: he immediately responds to Jesus' command and rises without hesitation to follow his directions. The greatest testimony the forgiven and healed man has to offer is the forward strides he makes on his way out the door. It is his actions more than his words that the Gospel chooses to highlight. Like the paralytic, his friends are also silent but active. Their movements command our attention and draw Jesus' attention. They accompany and assist

the paralyzed man, demonstrating faith, persistence, loving support, ingenuity, hope, boundary-breaking initiative, and the willingness to risk their
reputations for the sake of another's well-being. These unnamed heroes
embody faith in God and love for their neighbor, fulfilling the two great
commandments of Judaism and Christianity. In contrast to the scribes,
whose hearts reveal the beginning of resistance to Jesus' authority and
power, when Jesus looks into the hearts of the paralytic's friends he hears
what Paul speaks of in 2 Corinthians 1:18–22 (the Epistle reading that
accompanies this text in the lectionary for the Seventh Sunday of
Epiphany): faith that the promises of God find their "yes" in Jesus Christ.
The involvement of these friends suggests other lessons as well. They
teach us that healing is often facilitated by the help of others and that faithful action is a powerful form of intercessory prayer.

The paralytic man's friends remind us that Jesus is not the only one to
demonstrate boundary-breaking behavior in the Gospel of Mark, since
they are also willing to move beyond what is considered right or acceptable behavior in order to help someone else. A recent campaign by the
Association of Brethren Caregivers (a denominational agency of the
Church of the Brethren) urges congregations to "Embrace an 'Open Roof'
Policy" that allows all people to worship, serve, be served, learn, and grow
in the presence of God as valued members of Christian community. Many
churches and denominations know that advocating for the rights of persons with disabilities is not enough: God's love bids us to raise roofs,
install elevators, make worship and service opportunities accessible to the
hearing and visually impaired, and work with persons who are physically
challenged to seek God's loving intentions for one another.

Of course, one may also approach this story from the perspective of the
scribes. Unlike the friends who contribute to and participate in the paralytic's transformation, the scribes watch quietly from the sidelines. Their
silent resistance may remind us of painful patterns of quiet opposition and
passive-aggressive behavior practiced in our own faith communities.
Their growing opposition to Jesus' authority throughout this chapter
reminds us to consider our own points of resistance to God.

From the perspective of divine involvement, we can explore the many ways
this story reveals the identity, authority, and power of Jesus Christ. However much we may be drawn to the drama of the paralytic's experience
and the compassion of his friends, we must not forget that this is a story
about Jesus Christ. The paralytic's forgiveness and healing demonstrate
two vital aspects of Jesus' identity: his divine authority and power. Jesus
asserts divine authority when he declares that the paralytic's sins are forgiven, and he demonstrates divine power in healing him. He is more than

a priest who works outside traditional structures or a miracle worker who performs acts of healing; he is the Christ who has authority and power to do God's will. Jesus is provocateur and compassionate healer, forgiver and physician, mind reader and spiritual guide. He embodies the gospel, the good news of God's reign among us. When people come to Jesus to be healed, he sets the work of healing within the larger context of divine forgiveness and spiritual salvation. For those who tend to preach primarily about human needs and perspectives, this text provides meaningful material related to Jesus' divine identity.

From the perspective of divine-human interaction, it is also important to recognize that neither humans nor God act alone in this story but in relationship to one another. According to Mark's Gospel, divine authority and power reside in Jesus Christ alone, but humans participate fully as necessary partners in the fulfillment of God's just and loving reign. At times, people take the initiative in seeking help for a friend, or the crowd offers a chorus of praise and glory to God; at times, Jesus Christ takes the initiative in offering forgiveness at an unexpected moment or by confronting the silent resistance of others. But throughout this episode, both human and divine participants are essential to the fulfillment of God's life-giving intentions. Newness of life arises through a mysterious blend of divine-human interaction. Today we pray for God's help and may be surprised by the answer we hear or the abundance of grace we receive. We work to establish laws and policies that address the needs of persons with disabilities, but we need God to help reveal our prejudices and forge new pathways that we never could have imagined on our own.

CALLING AND EATING WITH SINNERS (2:13–17)

Exploring the text

This is the second of five controversial episodes between Jesus and the religious leaders. Just as he called Simon, Andrew, James, and John (1:16–20), Jesus is again walking beside the sea when he sees Levi the son of Alphaeus and issues his simple call, "Follow me." Unlike the others, Levi is not a fisherman but belongs to one of the most despised and corrupt professions. His place at the toll booth along the Via Maris (a well-known trade route that ran through the Sea of Galilee) meant that Levi did not collect income or poll taxes. He was a customs official at liberty to charge fishermen and other tradespeople whatever amount he wanted while collecting funds for Herod Antipas and hoarding the excess for himself. Greed and dishonesty were rampant among toll collectors, and Jesus' followers had good reason to be shocked by his call and the toll collector's response.[1] Levi is called to discipleship (*akolouteeo* is used elsewhere in Mark's Gospel with reference to discipleship–6:1; 8:34). Like the previous story (2:1–12) this account highlights Levi's immediate response as he rises to follow Jesus.

With scarcely a pause in the action, Mark takes us from seaside to table-side where a feast is underway (2:15–17). Most translations assume the location of the feast is Levi's home but, as one member of our Markan Bible study noted, the text is ambiguous about the location of this gathering.[2] Who is the host and who is the guest? It is possible that Levi or one of his friends called everyone together, but it is also possible that Jesus may have hosted the event, lending greater scandal to his actions in the eyes of the Pharisees. We do know, however, that the unusual guest list includes tax collectors and also "sinners," a reference to persons other than tax collectors who were considered social and religious outcasts. The scribes appear as party crashers, lingering about the doorway, puzzled and disturbed by Jesus' choice of dinner companions. After all, Levi and other tax collectors were known to have frequent commerce with persons considered ritually impure. Since dietary and other table regulations promoted Jewish identity and survival, we may sympathize with the scribes' concerns.

In contrast to the previous episode, the scribes do not keep their questions to themselves but ask Jesus' disciples why he chooses to eat with such people. Jesus answers them himself, quoting an ancient proverb that points out (with a measure of irony) that his mission is not to approve the righteous but to serve the sick. Like the scribes, we are left to ponder for ourselves who is righteous and who is in need of forgiveness. If the religious leaders could view themselves as sinners in need of God's grace and mercy, then they could also join the banquet.

One of the most important and least appreciated points to ponder with regard to this episode is that the call is not a call to repentance but to **discipleship**. The text does not report that Jesus insisted Levi turn his life around before following him, and it does not say that Levi repented of his misdeeds before joining Jesus at the table. Although the summons to discipleship includes repentance (it is, in fact, central to Jesus' proclamation of God's reign in 1:15), Jesus extends forgiveness and acceptance to Levi before repentance is voiced or demonstrated by the tax collector or any other guests gathered around the table. Jesus issues a call to discipleship, not judgment, and this call is the prelude to an eschatological banquet enjoyed by saints and sinners alike. Only God has the authority to declare what is right and who is acceptable. This episode declares that God's grace abounds.

Preaching and teaching the Word

Sermons related to the call of Levi and to Jesus' dinner with him and other tax collectors and sinners can develop various visual, theological, and/or metaphorical possibilities in the text.

Retelling the story. Sometimes the most moving way to engage current hearers with ancient stories is to present texts anew with the use of faithful imagination, current language, and theological integrity. There is something wonderfully graphic and visually appealing about these brief scenes by the seashore and tableside. For those inclined to make the most of their storytelling skills, this second confrontation between Jesus and religious leaders offers a great opportunity to develop sympathy for the many characters who inhabit the text, noting their backgrounds, daily lives, and religious commitments. Attending to the theological points raised earlier (and being careful not to invent psychological motives or to assign judgment when none is given), it is possible to elaborate on Levi's experience and to explore the banquet that follows in light of Jesus' radical acceptance of those who are despised.

Issuing a theological challenge. Focusing on Jesus' call to Levi and his mealtime fellowship with sinners, a sermon highlighting Jesus' radical acceptance of others could issue a challenge for us to consider anew those we have rejected or discounted. Many people look at Levi and see a sinner; Jesus sees a disciple. Like the scribes who peek around the doorway and witness a banquet in which they refuse to participate, the church would do well to wonder why Jesus chose to spend time with people who seem different from most "religious" people. But perhaps it is we ourselves who have crossed our names off the guest list. Why do we work so hard to draw boundary lines between ourselves and others? Are we not also the sinners Jesus calls to discipleship? New life abounds through Jesus' act of seeing others differently and approaching people with acceptance and compassion.

Speaking of metaphors: the messianic banquet. There can be no mistaking the celebratory tone and messianic connotations of this episode. In Levi's call and the banquet that follows we have a foretaste of God's gracious reign and the goodness we are invited to share with others in the company of Jesus Christ. In anticipation of the eschatological banquet, Jesus enjoys table fellowship with a surprising assortment of saints, sinners, and scoundrels whose company, we may well suspect, was a lot more enjoyable than that of most religious folk. Why is it that many religious persons do not know how to throw a good party or enjoy and engage the company of people who look and act differently? When Jesus joins the feast, he enjoys what the scribes could not: Levi's decision to follow Jesus.

Whether or not Levi's friends understood his new direction in life, they knew enough to join in his happiness. Irenaeus once said, "The beauty of God is a human being fully alive." Levi was nothing short of beautiful that day, and the banquet he enjoyed is one we all hope to join.

FASTING, FEASTING, AND SOMETHING NEW (2:18–22)

Exploring the text

As the third of five controversy stories, this passage represents a further escalation of tension between the religious leaders and Jesus. They confront him directly rather than speaking through his disciples (cf. 2:13–17), and Jesus responds by asserting the newness of God's reign.

This third confrontation combines two distinct units (vv. 18–20 and vv. 21–22) into a single teaching moment. The first describes an unidentified group of people who approach Jesus and ask why his disciples do not fast like those of John and the Pharisees. It appears likely that those who confront Jesus are the scribes and Pharisees spoken of in the surrounding episodes. Their question about fasting reflects a concern to define religious identity and promote independence amid a hostile environment. Fasting was not only prescribed on the Day of Atonement (Lev. 16:29; 23:26) but it was customary for religious leaders to institute public fasts during times of mourning and repentance. According to Luke 18:12, it was also common for Pharisees and other religious persons to fast twice a week. Evidently, John's disciples regularly joined in the practice of public fasting. Because rabbis were held responsible for the behavior of their disciples, the question about Jesus' disciples abstaining from the ritual of public fasting is hardly surprising.

Jesus' response does not disparage the practice but asserts the inappropriateness of fasting while he is with them. Invoking the image of a wedding, Jesus insists that his disciples must not fast while he, the bridegroom, is among them. The Pharisees and scribes, however, do not recognize the significance of this eschatological moment. Hebrew Scripture repeatedly associates God with the bridegroom whom Israel awaits (e.g., Isa. 62:5; Jer. 2:2), and the most obvious meaning of Jesus' words is that his disciples are now rejoicing in the eschatological gift of God's reign embodied in his coming. Disturbed by his message, the religious leaders will soon do all they can to get rid of him (3:6).

His followers, however, hear something else that alarms them: Jesus has announced that the bridegroom will soon be taken away. It is the first of many allusions Jesus will make in the Gospel of Mark to his forced departure and impending death. As early as the second chapter, Jesus intimates that his leaving will be painful and premature. The time of fasting will arrive soon enough.

The second part of this passage (vv. 21–22) proclaims the radical newness of **God's reign**. After speaking of the bridegroom, Jesus offers two other images in rapid succession: cloaks and wine. Both could be found at weddings and were staples of daily life. He uses the common activities of clothing repair and wine making to imagine the passing of old ways and the beginning of something new. If you patch an old garment with unshrunk cloth, the new cloth will pull away from the old, resulting in greater damage to both. Likewise, if you put new wine into old skins, the fermentation process of the young grapes will burst the skins, resulting in the loss of both skins and wine. As he describes the new being torn away from the old, we may recall Jesus' baptism when the heavens were torn apart and God's power was suddenly on the loose in the world (1:10). This word also arises later when the high priest tears his clothes at Jesus' trial (14:63) and when the temple curtain is torn in two at the time of Jesus' death (15:38). God's reign inaugurates a new way of being that cannot be sustained by old orders of religious conduct.

Jesus does not disparage old cloaks or wineskins and says nothing to indicate delight in their destruction. Instead, he insists that old ways of practicing faith are incongruous with God's new dominion. Announcing the inevitable passing of the present order, Mark reflects a greater level of tension between traditional Jewish faith and the new order inaugurated by Jesus Christ than is depicted in Matthew 9:16–17 or Luke 5:36–39. The tension between the former traditions of the elders and the eschatological newness of God's reign inaugurated by Christ undoubtedly reflects tensions between the traditions of first-century Judaism and the church.[1] However, Jesus' closing words in this third episode are less a renunciation than a rallying call: Put new wine in fresh wineskins! The power of God is alive among you. Drink the new wine and partake of the heavenly feast.

Preaching and teaching the Word

The two controversies depicted in 2:13–17 and 18–22 appear together among the lectionary readings for the Eighth Sunday of Epiphany, Year B. Yet the manner of Jesus' speaking, the images and parables he employs, and his insistence on the utterly new manifestation of God's reign in verses 18–22 provide more than enough ideas for one sermon. This and the other four confrontations of 2:1–3:6 lend themselves well to a five-part series related to ministering amid controversial and challenging circumstances.

One approach to preaching this episode is to recognize that every local congregation, denomination, and Christian organization has had to grapple with *the tension between old and new patterns of religious life.* This text announces God's call to recognize a radically different orientation to faith and religious priorities. Just as the early church often wrestled with its relationship to Judaism, religious communities today struggle to discern what it means to embody alternative forms of public worship, new ways of naming God, new media of communication, and new priorities in outreach and mission. How do we respect earlier traditions and at the same time embrace and advocate a new vision of God in our midst? Jesus' parables of old cloaks and new wine are especially helpful in this regard: they reflect radical interest in ancient practices yet insist on the radical reformation of them. In my own faith tradition as an Anabaptist, respect is given to the so-called Old Order churches (the Old Order Amish, Old Order Mennonites, and Old Order Brethren). However, our history as Anabaptists is riddled with numerous schisms marking the division between old and new ways of being church in the world. Sometimes old ways are put aside and new forms of church life take root and flourish; sometimes old ways of faith provide essential markers of a radical perspective that "new order" churches need to reclaim.

Another approach to this text is to explore the *practice of fasting* as it may help or hinder the life of faith. Mark 2:18–20 focuses on the communal experience of God's presence and power among us as it relates to this ancient practice. As noted earlier, Jesus' response to the Pharisees' question does not disparage fasting but recasts the discussion in terms of its purposes amid God's present and coming reign. Given the prevalence of eating disorders in our society, it is important to remember, as Jesus does, that there are indeed good reasons to abstain from this particular practice. To everything there is a season, and Jesus informs the Pharisees that while he is present among them, they do not need to grieve or fast. However, fasting may help us express our longing for God's just and loving reign and cultivate a spirit of readiness to participate in God's kingdom anew.

Jesus draws on *images from daily life* to help us glimpse the reality of God's new and powerful presence among us. The images and metaphors in this passage urge us to proclaim God's reign as we explore current events, daily activities, popular images, and stories. Jesus' parables both reveal and conceal God's reign and power in our midst as we are drawn into a realm of faithful imagination (see also Mark 4). Jesus speaks of God's reign as new wine thrown alongside former traditions and new patches sewn alongside old garments. Inevitably and dramatically, all will be transformed by God's new way of life in Jesus Christ.

SABBATH PROVISION (2:23–28)

Exploring the text

The fourth in a five-part series of controversies between Jesus and the religious authorities continues the motif of eating, but this time the confrontation takes place on the Sabbath. Under the scrupulous gaze of the Pharisees, Jesus' disciples pluck heads of grain and are criticized for working on the day of rest. The escalation of tension between Jesus and the Pharisees is evident in their abrupt attack: they no longer question Jesus and his disciples about breaking with Pharisaic tradition (2:18–22) but accuse them of doing what is not lawful on the Sabbath. It is no longer sins of omission that trouble the religious leaders but sins of commission.

It may help us to appreciate what is at stake in the Pharisees' accusation if we remember that the many laws governing Sabbath behavior are not only intended to encourage personal rest and recreation but to provide public markers of one's devotion to God and commitment to the community of faith. Among the Ten Commandments, none is so fully developed as the fourth, which pertains to the Sabbath (Exod. 20:8–11; Deut. 5:12–15). If we are willing to grant the Pharisees the best possible motive for their question, then they are not driven by petty legalistic concerns but a genuine fear of offending God and diminishing the life of faith. However, their question contains more self-interest than they are willing to admit: Jesus' radical freedom to authorize acceptable Sabbath behavior poses a threat to those who seek governance over these matters.[1]

Jesus' response to the Pharisees' accusation is remarkable for at least two reasons. First, *it focuses on God's life-giving purposes for the Sabbath.* Jesus cares about his disciples, supports their efforts to find something to eat, and places his concern for the provision of food within the context of Sabbath living. We have no reason to believe that the disciples were lazy, forgetful, or disrespectful when they plucked heads of grain on the Sabbath. Rather, Jesus explicitly mentions hunger and the need for food when he draws a comparison between his disciples' activity and the experience of David in 1 Samuel 21:1–6, who was blameless for eating the "bread of the presence." According to the law of Moses, the edges of a field are to be left ungleaned to provide grain for the poor and hungry (Lev. 19:9; 23:22) since God created the Sabbath for humankind and not humankind for the Sabbath. The Pharisees' preoccupation with methods of gleaning reveals a lack of empathy and a denial of God's life-giving intentions for the Sabbath.

Second, *Jesus' response asserts his divine authority.* Beginning with a rhetorical counterquestion, Jesus challenges the Pharisees' reading and interpretation of Scripture (2:25). He then develops an argument based on biblical precedent and cleverly associates himself with Davidic lines of authority and the bread of presence dedicated to God and designated for the priests' consumption on the Sabbath. At least two textual problems arise in our consideration of verses 25–26: it was not Abiathar but his father Ahimelech who served as high priest during David's incursion into the Temple (cf. 1 Sam. 30:7), and the text of 1 Samuel 21 does not indicate that David's companions were with him but that he deceived the priests rather than share the loaves of bread with others. It seems, then, that Jesus exercises a measure of hermeneutical ingenuity as he rehabilitates David's lie to the high priest and reshapes the biblical story for his own purposes.[2]

Jesus also asserts his authority through two prophetic announcements. In verse 27 he insists that the Pharisees have utterly reversed God's priorities when he announces, "The Sabbath was made for humankind, not humankind for the Sabbath." His assertion does not contradict the biblical mandate (Exod. 31:14) but pronounces God's will and intention for humanity. Also, in verse 28 Jesus announces, "The Son of Man is lord even of the sabbath." The self-designation "Son of Man" infuriates the Pharisees and asserts Jesus' divine prerogative to determine what is acceptable Sabbath practice (see **messianic titles**). The content and manner of Jesus' response to the Pharisees proclaim his role as final arbiter of religious faith and point to the Sabbath as a sign of the new age when God's provision for humanity will be fully realized and enjoyed.

Preaching and teaching the Word

For the Second Sunday following Pentecost in Year B, this passage is considered in the RCL alongside the fifth controversy, which also takes place on the Sabbath (3:1–6). These verses contain a great deal of practical wisdom for the church to ponder and pursue.

One way to approach this passage is to ask, *What are God's Sabbath purposes for us and the world today?* We would be wise to consider anew how God's life-giving intentions may be experienced and cultivated through regular Sabbath observance. Many of us struggle with competing demands for our time and energy, rampant consumerism, frenetic schedules, and/or feelings of intense loneliness within cultures that promote individual interests above community well-being. There is no shortage of "how to" manuals to encourage our interests. Fortunately, there are also a few other books to help us consider anew the meaning and possibilities of Sabbath observance.[3] Jesus insists that all of our ideas and arguments about the Sabbath must be understood in light of God's will to provide for our well-being and the well-being of others.

Theologically, there are at least six reasons for individuals and communities of faith to consider anew God's life-giving possibilities through Sabbath observance. First, the Sabbath is a day to remember our liberation from bondage to slavery and subjugation (for example, we break our bondage to consumerism when we cease for a day to visit markets and shopping malls). Second, the Sabbath is a day to reclaim the gift of rest (for example, we may cease working when the sun sets in order to begin our rest early and arise refreshed and attentive to God and those around us). Third, the Sabbath is a day to honor God's sovereignty as Lord and lover of life (for example, most Christians combine the day of Sabbath rest with services of public worship). Fourth, honoring the Sabbath expresses abiding trust in God as the ultimate source of our daily sustenance (for example, when we cease from our own labors we remember and proclaim our radical reliance on God to provide for our every need). Fifth, the Sabbath reminds us of God's life-giving intentions for all creation and unites us with nature and its abundant yet threatened resources (for example, time for outdoor activities and physical play may help restore our relationship with and accountability to nature). Sixth, the Sabbath is also a time to savor a foretaste of the messianic age, when we observe the peace of Christ and look for his living presence among us (for example, the Sabbath is a time to renew our efforts to make peace with others and to seek God's presence in all people).

We may also approach this text aware of *Jesus' passionate concern for the poor and all who hunger for daily provisions.* His dual references to hunger and the need for food in verse 25 indicate the high priority Jesus gives to these concerns. Jesus' care for the physical needs of all people is at the heart of the gospel, and his provision of food to the hungry is central to his ministry and to God's reign (6:30–44; 8:1–10). Because it is a Sabbath priority, Jesus' concern for the poor and hungry is intended to be a regular part of our focus and concern also. However, many of us do not know what it is like to be genuinely hungry. The Pharisees were certainly aware that Mosaic law provided a system of social security allowing persons in need to pluck grain along the edges of other people's fields (Lev. 19:9; 23:22)[4] but they were either not hungry enough or empathetic enough to associate the meeting of human needs with God's Sabbath purposes. Their inexplicable presence in the field that day suggests they are not there to pick grain but to pick a fight.

Finally, if we are honest with ourselves we may recognize at least *two tendencies we hold in common with the Pharisees.* First, many of us forget or refuse to acknowledge God's passionate concern for those who are hungry. Even the best intended religious persons become easily preoccupied with matters of personal conduct or morality while neglecting God's most pressing ethical concerns. We are fascinated with others' sexual behavior but largely unaware of those in our own community who are hungry. We spend inordinate amounts of time and energy advocating for the placement of the Ten Commandments in public places but have less enthusiasm for the commandment to love our neighbors as ourselves and advocate on behalf of the poor. We spend over a third of our federal budget on military-related expenses and less than 2 percent on hunger relief. Second, just as the Pharisees wanted to determine what constitutes right Sabbath practice, we also assert the right of self-determination in establishing or ignoring religious practices. We are guilty of denying Jesus' authority when we labor without ceasing and refuse to trust that God is the source of all that we need and desire.

SABBATH HEALING (3:1–6)

Exploring the text

Jesus' interactions with religious leaders throughout 2:1–3:6 set off sparks that ignite controversy and culminate in a firestorm of opposition. This final episode in a series of five controversies ends with the development of a plot to destroy him (3:6). The story of healing the man with a withered hand on the Sabbath continues the concerns raised in the previous episode and is set alongside it in the lectionary readings for the Second Sunday following Pentecost in Year B. Both episodes take place on the Sabbath and raise questions about Jesus' authority in relationship to Sabbath observance. The healing story provides lively testimony to Jesus' proclamation of God's reign amid heightened controversy and impending danger.

When Jesus arrives at the synagogue to worship God (cf. 1:21–28) he scarcely walks through the door before he sees a man with a withered hand. The Pharisees' eyes are on Jesus, but Jesus' eyes are looking in another direction. He sees one whose needs take precedence over religious infighting and whose malady prompts Jesus to demonstrate God's good and loving intentions. Verse 2 does not specify that the Pharisees are the only ones watching and waiting to accuse Jesus of violating the Sabbath, but it is clear from verse 6 that they and other detractors are present. Jesus' insight into their innermost thoughts parallels his prescience in the first controversy story (2:8). At that point, however, the scribes were simply raising questions as Jesus healed the paralytic and the crowd responded with amazement and praise. By the fifth episode, interlocutors have become adversaries who begin to plot his demise. Aware of the Pharisees' objections, Jesus turns his attention elsewhere.

The Greek phrase Jesus uses to bid the man forward (literally, "rise up to the middle") calls the man to the center of public attention as the locus of Jesus' care and concern. He refuses to engage the Pharisees in verbal sparring over rules of conduct or hypothetical cases. Instead, he focuses his hearers' attention on a particular human being who stands in their midst. For the second time in this episode Jesus acts as provocateur in confronting his detractors: "Is it lawful to do good or do harm on the Sabbath, to save life or to kill?" (3:4) His two-part question is not meant to avoid the Pharisees' objections but to redirect their concern. The Pharisees and other critics of Jesus' ministry know they cannot say it is lawful to do harm on the Sabbath. If someone's life is in danger, they know that Sabbath laws must be broken to rescue one in need.[1] However, later rabbinic tradition also argues that any disease that is not life-threatening is to be treated on a day other than the Sabbath.[2] Jesus' question therefore urges his hearers to consider anew what it means to do good and to fulfill God's compassionate intentions. His words and deeds proclaim the eschatological gift of Sabbath fulfillment as Jesus helps people experience healing, relief, and newness of life.

A dangerous silence fills the room. In the words of Robert Beck, "They oppose him in silence. Jesus has the word of power; they are impotent."[3] We could say that Jesus is not judicious in his use of rhetorical strategy; after all, his public humiliation of the Pharisees and other critics fuel the flames of resentment against him. But we could also say that God's wisdom and love is alive in Jesus as never before. He reacts to his opponent's silent reproach with compassion for the disabled man and feelings of anger and grief for his adversaries. Jesus' emotional response is significant. It not only reflects an intellectual or theoretical concern for others but an emotional and visceral one as well. His interlocutors have placed theological arguments above human well-being. The Pharisees' sclerotic response to persons in need recalls Pharaoh's hardness of heart that resulted in Israel's enslavement and Pharaoh's own demise.[4] Because the heart was considered the seat of human will, reflection, and emotion, Jesus' perception of the Pharisees' hardness of heart exposes their grievous resistance to God's just and loving reign (see also 6:52; 8:17; 10:5).

When Jesus commands the man to stretch out his hand, it is fully restored without even a touch or word of blessing (cf. 1:41). Since verbal communication can hardly be deemed work, it is ironic he is accused of violating the Sabbath. In fact, this passage bristles with irony: Not only is Jesus wrongly accused of violating the Sabbath, but the one who offers healing and the gift of life to others is threatened with losing his own life. Contrary to the rabbinic principle of saving life on the Sabbath, the Pharisees and Herodians are guilty of desecrating the Sabbath as they plot Jesus' death. By the end of this episode, these religious and political leaders join forces to plan his demise (cf. 11:18; 12:12; 14:1), just as it will take both religious and political leaders to bring about his crucifixion.

Preaching and teaching the Word

In addition to a reconsideration of Sabbath practices and their potential meaning for our lives (see "Preaching and teaching the Word" for 2:23–28, p. 47), these six verses urge us to consider the following topics:

In terms of Christian faith and ethics, *how have we neglected God's call to do good for others?* When we refuse to do good, whether through passivity, ignorance, or benign neglect, we become unwitting participants in evil. At great risk to his own reputation and well-being, Jesus chooses otherwise. In the aftermath of the hurricanes that ravaged Gulf Coast communities in 2005, Senator Barack Obama reacted to the federal government's lack of a coordinated and effective response to the victims by insisting, "Passive indifference is as bad as active malice."[5] According to Joel Marcus, "For Mark's Jesus, the eschatological war is already raging. . . . The cautious middle ground, upon which one might wait a few minutes before doing good, has disappeared."[6]

Various emotions are named in this brief story, and they invite us to reflect on *the role of emotion, empathy, and compassion in Christian faith and service.* Jesus' experience of anger and grief reveals something of the depth and vitality of his engagement with others. For most of us, however, anger and grief can be experienced as overpowering emotions that rob us of understanding or drain our energy. Scripture itself bears testimony to anger's diverse effects (e.g., Ps. 139:21–22; Jas. 1:19–20; 2 Cor. 7:10–12). Plato described the human personality as a chariot pulled by two horses, anger and desire, and driven by a charioteer, reason. Similarly, grief that is not acknowledged or honored threatens our well-being and that of others. Guided by love and compassion, Jesus' experience of anger and grief stands in potent contrast to the hardness of heart that characterizes his adversaries. When our hearts are hardened, Jesus calls us away from selfish preoccupations to empathize with others and work with compassion.[7]

This text opens the way for us to consider *services of healing and rituals of public blessing.* In my own faith tradition, services of anointing have been practiced for centuries in both private and public settings. They provide opportunities to confess our sin and/or need for God's help, to strengthen our faith, and to receive God's gifts of healing and wholeness, however they may be given.[8] With appreciation for the field of medicine and various healing arts, services of anointing involve the community of faith in the ministry of healing. Although we do not always (or often) experience a cure for what ails us, we may always experience healing as we entrust ourselves to God's care.

This passage also bids us to *recognize the dangerous consequences of proclaiming God's just and merciful reign.* It is the culmination of a series of five conflicts between Jesus and other religious leaders who resent and resist his authority. There is no doubt that violating the Sabbath is only one of his adversaries' many concerns: Jesus demonstrates divine power to overcome the forces of evil, declares the forgiveness of sins, proclaims God's will to accept those whom others despise, announces the radical newness of God's reign, names himself lord of the Sabbath, and offends the religious sensibilities of the most powerful leaders of his time. It is no wonder that people of power and influence feared him. It is more of a wonder that they did not kill him outright. The power of God is never more threatening to the powers that be than when it involves the radical practice of mercy toward all people. When members of Christian Peacemaker Teams act as advocates for families in Iraq whose members are imprisoned, they work without security guards in order to build trust and help people who suffer the consequences of the U.S. occupation. Many of these Christian Peacemakers have been beaten and arrested; one has been killed. In praying for allies and enemies, hostages and captors, we participate in God's reconciling love for all people, asking that God release us from bondage and the need to make enemies of those we might call friends.

Old Boundaries, New Possibilities

Mark 3:7–35

Immediately following the cycle of five controversies in 2:1–3:6, Jesus faces new and more disturbing efforts to slander his ministry and challenge his authority. Crowds continue to be drawn to his healing activity, but demons are the only ones to recognize his true identity. Twelve disciples are named as Jesus' closest followers, but we hear from the very outset that one will betray him. When Jesus returns home, family members suspect he is out of his mind, and religious dignitaries sent from Jerusalem attribute his power to satanic sources. Is it any wonder that Jesus refutes their accusations with images of plundered houses and warnings of damnation for those who refuse to recognize the work of the Holy Spirit among them?

JESUS HEALS THE DISEASED AND COMMISSIONS THE TWELVE (3:7–19a)

Exploring the text

Mark offers two episodes that communicate the dynamic and far-reaching possibilities of Jesus' ministry with others (vv. 7–12 and vv. 13–19a). Neither of these stories is included among the readings in the RCL, yet they communicate valuable information about Jesus' growing ministry and help us appreciate the nature of his ministry and the role of the disciples. The first episode is one of several summary statements in Mark's Gospel (see also 1:14–15, 38–39; 6:53–56) and recounts Jesus' growing popularity. The second offers a glimpse of the inner workings of Jesus' ministry as he calls several followers to a closer relationship with him, commissioning them to proclaim the gospel and cast out demons.

Healing People from Far and Wide (3:7–12)

Amid mounting opposition and controversy, Jesus experiences success and increased popularity as a healer. The narrative takes a decisive turn in verse 7 when, aware of the murderous plot against him, Jesus leaves the synagogue and seeks refuge with his disciples by the sea. However, instead of rest he finds a multitude of people from various regions who come to him for help and to receive his healing power. This summary of Jesus' healing ministry is then followed by an account of his naming the twelve disciples.[1]

The presence of the crowd signals at least three important aspects of Jesus' ministry. First, despite his extensive ministry, Jesus is still not recognized as the Son of God by anyone except the unclean spirits. Jesus' first priority is to proclaim the good news of God's reign (1:38), but there is no indication that the multitudes come to hear him preach. Instead, they want to receive healing (3:8b), and they appear no more aware of who Jesus is than the Pharisees and Herodians who plot his destruction in 3:6. Second, it is striking that those who seek healing long to touch him. Because human contact is not the only means to effect healing (see 7:24–30 and Luke 7:1–10, where Jesus is reported to have healed with a word), it is significant that people assume the need of physical contact and that Jesus himself seems to prefer modes of healing that include physical touch (see 1:40–45; 5:27–31; 6:56; 7:33; 8:22; 10:13). Jesus reaches out to Jews and Gentiles, men and women, and the ritually clean and unclean. At this point, strangers from all over seek contact with him. Third, the people who throng to Jesus' side come from a variety of regions that encompass a range of ethnic and religious identities. Word of his healing power has traveled far and wide, including to the north (Jerusalem) and south of Judea (Idumea), as well as to the eastern regions beyond the Jordan and the Greek cities of Tyre and Sidon, inhabited mostly by Gentiles. According to Blount and Charles, those who seek Jesus "come increasingly from beyond the boundaries of Jewish space. . . . The communal ground is shifting toward the impure and unholy, even toward the Gentiles."[2]

There are two other groups present throughout this episode. First, the disciples accompany Jesus and help secure a boat to ensure his safety and provide a platform for preaching. Throughout Mark's Gospel the sea is a frequent place of refuge and transformation (e.g., 4:35–41; 6:45–52) and the disciples often accompany Jesus as he ventures out to sea to find a place apart from the crowds or to travel to another area. Their quiet presence in this passage prepares us for the next episode, when Jesus will commission them to minister to others as his closest followers. In addition to the disciples, the unclean spirits also play an important role. They are the only ones to speak, but Jesus quickly silences their announcement of his identity as the Son of God (see **messianic titles**). There are several possible explanations for this. Perhaps he did not want the demons to name him because they were less than ideal character witnesses, or perhaps he did not want anyone to identify him as God's Son until after his crucifixion and resurrection (see **messianic secret**). Yet another explanation is suggested by the narrative context of this passage. Given Jesus' commissioning of the twelve (3:13–19a) and his insistence that those who do the will of God are his true brothers, sisters, and mother (3:31–35), it seems likely that Jesus did not want individuals testifying on his behalf who did not follow his way of life and embody his teachings. The unclean spirits do nothing except possess and damage others, whereas those who are filled with God's Spirit manifest God's compassion and resist all that destroys God's life-giving intentions for humanity (3:23–30).

Commissioning His Closest Followers (3:13–19a)

As Jesus moves from seaside to mountainside, he leaves the commotion of the crowds and calls together his closest followers. At this point in the Gospel Jesus is aware of opposition to his ministry (vv. 1–6), and he realizes that people pursue him primarily because of his healing power (vv. 7–12). The time has come to commission followers (see **disciples**) who will witness his ministry of preaching (chap. 4) and healing (chap. 5) and go forth to continue this ministry (6:7–13).

On the mountain, Jesus sets in motion the earliest stages of a new community of faith. "The mountain" recalls images of Moses at Sinai (Exod. 19; 24:1–4), and later in Mark's Gospel mountains are places of retreat (6:46), transformation, and revelation (9:1–8). Like Moses, Jesus initiates a transformative moment in the life of God's people: he does not simply "call" the twelve, for the Greek phrase suggests that Jesus "made" the twelve disciples his inner circle. Ched Myers points to the political dimensions of his commissioning as well: "By reenacting a 'new Sinai' covenant on the mountain, Jesus is attacking the ideological foundations of the dominant order. . . . Jesus, having repudiated the authority of the priestly/scribal order, now forms a kind of vanguard 'revolutionary committee,' a 'government in exile'! A community of resistance has been founded."[1] The number twelve, of course, has eschatological significance. In the first century CE, the reconstitution of all twelve tribal units was a distant hope to be fulfilled at the end of time when the ten lost tribes would be restored.[2] Jesus inaugurates an essential facet of God's reign, namely, the formation of a community that will witness his ministry. From this point on, the Gospel has as much to do with Jesus' followers as with Jesus.

There are two essential responsibilities that Jesus names for his disciples. Most importantly, he calls them to be with him. It is the first priority of discipleship and the surest mark of their loyalty to him. In contrast to the unclean spirits who fling themselves onto the scene then depart without further notice, Christ calls his followers to remain by his side in order to deepen their faith and strengthen their ministry. As chapters 4 and 5 of Mark's Gospel unfold, Jesus will preach, teach and heal others, with the disciples as his constant companions and apprentices. But before they can fulfill the second responsibility of proclaiming God's reign and casting out demons (as they are sent forth to do in 6:7–13), they must stay near him to receive his guidance, authority, and power. In contrast to the unclean spirits, his closest followers are commissioned to speak in his name and minister to others in word and deed (3:14–15). By the grace of God and the power of the Holy Spirit they will participate with Jesus Christ in the apocalyptic struggle to overcome the forces of evil by proclaiming the message of God's reign and casting out demons.

Mark notes that there are many others "whom [Jesus] wanted" to follow him up the mountain. No doubt these included disciples who are mentioned later in the Gospel, including several women (see 4:10; 10:32; 15:40–41). Peter, James, and John are often mentioned together (e.g., 9:2–13; 10:32–40). Simon the Cananaean (meaning "zealot" or "enthusiast") may have been a member of a nationalistic movement that resisted Roman rule. Judas Iscariot is named last as the betrayer of Jesus. The group of twelve represent a diverse collection of fishermen, tax collectors, those who may have opposed Roman rule, one who conspired with authorities to secure Jesus' arrest, and many others we never hear of again. Some of their names are Semitic (e.g., Simon, Matthew), others are of Greek origin (e.g., Philip, Andrew) while others are given new names (e.g., Peter, Sons of Thunder). Yet this disparate group comprises the inner circle of Jesus' followers who are simply called "the twelve" (e.g., 6:7; 9:35; 11:11; 14:17).[3] They are among his closest companions and are members of a new family of faith who, despite their failures and faithlessness, are entrusted with the good news of God's reign.

Preaching and teaching the Word

There is enough action in these two stories to draw us close to the water's edge or up the mountainside to be near Jesus. Whether considered separately or together, these passages offer several preaching and teaching opportunities.

The tension between silence and speaking, between demonic announcement and disciplined witness, bids us to consider *the stark contrast between those who are silenced and others who are commissioned to proclaim the good news of Jesus Christ.* For all the reasons noted above, Jesus did not want the unclean spirits to identify him as the **Son of God** (see also messianic secret). They neither accept nor practice Jesus' way of serving others in God's reign. Because most of us struggle to speak of Jesus publicly to friends and neighbors (let alone strangers), the bravado of these unclean spirits offends our social sensibilities, and we welcome Jesus' stern order for them to keep quiet. His admonishment serves as a warning to all people that it is not enough to correctly name Jesus or simply acknowledge his authority and power. Instead, the emphasis in 3:13–15 is on what his followers are called to do. Jesus calls people to proclaim the gospel in word and deed (see also 3:19b–35): to follow him closely, to act with his authority in casting out demons, and to provide loving testimony of God's reign.

There are *two necessary and vital dimensions of Jesus' call to discipleship: to be with him and to be sent out by him.* The translation of 3:14b–15 in the TEV helps to clarify and personalize the dual callings of Jesus evident in the text: "'I have chosen you to be with me,' he told them. 'I will also send you out to preach, and you will have authority to drive out demons.'" To be close to Jesus and to go out in service to others are both essential to Christian discipleship. Many of us tend to favor one or the other of these, to be pray-ers or do-ers, to dwell in Christ's presence or to serve Christ's people. But Jesus' call is to dwell with him and to minister to others so that piety and prophetic justice become loving companions in the life of faith. When we find ourselves lost in private seclusion with Jesus, his call for us to speak and act on his behalf draws us into new and challenging ministries. When we find ourselves weary in well-doing, prayer and dwelling in his presence offer us new life and hope. In his book *Space for God,* Don Postema writes, "Prayer opens us to a closeness with God, the compassionate God we know in Jesus Christ. And the closer we get to God, the closer we get to the people of the world. We find the world at the heart of God."[4] To be with Jesus and to be sent forth in ministry into the world by him are not separate activities but one and the same mission. Our nearness to God in Christ calls and empowers us to move with compassion in service to others.

These stories speak of *the community of faith as the locus of Jesus' presence and power.* The call to Christian discipleship comes to individuals but never to individuals alone. Throughout Mark's account, disciples are called into the company of others so that their ministries are not isolated acts of heroism but a shared mission of faith. Jesus also needed fellowship, and he longed to be surrounded by those he loved (3:13), just as he called the twelve to share a common mission (3:14–15). This new community is of a different kind than we are accustomed. Jesus does not attract an entourage of admirers who hover about, nor does he collect a group of secret agents or private bodyguards to act as bouncers when he is confronted by opponents.[5] Together the disciples worry and wonder about Jesus (4:35–41), go forth and serve those in need (6:7), eat and labor at his urging (6:30–44), struggle and compete with one another for his favor (10:35–41), and share in the same failure of faith when they desert him in his time of need (14:50). But they also share in the joy of his resurrection and the call that Jesus issues to join him in Galilee, where they will continue his ministry (16:6–7).

JESUS OVERPOWERS ENEMIES AND WELCOMES
A NEW FAMILY OF FAITH (3:19b–35)

A disturbing encounter with family members at home is interrupted by Jesus' confrontation with scribes who are visiting from Jerusalem. Immediately afterward, Jesus' encounter with his family is resumed as he defines kinship in terms of obedience to God's will. Mark's literary tactic of intercalation (interposing one episode within another) highlights the similarities and differences between each encounter (see also 5:21–43; 6:6–32). Crises erupt at every turn as Jesus is virulently opposed by those who should have been his most ardent supporters.

Exploring the text

At this point in the Gospel, Jesus moves from crossing boundaries and shattering barriers to drawing lines of division (cf. 1:40–45; 2:13–17). He has garnered the criticism of family, friends, and foes, who claim he is either deluded or demonic. Employing some of the sharpest rhetorical tools possible, Jesus provokes a theological crisis among those who question his sanity and challenge his allegiance to God. Using apocalyptic imagery and separatist tactics, he speaks of Satan on one side and the Holy Spirit on the other, kingdoms and households divided and new alliances forged, outsiders distanced from him and insiders near to him. Jesus urges his hearers to make a choice in the ongoing battle between divine will and demonic forces.

We feel the full effect of Jesus' response to the accusations of others through three successive movements. The first (3:19b–21) is signaled by Jesus' abrupt and intentional move from the mountain to his hometown. Similar to his first trip home (2:1), Jesus is met again by a crowd of interested supporters who are so numerous that there is no room to move about and prepare a meal. We may assume that their presence posed a threat to religious and political power brokers who wanted to control the authorization of religious tradition and temper popular opinion about Jesus. But it is not the religious authorities who are the first to offer their critique: his own family members are the first to confront him.

All four Gospels report that family members resisted Jesus, but only in Mark do we hear of their concern for his sanity and their will to restrain him. As his closest kin, they should be Jesus' surest source of personal support and his most dependable line of defense against aggression and assault. Instead, they have heard that he is out of his mind and decide to take matters into their own hands by removing him from public view (see also 6:1–6a). Perhaps they mean to ensure his safety and are concerned for his well-being. Or perhaps, in terms of negotiating ancient standards of honor and shame, they hope to protect the entire family from humiliation as he incites the criticism of religious authorities. Whatever their motives, Jesus' family members are the first to restrain him. The phrase *kratesai auton* is more accurately translated "to seize him by force" in keeping with its meaning elsewhere in Mark's Gospel (6:17; 12:12; 14:1, 44, 46, 49, 51).

In the second part of this extended narrative (3:22–30), Jesus' confrontation with family members is interrupted by accusations from scribal authorities. While his family suspects that Jesus is out of his mind, and while they may be motivated by concern for Jesus' well-being and a desire to prevent further damage to the family's reputation, the scribes have other concerns. They are anxious about Jesus' authority among the crowds and are angry that he interprets faith and religious practice in ways that threaten existing traditions and lines of authority. Although no one disputes Jesus' being able to perform miracles of healing and exorcism, the scribes are particularly threatened by his growing popularity and assertions of divine authority. Determined to damage his reputation, they accuse Jesus of being in league with Beelzebul, the ruler of demons.[1] Jesus is possessed, the scribes declare, and it is by the power of Satan that he is able to do what he does.

Jesus responds to these accusations with an **apocalyptic** battle of words that includes parabolic speech and prophetic denunciation. Although he uses parables in the next chapter as a favorite means of teaching, at this point they serve as a means of confronting and combating those who oppose the **reign of God** he represents on earth. Jesus announces that he has come with the authority and power of God to overthrow the rule of Satan and to cast out his minions. He speaks of the impossibility of Satan casting out Satan, since any kingdom at war with itself cannot maintain its own sovereignty and a divided household is sure to end in dissolution and ruin. First-century Jews and Christians were painfully aware of the catastrophic consequences of the division of Herod's kingdom and household. Jesus' words and images would have borne political as well as religious significance in the lives of his hearers.[2] There is no doubt that Jesus intends to overcome all that opposes God's rule, to bind the strong man and plunder his property just as the prophet Isaiah spoke of in 49:24–35. According to Ched Myers, Mark uses the word "kingdom" to symbolize the centralized state (see 6:23; 11:10; 13:8) and "house" as its symbolic center, the Temple (see 11:17; 13:34–35).[3] In overcoming the strong man, Jesus will break into the Temple in Jerusalem, cast out the real thieves, and overturn their goods (11:15–17), proving himself "the stronger one" heralded by John (1:8). Politically and socially, Jesus refers to himself in uncivilized terms as a terrorist who is determined to do battle with all who oppose God's reign.

In 3:28–30, Jesus uses the statement "Truly I tell you" to invoke his authority as divine spokesperson. His words declare that those who have denied the power of God at work in him deny the Spirit of God in their midst. Jesus is indeed possessed, but it is not by Satan as the scribes allege; he is possessed of the Holy Spirit, who empowers his ministry and authorizes his every word and deed. Jesus insists that those who attribute divine power to satanic sources are guilty of an unpardonable sin. Unless they recognize and acknowledge the movement of the Holy Spirit in him, they will be guilty of the very blasphemy they accuse him of (see 2:6).

It is important to note that Jesus does not assume the scribes are beyond the influence of his words. He warns them of impending judgment but leaves open the possibility that they will ultimately recognize the Spirit of God working among them. Also, Jesus promises that all other sins will be forgiven. This is not just good news; it is the best news. But for those who deny the power and presence of God's Spirit at work in the world and wrongly attribute it to demonic powers, Jesus warns of the disastrous consequences; they will suffer eternal alienation from God. In the words of Juan Luis Segundo, "The real sin against the Holy Spirit is refusing to recognize, with 'theological' joy, some concrete liberation that is taking place before one's very eyes."[4]

The third and final movement in this passage occurs in 3:31–35 when Jesus' family members reenter the scene to assert their presence. We can only guess their reasons for approaching Jesus again, since we do not know if they have come to seize him by force (3:21), quietly escort him home, issue an ultimatum, or request a private meeting. Given their initial concern for his sanity, however, we can safely surmise that their call to him is not benign. As persons who have stood closest to Jesus throughout his formative years, it is significant that they now stand at a distance. Twice we hear that his family members are "outside," and twice we hear that others are "sitting around" him as insiders who make up a new community of faith and discipleship. The contrast between his blood relations and the new community that is forming around him is suggested by the spatial distance between them.

Jesus looks at those nearest to him and declares that they are his brothers and mother. The family of God is made up of those who do God's will. Furthermore, the inclusion of "sister" in 13:35 reflects an awareness of the importance of women in the family of faith, who are among Jesus' most intimate followers. Just as Jesus' "insiders" include more than the twelve who are named in 3:14–19 (see, e.g., 3:13; 4:10), Jesus leaves open the possibility that anyone who does God's will—regardless of ethnic identity, gender, religious affiliation, or kinship ties—may be counted among the members of God's family (see Isa. 49:18–21; 60:4). Although the Gospel at this point does not disclose what in particular we must do to fulfill the will of God, obedience is a dominant theme in Hebrew Scripture (e.g., the Shema of Deut. 6:4–9 and the Decalogue of Exod. 20:1–17 and Deut. 5:1–21). The Gospels testify that the whole of Jesus' life embodies God's will. As we follow him to Gethsemane we learn that Jesus himself faces the painful decision to do the will of God even as he realizes it will lead to death (Mark 14:36; Matt. 26:39; Luke 22:42).

Preaching and teaching the Word

In Year B of the RCL, this passage inaugurates the vast season of Ordinary Time. Yet Jesus' exchanges with others are truly extraordinary. He provokes a crisis among those who hear him, and his words call forth a convictional response from all who are willing to listen to his message today.

Provocative imagery. When Jesus refers to himself as the strong man who has come to plunder Satan's house, he uses some of the most disturbing imagery possible. Like a thief, he has come to break in, steal, plunder, and rout the devil's household. Like a terrorist, he is on a holy crusade to bind Satan and hold captive his oppressors. This is the language of an extremist and, in the aftermath of 9/11, it rattles our sensibilities to think of God engaged in a holy war of any kind. What do we mean when we refer to Satan and the forces of evil today? Are we referring to manifestations of psychological and/or physical illness, demonic possession, natural disasters, personal sin, acts of prejudice and cruelty, consumerism run amok, or other political and social systems of oppression and deceit? In *Binding the Strong Man*, Ched Myers views Jesus' declaration of ideological war against Satan as the climactic campaign of his ministry.[5] His political reading of the Gospel presses us to be clear about what we mean when we speak of the prevalence of evil among us. If we are sensitive to Jesus' warning not to misinterpret good as evil and deny the Spirit's presence and power among us, we must be cautious in identifying our enemies with Satan. At a time when individuals, groups, and nations are willing to vilify others in the name of God, it is all the more important that we claim for ourselves Jesus' will to transform evil through loving our enemies without resorting to violence.

Blasphemy against the Holy Spirit. What exactly is this unpardonable sin that Jesus alludes to and so many Christians fear? I once heard a pastor say that if you worry about whether you have committed the unpardonable sin of blasphemy against the Holy Spirit, you probably have not. In this text, blasphemy suggests total opposition to Jesus and an utter rejection of his will among us. Rather than focusing on such absolute terms, it may be more fruitful (and troubling) to address a far more insidious sin that threatens the spiritual welfare of all people, namely, hardness of heart that precludes our recognizing and receiving the movement of God in our midst and drives us to deny God's goodness in others. It seems that many of us, including churchgoers, find it easier to name evil than good. As one member of our group Bible study said, "If I discredit the very source of my hope, what hope is there for me or anyone else?"[6]

Hardness of heart, stubbornness of spirit, and a refusal to open oneself to other persons and ideas are among the most damaging sins that human beings may commit against God and neighbors. Jesus recognized the hard-heartedness of those who opposed him in 3:5, and today we must be ever vigilant in opposing this tendency among us. In his short story "The Thanksgiving Visitor," Truman Capote recounts his childhood experience of being bullied by Odd Henderson. When Truman's favorite older cousin invites Odd to join them for Thanksgiving, Truman is appalled when he secretly witnesses Odd stealing his cousin's cameo brooch. At the dinner table, Truman triumphantly announces what he has just witnessed. In a surprising act of courage, Odd confesses his sin, returns the pin, and walks quietly away. Truman is shamed for his indictment of their guest and flees the table. Later when his cousin speaks with him in private she explains:

> Two wrongs never made a right. It was wrong of him to take the cameo. But we don't know why he took it. Maybe he never meant to keep it. Whatever his reason, it can't have been calculated. Which is why what you did was much worse: you *planned* to

humiliate him. It was deliberate. Now listen to me, Buddy: there is only one unpardonable sin—*deliberate cruelty.* All else can be forgiven. That, never.[7]

Doing the will of God despite opposition: the creation of a new family of faith. Perhaps the most poignant and disturbing aspect of Jesus' encounter with family members and scribal authorities is his realization that those who could be his closest companions misunderstand and/or reject him. We are wise to listen to the concerns of loved ones and the words of elders who recognize some failing we are not able to see in ourselves. But the accusations against Jesus were entirely false and represented the scribes' fear of losing authority and power. There are times when we need to assert God's grace and claim a new direction for our lives despite the strident objections of those closest to us. In her book *God's Troublemakers: How Women of Faith Are Changing the World,* Katharine Rhodes Henderson describes the work of religious women who have challenged the status quo and acted as "social entrepreneurs" in a world that is often suspicious of them. One of these women is Lee Hancock, who heads outreach ministries that focus on healing and AIDS/HIV issues. Hancock insists:

> I'm not a person who's willing to give up the church and just go out into the world and be an activist on health care issues. Because I think that whatever religion is about—and that is to say healing and wisdom and education and activism and justice—that all of those more substantial virtues and goals aren't raised up any other place. So I will continue to be rooted in religion, even though the church is currently far too small and far too self-involved.[8]

According to Jesus, those who follow him are more than a collection of admirers or curiosity seekers. They are a new family of faith united by Christ's love and obedient to God's will. However, this new family of faith poses opportunities as well as dangers. The church may name and encourage one another's gifts, gently correct its members' failings, patiently accompany each other through times of sorrow or distress, serve side by side in local communities, imagine and plan the great possibilities of Christian ministry, develop a household budget that provides for its needs and the needs of the world at large, and welcome strangers into the family of faith through outreach to others. But there are also dangers that may inflict the family of Christ, including dysfunctional patterns of relationship among leaders and members, a tendency to become its own reference point of interest or concern, the domestication of prophetic initiatives, suspicion of new ideas and members, taking one another for granted, and forgetting to celebrate life's joys and honor life's losses. Amid these potential opportunities and dangers, Jesus urges us to remember our common call to do the will of God. In other words, our hope resides not in our individual giftedness, outstanding leadership, or ideal program initiatives but in Jesus Christ, who calls us together, abides among us, and empowers us to do God's will.

The Parables of Jesus and the Power of God's Reign

Mark 4:1–34

Through metaphor, allegory, and simile, the **parables** of Jesus recounted in the fourth chapter reveal the power of God's reign among us, mysteriously hidden yet revealed in the proclamation of Jesus (4:10–12, 22–23). Verses 1–34 provide the first sustained presentation of Jesus' preaching in the Gospel of Mark, and verses 35–41 serve as an important transition between the fourth and fifth chapters. This primer on **discipleship** is joined together by repeated references to hearing (the verb *akouein* occurs thirteen times) as well as opening and closing references to parables that challenge us to consider God's reign and our relationship to it (4:2, 33–34). The fourth chapter also reflects a tone of apocalyptic urgency that pervades the whole of Mark's Gospel. Another extensive preaching section in Mark, the apocalyptic discourse of chapter 13, calls us to look, keep awake, and be alert for what is to come. Chapters 4 and 13 therefore reflect the dual responsibilities of hearing and seeing the gospel in the world around us amid the challenges of Christian discipleship.

We may well sympathize with Mark's first hearers. They experienced persecution at the hands of political authorities, volatile relations between various factions within Judaism, a society characterized by wide discrepancies between the rich and poor, and pressure to observe strict boundaries between ethnic and religious groups. When we hear of seeds sown amid difficult circumstances and the surprising abundance of God's harvest, we cannot help but marvel at God's power to give life despite the worst obstacles. The literary context of chapter 4 underscores the extraordinary nature of God's reign. It immediately follows fierce disagreements between Jesus and others who falsely accuse him (3:19b–35) and precedes his deeds of power among both Jews and Gentiles (4:35–5:43).

The fourth chapter suggests several themes that are relevant to the church today. First, Jesus' proclamation of **God's reign** asserts the undeniable power of God's rule, sometimes hidden but certain to flourish in the time to come. Although many people question Jesus' authority, doubt the viability of his teaching, and ignore or reject his boundary-breaking ministry to outsiders, these verses promise us that God's reign of divine love, justice, and reconciliation will flourish despite seemingly insurmountable circumstances. Second, this chapter highlights the contrast between failed response and successful response to God's word. As Luise Schottroff has demonstrated, failed hearing is a recurrent theme throughout chapter four (vv. 3–7, 12, 14–19, 25b), but successful hearing (that is, hearing that responds with active faith in God's reign) is also present and serves as the climax to Jesus' key parable and its interpretation (vv. 8, 11a, 20, 24, 25a, 34): "As a whole the discourse is to be read as an appeal for hearing," an appeal that is as timely today as it was nearly two thousand years ago (see vv. 3, 9, 23, 24, 33–34).[1] Third, the contrast between failed and successful hearing is related to the polarity of hiddenness and disclosure, mystery and revelation, that moves throughout Mark's Gospel. The reign of God is both a mystery that confounds us (vv. 11–12) and a manifestation of divine rule to be fully disclosed (vv. 21–22). The "now" and "not yet" reality of God's reign continues to challenge the church's sense of mission and identity. Fourth, Jesus insists that both speaking and hearing are necessary to receive the good news of God's reign. He calls people to receive the seeds he sows and to respond to the reign of God present among us even as he urges his followers to continue this twofold calling (6:7–13; 13:10; 16:7).

Finally, a brief word about parables is in order here. Although the term "parable" may refer to a range of rhetorical and literary types including short stories, metaphors, similes, aphorisms, and riddles, the literary context of the parables recounted in the fourth chapter of Mark highlights their significance as a means of communicating something vital about God's reign, namely, the promise of its fruitfulness and the importance of our participation in it. Although Jesus draws on parabolic speech regularly to confront or combat those who oppose his proclamation of the reign of God (e.g., 2:19–22; 13:28), his parables also serve as a favored means of teaching his disciples and imparting the mystery of God's reign to others.[2] He wants his followers to know what is essential to the life of faith: successful hearing of and obedience to the good news proclaimed by him. The parables, then, are not only concerned with Jesus' preaching but also with our hearing so that, like the seeds that take root in good soil, those who have ears to hear may receive God's words, repent, and participate in the extraordinary harvest of God's reign.

SOWER, SEED, AND SOIL (4:1–20)

Exploring the text

Mark 4:1–20 is a key reference point for understanding the whole of Mark's Gospel. For those who have ears to hear, Jesus' **parable** offers good news: despite resistance and failed response to God's word, the fullness of God's reign is sure to come and will produce a bumper crop among those who respond faithfully to his preaching. It also offers a word of warning: Many are the obstacles to hearing the gospel. Listen up, all who have ears to hear.

Three units, verses 1–9, 10–12, and 13–20, are set in close relation to one another so that the parable commands our sustained reflection on God's reign. With dramatic images, failed hearing (unproductive soil) is contrasted with successful hearing (a bountiful harvest), which is called forth by Jesus' sowing the word of God. Although human response is vital to the success of God's harvest, the abundance of God's reign comes as a gracious gift exceeding all human efforts to calculate, control, or manufacture its coming.

Two foundational concepts underlie this entire section and are essential to our understanding of it. First, Mark asserts the singular importance of the parable of the sower, seed, and soil for understanding the whole of Jesus' **proclamation**: the text commands us to listen both at the beginning and at the end of its initial presentation (vv. 3 and 9), it is offered as a singular example of the whole of Jesus' preaching (v. 2), and it is the only parable in Mark's Gospel to be followed by an allegorical explanation attributed to Jesus (vv. 14–20). Jesus insists that if his disciples cannot understand this parable, they cannot understand the others (v. 13). Second, underlying Jesus' ministry but also underlying his many admonitions to listen is the great commandment to hear the words of God in the Shema, from Deuteronomy 6:4–5.[1] Just as the people of Israel are commanded to hear and love God, Mark's version of the Shema in 12:29–30 commands us to love God with our whole lives–heart, soul, mind, and strength–and connects this with the command to love our neighbors as ourselves. The parable of the sower, seed, and soil also calls us to listen with the whole of our beings so that we may hear and faithfully respond to God with all our lives.

Remarkably, this passage is not listed among the readings of the RCL except in its parallel version in Matthew 13:1–9 during Ordinary Time in Year A. Significantly, the reading from Matthew does not include the troublesome verses in which Jesus describes parables as concealing the mystery of God's reign so that some may not understand their meaning (Matt.

13:10–17; cf. Mark 4:10–12). Given the importance of parables for Jesus' preaching ministry, preachers and teachers of the gospel would be wise to supplement and correct these omissions by reflecting on Jesus' parables in worship.

Listening to the Parable (4:1–9)

Once again Jesus is surrounded by an eager crowd beside the sea (cf. 2:13; 3:8–10). Throughout the Gospel, the disciples are asked to prepare a boat so that they may "go across to the other side." Boats become means of transportation and places of transformation in Mark's account (e.g., 4:35–41; 6:45–52). On this occasion, however, a boat provides Jesus with a safe platform from which to deliver his message. Assuming the posture of a teacher, Jesus is seated, and his voice carries more easily over water than it would on land. With these practical matters cared for, Jesus uses the occasion to "teach them many things in parables" (4:2), including one parable in particular that Mark has chosen to record as key to understanding the whole of Jesus' preaching and teaching.

When he speaks, Jesus begins and ends with the same imperative: "Listen!" (4:3, 9). Recalling the first word of the Shema and the command to love the God of Israel with all one's heart, soul, mind, and strength, this verb insists that God's people not only hear but obey. Verses 3–9 proclaim the inevitable success of God's present and future reign and call those with ears to hear to respond with faithful obedience to his proclamation and presence among them.

The picture Jesus paints in this parable is a familiar one and includes the most basic ingredients of agrarian life: sower, seed, and soil. Two of these, the sower and seed, remain constant throughout. But one, the soil, is described differently according to various locations and circumstances. However, all three ingredients are essential to the harvest promised in the climax of the parable.

At this point at least three facets of the story claim our attention. First, there can be no doubt that the sower spoken of in the parable is Jesus. The sower casts the seeds of God's word far and wide so that as many people as possible may have the opportunity to hear and respond. The practice described here is familiar: using a broadcast method of seeding, the sower's activity is neither reckless nor careless but purposeful and necessarily extravagant. Reflecting the economic realities of Palestinian agrarian life, the seeds are given wide birth and cast in a manner that maximizes their potential for growth. This parable seems to reflect the second sowing season of autumn, when seeds are first scattered then plowed under in hopes of producing a late harvest. According to Ched Myers, first-century Palestinian farmers who were fortunate enough to own a patch of land hoped to feed their families, pay rent, make tithes, cover taxes, barter for goods, tools, and supplies, and put away seeds for next year's crop.[2] When not enough was produced, the farmers easily fell into debt, lost their land, and were forced to sell their labor. Jesus' hearers likely found themselves relating to the precarious circumstances of agrarian life, and the sower was a character with whom they could readily identify amid lean and difficult seasons.

Second, the seeds being spread are cast amid a variety of circumstances, each of which could also be readily identified by Jesus' hearers. These circumstances not only include natural disaster, lack of sufficient resources, and pestilence of various kinds, but they can also be thought of in terms of trial by Satan, persecution at the hands of oppressors, and the temptation of worldly pursuits. Just as Jesus experienced resistance and rejection, his hearers experienced hardship and oppression that threatened their very existence, economic well-being, political autonomy, familial holdings, and religious freedom.

Third, the climax of the parable comes at its conclusion, so that the abundant harvest commands our attention and evokes a response. With which of the three soils do we identify? What will be the ultimate fruits that are born of our response to Jesus Christ? The miraculous bounty of grain that is harvested thirty-, sixty-, and a hundredfold would not only shatter the stranglehold of indebtedness that plagued many farmers; it also testifies to God's life-giving power and the eschatological hope of all who await God's reign as they live through oppression, hardship, and temptation.[3] Life in its abundant, God-given goodness awaits those who have ears to hear, eyes to see, and lives willing to participate in the mystery of God's work among us.

The Mystery of God's Reign (4:10–12)

Following his presentation to the crowd, Mark reports that Jesus is alone with the twelve disciples and other "insiders" who ask about his parables. We cannot help but sympathize with their longing to linger beside Jesus to receive his counsel and insight. But rather than provide clarity, Jesus complicates matters. According to these verses, the secret of **God's kingdom** has been given to those who surround Jesus, but everything comes in parables to those "outside" in order that they may not understand, turn, and be forgiven. This passage is among the most disturbing and enigmatic in all of Mark's Gospel. No wonder Matthew softens the blow by reporting that

Jesus does not speak in parables *in order to* confound his hearers but *because* they do not see, hear, and understand (Matt. 13:13). Jesus' words raise two vital questions: (1) What is the "mystery" that has been disclosed to those who follow Jesus? (2) Why does Jesus say that for those outside, the parables are given *in order that* they will not perceive, understand, and turn again to God?

First, with regard to the mystery of God's reign spoken of in 4:11, it is unfortunate that the word *musterion* is often translated as "secret." Whereas "secret" connotes a message whose disclosure depends on the somewhat capricious will of those who know its content, "mystery" as it is used in the New Testament refers to that which can only be known through the revelation of God. In other words, Jesus is not referring to some strange rite of initiation into a secret religious order but a divine mystery entrusted to his followers and awaiting full disclosure (v. 22).

One way of approaching the divine mystery of God's reign spoken of in verse 11 is to relate it to the mystery of Jesus' divine identity understood in light of his cross and resurrection (see **messianic secret**). Taken in this way, the informed reader of Mark's Gospel already knows of his impending death and resurrection, and those who do not recognize and understand this central matter of faith will not turn and receive God's forgiveness. According to this view, these verses provide a harsh and potent warning against a shallow faith that is willing to follow Jesus only when it is convenient or comfortable to do so, without accepting the full cost of discipleship.

However, a plain reading of chapters 1–4 reveals that at this point in Mark's narrative Jesus has not yet shared with his followers word of his impending death and resurrection. It is not until Peter announces that Jesus is the Messiah in 8:27 that Mark records the first of three occasions when Jesus discloses his imminent suffering, death, and resurrection (8:31–38; 9:30–32; 10:32–34). In the context of Mark's fourth chapter, another more immediate mystery has arisen: the division between those who reject and those who accept Jesus' proclamation of God's reign. The tension between those who respond in faith to Jesus' proclamation (fruitful soil) and those who resist his teaching for various reasons (unproductive soil) is keen. From this perspective, the mystery entrusted to Jesus' followers is that despite all appearances to the contrary, amid rejection and apparent defeat, the reign of God will yet flourish–but only to those who have eyes to see, ears to hear, and hearts and minds open to receiving the words of Jesus Christ.

Yet another insight related to the mystery of God's reign arises out of our consideration of the literary context. In the first three chapters of the

Gospel, Jesus proclaimed God's reign through his ministry of compassion to lepers (1:40–45), paralytics (2:1–12), and tax collectors and sinners (2:13–18). Ironically, he was cast outside official circles of recognition and authority because he welcomed the most despised members of society in God's name. But these outcasts recognized the mystery of God's reign: they had become insiders who now knew that the reign of God was evident in Christ's boundary-breaking activity among persons who were despised by others. Through Jesus Christ, God chooses to reveal power by helping those who are powerless, God reveals greatness by attending to the least, and God's reign reaches beyond boundaries of our own making to include those who are rejected by others. In other words, the mystery of God's reign is given to those who witness and follow the boundary-breaking ministry of Jesus Christ.

The second question, related to Jesus' assertion that for those "outside" he preaches in parables *in order that* they will not perceive, understand, and turn again to God, is even more problematic and complicated than the first. Is Jesus suggesting that God intends for some to hear his parables and not understand, repent, and be forgiven? Once again, the literary context offers clues to aid our understanding. It also helps to clarify what Jesus means when he speaks of "insiders" and "outsiders." According to chapters 1–3 and in contrast to society as a whole, Jesus does not treat lepers, paralytics, tax collectors, and sinners as "outsiders." In God's reign, "outsiders" now become "insiders," so that several strange characters are numbered among Jesus' followers (e.g., 3:13; 4:10). From this perspective, Jesus is once again announcing that divine norms of social and religious acceptability are radically other than what we assume.

But the harshness of Jesus' words still rings in our ears. What does it mean to say that for those who are outside the immediate circle of his followers, parables are given *in order that* they may not perceive, understand, and be forgiven? Is Jesus saying that parables are intended to conceal or obscure understanding so that some people will not be able to turn again and be forgiven? At least two factors mitigate against reading the text in this manner. First, Jesus is emphatic that God's intention is to reveal what is hidden and to disclose what has been made secret (4:21–23). His ministry has consistently called people to repent and participate in God's reign (e.g., 1:14–15, 38). Similarly, the parable of the sower, seed, and soil urges people to consider the stark contrast between unproductive and productive soil, between failed hearing and successful hearing, and ends with a plea to consider the abundant harvest of God, which will be experienced by those who respond faithfully to Jesus' words (4:8–9). We have every reason to believe that Jesus intended for his preaching to help people come to a clearer, more decisive understanding of God's just and gracious rule even as he pressed his hearers toward an ever deeper encounter with it.

Second, the sense of apocalyptic urgency that moves throughout Mark's Gospel is evident in Jesus' quote from Isaiah 6, which reflects a setting of conflict and despair over the faithlessness of God's people. In the prophetic call narrative of Isaiah, the people of Israel have offended divine justice by calling evil good and good evil (Isa. 5:20–25). God commands the prophet to speak to this hard-hearted and obdurate people and make clear to them that they do not understand. Similarly, Jesus recognizes that many have rejected the reign of God he proclaims. According to Myers, Jesus employs apocalyptic rhetoric not to "articulate a theology of divine predestination, but to paint a picture of a people in denial."[4] There is indeed a word of divine judgment here but, nestled between Jesus' parable of the sower, seed, and soil (4:3–9) and his explanation of it (vv. 13–20), these difficult verses call forth a faithful response to the word of God sown in Jesus' parables.[5]

Understanding the Parable (4:13–20)

The extended explanation of the parable in 4:13–20 guides hearers through an allegorical consideration of its various parts. Although some scholars view this section as an invention of the early church, Schottroff and other scholars interpret these verses in light of the history of Jewish parable culture, written and oral, which does not make a sharp distinction between parable and allegory but understands verses 13–20 "as the application of the parable in 4:3–8 to the contemporary situation."[1] In this view, these verses explore in greater detail various aspects of life reflected in the early church, including experiences of spiritual, political, and material hardship.

Jesus begins by voicing his frustration and concern when his followers do not understand this pivotal parable (v. 13). His comments move quickly to words of grace: the sower moves in our midst, casting the seeds of God's reign among us (v. 14). The final words of Jesus' parable are also words of grace: God and God alone has the power to produce a harvest of goodness, justice, and mercy that is more abundant than we could possibly imagine or manufacture by our own effort (v. 20). But every word in between, every soil spoken of, and every circumstance described, speaks another word: Jesus calls for humans to respond to the words he proclaims and to participate in God's just and loving reign among us.

At one level, the parable of the sower, seed, and soil reflects the challenge of agrarian life amid circumstances of pestilence, natural disaster, economic hardship, and competition with large landowners. For those suffering under these conditions, the parable promises the fulfillment of God's just and loving reign as they listen and receive Christ's words of hope. At another level, the allegorical explanation of the parable presses hearers to recognize other aspects of life that work against a faithful hearing of the gospel, including demonic possession, persecution at the hands of political oppressors, and the temptation of worldly pursuits. Having encountered demonic possession earlier in Mark's Gospel, the hearer is aware of Jesus' power to free those who are tormented by evil forces (1:25–26, 39) and his will to bind the "strong man" who threatens to overpower God's reign (3:23–27). Those who experience persecution or pledge their allegiance to powers other than God can recognize the rocky terrain that Jesus' first disciples stumbled upon (e.g., 13:9–13; 14:37–42, 66–72). Jesus' parable also speaks to those who are susceptible to greed and worldly acclaim (e.g., 9:33–37; 10:17–22). At the climax of Jesus' message, the good soil produces fruit beyond measure. Those who hear Jesus' words and bear good fruit will experience a miraculous harvest that exceeds their every need, pays off their debts, and ensures their well-being.

Amid the many facets and multilayered meanings of this story, we must not forget that the parable of the sower, seed, and soil describes two fundamentally different responses to the reign of God proclaimed by Jesus Christ. There are those who hear Jesus' message and, by receiving and cultivating his words, bear fruit that is blessed by God. But there are many others (occupying fully three-fourths of the parable explanation) who hear but are either unable or unwilling to receive and cultivate his words. Among these, no fruit is harvested. Both divine grace and human involvement are integral to the gospel proclaimed by Jesus Christ. Although soil may be thought of as a passive entity that is unable to "decide" whether to be fruitful or fallow, its productivity or lack thereof reflects a dynamic potential that Jesus calls forth from those who hear him.[2] The parable of the sower, seed, and soil urges us to recognize the dynamic potential of God's promises and the ability to respond that is inherent in all persons who are able and willing to participate in God's reign. By the end of Mark's Gospel, we hear that the relationship between God and human participants is strained to the breaking point. The disciples misunderstand Jesus, abandon him in his time of need, and flee in fear. Even those who have been given the mystery of God's reign are subject to the same vulnerabilities, struggles, and hard-heartedness as others. But this also is not the last word. Despite human failures and faithlessness, the Spirit of God continues to work among us. The parable of the sower, seed, and soil proclaims the message of divine grace and human activity as Jesus seeks to provoke a convictional response from all who have ears to hear.

Preaching and teaching the Word

The parable of the sower, seed, and soil is familiar enough to many Christians that it begs a new hearing. An oral presentation of this passage (either by script or memory, as a solo presentation or shared among multiple voices) could serve as a powerful introduction to Jesus' parables of God's reign. Although the lectionary does not include 4:10–12 or any of its parallels in the other Gospels, this passage is worthy of our efforts to wrestle with its meaning. If care is given to its context in Mark (and/or a comparison is made with other versions in Matt. 13:13–17 and Luke 8:9–10), an interesting and important message may emerge related to the mystery of God's reign and its hidden and disclosed presence among us. In the spirit of 4:14–20, a sermon could challenge listeners to respond to the gospel amid the various obstacles to hearing and/or could focus on the promise of God's abundant harvest. Several foci may help illumine the text.

The importance of listening. With its many references to listening and hearing, 4:1–20 urges us to keep attuned to God's word alive among us. Jesus' command to listen in verses 3 and 9 parallels the Shema from Deuteronomy 6:4–5 with its command to hear, take heed, and obey God with the whole of our lives. A sermon that focuses on listening to God's word and seeking God's reign can point the way to listening to the Spirit of Christ, who continues to sow seeds of hope among us. The practice of listening is more difficult than we may realize. Not only family members but neighbors and nations find it challenging to hear one another, especially across ethnic and religious divides. Sometimes a more playful approach may be of help. In the children's book *Listen Buddy!*, a bunny with enormous ears refuses to listen to his parents: when they ask him for a pen, he brings them a hen, and when they send him to fetch fifteen tomatoes, he returns home with fifty potatoes.[3] Finally, Buddy faces the consequences and comes face to face with the terrible Scruffy Varmint. Outrunning the giant villain, he returns home safe and sound with ears wide open, attentive to his parents' teaching. Ah, if only the people of God would have ears to hear and hearts eager to respond to the words of Christ alive among us.

Speaking words, sowing faith. When Jesus was faced with opposition from religious authorities and family members alike, he did not take up arms against his enemies, urge his followers to form a new political party, or try to impress others with his miraculous powers. Instead, he undertook the most radical and threatening ministry possible: he **proclaimed** the power of God's reign and announced the fulfillment of God's promises in the face of fierce opposition from others. What could be more audacious than to believe that words, even God's words, have the power to overcome evil?

On the one hand, words can seem a feeble weapon when opposing military regimes, arsenals of weapons, seemingly endless economic resources, the pretense of intellectual superiority, and the righteous indignation of religious leaders. For those who have ears numbed by a constant barrage of advertising and instant messages, words can seem a weak and tired medium to convey the power of God. On the other hand, it was the weapon Jesus chose time and again as he proclaimed God's reign on the loose among us. Jesus' faith was centered on God's word in Hebrew Scripture, and the words he sowed reflect God's voice. Not only is the pen mightier than the sword, but the gospel Jesus proclaims has the power to create new worlds or crush the forces of evil at work in this world. In the words of Martin Luther's well-known hymn, "The prince of darkness grim, we tremble not for him. His rage we can endure for lo, his doom is sure. One little word shall fell him."[4] Through parable and poetic imagery, seeds are sown among us—not only by the Spirit of Christ but also by those whom Christ calls to spread the gospel far and wide.

A word of warning, a word of hope, and a word of challenge. The parable of the sower, seed, and soil does not offer a one-dimensional picture of God's reign but helps us glimpse the complexity of faith amid the realities of daily living. Jesus issues a word of *warning* and a wake-up call to respond to his words. There is evil at work among us. Jesus alerts us to the apocalyptic crisis at hand so that we will trust in the harvest to come even as we participate in God's will for the world right now. Jesus also offers a word of *hope* and comfort amid times of crisis. He sets a vision of God's reign before us that declares the fulfillment of God's promises and life-giving intentions for creation. Although we may not always see the fruit of our endeavors, Jesus' parable assures us that the reign of God has already been sown and is growing toward future fulfillment.

Jesus offers another word as well. Between crisis and hope, we face *challenges* to our faith that sometimes propel us onward but often push against our resolve or strangle our hope. There are forces of evil, patterns of oppression, political pressures, economic hardships, and personal addictions that afflict us. Jesus' parable urges us to recognize these and to name all that opposes God's rule. Amid the many challenges of day-to-day living, preachers and teachers of the gospel can encourage people to respond to God's grace and goodness amid the adversity of life even as we hope for the coming fullness of God's reign.

The mystery of God's reign. Where do we see glimpses of God's dominion or hear murmurings of God's rule? The "mystery" of God's reign is not a distant reality that will only be experienced at some later time, nor is it entirely unknown or unrecognizable in the present. Rather, the "mystery" is that God's reign is given to us even now and is apparent to those who seek God with the eyes and ears of faith. Even Jesus' closest followers struggled to recognize who Jesus was and failed to understand his teachings. But Mark's Gospel surprises us with persons who are able to see and respond in faith to the power of God in Jesus Christ (e.g., the woman with hemorrhages in 5:25–34, the Syrophoenician woman in 7:24–30, the father of the epileptic boy in 9:24). Jesus' parable reflects something of God's reign and urges us to recognize and respond to God's rule among us.

MORE PARABLES OF GOD'S REIGN (4:21–34)

Jesus' preaching about **God's reign** continues with this collection of sayings and parables. The narrator's repeated use of the words "He said to them" (4:21, 24, 26, 30) signals that several distinct episodes have been placed in quick and purposeful succession. Verses 21–25 include four brief sayings or **parables** about paying attention to God's hidden yet present reign. Verses 26–32 include two additional seed parables (see vv. 3–9) that proclaim the inevitable fullness of God's reign. The section concludes with verses 33–34 announcing the importance of parables for Jesus' preaching and teaching.

Exploring the text

Lessons on Seeing, Hearing, and Giving (4:21–25)

The hiddenness of God's reign will not last forever. Like a lamp brought into a darkened room, God's call is intended for everyone to see and hear. Mark uses the active tense when speaking of the lamp "coming" as a way of suggesting that Jesus himself is the lamp who brings light to our darkness. The problem, of course, is that not everyone recognizes or welcomes Jesus as the one who illumines God's way. According to Blount, "The secret now is, as it were, hiding in plain sight. The mystery that Jesus represents God's divine kingdom strategy is constantly being revealed as if it were a lamp on a stand and yet it remains a mystery precisely because the evidence is being misread."[1] Even Jesus' disciples don't understand him. Yet the gospel proclaims that seeds are intended to grow, light is meant to illumine, and God's word is meant to be heard—not only in the future but the present. In Mark's apocalyptic context, Jesus' coming, like a lamp on a lampstand, reveals God's reign so that everyone who pays attention may know God's life-giving intentions for the world. Mark punctuates his point with the same words he used to conclude the parable of the sower, seed, and soil: "Let anyone with ears to hear listen!"

The next two sayings, in 4:24–25, are introduced with a command to "pay attention to what you hear." On the one hand, Jesus' admonition may simply be a way of urging his hearers to listen carefully to what he is about to tell them. On the other hand, Jesus may be offering a more general word of advice about paying attention to *everything* we hear. Given the number of concerns that clamor for our attention and allegiance, Jesus counsels us to consider carefully what we are hearing. According to Marcus, "In a world that is still, in some sense, Satan's house and dominion (cf. 3:23–26), not all the voices that may be heard *ought* to be heard."[2] Those who seek insight into the gospel that Jesus proclaims will receive an even greater measure of insight, but those who reject his proclamation will lose what little they thought they possessed of God's righteousness. The wise will become wiser, but those who claim to already know God's ways yet reject the gospel of Jesus Christ will have even less than they first imagined.

Verses 24–25 have at times been taken out of context and misapplied to matters of monetary wealth and material reward. Jesus is not urging people to give money to religious leaders and organizations so that God may bless their generosity with financial success. The context of this passage amid Jesus' fierce disagreements with religious leaders and others who reject his vision of God's reign (see 3:6, 19b–35) can leave no doubt that Jesus is not advocating a gospel of wealth. Instead, Jesus' parables in 4:21–25 urge people to listen and accept the reign of God he has been proclaiming through his ministry of compassion and outreach to others. Given his own example of serving without receiving monetary reward and his teaching about giving to others at the expense of oneself (e.g., 10:17–27), it is a gross perversion of Scripture to suggest that Jesus proclaims a system of material reward and punishment.

Secret and Subtle Seeds (4:26–34)

The last two parables in the fourth chapter return once again to the image of seeds (cf. 4:3–20). Both parables begin with sowing and end with descriptions of the full-grown, public manifestation of God's reign.[1] But each emphasizes different aspects of God's impending reign, with the first parable focusing on the silent but sure growth of the seed and the second focusing on the remarkable contrast between the size of the mustard seed and the plant it produces. The entire section is rounded off with concluding words about the importance of all Jesus' parables.

The parable of the seed growing secretly (vv. 26–29) compares the kingdom of God with the sure and steady growth of the coming harvest. Seeds grow of their own mysterious momentum, not according to the schedule or direction of the farmer but automatically (from the Greek word *automatē* in v. 28). Those with eyes to see may observe their incremental progress from stalk to head to full grain in the head. Whereas the growth of the seeds in Jesus' parable of the sower, seed, and soil was interrupted at various stages by birds, rocks, and thorns, the seeds scattered in verses 26–29 move through their progressive stages with uninterrupted success. Propelled by divine determination and power, they culminate in a full harvest that awaits the farmer's sickle.

The sure and steady growth of the seeds in this parable has sometimes been likened to the church's progress through successive stages of development as it prepares itself for Jesus' final return. However, the center of gravity in this passage is not the farmer's efforts to cultivate what has been sown but the mysterious and sure growth of the seeds, which develop according to their God-given momentum. More pronounced in this passage are phrases and images drawn from prophetic literature. We hear allusions to Isaiah 61:11, which foretells the day when God's righteousness will, like a garden, "spring up before all nations," and to Joel 3:13, with its prophetic oracle of divine justice: "Put in the sickle, for the harvest is ripe." In the midst of imperial rule and Roman oppression, Jesus' parable of God's reign speaks with determination and power to a beleaguered people who may have been tempted to take up arms against the dominant regime.[2] The parable insists that Mark's hearers can no more procure the kingdom's coming by willful effort than they can force its fulfillment by military intervention. As any good farmer will tell you, patience and hope are the spiritual sustenance of those who labor in God's fields.

The last parable in this section (vv. 30–32) highlights the contrast between the minuscule mustard seed and the plant it produces. Through this simple yet startling image, Jesus declares that the reign of God may seem insignificant and vulnerable right now but will someday become a sturdy shelter for all who seek refuge in its branches. On the one hand, those who are oppressed by political regimes and others would consider themselves "the smallest of all the seeds on earth" amid an overwhelming forest of opponents. On the other hand, Jesus' parable offers genuine comfort, since this strange seed is destined for greatness. Once again,

Jesus draws on prophetic images and in this case adapts them for his purpose: the mighty cedar that provides a resting place for all nations (Ezek. 17:22–24; Dan. 4:19–22) is a tiny seed that grows into a bush of enormous proportions. The parable announces that the present oppressive situation will give way to the full realization of God's gracious rule. When this happens, the kingdom of God will offer a safe haven to "the birds of the air" (a frequent symbol for the nations of the world, i.e., Gentiles) so that all people may find a home in its branches. That which is least will become greatest (see 9:35; 10:31, 42–45; cf. Ezek. 17:24).

The collection of parables in Mark 4 concludes with the statement that Jesus spoke "the word" with many such parables (v. 14). We may therefore assume that Mark has carefully selected the parables recorded in verses 1–32 as representative of Jesus' preaching and integral to understanding the whole of his kingdom message. As Jesus' chosen mode of discourse, the parables are accessible to all who have ears to hear and are meant to illumine the mystery of God's hidden yet present reign amid circumstances of oppression and uncertainty. The parables are challenging but not impossible to understand: their very difficulty lies in the nature of God's reign with its demanding claim upon the lives of all who hear Jesus' message and witness his ministry. Not everyone was receptive, and many resisted or rejected Jesus' teaching. Yet he spoke the word to them "as they were able to hear it" and offered his disciples private instruction to encourage their understanding.

Preaching and teaching the Word

It is the genius of parables to communicate big lessons through little stories, and in the case of Jesus' parables to do so in ways that provoke our deeper understanding of God's present and coming reign. The parables recounted in 4:21–32 are especially brief and proclaim the word of God through tangible images of lamps and seeds while making subtle references to hidden and revealed greatness. It would certainly be possible to prepare a sermon that links the parable of the sower, seed, and soil in verses 1–20 with verses 21–32. However, each of the parables in verses 21–32 and the closing comments that follow in verses 33–34 reflect valuable and distinct aspects of God's reign that are worthy of our attention.

Perhaps the most important message to be communicated through these parables is that God intends to disclose what is now hidden and to *reveal the fullness of God's reign as light, harvest, and shelter for all people.* Jesus speaks of God's reign in positive if not peculiar language: as light that shines from a lampstand, as fields that bear fruit through the inner power and grace of God's life within them, and as a tenacious bush that offers protection for all nations. The joy and hope that permeate these parables is good news for everyone, since God's mercy illumines our blindness and offers refuge from all that threatens and oppresses us. But words of warning are also woven into God's promises: Jesus asserts that those who think they already understand God's righteousness without receiving his kingdom message will lose whatever hold they thought they had on holiness (v. 25). Jesus' parables assure us that God's reign secures the well-being of all people and nations. In the words of one member of our group Bible study, "The bush does not grow for its own sake alone but for the sake of others who may come and take refuge in its branches."[3] At a time when our nation wrestles with privacy rights, issues of secret surveillance, the Patriot Act, and various immigration laws, it is especially important to point the church toward Jesus' vision of God's reign as that which seeks to protect and empower the least and most vulnerable persons who seek refuge among us.

Jesus' passion for *parabolic preaching* is also significant for the church's ministry and understanding of God's reign. Remembering that the Greek word for "parable" (*parabolē*) refers to something "thrown alongside" something else, Mark's insistence that Jesus only spoke in parables (v. 34) suggests that Jesus intentionally chose to speak and act in ways that proclaimed God's reign "thrown alongside" the reigns of this world. According to Clifton Black, "Wherever Jesus treads, God's parable pops."[4] Preaching that is parabolic, then, may or may not include short stories, but it certainly proclaims God's power on the loose among us, confronting us with an alternative view of reality.[5]

In the spirit of Christ's parables, our preaching and teaching points to the power of God at work in this blessed but broken world. For example, when a German soldier during World War II fell ill with typhoid fever on the Russian front, a Russian Mennonite woman who worked at the hospital befriended him. At great personal risk, she forged a change in the transport papers, ensuring his safe passage home. Years later the man moved to the United States and became wealthy. Without family members or a religious community to which he belonged, he remembered the nurse who had helped him years before and looked for a Mennonite congregation in the phone directory. Visiting with the pastor he asked, "What would your congregation do if you had access to two million dollars?" In the months that followed, a committee was established to oversee the stewardship of the man's resources through the development of a Service and Education Fund that encourages voluntary service overseas and in the United States, builds homes for Habitat for Humanity, sponsors numerous disaster response projects, donates money to antiwar efforts, establishes grants for youth attending Christian colleges in exchange for

one year of voluntary service, and so forth. The seeds sown fifty years earlier continue to produce a harvest of hope among those who cultivate
God's gifts.

Care of the earth and the stewardship of creation are assumed throughout
Jesus' parables and are timely concerns for us today. Land, soil, seed, and
farmer are integrally related to one another and necessary to the care and
cultivation of the world around us. With oceans overfished, forests over-
cut, the climate overheated, and 40 percent fewer creatures inhabiting the
earth today compared with thirty-five years ago, preachers and teachers
of the gospel need to proclaim God's life-giving intentions for all creation
and declare our mutual responsibility for sowing seeds, cultivating
resources, and producing goods in ways that benefit all the world's inhabitants. Jesus' first-century hearers were likely to have been well aware of
the painful consequences of agrarian poverty, whereas most North American or European congregants today have much to learn about the
inequitable distribution of natural resources that citizens of wealthy countries enjoy in the global economy, the abuses committed by large corpo-
rations and business interests that irrevocably damage the environment,
and the egregious slaughter of the original inhabitants of North America.
Jesus' parables of the earth reflect God's vision of abundance that is to be
shared with others rather than hoarded by a few.

JESUS CALMS THE STORM (4:35–41)

Exploring the text

Mark's dramatic description of the storm at sea and the disciples' plea
for help elicits our immediate and sympathetic response. It also reflects
significant connections to what precedes and follows this episode and signals several important emphases of subsequent chapters.

The text begins by noting that Jesus' calming of the storm takes place
"on that day" when Jesus was preaching the parables (4:1–34). By the end
of this episode, the disciples struggle to understand Jesus' authority and
power just as they struggled to grasp the full meaning of his parables (vv.
10, 13, 34). They continue to need Jesus' help later in the Gospel to understand his identity and mission (e.g., 8:14–21, 31–38; 9:28–29, 38–48). References to Jesus' deep sleep during the storm and his rising at the disciples'
urging (4:38) parallel the farmer who sleeps while trusting in the seed's
growth (vv. 26–29) and may be contrasted with the sluggish sleep of his
followers later at Gethsemane (14:32–42). Similarly, the Greek word for
"great" (*megalē*) occurs three times in this story (a great windstorm, great
calm, great awe), just as the greatness of the mustard seed is underscored

in 4:32 and Jesus later speaks of greatness in unexpected ways (e.g., 9:33–35). When Jesus rebukes the wind during the storm we remember his ministry of rebuking demons (e.g., 1:25; 3:12; 9:25). Finally, intertextual references abound as God's power to calm the sea recalls Psalms 18, 89, 106, and 107 as well as the story of the prophet Jonah.

The story of the storm at sea also highlights several of the Gospel's most important theological themes. In directing his disciples to "go across to the other side," Jesus moves his followers from Jewish to Gentile territory across the Sea of Galilee. As the first of several journeys undertaken by Jesus and his closest followers (see also 5:21; 6:45–53; 7:31; 8:10, 13; 9:30), the story of Jesus' calming the storm reveals an opening in the disciples' awareness of God's **power** and will to reach all people and places. A shift in thematic emphasis is also experienced as the text moves from recounting Jesus' powerful words (the parables of chap. 4) to his powerful works (the miracles of chap. 5). Jesus demonstrates his power over natural forces (4:35–41), demonic forces (5:1–20), and death itself (5:21–43). The theme of fear also arises in this story. Jesus' comment in 4:40 suggests that fear has overwhelmed whatever faith the disciples may have had in him, and their fearfulness stands in stark contrast to Jesus' own peaceful repose at the back of the boat. Hooker notes that Jesus' sleep not only represents his trust in God but also confidence in the disciples' seamanship, a sense of trust and confidence that the disciples seem to lack.[1]

The story concludes with a question that is central to the whole of Mark's Gospel: "Who then is this, that even the wind and the sea obey him?" Having witnessed his power to calm the sea, it is significant that the disciples do not ask *how* Jesus accomplished this mighty act but *who* it is that stands before them as lord of wind and sea (4:41). Earlier in Mark's account, Jesus' identity is declared in the opening verse (1:1), the voice of God declares Jesus' sonship at the time of his baptism (1:11), demons call him the Holy One of God (1:24), and Jesus names his divine authority at pivotal moments in his ministry (2:5–11; 3:23–27). But in this story of Jesus calming the sea, the power of God in Christ is demonstrated rather than declared. Mark's Gospel would have us know that Jesus' identity is evidenced not only by divine titles and human acclaim but also by the power of God at work in him (see **messianic titles**). As creator of the sea, God alone can calm its powerful momentum (Ps. 89:9).

Preaching and teaching the Word

There are more than a few ways to preach and teach about this remarkable text. In addition to its place among the RCL readings for the Third Sunday following Pentecost in Year B, it may be interesting to compare this story to another seafaring episode in Mark 6:47–53. A series of sermons related to human fear and divine intervention could be offered based on both of these Markan stories as well as other texts relating storms at sea found in Hebrew Scripture (e.g., Ps. 107:23–32; Jonah 1:17–2:10).

Intertextually, a dynamic comparison can be made between the disciples' experiences during the storm and Jonah's story in the Hebrew Bible. In addition to various word parallels and idiomatic similarities (e.g., the storm "died down," "they feared a great fear"), several similarities and differences exist between the two accounts. In his exploration of Matthew's account of the disciples at sea (Matt. 8:18, 23–27), Cope notes the following parallels between Jonah's experience and that of Jesus and his disciples: departure by boat, a raging storm, a sleeping character, frightened sailors, the miraculous calming of the sea, and the sailors' awed response.[2] The differences between the two stories are also pronounced: unlike Jonah, Jesus does not flee from God but seeks to accomplish God's will, and the disciples do not ask Jesus to intercede with God but call on Jesus himself to save them.[3] Mark's story proclaims that the very person and presence of Jesus Christ is the power of God at work in the world.

Symbolically, the story of the storm at sea provides an enduring picture of Christian discipleship. Boats have long symbolized the church throughout its troublesome and tempestuous history. Theologians and laity alike struggle to understand the journey of faith that sometimes takes us through tumultuous waters. The French Romantic painter Eugène Delacroix (1798–1863) was fascinated with the story of Christ on the Sea of Galilee and produced several paintings of this scene based on his interpretation of the accounts in all three Gospels. In one painting, nine disciples are tossed about a rowboat in utter disarray while Jesus sleeps in the stern with enormous dark green waves beating ominously around them. Two disciples are rowing, one is clinging to the tiller, another is cowering at the bow, yet another is pointing at the raging waters, and the four remaining disciples are turned toward Christ, with one of them asleep beneath his enormous cloak. In another painting, six disciples are shown in a sailboat, with five of them working together as they attempt to manage the tiller and sails while the sixth rouses Jesus from sleep. Each depicts a very different approach to the disciples' confrontation with the raging elements, and each reflects different expressions of human effort to meet the crisis at hand while Christ sleeps serenely among them. Delacroix's creative use of color and light as well as his varied depictions of the disciples' experience at sea inspire us to imagine our own place on the boat and the shared fate of those who journey together in fear and faith.

Theologically, several important themes claim our attention. The words "go across to the other side" remind us of Jesus' boundary-breaking ministry throughout the Gospel and urge us to attend to the transforming possibilities of Christ's presence and power. The story of Jesus calming the sea also confirms his identity as the Son of God who commands the forces of nature. We view his divine authority and power through the eyes of persons who have just struggled for their survival and who wrestle internally with fear and faith. Although Jesus chides the disciples, we may find ourselves sympathizing with their experience and those of other persons who have known the terror of hurricanes and other natural disasters. Whenever we are threatened by forces beyond our control, fear and faith compete for our allegiance, and we wonder what will become of us and those we love. Of course, it is entirely possible that the disciples feared something even worse than the storm: Jesus' indifference to their plight. If that is the case, then it is their faith and ours that need to be awakened during times of crisis and not Jesus Christ. He is there with us, the very presence of God promising to share our most perilous journeys.

This story also provides an opportunity to discuss miracles. There are those who do not believe that God intervenes in human events, interrupts the laws of nature, or intercedes on our behalf. We may certainly name countless examples of bad things happening to good people, and the Bible itself testifies to humanity's fierce accusations against God's presumed indifference to human suffering. There are also those who believe in God's miraculous power manifest among us through extraordinary experiences of physical healing, interventions in daily activities, and the unaccountable success of community service projects that bear fruits beyond the sum of human involvement. We may attribute these events to God's work among us just as Scripture also testifies to God's purposeful intervention in human history. The story of Jesus' calming the sea speaks to both. It is intended for people of faith and people who doubt. It reflects a messy mix of fear and resolve, of human angst and divine serenity, of chaotic forces and peaceful resolve. Jesus' calming the sea carries us along currents of human anxiety and divine determination as it proclaims Christ's power over chaos.

Exorcism, Healing, and Overcoming Death

Mark 5:1–43

J ust as the fourth chapter of Mark's Gospel recounts Jesus' powerful words, the fifth recounts his powerful works. In both chapters, Jesus engages others in the good news of God's ready reign and proclaims God's will to defeat the forces of evil that threaten to destroy the gift of life entrusted to us. However, while Jesus' parables challenge us to consider what is hidden beneath the surface of daily life, the stories of his mighty acts confront us with dramatic examples of divine **power** bursting onto the landscape of our lives. Whether these stories startle, comfort, inspire, embarrass, or baffle us, we cannot avoid their presence in the text. They are evidence that Jesus is not only the herald of **God's reign** but that he secures God's rule in the world by overcoming the forces of chaos, Satan, illness, and death itself. Jesus will not leave us alone but assures us of God's merciful intentions for all humanity.

This chapter bears witness to three miracles. Crossing into Gentile territory, Jesus overpowers the forces of Satan before returning to a predominantly Jewish area, where he heals a woman of chronic illness and resurrects a young girl who has died at home. There is an unstoppable quality to all of these events that recalls Jesus' announcement of God's impending reign (1:15) and the parable of binding the strong man (3:27). Jesus reveals the extent and character of God's power manifest in him. With compassion, tenderness, and purposeful attention to outsiders, Jesus crosses geographic, ethnic, social, and economic boundaries for the sake of God's love for all people.

MORE POWERFUL THAN DEMONS (5:1–20)

Exploring the text

Few North Americans or Europeans are comfortable with stories of exorcism, let alone the possibility of demon possession. Our personal and cultural resistance to services of exorcism combined with the awkward wording of 5:1–20 are reason enough for many of us to avoid this text. But let the hearer beware: the stories we often ignore are most often the ones we need to hear. If we are willing to withdraw our resistance long enough to listen carefully to the questions and impressions that emerge from our encounter with this event, a word may arise that surprises our expectations and calls to life the imaginative potential of this strange story.

Whereas Luke attempts to tidy up the Gerasene's story (Luke 8:26–30) and Matthew abbreviates it (Matt. 8:28–34), Mark spares no details and offers the most extensive account of exorcism and its aftermath in all of biblical literature. Given the repeated phrases and cumbersome wording of 5:1–20, it seems likely that Mark's account reflects the synthesis of two separate but similar healing events, or two reports of the same event. In many ways this story reflects what is typically found in ancient exorcism accounts: an initial meeting with the demoniac (vv. 2, 6), a description of the possessed person's condition (vv. 3–5), the demon's recognition of the exorcist (vv. 6–7), the act of exorcism itself (vv. 9–13a), evidence of the demon's departure (vv. 13b–15), and the responses of those who are impacted by this event (vv. 15–20). The Gospel's final editing, however, gives significant attention to two facets of the story. First, the condition of the possessed man is described in great detail, highlighting the pathos of his situation, the power of the demons who possess him and, by implication, the even greater **power** of God in Christ, who defeats the forces of Satan. Second, the responses of the townsfolk, Jesus, and the healed man are also highlighted, underscoring the implications of Jesus' ministry for those who witness the power of God at work in him.

Also characteristic of Mark's narrative are allusions to the prophets and events recorded in Hebrew Scripture. The story of the demoniac recalls Isaiah 65:1–7, in which God reaches out to a defiled people sitting in tombs and eating the flesh of pigs. It also recalls Exodus 15:14–16 and the story of Israel's liberation from captivity to the Egyptians.[1] Just as God defeated the enemies of Israel by drowning them in the Reed Sea, Jesus expels the demons who enter into pigs and rush into the sea and drown. Just as foreign nations respond in fear and trembling when they hear what God has done for Israel, the townsfolk who see the man freed of demonic possession react with astonishment and fear. Both events declare that God is at work in the world to overcome the forces of evil and free the oppressed.

This story also bears strong similarities to Jesus' earlier encounter with the possessed person in the synagogue at Capernaum (1:21–28). In both stories, Jesus is confronted by demons who acknowledge his authority in a public setting, and in both cases he successfully frees the possessed men. However, the earlier episode takes place in Jewish territory and in a sacred space (the synagogue), whereas the second takes place in Gentile territory and in an unclean place (amid pigs and tombs). Of particular importance in the second story is that the healed man begs to accompany Jesus and is commanded to return home to proclaim what God has done for him. The theme of proclaiming the good news of God's reign that began in the first chapter and was further developed in chapters 2 through 4 continues in this remarkable story of the demoniac's healing. But in this case Jesus entrusts the gospel to a Gentile, who serves as the first evangelist to people outside Israel.

Four movements or sections may be identified within the Gerasene's story. First, in 5:1–5, Jesus and his disciples arrive by boat on the other side of the Sea of Galilee, where they immediately encounter a man with an unclean spirit. Although scholars disagree as to the exact location of this event, we know from verse 20 that it takes place somewhere in the region of the Decapolis, an alliance of ten cities to the south and east of the Sea of Galilee, largely populated by Gentiles. The presence of pigs and swineherds (noted in vv. 13–14) also signals that Jesus has entered Gentile territory. Most importantly, Jesus hardly steps foot on shore when he and his disciples are confronted with a strange welcoming committee. The demoniac rushes toward Jesus, and quite suddenly we are aware of the terrible offense to Jewish faith and practice evoked by this scene: the possessed man who greets Jesus is tormented by an unclean spirit, he is surrounded by unclean animals, and he resides among the tombs where he risks contamination. Tombs are mentioned three times in the opening verses so that we may be aware of the life-and-death battle Jesus is called to confront.

The man's condition is at once pathetic and terrifying. He not only dwells among the dead but is constantly bruising himself against stones, howling in agony. Spiritually, he struggles on the margins of life and death. Psychologically, the unclean spirit has perverted the man's self-identity so that he has become his own worst enemy. Emotionally, demons have control of his feelings and voice so that all he can do is howl in agony over his unending torment. Physically, the unclean spirit overpowers the man so that chains no longer restrain him and no one has the power to subdue him. His heart, soul, mind, and strength are continually tormented by Satan's power. No one is able to bind him because he is bound by Satan. Alienated from friends and family, the possessed man is destitute of hope—until Jesus steps out of the boat. In one fateful moment the demoniac rushes toward him with words that reveal a mixture of fascination and fear.

The second major movement of this story, verses 6–13, recounts the verbal exchange between Jesus and the demoniac followed by the dramatic exorcism of the unclean spirit(s). The awkward retelling of this event mirrors the chaotic effects of Satan's power. Not only does the demoniac shift between single and plural self-references, but the order of events is somewhat confused: it is only after the demoniac pleads with Jesus not to torment him (v. 7) that we learn Jesus has already confronted him (v. 8). When the demoniac falls at Jesus' feet, it is less likely an act of worship than a reflection of his anxiety about Jesus' superior power. Similarly, when the possessed man refers to Jesus as Son of the "Most High God," he is not making a confession of faith but using a familiar title among non-Jewish people when referring to the God of Israel (see **messianic titles**). The unclean spirit is clearly threatened by Jesus' power; the spirit fears it will be exiled. A terrible fusion of identity has taken place between possessor and possessed. Ironically, the unclean spirit has claimed the role of exorcist and invokes the source of Jesus' power while demanding that he not be tormented.

But Jesus will not be deterred. He recognizes what is at stake in this situation and pursues the man's liberation. In asking for the name of the unclean spirit, Jesus seeks to name the demons in order to overpower and expel them. However, the unclean spirit evades his efforts by saying, "My name is Legion; for we are many." Demons in ancient times were thought to be associated with particular geographic regions, and in this episode they ask not to be sent out of the country but into a herd of swine grazing on the hillside.[2] In agreeing to their request, it seems that Jesus is conceding to their wishes but, ironically, the unclean animals who are possessed by unclean spirits rush into the water and are consumed by the sea. Just as Pharaoh's army was overtaken by the Reed Sea, Satan's Legion is drowned by water. Creatures are destroyed not by Jesus' choice but by the mistaken choice of those who think they have the authority to overpower and control the lives of others.

This section of the story is permeated with military references: the word "Legion" denotes a division of several thousand Roman soldiers, "herd" or "band" is often used to refer to a group of military recruits, the pigs "rush" or "charge" into the sea, and they recall the emblem of a wild boar that was worn on the tunic of Roman soldiers who occupied Palestine during that time. The story speaks, then, not only of one man's experience of demon possession but it addresses the experience of nations and people who are dominated by unwelcome forces. According to Myers, "This unlikely story offers a symbolic portrait of how Roman imperialism was destroying the hearts and minds of a colonized people."[3] Jesus' extraordinary ability to conquer the forces of Satan demonstrates the power of God to overcome the mightiest forces on earth. The text also highlights the way in which Jesus accomplishes his liberating purposes. In contrast to the uncontrollable violence exerted by the unclean spirit, the power of Jesus Christ does not destroy or coerce others but consistently chooses nonviolent means of effecting change.

In the third movement of this story, verses 14–17, word of this strange event quickly travels far and wide. Before long, people from all over arrive to see Jesus and the healed man sitting by his side, now dressed and in his right mind. Mark's account gives an unusual amount of attention to the people's reaction. Not only are they astonished, but they are afraid. Instead of celebrating the demoniac's recovery, they are seized by fear and beg Jesus to leave the area. The people recognize a power alive in Jesus that no one can control, neither Satan nor human beings.[4] Whatever economic losses they suffer as a result of the pigs' destruction is nothing compared to the fear they feel in the presence of Jesus Christ. The healed man is living testimony that God will not leave things as they are. It is easier to accept the presence of a crazy person outside the boundaries of town than a healed man who will walk among them, confronting them with the reality of God's transforming power in their midst.

In the fourth and final section, verses 18–20, we hear a surprise ending to this strange story. Just as the unclean spirit begs to remain in the region and enter the swine (vv. 10–11), and just as the people beg Jesus to depart the region and leave them alone (v. 17), the man healed of demon possession now begs to accompany Jesus as he steps into the boat (v. 18). He is undoubtedly aware of the hardships he will endure if he remains at home. However, Mark's account reveals that he is motivated by something other than anxiety or fear: the wording of his plea to "be with [Jesus]" echoes a phrase used earlier when Jesus calls his **disciples** to "be with him" (3:14). Here is a person who earnestly desires to be a disciple of Jesus Christ.

Jesus' response comes as an utter surprise. He urges the man to go home, live among his friends, and tell them what God's mercy has done for him. Previously, Jesus silenced demons and forbade people to tell others what he had done for them (e.g., 1:25, 34, 43; 5:43; 7:36), but on this occasion he urges the man to tell his neighbors about God's healing mercy. To understand these seemingly incongruous commands, we must recognize that Jesus urges people to fulfill the call to discipleship in radically different ways at different times and places. On this occasion, he commissions a Gentile to serve as the first missionary to his own people. A man who was cast outside the edges of social acceptability is thrown back into the heart of his hometown. A land that was considered "out of bounds" for Jews is now blessed to receive God's word among them. A man who previously spoke with the voice of demons now speaks the words of God. One further shift is important to note. Whereas Jesus urges him to tell others how much *the Lord* has done for him, the man proclaims how much *Jesus* has done for him. There can be no doubt of the source of his healing and liberation. Everywhere he goes, he proclaims the **gospel** of Jesus Christ, the good news of divine mercy, salvation, healing, and liberation for all people. No wonder the story ends by reporting that everyone is amazed.

Preaching and teaching the Word

In the early 1990s when the American Bible Society decided to produce a series of videos on New Testament stories for young adults, research suggested that the target audience identified more strongly with the account of Jesus and the Gerasene demoniac than with any other story in the New Testament.[5] Perhaps it is a shared sense of chaos and frenetic behavior that draws us into the orbit of the Gerasene's story. Or perhaps we relate to the demoniac's extreme isolation or experiences of being overpowered by forces beyond his control. Whether we resist the idea of demon possession or are fascinated by it, there are several ways to approach the story of Jesus' encounter with the Gerasene demoniac.

Possession and the power of evil. Because some of us wholly embrace and others utterly reject the possibility of demon possession, it is wise for preachers and teachers of the gospel to carefully consider the obstacles we encounter on the way to understanding the story of Jesus and the Gerasene demoniac. For example, there is good reason to challenge the belief that satanic powers are able to prevent us from confronting evil in its many personal and systemic guises. Conversely, we must guard against public services of exorcism that seek to showcase a preacher's holiness (see 8:11–12). This passage in no way suggests that God willed the demoniac's possession in order to demonstrate Jesus' power.

However, the demoniac's story reminds us not to deny the power of evil at work among us. We are wise to resist an attitude of skepticism that dismisses the very real personal, interpersonal, and corporate effects of overwhelming evil in our midst. We risk trivializing the demoniac's experience by comparing it to lesser struggles, such as the tendency to repeat the same mistakes or the irritations we face in changing our personal habits. The story of the demoniac is the story of a person gripped heart, soul, mind, and body by the overwhelming power of evil. Whether or not we name this force as Satan, the possessed man has lost his life to forces beyond his control. Like the fierce grip of AIDS, terminal cancer, sexual abuse, chronic mental illness, material deprivation, and war, the demoniac is overcome by powers that intend his destruction.

Similarly, his experience urges us to carefully name the sources of evil we encounter so that we do not misattribute or misunderstand them. In serving as a psychiatric chaplain at a state mental hospital, I came to know quite well a patient who had been repeatedly raped by family members throughout her childhood. Although her illness was diagnosed as chronic depression, staff members knew that she not only needed medical, psychological and spiritual care but the help of persons who could arrest and convict the men who abused her. Her story reminds us that evil comes to us in many ways and that we need to name each of these and work with one another to overcome evil and facilitate the healthful integration of body, mind, soul, and heart. God is as determined to overcome evil as Jesus was determined to exorcize the demon from the possessed man.

Different "levels" of liberation. The story of Jesus and the Gerasene demoniac reflects healing, release, and liberation at different levels of human experience. After his encounter with Jesus, the social and inner-personal dimensions of the demoniac's liberation are reflected in the description of him sitting beside Jesus, "clothed and in his right mind." At the level of social relationships, the healed man could now reenter his community and participate in circles of commerce, discourse, and friendship. At an inner-personal level, being in his right mind meant that he was restored inwardly and experienced the renewal of his identity. Having restored the man's sense of self and his place among others, Jesus then gives him a voice and vocation (from the Latin *vocare*, "to call"). Now he can share the good news of God's mercy openly. Like the demoniac, many people today are ostracized because of mental illness, race, sexual orientation, addictive behaviors, or AIDS. They too need to experience social and inner-personal healing and to be liberated *from* evil and *for* ministry.

There is yet another level of liberation suggested by the story of Jesus and the Gerasene demoniac. Mark's account offers intimations of God's power to overcome the Roman Empire whose military forces had overrun the nations of the Middle East. The Roman legions occupied the people of Palestine as violently as the legion of demons had possessed the Gerasene demoniac. Similarly, the liberation experienced by the demoniac was desired by all who had suffered from Rome's coercive and violent occupation. The text insists that liberation is assured through the nonviolent intervention of God in Jesus Christ. He alone is powerful enough to overcome the sources of evil within and around us. In the aftermath of the U.S. invasion of Iraq, there is a sobering and hard word here for any nation that seeks to overthrow or control the destiny of other countries. Violence is utterly rejected by God, who relentlessly pursues the well-being of people and nations through nonviolent acts of compassion, mercy, and healing.

Divine power and other kinds of power. A sermon focusing on the power of God could recognize the ways in which Jesus exercises divine power. He is the still, calm center in the midst of chaos, exerting God's power for the well-being of others. Jesus' words and deeds stand in stark contrast to those of the unclean spirit: whereas the unclean spirit alienates persons from themselves and others, Jesus integrates individuals within themselves and draws them into relationship with others; whereas Satan uses violence to coerce and destroy enemies, Christ expels evil by confronting it with its own destructive purposes. Amid the power plays of corporate America and the petty intrigues of smaller institutions, it is important to keep our eyes on Jesus. He does not seek his own advancement but the empowerment of others; he does not work to possess people or accumulate allies but helps people to be in full possession of themselves, ready and able to serve God and neighbors.

Ironies abound. Tragic and comic ironies arise in this text and reflect the reality of our world bumping up against the reality of God's reign. Ironically, when people see the man bound by Satan's power, they try to bind him with chains; similarly, our efforts to "help" others often serve to aggravate their condition and reflect our desire to prevent their harming or embarrassing us. Ironically, people fear Jesus' power and chase him away; similarly, we would rather get rid of what is helpful to us than face the possibility of change. Ironically, the unclean spirit acts as its own exorcist and invokes "the Most High God" in order to stay in the region. That request is fulfilled but, ironically, results in the unclean pigs being "cleansed" in the waters that consume them. Their immersion reminds us of the waters of baptism that bear us through life and death to newness of life. Finally, the man healed of demon possession experiences several ironic twists as well: he is an outcast suddenly thrown back into the social order that restrained and rejected him; he once spoke with the voice of Satan but now speaks the words of God; as the first evangelist to Gentiles, he opens God's way to a region and people considered "out of bounds" by Jews. Life is often not as we expect it will be, and God seems to take particular delight in overturning our expectations along the way. Amid the uncertainties and surprises, however, we can be sure of one thing: God will not leave things as they are but moves powerfully to bring the divine reign of mercy, justice, healing, and hope to all people.

POWER TO OVERCOME ILLNESS AND DEATH:
THE STORY OF JESUS AND TWO WOMEN (5:21–43)

Jesus' powerful activity continues with two extraordinary healing events woven together into one extended account. In 5:21–43, Jesus' intention of aiding a young girl who is near death is unexpectedly interrupted by a woman in desperate need of healing. The juxtaposition of these two events urges us to explore their differences and similarities, as well as the various themes that arise in our encounter with these two women. The literary technique of intercalation is a common feature of Mark's Gospel, serving to underscore parallel themes and to heighten our sense of expectation, fulfillment, and/or contrast in the progression of narrative events (e.g., 11:12–26; 14:26–72). This portion of the Gospel reveals insights into the nature of divine **power** embodied in Jesus Christ and the kingdom he inaugurates. Just as importantly, we learn of God's power through the indispensable witness of two women whose own power is experienced and enlivened through contact with Jesus Christ.

Exploring the text

By verse 21, Jesus has crossed the Sea of Galilee and is once again on Jewish territory. A large crowd greets him by the sea and is mentioned five times in the first fourteen verses. In contrast to family members and neighbors from his hometown who will soon reject Jesus (6:1–6), the crowds who press near to him are favorably disposed and fascinated by his wonder-working power. A leader of the synagogue also appears on the scene and makes a desperate plea for help. His presence in the narrative reveals that not all Jewish leaders were opposed to Jesus (see also 12:28–34). The fact that he "sees" Jesus is significant, because Jesus himself possesses a penetrating gaze (5:32), and visual sight often signifies spiritual perception in Mark's Gospel (e.g., 10:46–52). Jairus falls at Jesus' feet and begs him repeatedly to come help his daughter. The account uses brief phrases in rapid succession to underscore the urgency of the moment. Jairus quickly communicates his daughter's near-death condition, begs Jesus to lay his hands on her "so that she may be made well [saved], and live" (5:23). Here as elsewhere in Mark's Gospel, the word "save" suggests the restoration of physical and spiritual well-being as well as eschatological deliverance at the end of time (see 8:35; 10:23–26; 13:13–20). Without hesitation, Jesus goes with Jairus to help his daughter.

The narrative is suddenly interrupted in 5:25 by the presence of a solitary and silent figure in the crowd. In four successive phrases we hear of a woman who has suffered twelve years from a flow of blood, endured

much under many physicians, spent all the money she had without prof-
iting from it (see also 8:36), and is worse off now than before. According
to Marcus, the phrase "fountain of her blood" in 5:29 is related to the
statute in Leviticus 15:19–33 pertaining to the ritual uncleanness of a
woman with a discharge of blood outside the time of her regular men-
strual period.[1] However, Mark's account is not preoccupied with matters
of uncleanness and ritual impurity. Spencer notes that the main restric-
tions for a person in her condition would have been against entering the
Temple, having sexual intercourse with her husband, or having someone
touch the place where she was seated—none of which apply to her contact
with Jesus in the crowd.[2] Also, Mark does not name uncleanness or ritual
impurity in describing her condition (cf. 1:40–45). Instead, the narrative
focuses on her illness and the exploitation she experienced at the hands
of ineffectual medical practitioners. Through several carefully noted
details, the Gospel draws our attention to the severity of her condition and
the dire consequences of what has happened, including long-term suffering and poverty (cf. Luke 8:40–56; Matt. 9:18–26). Mark's portrayal of the
woman's condition emphasizes that she does not need to be cleansed but
healed; she does not need to be released from impurity but from inadequate and unfair medical practices. In contrast to these faulty practitioners, Jesus is the caring physician (2:17) whose healing power cannot be
contained but moves irresistibly toward those who need him.

The woman's movements and thoughts are also carefully noted by
Mark. Having heard about Jesus, she perceives his spiritual power and is
desperate to be healed. The woman has faith that by simply touching his
cloak she will be made well (5:34). Often, Jesus is the one to reach out to
others (see 5:41 as well as 1:31; 1:41; 7:33), but on this occasion the
woman with the chronic hemorrhage takes the initiative, summoning
reserves of faith and hope within her to seek what she needs. Here as elsewhere in Mark's Gospel, Jesus is not contaminated by contact with one
who is ill but is the conduit of transformative power for those in need of
divine help. As soon as the woman touches his garment, she feels that her
hemorrhage has ceased. Her body realizes what her heart has long
desired: she has been healed of her disease.

Just as quickly, however, Jesus also senses that power has gone forth
from him (5:30). The flow of blood in the woman's body is replaced with
a flow of power that moves without reservation between healer and
healed. Jesus turns to the crowd, eager to know who has touched his
clothes. The disciples are mentioned for the first time in this story in verse
31, and the Gospel depicts them as largely unaware of what is happening
around them. Jesus, however, continues his penetrating gaze through the

crowd and searches for the one who has touched him. With fear and trembling, the healed woman steps forward and falls down at his feet. Her humble posture and full response to Jesus' query stand in marked contrast to the behavior of the disciples.

In calling her out, Jesus provides an opportunity for the woman to publicly share what has happened and confess her faith before others (v. 33). There is a judicial tone to these proceedings: she speaks "the whole truth" of what has happened to her, and there is little doubt that her confession includes testimony of Jesus' healing power as well as mention of what she suffered due to irresponsible and fraudulent medical treatment (as recorded in vv. 25–26). In response to her testimony, Jesus calls her "daughter" and acknowledges her kinship as a beloved member of God's family (cf. 2:5b; 3:33–35; 5:23). In contrast to the disciples, the woman has faith in Christ's power. His blessing of peace indicates that she has received God's gift of wholeness. His final words to her, "Be healed of your disease," include an imperative announcing her full healing and continued restoration.

The condition, thoughts, and movements of the woman are in dramatic contrast to those of Jairus. He is named; she is not. He is counted as part of the necessary quorum required for public worship; her presence or absence in worship is of no public consequence.[3] He is a respected leader of the synagogue; she possesses no title or official status. Jairus speaks; the woman is silent until Jesus calls on her. Jairus confronts Jesus face to face; the woman approaches him surreptitiously. Jairus is a man of considerable wealth and social support; she has lost her wealth and has no one to advocate on her behalf. He is a respected member of society; she is on the margins of social acceptability. All of these differences render her the least likely recipient of attention, yet Jesus stops his journey to attend to this woman and listen to her story.

The narrative is again interrupted when word arrives by messenger that Jairus's twelve-year-old daughter has died (v. 35). At first it may appear that the healing of one has delayed the treatment of another and resulted in the girl's death. But Jesus would not have Jairus or others assume that God's power is limited in this way. Instead, he urges Jairus not to fear but believe, just as the woman healed of her hemorrhage had faith in him. In the economy of divine grace, there is no shortage of power and no lack of compassion. Remembering that Jesus' deeds of power point us toward the fullness of **God's reign** and the culmination of history, these stories remind us that "there is more than enough eschatological power to go around."[4]

Turning from Jairus to his disciples, Jesus summons Peter, James, and

John to accompany him (5:37; see also 9:2 and 14:33). Since it was not uncommon for wealthy persons to hire professional mourners, Jesus and his companions arrive to a loud commotion outside Jairus's house. When Jesus enters he asks why they are weeping, since "the child is not dead but sleeping" (5:39). Jesus is not questioning their diagnosis of her condition but their faith in his restorative powers. She is neither resting nor unconscious, but Jesus, as is the case elsewhere in Scripture (e.g., Dan. 12:7; 1 Thess. 5:10; 1 Cor. 15:6), refers to death as sleep. After the assembly laughs at him, Jesus ushers the people outside and takes the girl's parents and his three companions inside. Jesus takes her by the hand, ignoring the prohibitions against touching the dead and confident that it is not her outward condition that renders the girl unclean or unacceptable (see 7:17–23). Jesus commands her, "Talitha cum." These Aramaic words are literally translated, "Little lamb, arise," an endearing phrase that recalls other instances in Mark's Gospel when people arise just as Christ will arise from the dead (e.g., 2:11–12; 9:27; 16:6). The use of Aramaic and its translation in the text reveal that no magical formulas were spoken by Jesus and that he used the common language of daily discourse when raising her to life (see also 7:34).[5]

The girl immediately responds to Jesus' touch and command (5:42). She rises and walks around, an indication of her good health and liveliness. Those in attendance respond with amazement (16:8). Remarkably, Jesus orders those who are present to tell no one what has happened and to give the girl something to eat. Jesus is often concerned with the physical needs of others (see also 6:35–42). Eating demonstrates that the girl is fully recovered. Less obvious are his reasons for commanding their **silence** (see **messianic secret**). It is indeed strange that Jesus urges them to say nothing to anyone, since it will soon be apparent to everyone outside the house that the child is now alive and well.

In her analysis of the several occasions when Jesus commands people to keep silent about his identity or activity, Mitchell recognizes patterns in Mark's narrative that may help us appreciate Jesus' admonition to be silent in this particular text.[6] Although Jesus often urges his closest disciples and others not to speak of him before he reaches Jerusalem, there are a few unnamed characters in Mark's Gospel who cannot contain themselves (see 1:45; 7:36), or whom Jesus urges to speak freely of what has happened (5:19–20), or whom he urges to confess their faith openly in public (5:33). In each of these cases, the speaker is unnamed and is an unlikely witness to the gospel. Mitchell argues that such instances of gospel proclamation by anonymous and marginalized persons help us appreciate the reversal of expectation that occurs when Jesus' closest disciples fail to proclaim their allegiance to Jesus as he approaches the cross.[7] In other words, Mark notes lesser known and marginalized characters as the first to proclaim the good news of Jesus Christ rather than his followers or other persons of privilege (such as Jairus and his family). This reversal encourages us to look beyond the pages of the text to anticipate other unlikely witnesses who will proclaim the good news of Jesus Christ.

Finally, there are several parallels in Mark's narrative between the diseased woman and the dying girl. Both accounts feature "twelve years," "daughter," a life-threatening illness, healing through Jesus' touch, and, of course, both stories are about women. Miller notes, "Blood stops flowing in both, bringing life to one and death to the other."[8] Also, the severity of their situations is highlighted in Mark's account through mentioning the long-suffering of the woman with chronic hemorrhaging and the fatal consequences of the girl's condition. There is an additional bond between them. After twelve years of illness or childhood, both women have been robbed of their creative, life-giving potential, and both receive renewed life in their encounter with Jesus Christ. The power of these women, like the power of Jesus Christ, reveals God's passion for life: their suffering, the marginality of their experience as women, and their life-giving potential reflect a positive relationship between divine and human dimensions of longing and power.

Preaching and teaching the Word

Mark's account of the woman healed of chronic hemorrhaging and the girl raised from the dead arise in the RCL during the Fourth Sunday following Pentecost in Year B. These events bear witness to Jesus' extraordinary power and suggest several possibilities for sermons and lessons.

The power of women and the power of God. The story of these two women offers a wonderful opportunity to preach and teach about the power of women and God's power at work through them.[9] Although it is God in Christ who heals the woman's disease and raises the girl from the dead, the power of both of these women is featured prominently and favorably in the Gospel account. The woman with the twelve-year hemorrhage takes bold initiative in reaching out to Jesus and, when given the opportunity, speaks the whole truth of her experience. The young woman raised from the dead offers her active response to Jesus' healing touch and, at twelve years of age, returns to life as one who is empowered with life-giving potential. Although Jairus plays an important role in this extended drama, he serves primarily as a facilitator of his daughter's healing and recedes into the background when the healed woman takes center stage as an exemplar of faith. A sermon that honors these women may also relate stories of other nameless women of faith today whose quiet initiative, words of truth, and/or eager response to God's gift of life continue to proclaim the good news among us.

The desire for life that both women demonstrate through their contact with Christ also reflects some of the most powerful and positive aspects of sacred *erōs* imaginable. Although *erōs* has often been construed negatively or as less holy than *agapē*, the stories of these women testify to a divinely blessed longing for life that is expressed through communion with God amid the real passions and struggles of life. Both women embody the gospel truth of human suffering and divine mercy. Both women share a vigorous desire for life and connection with others. Both women are blessed with divine potential and/or the capacity to bear new life. Both women begin life anew through their contact with Jesus, whose own power is not diminished but enlivened by his encounter with them. The charge of energy that moves through Jesus and the woman with the chronic blood disease and the intimate connection he makes with the young girl who has died embody the power of divine *erōs* through these generative encounters. The interactions of these two women with Jesus energize the divine power to create, restore, and resurrect life among us. In her book *The Wounding and Healing of Desire*, Wendy Farley describes *erōs* as "the power of love in the form of desire. . . . This power manifests in feeling, and we call it love, but more fundamentally love *is* power."[10] This desire, this sacred *erōs* that is divine love and power, thrives among those who know God's suffering and longing as their own and seek God's generativity among us.

However, erotic power has often been misunderstood or violated. If erotic power is misconstrued as one person's manipulation of another, or if it is experienced as the domination of one person over another, then God's life-giving intentions for women and men have been violated at the most basic level. For example, it often takes several months or years for women who experience the damning effects of sexual abuse to reclaim the God-given power they possess within themselves and to find new ways of engaging their life-giving potential as women, mothers, lovers, friends, workers, and persons of faith. Most stories of sexual abuse or violation are untold. But these stories, like those of the two women healed by Jesus, draw our attention to women's suffering and the gospel's power to bring new life to all people.

A sermon that addresses women's power must also recognize the social, economic, political, and religious forces that oppress women who speak the truth about their lives and world. Just as women in first-century Palestine were subject to familial control, restricted by rigid rules of social conduct, and had little or no independent access to material resources, many women around the world today face significant challenges in confronting oppression of various kinds. For example, Godana is a forty-eight-year-old woman living in Yabelo, Ethiopia, who broke tradition by attending meetings and speaking up on issues related to women's health such as family planning, HIV/AIDS prevention, and reproductive health. In addition to caring for her nine children, she now works for CARE to educate women about family planning. While many women are without voice or a means of addressing the oppression they suffer, Godana's work reminds us of the power of God to bring health and wholeness to all people.[11]

Not only women's power but God's power comes to light in new ways through our encounter with this text. In Jesus' interaction with the woman healed of chronic bleeding, the flow of divine power moves irresistibly and without reservation between healer and the one who is healed. He is willing to stop his journey in order to see and hear the unnamed woman—an indication of the priority God gives to those who are impoverished and otherwise unrecognized by society at large. Jesus draws the woman out of anonymity and offers her an opportunity to speak publicly the whole truth of her situation, blessing her ministry of proclamation. With regard to the ancient dynamic of honor-shame, he reverses expectations by not seeking public recognition for healing the woman but "grants the honor of the cure to her, by virtue of her 'faith,' the decision she took to touch him."[12] This encounter does not drain him, but he moves on to raise the young girl from the dead, proving that there is more than enough healing power for all people. Addressing her as "little lamb" and taking her by the hand, Jesus shows great tenderness and willingness to risk contamination for the sake of contact and intimacy with one who has died. Jesus honors and respects these women; he is willing to be led by the bold initiative of one, and he carefully responds to the vulnerability of the other. He shows that divine power not only seeks the well-being of others but their empowerment. How strange and wonderful is the power of God in Jesus Christ.

Poverty and the public health care crisis. The story of the woman who suffered for twelve years from chronic hemorrhaging highlights her impoverishment and disease, opening a way for us to preach and teach about poverty and the public health care crisis. Jesus interrupts his journey to the home of a wealthy and respected leader of the synagogue in order to attend to someone without material wealth or social status. Yet he also attends to the young girl. His actions do not outline a clear and simple health care plan for ours or any nation, but they do suggest several points to consider as we debate the availability of adequate health care for all people.

First, by interrupting his journey to Jairus's home, Jesus demonstrates the divine priority given to persons who are suffering, marginalized, and poor. With more than nine million children under the age of nineteen in the United States without health insurance (and nearly 90 percent of them from working families), preachers and teachers of the gospel have every reason to speak of the need for comprehensive health care coverage for those who are most vulnerable and least protected by our society.[13] Like the woman who suffered from the "care" of inadequate and exploitative medical practitioners, there are many among us who suffer silently for want of adequate and affordable health care. Second, Jesus' care for both women demonstrates that the power of God's healing is not reserved for a few but intended for all; it is not a "zero sum" equation that results in some people being blessed while others are ignored. Rather, there is a generous and comprehensive spirit to Jesus' actions that encourages us to seek ways of extending health care coverage to all who need medical attention. Finally, Jesus affords the unnamed woman an opportunity to speak publicly about what has happened to her. He directs our attention to those who have no public voice and are relegated to the margins of social concern. In calling for her testimony, Jesus encourages us to hear the testimonies of other persons who experience injustice. In this way we may draw into the center of our conversations persons who have been pushed to the margins of social concern.

Truth telling. One of the most captivating phrases in this passage arises when the woman falls at Jesus' feet and tells him "the whole truth." Her testimony no doubt reflects her faith in Jesus and how she experienced his healing power. But given the lengthy description of her condition and Jesus' response afterward, we have every reason to believe that her testimony also includes a truthful account of what she endured under many physicians who drained her financial resources and prolonged her misery. Truth telling of this kind does more than publicly recognize who is at fault or seek restitution for injuries; it is basic to God's reign of divine justice and mercy. In the aftermath of apartheid, the South African Truth and Reconciliation Commission established by the Government of National Unity conducted hearings and court cases to address the violence and human rights abuses suffered by South Africans during the apartheid regime. Instances of human suffering revealed in these hearings needed to be publicly spoken and heard. Just so, Jesus' encounter with the woman who touches his cloak speaks to the importance of human initiative, truth telling, and the divine capacity to experience life anew in light of what we have suffered.

Faith that overcomes fear. Fear is named throughout Mark's Gospel and is experienced by many people for many different reasons: the disciples respond in fear when Jesus calms the storm (4:40), people are afraid when Jesus heals the demoniac (5:15), the healed woman is afraid when she falls at Jesus' feet (5:33), and Jairus is urged by Jesus not to fear but to believe (5:36). In all these instances of fear, only the woman who is healed of the chronic hemorrhage manages to overcome fear by faith. Her story culminates in Jesus' announcement that her faith has made her well. In contrast to the disciples, who trudge alongside Jesus with little insight or initiative, she is quite aware of what has happened to her and moves beyond fear to publicly speak the truth of what she has experienced. This woman is not endowed with any extraordinary abilities, nor does she possess any material or physical advantage over others. But she has faith. She is not commended for having courage—that is, confidence in one's own inner resources to confront one's fears. Instead, Jesus commends her faith and her faithful way of actively seeking divine resources to overcome disease and injustice. Whether our witness is public or private, great or small, it is our faith in God that encourages us to look beyond ourselves and recognize God's grace alive among us.

Prophetic Ministry
and Gospel Power

Mark 6:1–8:21

As Jesus' ministry continues to move beyond his hometown in Capernaum to neighboring regions and the cities of the Decapolis, the gospel extends its reach as never before. Many of the episodes included in 6:1–8:26 reflect themes encountered earlier in the Gospel. For example, we not only hear that Jesus experiences further opposition from family members and religious leaders, but his rejection at Nazareth is described in terms that sharpen our awareness of Jesus' prophetic role in Mark's Gospel (6:4–6a). The nature of prophetic witness is also evident in the rejection anticipated by Jesus' disciples and experienced by John the Baptist (6:11, 17–29). Other themes recur as well–the **disciples** play an ever more prominent role, and Jesus continues to proclaim the **gospel** through teaching and healing–but Jesus also shares the good news through feeding the multitudes and walking on water. He is willing to change his priorities in light of an encounter with a Syrophoenician woman, and he denounces those who define religious acceptability in terms of purity codes. These chapters convey the fullness of **God's reign**, offering us visions of relentless grace, redeeming power, and eschatological hope.

PROPHETIC WITNESS (6:1–29)

Exploring the text

When Jesus returns to his hometown in 6:1, the sudden shift in geographical location focuses our attention on the prophetic role of Jesus and his followers, who experience rejection at home and abroad. The first half of chapter 6 sharpens our sense of what is at stake in Jesus' ministry; it tests our understanding of his identity when the prophetic witness of the gospel results in rejection, hardship, and death.

Jesus the Prophet and His Rejection at Nazareth (6:1–6a)

This passage provides an important transition. If we consider it in light of the preceding stories that recount Jesus' many deeds of power (4:35–5:43), we become keenly aware of the sudden and surprising limitation of Jesus' **power** when he returns home and encounters the disbelief of his neighbors and kinfolk. However, if we view 6:1–6a as the first of three episodes that highlight Jesus' prophetic role and that of others who follow him, then his self-identification as prophet and rejection at his hometown lends particular meaning to his commissioning of the twelve disciples in verses 6b–13 and 30 and sharpens the association we make between Jesus' rejection and the death of his prophetic forerunner, John the Baptist, in verses 14–29.

Several facets of this story merit our attention. Although this is the third time Jesus has taught in a synagogue on the Sabbath and the third time he has experienced opposition to his teaching, on this occasion it is not demons or religious authorities who oppose him but his neighbors and closest kin (cf. 1:21–28; 3:1–6). They are scandalized by his message. The imperfect tense used here suggests that the people continue to take offense at his preaching. Through a series of five questions spread over two verses we witness the marked shift among townsfolk who wonder about the source of Jesus' power and wisdom, the reports of his miraculous deeds, and his lineage and relationship to kinfolk who still live close to home. It was unusual to identify a son in relation to his mother rather than his father, and it is possible the words "son of Mary" are intended as a slur that implies dubious paternity. Earlier in the Gospel, Jesus' biological family suspected he was insane (3:21), and he redefined kinship in terms of faithfulness to God's will (3:31–35). Later he speaks of the importance of familial support (7:9–13) and promises new familial ties in the age to come (10:29–31). But at this point, his family members are counted among those who reject Jesus' authority and power.

Most remarkably, Jesus identifies himself as a prophet. Although the Gospel asserts that he is more than this (e.g., 8:27–30), Jesus' self-identification as prophet places his ministry within the biblical pattern of prophetic witness, rejection, and vindication realized earlier in Israel's history and recounted throughout Hebrew Scripture (e.g., 2 Chr. 36:15–16; Jer. 35:15–17; Hos. 9:7). His words in 6:4 probably reflect an ancient aphorism. Jesus' neighbors and family members were unable to recognize his authority or accept his power as bearer of God's prophetic word. Consequently, Jesus could do no deed of power among them, except to lay his hands on a few people and heal them.

The fact that the text closely associates the diminishment of Jesus' power with the crowd's unbelief raises important questions. Is Jesus not capable of working miracles when others do not have faith in him? Or is he resentful and unwilling to help those who do not recognize his authority and power? According to Witherington, it seems the people's "lack of faith limits the reception of help readily available from Jesus."[1] Throughout Mark's Gospel, faith is a means of participating in God's healing purposes among us. He is indeed able to continue his healing ministry in subsequent chapters of Mark's Gospel (e.g., 6:56; 8:22; 9:25), but Jesus is not willing to coerce belief by manipulating events to prove his prophetic and divine identity. The text ends by noting that Jesus is amazed at their unbelief. This comment may serve to remind us of Jesus' human struggle to accept the resistance of those whom he knew and loved most intimately.

Sending Forth the Twelve (6:6b–13)

Another shift in the narrative takes place as Jesus leaves his hometown to teach and preach in the surrounding villages. Earlier in the Gospel when he experienced fierce opposition from religious leaders (3:1–6), Jesus departed with his disciples and called forth twelve to proclaim the gospel and cast out demons (3:7–19). Here also Jesus experiences rejection (6:1–6a) then sends forth the twelve to minister to others (6:6b–13). Later, in verse 30, they give their report to Jesus (see **disciples**).

The relationship between the disciples' ministry and that of their master is described in the closest terms possible. Like Jesus, they follow his pattern of proclaiming repentance, overcoming evil spirits, and healing the sick (6:12–13). However much the disciples may fail or frustrate Jesus in the chapters to come, in this episode there is no mistaking their amazing success: by his authority and power they participate in the eschatological realization of God's just and merciful reign. By sending them out two by two, Jesus ensures their companionship and safety along the way and provides the minimum of two witnesses required by Jewish law to establish legal testimony (see Deut. 19:15).

Verses 8–11 provide the details of Jesus' instructions. In short, the disciples are to travel lightly and depend on the hospitality of others to supply their most basic needs.[1] Marcus notes that there are several parallels between the Markan description of the disciples' itinerant ministry and Old Testament portrayals of Israel's movement through the wilderness.[2] Both the exodus story and Mark's version of Jesus' instructions suggest that the traveler carry a staff, bring no bread or money for the journey, and wear sandals and only one tunic or garment of clothing (see Exod. 12 and 16; Deut. 8 and 29). Not much is needed for the work of prophets and itinerant preachers who continue the exodus journey of faith. When the disciples enter a house, Jesus instructs them to remain there—perhaps to promote a sense of community and to discourage competition among potential hosts inclined to outdo one another with generosity. When people refuse to hear them, Jesus urges his followers to shake the dust from their feet as a testimony against them. This gesture appears to be a prophetic and symbolic action that denotes judgment on those who refuse to receive the disciples' message, and it may reflect the Jewish custom of shaking the dust of foreign territory from one's feet before returning to the Holy Land. As prophetic witnesses of the gospel, the disciples can expect rejection and opposition just as Jesus experienced at his hometown (6:1–6a).

In verses 12–13 we learn that the disciples, like Jesus, went forth to proclaim repentance, cast out demons, and anoint and cure many who were sick. Although Mark's Gospel does not record instances of Jesus anointing those who are sick, he himself is anointed shortly before his trial and crucifixion (14:3–9), and the early church incorporated the practice of anointing as an ordinance of Christ's followers (Jas. 5:3–5). Interestingly, the disciples' preaching more closely resembles that of John, who proclaimed repentance for the forgiveness of sins (1:4) than that of Jesus, who also announced the good news of God's impending reign (1:15). Perhaps, like John, the disciples are serving here as prophetic witnesses pointing to one more powerful than they who may be heard and followed in person. Indeed, Herod's reaction to the disciples' ministry in the following verses suggests that they were successful in continuing the work of Jesus and John (6:14–16).

A Gruesome Banquet, a Cruel Death (6:14–29)

Mark intentionally places the terrible account of John's beheading amid material that highlights Jesus' prophetic witness (6:1–6a) and that of his disciples (6:7–13, 30), alerting us to the costly consequences of gospel faith. John's death provides a cruel picture of the prophet's fate—and an ominous glimpse into the prophetic destiny of Jesus and his followers (see also 13:9–13).

According to 6:14–15, news of the disciples' success spread far and wide, garnering the attention of common folk and political leaders alike. Here as elsewhere the question of Jesus' identity rises to the surface (see also 2:7; 3:22; 4:41; 6:2–3), but on this occasion people's notions of who

Jesus is and what is he about are centered around his prophetic activity and identity. The text tells us that some believed Jesus was John the Baptist raised from the dead, in whom John's powers were reenacted. However, none of the Gospels record miraculous deeds performed by John, and Mark describes him as less powerful than Jesus (1:4–8). Others insisted that Jesus was Elijah, the ninth-century prophet who confronted royal powers and was expected to return to announce the Messiah's coming (1 Kgs. 17–19, 21; 2 Kgs. 1–2; Mal. 4:5–6). As Witherington points out, Elijah was also considered the patron saint of the poor and needy, a further reason for people to have confused him with Jesus.[1] However, according to Mark's Gospel, Elijah more closely resembles John than Jesus; John functions as Jesus' forerunner in the first chapter, and in the ninth chapter Jesus himself associates John with Elijah (9:11–13). Still others say that Jesus was "one of the prophets of old." While this assessment affirms Jesus' prophetic authority, it does not fully account for his identity. This becomes apparent in the next several chapters when Peter confesses that Jesus is the Christ (8:27–30) and the cross and empty tomb bear witness to his messianic identity. Finally, 6:14–16 begins and ends with references to Herod. When he hears of the disciples' extraordinary ministry, Herod immediately thinks of Jesus (v. 14a) and fears that John has been raised from the dead (v. 16). Perhaps it is the prophetic witness of Jesus' disciples that inspires Herod to think of their teacher and of his prophetic forerunner, John the Baptist. Or perhaps Herod's anxiety is roused because of his role in the prophet's death, recounted in the story that follows.

The flashback in 6:17–29 discloses the story of John's death and is the only occasion when the Gospel focuses at length on a character other than Jesus. But even John remains hidden from sight and secluded in prison until he makes a cameo appearance as the final course at Herod's gruesome banquet. Instead, the story busily pursues the machinations of Herod, his wife Herodias, and her daughter Salome. Interestingly enough, their familial intrigues are also recorded by the Jewish historian Josephus, who correctly identifies Herod by his rightful title of tetrarch (see Luke 3:1). Josephus plainly states that Herod imprisoned and executed John because he feared an uprising from the Baptist and his supporters. By contrast, Mark portrays Herod as interested in John's message and even protective of him personally (6:20).[2] However, Mark's more sympathetic depiction of Herod does not ignore the political implications of John's message. Since intermarriage consolidated royal dynasties, writes Myers and his coauthors, "John's objection that Herod should not marry his brother's wife could scarcely be more political (6:17f). The half-

Jew Herod conformed to Jewish law only when he deemed it politically expedient. . . . By insisting that Herod be accountable to Torah (6:18), then, John was raising a volatile political issue in colonial Palestine."[3] In other words, John's objections to Herod's alliance with Herodias (based on Lev. 18:16; 20:21) were not only pious but political.

The relationship between Herod and Herodias is also of particular interest. The Gospel reports that Herodias had a grudge against John and wanted to kill him, whereas Herod was drawn to the prophet's fiery message and believed him to be a righteous and holy man. As the story progresses, however, the two are less antagonists to one another than collaborators in John's demise, with Salome being drawn into their incestuous power play. Both Herod and Herodias suffer the consequences of John's accusations, both seek to maintain their marriage alliance, and both want to avoid the overthrow of Herod's rule. Although Herodias is guilty of provoking John's death and utilizes whatever power is at her disposal to procure it, we must not be quick to interpret Herod's sympathy toward the Baptist as reason to excuse his full participation in John's murder. As Spencer points out, "Herodias does indeed seize the 'opportune' (*eukairos*, 6:21) moment to provoke her husband into satisfying her blood vengeance against John. But she doesn't, as is sometimes thought, create the opportunity. She hatches no sinister plot."[4] Herod's excessive offer to Salome, his repeated oath to give her anything she asks, and his decision to save face before his guests rather than spare John's life culminate in his fateful decision to issue the order for John's beheading. Whatever ambivalence or remorse Herod may have felt is overruled by the cruel expediency of his decision. In the words of one young member of our Markan Bible study, "Herod commits an especially awful deed by killing someone he likes."[5]

Salome also deserves our careful consideration. She suddenly appears at her father's birthday party to dance and provides an unusual instance of a female member of the royal family who puts herself on public display. However, we must be careful not to read into the text what is not present: Mark does not tell us whether she arrives because of her father's request, her mother's urging, or her own desire. Neither does the text say that her manner of dress was seductive or that her dance was sexually provocative. It does report that she enters the circle of court nobles, army officers, and leading politicians of Galilee and becomes the willing agent of her mother's cruel plot and her father's failed conscience. Salome runs back and forth between Herodias and Herod, not only accepting her mother's errand but adding to her macabre plot by demanding that John's head be placed on a platter. Although strong similarities exist between her story and those of Esther and King Ahasuerus (Esth. 2, 7); Judith, who beguiles and beheads Holofernes (Jdt. 13); and Jezebel, who seeks to kill the prophet Elijah (1 Kgs. 19:1–3), we must not assume that Salome entered the banquet with any intention other than that of entertaining or pleasing Herod and his guests.[6]

We may also compare Salome and Herodias to other women in Mark's account, including the woman healed of her twelve-year hemorrhage (5:25–34) and the Syrophoenician woman who pleads for her daughter's well-being (7:24–30). All of these women use whatever personal or familial sources of power are available to them. But in seeking what they most desire, they engage power quite differently. For Herodias and Salome, power derives from their ability to please men as they seek recognition, status, and personal security in arranging the death of an enemy. For the unnamed women in Mark 5 and 7, divine power is enlivened through their faith-filled encounters with Jesus Christ. By faith, they provoke his compassionate response and participate in the transforming power of God for themselves and those they love.

The terrible story of John's death invites other comparisons as well. Most notable are the similarities between John's fate and that of Jesus. Just as John's ministry in the wilderness foreshadowed that of Jesus, so does his death. Both John and Jesus garner the attention and respect of political leaders who ultimately issue the orders for their executions. Both are arrested, bound, cruelly executed, and buried. Just as the Baptist preaches and is delivered unto death, so Jesus preaches and is delivered unto death. The pattern bodes ominously for Jesus' followers as well. When the disciples return from their first ministry endeavor to share with Jesus all that they have done and taught (6:30), their success strikes us differently in light of John's story. His death is a reminder of what is to come not only for Jesus but for others who proclaim his message of repentance and good news to all the nations (13:9–13).

Preaching and teaching the Word

The RCL divides 6:1–29 into two portions, with verses 1–13 among the readings for the Fourteenth Sunday of Ordinary Time in Year B and verses 14–29 for the Fifteenth Sunday. In sequence, these texts can provide the basis for sermons or lessons highlighting the prophetic witness of the gospel at home and at large. A consideration of one's particular setting, seasonal interests, churchly needs, and worldly questions will draw attention to various aspects of these lively and disturbing stories of prophetic witness.

The fullness of prophetic witness for all Christ's followers. The prophetic witness of the gospel comes to life in these stories through Jesus' self-identification as a prophet (v. 4) and his commissioning of the disciples to confront and cast out evil, heal the diseased, and proclaim repentance and good news to all people (see also 13:9–13). There is no arbitrary division of labor, as if some are given the task of evangelism, others the ministry of healing, and still others the work of confronting and casting out evil. In partnership with one another, they work together to proclaim the fullness of God's reign through compassionate and revolutionary activities. Since most congregations today tend to advocate one aspect of the church's calling as superior to another (either evangelism or justice, either outreach to the poor in spirit or to the economically impoverished), sermons and lessons reflecting on Mark 6 can recall Christ's vision of ministry that addresses the breadth of human need and longing.

The costliness of prophetic witness for all Christ's followers. Mark 6:1–29 also depicts the inevitability of rejection and suffering as Jesus and his followers fulfill their prophetic calling. The stories in the first half of Mark 6 anticipate the pattern of proclamation, rejection, and vindication that recurs in the prophetic books of Scripture. Some of our most painful and wrenching experiences arise when kinfolk, community leaders, and members of our own congregations are scandalized by what we believe are divinely given insights and directions. When this happens, processes of discernment and reconciliation can be quite helpful. But when our ministry is met with resolute unbelief, refusal to listen, or impenetrable arrogance, Jesus would not have us surprised by the cruelty of others. Instead, he urges us to keep moving along, in good company and with the blessed assurance of his resurrection power to bring all creation to newness of life.

Traveling lightly. It is remarkable that in his instructions to the disciples in Mark 6:6b–13 Jesus does not say a thing about what they are to preach or teach. Instead, his entire focus is on the manner of their ministry, the way they are to go about their witness in the world. Although there is no need to debate the real value or imitate the exact details of Jesus' instructions (e.g., whether Jesus' followers should wear sandals or shoes, whether they should remain in the same setting for a few days or several years), there is no mistaking the spirit of Jesus' intentions. His followers are to travel lightly. They are not to worry about their provisions but are to humbly accept the hospitality of others even as they freely offer their own gifts to those around them. When others refuse to receive their message, they must not respond with rebuttals or violence but, shaking the dust from their feet, acknowledge the error of their detractors and continue their witness elsewhere. Also, they must minister in the company of another, sharing the companionship, encouragement, and accountability of fellow witnesses in the work of ministry—peacefully, simply, together.[7]

However, Jesus' relatively simple admonitions are more difficult to practice than to preach. We hardly notice the opportunities and encounters that arise daily as all God's people are called to share the gospel with others. When people train for Brethren Volunteer Service (an outreach ministry of the Church of the Brethren), their final exercises sometimes involve being dropped off with another volunteer several hours away from the training center. With only fifty cents in their pockets (in case they need to make an emergency phone call), they are given instructions to work for anyone who is willing to engage them in exchange for meals and transportation back to the training center later that day. They are not allowed to receive money for their labor. Of course, they are encouraged to share the gospel in whatever ways the Spirit moves them and seems appropriate to the situation. Volunteers return with sad and humorous stories: some people turn them away, others keep trying to pay them money, and still others, when hearing them sing hymns while working, ask questions about their faith. Nearly all volunteers express some sense of how difficult it is to be vulnerable and beholden to others. We do not need to practice itinerant ministry in order to be faithful disciples of Jesus Christ, but neither is it such a bad idea to remember our interdependence with others as we share the gospel in word and deed.

Politics and religion. There is no mistaking the political implications of John's message to Herod: marrying Herodias not only violated levitical law but fortified the royal court's alliances with others. Most of us have a very limited view of the intersection of politics and religion; it arises only during discussions of the Ten Commandments posted around local courthouses, teaching evolution in public schools, or making decisions related to the beginning and end of life. Besides these "hot topics," most people seem unaware or unwilling to acknowledge that the gospel speaks to our corporate and political concerns in myriad other ways as well, including care for the poor and nonviolent approaches to enemies. In his book *The Politics of Jesus,* John Howard Yoder challenges us to deepen and enlarge our understanding of Jesus' life, death, and resurrection, as these hold political implications as well: "Jesus was, in his divinely mandated (i.e., promised, anointed, messianic) prophethood, priesthood and kingship, the bearer of a new possibility of human, social, and therefore political relationships."[8] A sermon related to the story of John the Baptist may challenge listeners to consider the prophetic and political implications of our alliances, business transactions, and government decisions. John helps us remember the necessary relationship between divine priorities and human policies as we proclaim the gospel in word and deed.

Shared sin. Sin often occurs in collusion with others, as it did with Herod,

Herodias, and Salome. This strange and disturbing tale of political intrigue, sexual liaisons, and violence is not only the stuff of grocery store tabloids; it involves everyone who attended Herod's banquet and all of us who are pulled into this strange and intriguing drama. If we are honest with ourselves, we are less likely to identify with John than we are with the sinful inclinations of Herod, his household, and other guests. Perhaps it is the aggressive push for power, prestige, and possessions evidenced by the courtiers and royal family that cuts our consciences to the quick as we seek to advance our own interests rather than the interests of others. Perhaps we can relate to Herod's need to save face and appear to be in control, or his inclination to be ruled by the desires of others rather than his own sense of what is right. Perhaps we recognize some of Herodias's manipulative or passive-aggressive behavior creeping into our words and deeds. Perhaps there is a streak of Salome's exhibitionism in us that would rather draw the attention of others than recognize our culpability in the process of someone else's demise. Or perhaps we are as silent as Herod's guests, choosing to be spectators entertained by the gruesome games we witness instead of rising to protest the violence we unwittingly support. The cruel death of John the Baptist reminds us that sin abounds and that there are many ways to destroy God's messengers and undermine the prophetic witness of the gospel.

PASTORAL MIRACLES (6:30–56)

The episodes that comprise the second half of Mark 6 relate several distinct yet related miracles: distinct because they manifest divine power in various ways among different people and settings; related because all of these events reveal Jesus' compassion and determination to serve those who need him. One member of our Markan Bible study noted that these events highlight Jesus' ministry of nurture: he encourages the disciples to rest (v. 31), feeds strangers who unexpectedly arrive for supper (vv. 37–41), arranges for his disciples to get away from the crowd (v. 45), finds a place of personal solitude and prayer (v. 46), calms yet another stormy sea (v. 51; cf. 4:39) and ministers to all who are ailing (vv. 53–56).[1] God's grace and kindness abound. There are also several allusions to Israel's past, and these episodes take place in predominantly Jewish regions (cf. 8:1–21).

Exploring the text

Feeding Five Thousand (6:30–44)

The feeding of five thousand in Mark is not quite a potluck or a picnic, an earthly banquet or a messianic feast. Yet it contains elements of each, with people sharing food, reclining on green grass, and enjoying an abundance of bread and fish in the presence of Jesus Christ. It is the only miracle story to appear in all four Gospels. However, Mark's version is uncharacteristically long, and this Gospel also includes the story of another miraculous meal that serves about four thousand guests (8:1–10). The latter takes place in Gentile territory, but this first feast is near Capernaum and bears striking similarities to other events in Israel's history. The feeding of five thousand not only alludes to the past but anticipates the future, when Jesus will take, bless, break, and share bread with his disciples at the Last Supper and enjoy their company at the messianic banquet in the kingdom to come.

Placed beside the story of Herod's banquet in 6:17–29, the story of the feeding of the five thousand invites comparison. Herod vacillates in his allegiance to John, while Jesus is resolute in showing compassion toward others. Herod hosts a banquet in his own honor, issuing invitations to the most prestigious members of society, and Jesus blesses bread in God's name, offering food to anyone who is hungry. Herod's family takes the initiative in plotting the death of John, and the reluctant disciples are commanded by Jesus to serve others. Finally, the royal banquet concludes with John's head on a platter, and Jesus' feast draws to a close with everyone satisfied and twelve baskets of food left over.

The disciples also play a prominent role in this incident. Verse 30 is the only instance when Mark refers to Jesus' closest followers as apostles, persons who are "sent out" by Jesus. The term does not represent an official title as much as a description of their role and how they function in the Gospel. After reporting the success of their first missionary venture, Jesus urges the disciples to come away to a quiet place and rest for a while. The phrase "deserted place" occurs three times in the first few verses, combining the disciples' need for solitude with images of Israel's sojourn in the wilderness. But Jesus' efforts to secure a place for them apart from the crowds are in vain. Although they travel by boat to another shore, the people follow their movements and hurry ahead by foot.[1]

Stepping ashore, Jesus sees the crowd and feels compassion for them. Amid the press and clamor of people, his heart never seems to harden (cf. 3:5; 6:52). He reaches out to these strangers (see also 8:2; 9:22), who are more like sheep in need of a shepherd than an unruly mob in need of control. He takes this opportunity to offer words of instruction and hope (6:34). As Marcus points out, this story includes several elements of a Moses typology: it references the wilderness location, the crowd pursues Jesus "like sheep without a shepherd" (Num. 27:17), people are arranged in large groups (Exod. 18:21, 25; Deut. 1:15), and Jesus teaches them just as Moses taught Israel the Torah.[2] Like Elisha, Jesus also unexpectedly feeds all who are hungry (cf. 2 Kgs. 4:42–44), yet the abundance of his provision surpasses that of Moses and Elijah. He may be a prophet (6:4), but he is more than this (8:27–30).

The exchange between Jesus and his disciples forms the centerpiece of this miraculous event (6:35–39). The disciples have not eaten for quite some time (v. 31), and the hour is late when Jesus finishes teaching (v. 35). Their hunger pangs are no doubt as sharp as their tongues when they urge Jesus to send the people away to fend for themselves. Jesus' reply is short and commanding: "You give them something to eat." But the disciples do not hesitate to make their rebuttal: even if there were a deli in sight, it would take a half-year's wages to pay for enough bread to feed this crowd.[3] Whether exasperated, exhausted, or simply incredulous, they cannot imagine what Jesus intends or what their role will be in caring for the crowd. After Jesus asks them how many loaves they have, he sends them out into the crowd to see what is available. They return to him with their meager offering of five loaves and two fish.

Next, Jesus instructs his disciples to order the people to sit in groups of hundreds and fifties on the green grass. Like the shepherd of Psalm 23, he will see to it that the people have what they need; like Moses in Exodus 18:21 and 25, he arranges for others to assist him in serving. Jesus calls the disciples to the work of servanthood, to continue the ministry they enacted elsewhere (Mark 6:6b–13). Their work includes not only being sent out to preach and heal but to serve those they unexpectedly encounter in their daily living. The disciples watch as Jesus takes, blesses, breaks, and gives the bread and fish to them, directing them to distribute these gifts to others. In the midst of serving, God multiplies their simple offerings. The disciples are instrumental to the work of Jesus, and his work involves multiplying the gifts of others. By Christ's hands and the hands of his followers, all are fed.

Some have attempted to explain away the miraculous nature of this event by arguing that the multiplication of bread and fish was due to the generosity of a few that inspired others to share whatever food they had brought along. But the Gospel does not support this interpretation of events. Instead, it describes a supernatural event as Jesus Christ works with others to procure more food than anyone could humanly account for. Everyone ate and was fully satisfied. By the end, the disciples gathered up twelve baskets of leftovers, perhaps a symbolic reference to the twelve tribes of Israel. The broken pieces, like the human beings the disciples served, are gathered together so that nothing is lost. By the end of the feast,

God provided more than was needed and far beyond what seemed humanly possible. Mark does not comment on the crowd's response, and we learn that the disciples did not understand the meaning of this miracle (6:52). Yet they witnessed an extraordinary event as Jesus satisfied the hunger of human hearts and bodies.

Walking on Water (6:45–52)

Mark's account of Jesus walking on water continues the theme of God's compassion and care for others. The action and initiative belong entirely to Jesus: he guides the disciples onto a boat, dismisses the crowd, goes up the mountain to pray, sees the disciples struggling against the wind, walks on water to meet them, speaks words of comfort, calms the wind, then joins the disciples on their journey to the other side of the sea. This is the second of three boat scenes, and each episode represents a revelatory encounter between Jesus and the twelve disciples (see also 4:35–41; 8:13–21). But this event, more than any other seafaring miracle, identifies Jesus with the God of Israel who steadfastly pursues the well-being of God's people.

The introductory verses set the stage for the ensuing drama (6:45–46). Jesus urges his disciples onto a boat and sends them off to the other side of the sea just as he urged them earlier to find a place away from the crowd to rest for a while (v. 30). It seems somewhat odd that Jesus insists on their leaving him before the crowd is dismissed, but perhaps he chooses to attend to the crowd himself so that the disciples may be free to get away. After saying farewell to the people on shore, Jesus seeks his own place to pray. It is on the mountain that he finds a place of divine encounter and, like Moses, communes with God (Exod. 3:1).

During the night, Jesus notices that the disciples are straining at the oars (6:47–48). It is remarkable that he can see the disciples across the lake during a windstorm in the middle of the night (literally, "the fourth watch," between 3 and 6 a.m.), since both distance and darkness conspire against visual acuity. His penetrating gaze and spiritual insight reflect divine powers not normally experienced by others (see also 2:5–8; 3:5; 3:34–35; 10:14). Just as importantly, Jesus is concerned about the disciples' well-being. Seeing them strain at the oars (literally, "being tortured in rowing"),[1] he goes in pursuit of the disciples amid the fury of the storm. Some commentators have attempted to explain away the miraculous nature of this event by asserting that Jesus could have walked across submerged stones, along the shoreline, or perhaps on a layer of ice that had accumulated during the winter. But speculations like these distract us from the miraculous impression the story conveys. Jesus has power to overcome the forces of nature and is determined to transform the worst situations into an opportunity for divine grace.

More troublesome is Mark's comment that Jesus intended to pass them by (6:48; cf. Matt. 14:22–33; John 6:15–21). Why would Jesus cross the water and want to be seen by the disciples yet refuse to offer help in their time of need? The most satisfactory answer is offered by Marcus, who interprets this text in light of Moses' encounter with God when God does not face him but passes him by in order to reveal divine glory without jeopardizing Moses' safety (Exod. 33:17–34:8). According to Marcus, "Mark, similarly, has introduced the motif of Jesus 'passing by' into the narrative of the walking on the water because of its epiphanic connotation, but since he needs to end the story by having Jesus united with the disciples in the boat, he writes only that Jesus *wanted* to pass them, not that he *did* so."[2]

Two other parallels may be noted between this event and Israel's encounters with God in the Hebrew Bible. First, God's power in overcoming the forces of the sea is well attested in Hebrew Scripture (e.g., Gen. 8:1–3; Job 9:8; Ps. 33:7; Jonah 1:11–16). Second, the great "I am" spoken by the God of Israel (Exod. 3:14) is reiterated by Jesus as he approaches the disciples on the stormy sea. Jesus announces "I am here" or "It is I" (*egō eimi*), proclaiming God's saving presence and revealing his divine nature (see also 14:62).[3] Thus, this story of divine rescue is also a story of divine revelation. He is the great *I AM* who is present to his disciples during the worst of times and has power to transform the forces of death.

The story ends by noting the disciples' utter astonishment and their hardness of heart (6:51b–52). However callous or ignorant their reaction may sound, it is helpful to remember that they began the day with the promise of rest (vv. 30–32), were soon busy with the work of serving others (vv. 33–44), and ended the evening with a near-death experience at sea. Although the Gospel keeps our eyes focused on Jesus, Mark is careful to include several comments describing the disciples' feelings and reactions throughout the storm. They are tortured by incessant rowing (v. 48), terrified by an apparition (vv. 49–50), astonished at Jesus' unexpected presence (v. 51), and dumbfounded by all that has happened (v. 52). It is possible to imagine that the disciples were also angry at Jesus for not accompanying them when they first set sail, since he earlier demonstrated his power over the sea (4:35–41). Whatever their feelings, the text clearly points us back to the feeding miracle that immediately precedes the storm at sea. Mark comments that "they did not understand about the loaves, but their hearts were hardened" (6:52). The disciples seem increasingly unable to recognize the significance of Jesus' power and authority. Like Jesus' worst enemies (3:5) and Pharaoh himself (Exod. 11:10), they are also susceptible to hardness of heart (see Mark 8:17).

Healing the Diseased (6:53–56)

The summary verses at the close of chapter 6 highlight Jesus' miraculous healing power through a combination of generalization and vivid detail. In general terms, we learn that Jesus' popularity continues to grow among the people at large. He travels extensively through the towns and countryside of the region and is able to heal everyone who reaches out to him for help. Like other summary passages in Mark's account (e.g., 1:32–34; 3:7–12), these verses remind us that Jesus' ministry extends beyond the confines of the written page to include events and encounters too numerous to record. We may also compare what is described here to 6:1–6a when Jesus "could do no deed of power," presumably because of the unbelief of family members and friends. Now, however, we hear that Jesus' powers are flourishing, which suggests faith among those who long for his gifts of mercy and healing.

Several details are also worth noting. The text reports that the boat landed at Gennesaret on the northwest shore of the Sea of Galilee rather than the original destination of Bethsaida (6:45). The shift in geographical locations most likely indicates that Mark has inserted other materials into this sequence of stories, since it is not until 8:22 that Jesus and the disciples arrive in Bethsaida. As soon as they step ashore, the crowd immediately recognizes Jesus—something that the twelve were not able to do just a few verses earlier (6:49). They also hurry to gather up loved ones who are sick to bring them to Jesus for healing, just as the twelve and other disciples are to go about the work of gathering God's people (vv. 42–44). Jesus cannot help but extend God's grace to all who are in need, and there is not one who leaves bereft of his power. If the chapter begins with people asking who Jesus is (vv. 2–3), it ends by showing us the breadth and depth of his compassion and power.

Preaching and teaching the Word

The RCL includes only verses 30–34 and 53–56 as the Gospel readings for the Sixteenth Sunday of Ordinary Time in Year B. However, numerous connections run throughout this chapter of the Gospel, tempting preachers to address several themes.

1. Our Need for Daily Bread and Spiritual Sustenance. This need runs throughout these stories as we encounter Jesus' resolute determination to help others. Although we may explore the eucharistic imagery in this event, some of the most compelling aspects of this story include our perennial hunger for physical and spiritual sustenance and God's will to fulfill these needs. A comparison between the feeding of the five thousand and the story of Herod's feast in the verses that immediately precede it yields some striking points of contrast (see "Preaching and teaching the Word" for 6:14–29, p. 108). Both the remarkable feast that Jesus provides with the help of his disciples and the stories that follow suggest several focal points for preaching and teaching.

• *Being fed by Jesus Christ.* What does it mean to be fed by Jesus? For some, it may be as simple as a weekly "fill-up" on Sunday morning. But the story of Jesus' feeding the five thousand reaches beyond the pages of Scripture to touch upon one of the most universal of human experiences– the need for both daily sustenance and spiritual hope. Just as Christians around the world pray, "Give us this day our daily bread," the Gospel tells us of God's deepest desire to satisfy the hungers of our souls and bodies. Jesus did not simply preach and then leave. His ministry to the five thousand who hunger for divine guidance and daily bread fulfills the words of the ancient Spanish prayer: "Lord, give bread to those who are hungry and hunger of you to those who have bread."

Mark 6:30–56 reveals many ways to be fed by Jesus, many ways God meets the most basic human needs of spiritual and bodily hunger. To be fed by Jesus is to seek his presence and listen to his teaching. To be fed by Jesus is to sit and rest a while. To be fed by Jesus is to encounter God in a stranger and be surprised by divine guidance. To be fed by Jesus is to find company and companionship among others who hunger and thirst. To be fed by Jesus is to recognize the sacred gift of daily bread. To be fed by Jesus is to be encouraged to share whatever gifts we have, knowing that our simple offerings will be multiplied by God for the good of all people.

• *Communion and other holy meals.* Whether or not Mark's text was written to reflect eucharistic images, there is no mistaking the holy nature of this simple meal. Jesus shares the abundance of God by taking, blessing, breaking, and giving bread to all who are hungry. In typical Jewish fashion, he offers a blessing before the meal. Yet it is not entirely clear whether Jesus is blessing the bread or God. The traditional Jewish grace declares, "Blessed are you, O Lord our God, ruler of the universe, who brings forth bread from the earth." But we too are blessed in the breaking and sharing of bread. Looking back, we are blessed with memories of God's amazing gift of manna in the wilderness, potlucks following Sunday worship, and other occasions when

God provided for our every need. Looking forward, we are blessed to anticipate the heavenly banquet when all creation will join in the messianic feast. Looking to the present moment, we encounter God's gifts in abundance whenever we share a meal and enjoy the fruits of creation with others. When my children and I bake our weekly bread, we often sing, "Be gentle when you touch bread. The earth has caressed it. Lord Jesus he blessed it. So be gentle when you touch bread."[1] Every meal is an opportunity to recognize and receive God's blessings–and to share those blessings with others.

• *Serving one another.* I wonder if it was something of a shock to the disciples to have returned from a wildly successful missionary journey only to be sent by Jesus to search for carry-out food for five thousand! Ministry often involves the less-than-glamorous work of attending to the needs of others and serving where we are most needed. Since the urge for recognition and reward pushes us to pursue the largest possible salary or to compare ourselves with others, a sermon recalling the vitality of serving can help us remember that God continues to enact miracles of mercy and kindness through those who are willing to lend themselves in service to others. Serving others is at the heart of discipleship, and this story highlights this most important aspect of faithful living. The term "apostle" refers to those who are "sent out," and it does not describe the disciples' status as much as their function or role in being called to Christlike service. The disciples assessed available resources, gathered people together, arranged seating, distributed bread and fish, made sure everyone was fed, and then organized the cleanup. The miracle of feeding several thousand people became a reality because of their obedience to Jesus' command, just as Jesus calls us to assess the needs and gifts of those around us, offer help with disaster relief projects, volunteer to coordinate local and ecumenical service work, and see the hunger of the world as our own.

• *Food and mercy for all people.* When it comes to God's mercy there is no such thing as small portions. Everyone was given a place on the grass, all were fed, and there was more than enough left over. In the economy of God's grace, there is more than "a little justice," and it is not reserved for a select few. Jesus did not ask the disciples to assess the people's religious commitment, the extent of their hunger, the depth of their appreciation, or their ability to repay him before he sent them out to distribute food. Instead, the miraculous feeding of the multitude underscores the abundance of God's mercy for all people through a radical act of divine generosity.

It is disturbing to think that in a land of plenty so many people are hungry, in a country of abundant resources most of the wealth is owned or controlled by very few, and throughout our nation many immigrants are turned away for wanting to pursue an honest living. It seems that we live in constant fear of never having enough as we continue to reach for more. Perhaps the alarming rise in obesity among Americans is symptomatic of this desire to hoard more than we need and reflects our inability to savor the simple gifts of daily bread. Have we forgotten what it is to be satisfied and the joy that is to be found in helping to satisfy the needs of others? According to economist Jeffrey Sachs, more than eight million people around the world die each year because they are simply too poor to stay alive—and yet the end of poverty by the year 2025 is a realistic possibility if governments and their citizens decide to address the most basic needs of health care, education, and infrastructure to promote life and economic security among nations.[2] Those who know the goodness of God revealed in Jesus Christ need not fear the scarcity of goods but are called to trust in the goodness of God, who provides for our every need and calls us to share God's gifts with others.

2. Pastoral Caregiving. This is particularly evident in the story of Jesus walking on water to save the disciples (6:45–52) and his healing ministry to others (6:53–56). These texts suggest several focal points for preaching.

• *Caring for others and caring for ourselves.* In the events leading up to the disciples' experience of the storm at sea, Mark demonstrates how demanding the work of discipleship really is. Like many of us, Jesus and his disciples found it difficult to take time to rest, pray, eat, and enjoy one another's company. A sermon based on the story of the storm at sea could name the many tensions Jesus and his followers felt: between caring for others and caring for themselves, activity and rest, companionship and solitude, laboring and celebrating, pulling at the oars and seeking divine intervention. Jesus' response to the fullness of his life and theirs was to seek time alone to rest and pray. More than an item on the never-ending list of things to do, prayer is an indispensable source of transformation and renewal, drawing us into attentive awareness of God. Because of prayer, Jesus was able to see the struggles of his disciples and rise to meet them in their moment of crisis. In the words of Desmond Tutu, "We are always in the presence of God. Prayer is acknowledging that we are in that presence."[3]

• *Sympathy for life's struggles and storms.* Another pastoral concern arises when we consider the feelings and struggles of the disciples as they make their way through the storm at sea. Our sympathy is easily roused by their predicament when we recognize how hard they labored that day and how exhausted they must have been. Yet it is sobering to realize that after Jesus calmed the sea and saved them from death, the disciples did not experience greater understanding of him or his ministry but hardness of heart (6:52). All of us can find just cause to harden our hearts against God at some time or other in our lives. Our troubles can lead us to clarity of compassion and insight, or we may harden our hearts through bitter resentment and anger. Although we are all susceptible to this most perilous of spiritual conditions, hardness of heart need not be a fatal condition. For example, remembering the horrors of the Holocaust, many Jews have reacted strongly to the genocide and continued escalation of violence in Darfur and have rallied incessantly for an international peacekeeping force to protect civilians threatened by war.[4] Death and destruction are not the end of the story. Because of God's resolute determination to be with us, to teach us, to redeem us, we too may rise in the darkness of night with our eyes focused on the suffering of others as we recognize Christ's presence and power among us.

• *The person and work of Jesus Christ.* There is perhaps no more pastoral message than one that assures us of Christ's presence among us, a presence that is neither benign nor unaware of our struggles. The pastoral miracles of Mark 6:30–56 reveal Jesus' authority and power as the Christ who meets people in the midst of various needs and crises. Throughout all of his encounters with others, Jesus extends divine mercy and compassion to everyone he meets. He is the compassionate shepherd, provider of daily bread, Lord of the sea, and the great physician. Fully human and fully divine, he is the model of servanthood for his followers and the fulfillment of God's promises to humanity. We cannot be who he is or do all that he does, but through the presence of Christ's Spirit we are empowered to continue his compassionate outreach to others and to participate in his wonder-working power on earth.

THE HEART OF HOLINESS (7:1–23)

For the first time since chapter 3, Jesus is confronted by **religious authorities** who challenge his authority and question his followers (cf. 2:1–3:6). When scribes and Pharisees openly question the behavior of Jesus' disciples, it feels as though we are overhearing an in-house argument about what is clean and unclean, including narrative interruptions to explain or elaborate on specific details. However, in the course of a few short verses, Jesus turns the conversation in another direction and accuses his critics of abandoning the heart of God's commandments while pursuing practices that focus on their own interests and limited understanding of ritual purity. The opening half of chapter 7 not only draws our attention to the rising opposition to Jesus and his followers among religious leaders in Jerusalem but also serves as a transition to his ministry among Gentiles in subsequent sections of the Gospel (7:24–30, 31–37; 8:1–10). The dense assortment of controversies, sayings, and arguments included in this passage may be traced to Jesus, the early church, and Mark's editorial efforts to grapple with key issues related to the church's identity and practices.

Two literary forms are evident in 7:1–23.[1] As a *controversy narrative*, this passage includes a question posed by religious leaders who are openly critical of Jesus' disciples. Their accusatory question is then followed by Jesus' sharp response, including an incisive critique of those who "abandon the commandment of God and hold to human tradition" (v. 8). As a *teaching narrative*, this passage includes Jesus' appeal to Hebrew Scripture (vv. 6–8), an argument based on a specific example (vv. 9–13), followed by a parabolic saying (v. 15) that he later explains to his closest followers (vv. 17–23). Each of the following three sections explores Jesus' understanding of what is at the heart of holiness as he teaches his followers what is clean and unclean in religious faith and practice.

Exploring the text

Conflict Concerning Cleanliness and the Tradition of the Elders (7:1–8)

There is something ominous about the sudden mention of **Pharisees** and **scribes** who travel from Jerusalem to observe Jesus and his disciples. In 2:1–3:6 scribes and Pharisees confront Jesus five times, culminating in a conspiracy against him. Also, in 3:22 scribes from Jerusalem accuse him of being possessed by Beelzebul. When a delegation from the Holy City arrives to interrogate Jesus in 7:1–5, it does not bode well. The scribes and Pharisees are united in their critical appraisal of Jesus and his disciples. It is somewhat strange that these religious leaders choose to focus their criticism on his followers rather than Jesus. However, this may well reflect his enormous popularity and their reluctance to appear hostile to Jesus in front of the crowds.

Two questions are of immediate concern to the scribes and Pharisees: Why do the disciples eat with unclean hands, and why do they not observe the tradition of the elders? According to the Torah, handwashing before eating is only required of priests and their households when partaking of food that is dedicated to God (see Num. 18:8–13).[1] Eating with unclean or "common hands" was not of particular concern for laity. But the oral tradition of the elders expanded this practice to include all persons eating bread on any occasion, and as Jesus' closest followers, the disciples were closely observed to see how their manner of living reflected Jewish teaching and tradition.[2] By advocating the tradition of the elders, the Pharisees' goal was to sanctify all of life in order that the commands of God could be applied to every facet of daily living. According to this positive assessment of the scribes and Pharisees, their questions related to ritual purity are not matters of trivial pursuit. The religious leaders inquire about the disciples' handwashing to ascertain whether they demonstrate reverence and holiness in every facet of their lives.

However, the narrative affords us a more complicated interpretation of their concern. Jesus' strident response to the question of handwashing indicates his frustration over the scribes and Pharisees' preoccupation with such practices at the expense of God's commandment (7:8). The word "traditions" (*paradosin*) is used five times in the first eight verses and reflects something more than the Pharisees' interest in promoting personal piety through acts of cleanliness. According to Marcus, the ritual of handwashing before meals served as "a 'boundary marker' by which Jews both identified themselves and were identified by outsiders as being set apart from their neighbors."[3] Apparently, the religious leaders discriminated between those who did and did not conform to prescribed practice. Jesus criticized them for abandoning God's commandments in favor of their own measures of holiness (v. 8) and promoting their own self-interests while violating the Torah (vv. 7–13). Quoting Isaiah 29:13, Jesus accuses of hypocrisy those who give lip service to God in worship yet replace God's commands with their own ideas of what is right and acceptable. In his critical assessment of the scribes and Pharisees, Jesus views them as far from God and perilously close to that most fatal of human conditions—hardness of heart (v. 6; see also 3:5; 6:52).

This negative portrayal of Jewish leaders is highly problematic. We too would be guilty of hardness of heart if we simply assumed that all scribes, Pharisees, and other religious leaders in the Gospel abandoned God's purposes and pursued their own selfish interests (see e.g., 5:21–24, 35–43; 12:28–34). The literary role these characters serve as antagonists of Jesus in 7:1–8 must not be confused with the historical and spiritual significance of their role in Judaism. When Jesus quotes Isaiah 7:6–7, he is concerned that people of faith not confuse their own understanding of holiness with God's deeper purposes. His denunciation of the corrupt practices he sees in his own faith tradition calls us to examine our own religious practices more carefully in order that our lives may reveal God's loving intentions for all people.

A Case in Point: The Corban (7:9–13)

As an example of the way in which the tradition of the elders violated the commandment of God, Jesus cites the practice of Corban. Beginning with the law of Moses, he quotes the command to honor father and mother (Exod. 20:12; Deut. 5:16) and includes an additional citation from the Torah asserting that those who speak against one's parents must surely die (Exod. 21:17). Although the latter rule does not seem to have been enforced, there was no doubt that children were held responsible for providing material support for their parents and that those who sought to avoid this obligation were thought to be cursed by God.[1] Jesus then contrasts the commandment to honor one's parents with the tradition of the elders that allowed people to avoid this sacred obligation. The oral tradition permitted people to make an oath (*corban*) that set aside property to be used by the Temple for religious purposes. Once the oath was made, the profits to be gained by these goods and property belonged solely to the Temple and were not available for use by one's parents. According to Myers and his coauthors, "Because this practice leaves one's parents financially ostracized, Jesus argues, the 'vow' to the Temple becomes a 'curse' upon the elderly (7:12), and 'nullifies the command of God' (7:13)."[2]

The fact that Jesus chose this example of corruption among many other potential offenses (7:13) indicates his outrage over matters of economic hardship and injustice. It also suggests that Jesus was not simply interested in dismantling familial relationships but sought to reorient them according to humane, compassionate, and divinely directed standards of behavior (cf. 3:33–35). No doubt the Pharisees did not intend to nullify the law of Moses or to threaten the financial security of older persons in allowing the practice of Corban. Yet these were the consequences of their teaching and practice. Although Jesus does not advocate the complete abandonment of the oral tradition, he argues for its radical reassessment in light of the Torah and, as the next section attests, pronounces his own understanding of holiness.

New Teaching about Clean and Unclean (7:14–23)

In this section, Jesus takes the matter of holiness in a very different direction. He returns to the question of cleanliness raised by the scribes and Pharisees in 7:5 but issues a dramatic pronouncement that must have shocked the religious leaders and other hearers of Mark's Gospel. In the previous verses he upheld the law of Moses and criticized those who abandoned and violated God's commands. Here he asserts an entirely different under-standing of holiness, one that is not present in the Torah or the tradition of the elders. As the narrative unfolds, Jesus calls for a new understand-ing of what it means to be clean and unclean.

The passage begins with Jesus turning from the scribes and Pharisees to the crowd (v. 14). It is to these more receptive hearers that he directs his new teaching, although we may assume that the delegation from Jerusalem and Jesus' disciples are also in attendance. Jesus begins with the admonition to listen, just as he did in chapter 4 when preaching about the parable of the sower, seed, and soil (4:3). Similarly, if we accept 7:16 as original to the text, the conclusion of his opening argument parallels the closing of the parable of the sower, seed, and soil with Jesus' words, "Let anyone with ears to hear listen" (4:9). Jesus calls people to attention and with divine authority pronounces a new teaching: it is not what enters a person from the outside that makes one unclean but what comes out of a person from the inside that renders one unclean (7:15). This sermon-in-a-sentence is both provocative and innovative, reminiscent of a wisdom saying and a parable. Jesus speaks with prophetic authority, announcing a new word even as he enacts a new understanding of holiness. Marcus argues that "Jesus' saying about purity in 7:15 is a performative pro-nouncement, one that *accomplishes* the purification it announces. . . . Jesus is not just holding a mirror up to nature, depicting what has always been the case, but actually *changing things* by his apocalyptic pronouncement that all foods are (now) clean."[1]

The disciples, however, do not understand (7:17). Earlier they were inflicted with hardness of heart (6:52), and as the narrative unfolds they seem less and less able to understand or accept what Jesus says and does. Jesus' saying perplexes them and, like the parable of the sower, seed, and soil (4:10), they ask him to explain what he means. With evident frustra-tion, Jesus offers two responses. First, in 7:18–19 he argues that it is not what enters a person's stomach that is the cause of defilement, since food does not go through the heart but passes on to the sewer. Only that which passes through the human heart can render a person clean or unclean. The mention of "heart" is of particular significance, since the heart was thought to be the center of one's will and decision-making abilities and the Gospel often refers to hardness of heart as the most grievous of spiri-tual conditions (e.g., 3:5; 6:52). Jesus' explanation is then interrupted by a narrative comment in 7:19b announcing that he thus declared all foods clean. The abrupt placement of this comment suggests that it represents a later insertion into the narrative.[2]

The narrative then continues with Jesus offering a series of comments elaborating on the source of human defilement (7:20–23). It is what comes out of a person's heart that renders one unclean, since evil intentions arise within human beings and extend outward in their damaging effects. In short, "sin is a matter of the heart, the will, rather than a matter of violating laws of purity."[3] The list of evil inclinations that follows includes dispositions and activities that are harmful to one's neighbors and repugnant to God. Such catalogues were common among Stoic writers and Hellenistic Jewish philosophers, and several are found within the New Testament (e.g., Rom. 1:29–31; Gal. 5:19–21; Col. 3:5–8). In Jesus' list, personal attitudes and actions are intermingled, so that we cannot say one is of greater or lesser significance than another. Both individual attitudes and actions reflect the orientation of the human heart and impact one's relationship with others.[4] Here Jesus pushes his hearers to consider defilement or impurity as a matter of personal sin that has social impact. The heart of holiness, then, is not a matter of ritual purity, of distancing oneself from objects, foods, or persons believed to be unclean. It is a matter of the will to love God and neighbor.

The cumulative effect of Jesus' teaching in 7:1–23 is startling. On the one hand, he criticizes the scribes and Pharisees for abandoning the Torah (vv. 1–13). On the other, Jesus abrogates levitical law and claims divine authority to pronounce a new understanding of holiness (vv. 14–23). He insists that holiness is not a matter of identifying what is clean or unclean outside of oneself or apart from others. Instead, holiness is a matter of individual attitudes and actions that have profoundly social consequences. Jesus is passionately concerned with fulfilling the purposes of God's law as these are reflected in our care of kin and neighbors. He urges those with ears to hear to examine their own defiled hearts rather than their neighbors' dirty hands. According to Christ, the heart of holiness is loving what God loves and doing what God does.

Preaching and teaching the Word

The terms "holiness," "cleanliness," "defiled," and "tradition of the elders" are not often used by Christians today. Yet we have come to develop our own vocabulary of "practices," "values," and "spiritual disciplines" to express the church's ongoing interest in activities that encourage faithful living. This text prompts us to ask which practices fully reflect God's purposes. It also requires careful study so we can avoid hasty comparisons and refrain from unfair judgments about Jewish leaders represented in this passage. In particular, it is important to appreciate the vitality and ingenuity of Judaism, which is the wellspring of Jesus' faith and the source of our own. Like his prophetic forebears, Jesus sought to correct the community of faith of which he was a part and did so by denouncing practices that offended God's law and its purposes. His radical pronouncements challenge us to ask questions and pursue with integrity our own religious rituals and practices.

What are the holy practices we pursue today, and why do we pursue them? Most Christians today do not think in terms of what is clean or unclean when it comes to worship and spiritual disciplines but, like Jesus' interlocutors, we hope to establish patterns of behavior that encourage our love for God and reflect our commitment to follow Jesus Christ. Over the past several years, the work of Dorothy Bass, Stephanie Paulsell, and others confirm a growing interest in Christian practices that cultivate a more meaningful relationship with God through faith-filled activities.[5] If the ritual of handwashing before meals and the practice of Corban no longer reflect our devotion to God and care for kin, what kinds of activities and practices develop our spiritual lives and identities? How do practices of hospitality, public worship, private prayer, Sabbath keeping, service work, and forgiveness deepen our sense of God's presence and confirm our identity as Christ's followers?

Jesus' response to his interlocutors urges us to consider both the purposes behind our practices as well as the potential pitfalls that may arise as we engage in various rituals and practices. In terms of the *purposes behind our practices,* Jesus reminds us that our worship of God and care for others need to be closely related to one another (7:6–7). For example, in 7:9–13 he insists that the religious practice of Corban must not violate God's command to honor and care for one's father and mother. Thus, care and vigilance is called for in discerning which practices are important to cultivate and which to forgo. Do our Sabbath-keeping practices encourage restfulness and a renewed sense of trust in God as we cease from our labors, or do they perpetuate a preoccupation with church-related meetings and frenetic leisure-time activities?

In terms of the *potential pitfalls,* Jesus would have us regularly assess the real consequences of our religious practices so that we understand how they affect ourselves and others. It is all too easy to succumb to moral rigidity or spiritual self-satisfaction. Traditions of special foods at potlucks, songs sung in worship, or phrases used in public prayer are passed on from one generation to the next and are seldom altered in light of new members or different settings for worship—and God help the pastor or layperson who initiates changes in these beloved practices! With wisdom and care, the church needs to regularly assess how our practices help and hinder genuine faith in God. Yet another potential pitfall is evident just beneath the surface of Jesus' words: Christ warns us to beware of pointing out the dirty hands of others when our own hearts are filled with evil intentions (7:14–23). We must not confuse our efforts to develop habits of holiness with a sense of superiority over others. Vanity and pride lead us to believe we can secure our righteousness by holy habits or by distancing ourselves from those we consider unclean. Instead, Christ shows us that God longs to draw near to all people and longs for us to practice our love for others.

In very *practical terms,* Jesus' teaching focuses not only on our attitudes but also our actions. Although we may find within our hearts any number of evil inclinations, such as deceit, fear, moral rigidity, and envy, Jesus urges us to renew and reorient our lives according to his teachings of mercy, love, and justice. His comments about the practice of Corban provide us with a very specific example of how deeply religious persons exhibit callous behavior in the name of religious practice. The weaknesses of the scribes and Pharisees are really not far removed from our own: if we examine our own church budgets, what portion of our resources is given to serving persons outside our congregation? Jesus cared deeply about the needs of others, and his compassion was evident in concrete ways.

Finally, the *heart of faith* is central to Jesus' teaching. In biblical terms, the heart is the seat of the will that guides our daily living. When Jesus quotes Isaiah, he accuses of hypocrisy those whose hearts are turned away from God because their deeds are at odds with the words they speak in worship (Mark 7:6–7). Many of us accept God's forgiveness of sins as part of our weekly worship yet harbor long-term resentment toward those who offend us; we speak of honoring our parents yet do not listen to what they need; we sing praise to the Prince of Peace yet respond violently to enemies. Slowly but surely we become numb to the pain we inflict on others as well as ourselves. Hardness of heart is perhaps the most dangerous and damning of spiritual conditions since, in the words of one Bible study member, "the whole of Jesus' story is about compassion for all people."[6] Throughout Christ's teaching, preaching, miracles, and other mighty deeds runs the strong current of compassion that is fueled by divine love. The more deeply we cultivate practices of mercy, justice, and compassion in our own lives, the more thoroughly we embody God's love and bear witness to the heart of our faith.

MINISTRY AMONG GENTILES (7:24–37)

Just after Jesus' confrontation with the scribes and Pharisees over what is clean and unclean (7:1–23), three stories in quick succession recount Jesus' ministry among Gentiles: He is persuaded by a Syrophoenician woman to feed "the dogs under the table" (vv. 24–30), he heals a deaf mute (vv. 31–37), and he feeds a hungry crowd (8:1–10). Immediately afterward, Jesus is confronted by Pharisees who ask him to provide a heavenly sign (8:11–13), and Jesus' own disciples seem utterly unable to comprehend the miracles and meaning of the events they have witnessed (8:14–21). As the first major section of Mark's Gospel draws to a close, several important themes are intensified and reiterated anew.

Exploring the text

Jesus' Encounter with the Syrophoenician Woman (7:24–30)

The story of the Syrophoenician woman who confronts Jesus on behalf of her daughter is one of the most intriguing and disturbing events recorded in Mark's Gospel. Given her status and role as a Gentile woman, it is extraordinary that she approaches Jesus in the privacy of a home where he has come to find anonymity and rest. Their exchange is all the more remarkable since she is the only person in Scripture to argue with Jesus and win. She is witty and wise, while he appears callous and unyielding. Hearing her words, Jesus experiences a change of heart and a shift in perspective: he continues to minister to Israel but reaches out to Gentiles as well. This passage affirms and anticipates the church's widening ministry beyond the boundaries of Judaism.

The social setting and context of this encounter contribute to its provocative impact. The city of Tyre is located northwest of Galilee in the province of Syria, in present-day Lebanon. Although the majority of the inhabitants in Tyre were Gentiles, the surrounding villages and farmlands included many Jews who depended on the urban market for their survival.[1] It is likely that Jesus is visiting the home of Jews and that he sought refuge among sympathetic supporters in the aftermath of his confrontation with religious leaders from Jerusalem (7:1–23). The Syrophoenician woman, however, represents a very different ethnic group and regional setting. As one of the Gentile city dwellers, writes Sharon Ringe, "she is portrayed as part of the group in that region whose policies and lifestyle would have been a source of suffering for her mostly poorer, rural, Jewish neighbors."[2] It is entirely possible that Jesus' initial impression of this woman was that she belonged to the financially privileged members of society, while his sympathy was roused on behalf of the impoverished rural, Jewish residents.

The text focuses our attention on the exchange between Jesus and the woman more than it does the healing event itself. Crossing boundaries of gender, ethnicity, and socioeconomic standing, she falls at his feet and pleads with Jesus to cast the demon out of her daughter (v. 25). The cruelty of his response rings in our ears: "Let the children [of Israel] be fed first, for it is not fair to take the children's food and throw it to the [Gentile] dogs" (v. 27). His words are especially severe if we remember that nearly all dogs at that time were scavengers and not beloved household pets.[3] It is somehow not enough to say that Jesus was exhausted from his extensive ministry and that the woman has caught him in an "un-Christlike" moment. Neither is it satisfying to say that Jesus was simply announcing his priority of witnessing first to Jews, since it was unnecessary for him to use such insulting language toward Gentiles. The more likely explanation is that Jesus sympathized with Jews who suffered material deprivation at the hands of the Gentile elite.[4] This is consistent with his passion for the economic well-being of all people, especially the poor (e.g., 7:9–13; 10:17–22; 12:38–44). Nevertheless, given his generosity toward another Gentile (namely, the Gerasene demoniac in 5:1–20) and his recent confrontation with Jewish authorities over what comes out of a person's heart (7:14–23), his callous outburst is surprising.

Even more surprising than Jesus' retort is the woman's response. She listens carefully to what Jesus says and accepts the priority of his mission to the people of Israel. But she is not satisfied with Jesus' vision and is passionate about the well-being of her daughter. With ingenuity and skill, she subverts Jesus' image of throwing food to the dogs and calls him to an alternative view of ministry—one that includes her, her daughter, and other Gentiles. She not only has faith in his power to cast out demons but believes that his mission extends to those outside the household of Israel. Her faith and vision of God's reign not only exceed that of the scribes and Pharisees—they momentarily exceed that of Jesus himself. She is able to see what he resists, namely, that his mission is larger than he had originally imagined or determined. With wisdom and wit, persistence and passion, she calls forth a larger vision of the power of God's presence.

Her words make all the difference in the world. Jesus has a change of heart and a shift in perspective. He commends her for speaking to him and urges her to go see her daughter, who is no longer possessed by a demon (7:29). This final response to the Syrophoenician woman is noteworthy for three reasons. First, it is significant that Jesus commends the woman for speaking to him as she did. Here as elsewhere in Mark's narrative, words have the **power** to proclaim an alternative reality and to transform the hearts and minds of others (e.g., 1:14–15, 39; 6:12–13; cf. Matt. 15:28). Second, the fact that Jesus is able to heal the woman's daughter from a distance tells us that his power reaches beyond the confines of physical proximity to expel the forces of evil. There is no demon, near or far, that he cannot overthrow, and there is no barrier of clan or gender he will not cross.

Finally, it is nothing short of amazing that Jesus' vision and vocation are radically reoriented. He refuses to harden his heart against the Syrophoenician woman just as he warns his followers against hardness of heart in the next few chapters (see 8:17; 9:32–37). He is led to think and act in ways that call forth the fullness of God's vision for humanity, and the voice of the Syrophoenician woman is essential to this reorientation. Her story, like that of other remarkable women in Mark's Gospel (e.g., 5:24–34), offers us important insights into the good news of Jesus Christ.[5]

Preaching and teaching the Word

Although this story and the healing event that follows in 7:31–37 appear together in the RCL, the insights noted above suggest that Jesus' encounter with the Syrophoenician woman deserves particular attention.

The actions of the Syrophoenician woman suggest that it is not enough to sit at home and lament the suffering of those we love. Sometimes we must rise from the midst of grief to work for the well-being of others. There are times when it is important to risk offense, to summon whatever internal resources of faith and hope we have within us, and to hound the powers that be for the sake of those who cannot speak for themselves. The Syrophoenician woman took initiative and acted with a remarkable combination of boldness and humility. She may have been desperate, but she did not despair. Instead, she approached Jesus, fell at his feet, asked for what she needed, listened carefully to his response, then turned some of his own words around to appeal to a larger vision of divine grace and compassion.

Her words remind us of the *potential of words to shape an alternative reality* and to call forth a larger, more faithful vision of God's reign among us. Those who seek nonviolent means of transformation must not only act creatively but speak effectively through conversation, confrontation, debate, and other modes of mediation and provocative speech. This is true not only in our own congregations and local neighborhoods but in broader religious and political contexts as well. At the Watu Wa Amani (People of Peace) conference in Kenya in 2005 (as part of the World Council of Churches' "Decade to Overcome Violence"), leaders and members of the historic peace churches (Brethren, Mennonites, Quakers) shared countless stories of confronting political and religious leaders who were responsible for violence inflicted on them and their churches. For example, in Burkina Faso during the 1990s, Mennonite church leaders witnessed brutal killings and abuse committed against their family members and congregations. Several pastors made the journey to the prime minister's residence and stood outside, requesting admission and a hearing. To their astonishment, they were admitted into the prime minister's office and granted the opportunity to share their stories, many of which implicated government leaders. Expecting that they would be executed for bearing witness to what they had seen, these church leaders were amazed when the prime minister called them back later to announce that he was establishing a Council of Sages to examine the root causes of the violence and to propose solutions.[6] Words do matter. In large and small ways, God opens the way for us to shape the world through the words we share.

It may either disturb or delight us to think of *Christ as changing his mind* when he is confronted by the Syrophoenician woman. Although nearly everyone who hears this story is repulsed by Jesus' initial rejection of her, there is great drama in his complete turnaround. Whatever the cause of his harsh retort, Jesus listens to her insightful response and empathizes with her words. He follows the lead of the Syrophoenician woman, acknowledging that her vision of God's reign is indeed faithful. Consequently, there is no diminishment of Jesus' power but an expansion of it. All too often we, too, judge others harshly and need to be confronted by those who challenge our perceptions and help us experience a change of heart, widening the reach of our own mercy and compassion. The story of Jesus with the Syrophoenician woman alerts us to the possibility that if Jesus can experience a wider vision of God's reign, so can we.

Another facet of Jesus' power that claims our attention is his ability to heal the woman's daughter from a distance. This may inspire hope that God is able to work on behalf of those we care about even when we cannot help them ourselves or even when it appears that God is far from us. For those who fear God is disinterested or dispassionate about the fate or the well-being of those we love, the story of Jesus' transformative experience with the Syrophoenician woman offers comfort and hope that our pleas will also be heard and that the heart of God responds to human need, near and far.

Jesus Heals a Man Who Is Deaf and Mute (7:31–37)

Exploring the text

Jesus' encounter with a man who is deaf and mute is the second of three stories in swift succession that record his ministry among Gentiles. This healing event takes place in the region of the Decapolis, but the itinerary given in 7:31 seems strangely illogical: Jesus is said to travel far north of Tyre to the city of Sidon in order to make his way south of Tyre to the region of the Decapolis. Either Mark has confused the geographical locations or, as

Hooker suggests, the Gospel is offering us "a compressed summary of a journey which he believes Jesus to have made in the north."[1] The most important point to be taken from the geographical details in verse 31 is that the various cities mentioned are populated predominately by Gentiles.

Rather abruptly, the next verse announces that a group of people brought to Jesus a man who was deaf and mute. They beg him to lay his hand on their friend in order to heal him. Like those who plead on behalf of the blind man in 8:22–26, it is not the faith of the disabled person that brings about his healing but that of his faithful companions (see also 2:1–12). There are several other parallels between the healing of the deaf mute and that of the blind man: both events take place apart from the crowds, they involve extensive or repeated physical contact, both men are fully healed, and in both cases Jesus urges people to keep silent. Also, both stories recall Isaiah's vision of the restoration of Zion when the blind will see, the deaf hear, and the mute shout for joy (Isa. 35:5–6). Jesus does not simply announce the arrival of God's reign. He brings about its coming and enacts God's will among us. Beyond physical healing, spiritual transformation is also suggested. Those who see are able to recognize Jesus Christ, those who hear are able to receive his good news, and those who speak proclaim the gospel to others.

A great deal of attention is also given to the physical details of the healing process. The intimacy of the setting is underscored by three different terms: Jesus purposely takes the man "aside," "in private," and "away from the crowd" (7:33). He uses several gestures that are reminiscent of ancient healing practices: by thrusting his fingers into the man's ears Jesus may have intended to open a passageway for hearing; the use of saliva for healing was a common remedy, since many believed in its medicinal and magical properties; and physical contact with the man's tongue was not unusual, since it allowed direct contact with the infected or disabled body part. Three other features are worth noting: immediately before the healing takes place, Jesus looks to heaven, sighs, and speaks a single word. These gestures suggest Jesus' prayerfulness and compassion more than they reflect specific healing techniques. The translation of the Aramaic term *Ephphatha* also indicates that Mark wants us to know that Jesus did not use a magical incantation but invoked divine power to heal the man's ears and tongue.

Immediately after his ears are opened and his tongue is healed, the man speaks (v. 35). Just as quickly, Jesus tries to **silence** him (v. 36)! He also orders those who witnessed this amazing event to tell no one–an impossible request since all who have known the deaf man cannot help but to recognize the miraculous change in his condition. But their words are beyond Jesus' control, and the more he tries to quiet them the more they speak. Here as elsewhere there is the sense that the time for **proclamation** has not yet arrived, but neither can it be contained (e.g., 1:43; 5:43). According to Juel, at this point in the narrative we are given "a glimpse of what is to come—a mission carried out by those whose ears have been opened and whose tongues have been released, and who therefore simply cannot be silent. . . . Nothing is hidden except to be made known. The whole [gospel] story, like this healing, presses toward disclosure."[2]

Although we hear nothing of the healed man's personal reaction to what has happened, Mark says a great deal about the response of those around the man. They not only share openly the good news with others, but their comments leave no doubt as to the significance of this event. Superlatives abound: they speak all the more, they are astounded beyond measure, and they report that Jesus does everything well. Marcus points out that the perfect tense in 7:37 ("He has done everything well") emphasizes that Jesus' past actions have continuing effect and that the present tense later in the same verse indicates that Jesus continues to heal the deaf and speechless in the present age ("he makes the deaf to hear and the mute to speak").[3] If he can heal the deaf and mute, then there is hope for all of us—even those who, like his disciples in the following chapter, continue to misunderstand his mission and ministry.

Preaching and teaching the Word

Both this story and the preceding account of Jesus' interaction with the Syrophoenician woman appear together among the RCL readings for the Twenty-Third Sunday of Ordinary Time in Year B. The most obvious similarities between the two events are that they both take place in Gentile territory and that the persons who are healed do not approach Jesus themselves but are aided by others (the possessed girl's mother, the deaf man's friends). However, like the story of Jesus' encounter with the Syrophoenician woman, the story of healing the deaf mute suggests its own lively possibilities for preaching and teaching.

Although we do not want in any way to denigrate the physical hardship of the man who is brought to Jesus for healing, the story of his ears being opened and his tongue being loosed inspires us to *consider the ways in which we may be spiritually deaf to God and the world around us.* If not only physical but spiritual disabilities are suggested by the deaf mute's condition, then we may consider what we are willing or unwilling, able or unable, to hear from God, our neighbors, and the larger world of which we are a part. We are assaulted by a barrage of sound bites and chatter that dulls our ears and deadens our attention to more important concerns.

But there is a part of us that does not mind these distractions in the least, and we find safety, security, and comfort in the clutter around us. Ironically, twenty-four-hour news shows have not made us more compassionate or aware of the world at large but have dulled our sense of urgency and relationship to the crises we witness. In his book *The End of Words*, Richard Lischer describes a "growing dissonance between message and sensorium, between the gospel and the all-encompassing sea of words, images, and ideologies within which we attempt to communicate it. . . . The preacher does not contend with competing messages that are easily named but with principalities and powers that envelop us and swim effortlessly beside us in the sea of words."[4] Some of us need to listen more broadly and widely to hear a new and transforming word of God; others of us need to discern among the competing voices a true and life-giving word that offers hope and recognizes Christ's saving interest among us.

This story also challenges us to consider our own muteness and *resistance to speaking about the gospel*. The healed man displays an irresistible movement toward confession that proclaims the good news of God's presence and power. However, many of us are reluctant to share our faith with others and have found satisfying reasons to remain silent: "My deeds speak more loudly than my words," "I will do more damage than good if I try to explain my faith to someone else," "I have never been very good at speaking, so I will leave it to others to fulfill that part of the gospel mandate." If the healed man and his friends could not help but to proclaim the good news of Jesus Christ even before they knew of his cross and resurrection, then how much more do we who live on this side of the resurrection have to offer when we speak of God's goodness to others! If we are intimidated by the prospect of speaking, perhaps we may do as the healed man and his friends did—that is, focus our words on some particular evidence of God's goodness or mercy among us and keep pointing people toward God.

This story also suggests an *intimate and necessary connection between hearing and speaking*. The deaf mute does not speak until after he has been healed of both his deafness and his severe speech impediment. As the saying goes, God gave us two ears and one mouth so that we might listen twice as much as we speak. But listening is not enough. We must also learn to hear. To listen, we must have the physical apparatus to comprehend sounds; to hear, we must pay attention to what is being said. The greatest commandment begins with the words "Hear, O Israel" (Deut. 6:4–9). We are called not only to listen for God but to hear God and then to speak what we hear to one another. The first Bible verse I remember hearing as a child was spoken by my next-door neighbor during a conversation we shared as he leaned over the backyard fence. A deeply religious man, he chose his text well and found a verse that included my name: "Let us know, let us press on to know the LORD; his appearing is as sure as the dawn" (Hos. 6:3). When I repeated the phrase back to him, however, I realized that more than hearing my name I liked the idea behind the words: we must always press on to know God who is ever ahead of us. My neighbor had listened to me enough to know that I was a curious child, and he found a way of speaking to me about faith using God's words when he could not find his own. For those who have eyes to see, ears to hear, and tongues to speak, the gospel claims our attention and urges us to share the good news with others.

LOAVES AND LEAVEN (8:1–21)

The eighth chapter of Mark's Gospel continues with Jesus' ministry among Gentiles. Similar to his earlier feeding miracle among Jews in the sixth chapter, Jesus extends God's gracious provision of bread and fish to a crowd of four thousand people that includes both Jews and Gentiles. Afterward, however, the Pharisees continue to argue with Jesus and ask him for a heavenly sign to validate his ministry (8:11–13). After leaving them, Jesus warns his disciples to watch out for the leaven of the Pharisees and Herod, but his followers misinterpret Jesus' warning as a reprimand for not bringing along enough bread for the journey (vv. 14–21). Jesus is frustrated and concerned that they, like the Pharisees and Herod, have hardened their hearts and do not see, hear, or perceive the power of God's reign among them. By the end of this section we long for some glimmer of hope, some reason to believe that the disciples may open their eyes, ears, and hearts anew to the gospel of Jesus Christ.

Exploring the text

Feeding Four Thousand Gentiles (8:1–9)

Following his ministry among Gentiles in the city of Tyre and the Decapolis (7:24–37), Jesus feeds another crowd of people (cf. 6:30–44). Jesus had "compassion" on them because they had nothing to eat. The word for compassion is used elsewhere to describe Jesus' response to those who are suffering from illness (1:41), hunger (6:34), and demon possession (9:22). At this point, he is sympathetic because the crowd has been with him for three days and many of them will have to travel a great distance before returning home.

The most important difference between this story and Jesus' earlier feeding miracle is that it takes place in Gentile territory and most certainly includes a combination of Jews and Gentiles. Overall, however, it contains more similarities than differences with Mark's previous feeding miracle among Jews. Both events take place in isolated areas and reflect strong associations with Israel's experiences of wandering in the wilderness. The language used in both stories also mirrors Jesus' last supper with his disciples when he takes, blesses, breaks, and shares the loaves with others. In both cases the disciples play an important role in distributing the bread and fish to the crowd of people, embodying Jesus' command to share what is given. Yet his disciples do not understand the meaning or significance of what they are participating in (6:52; 8:17–21), a fact that greatly frustrates Jesus, especially after the second feeding miracle. Just as important as the act of distributing the bread (the verb is repeated three times in 8:6–7), both stories underscore the fact that everyone present ate to their satisfaction and that there were several baskets of food left over.

A few minor differences are also evident between the two accounts. In 8:1–9, the people have been with Jesus for three days rather than one, the fish are served separately, a different word is used for the baskets that hold the leftover fragments,[1] the verb "giving thanks" (*eucharisteō*) is employed instead of "blessing," and the number of people and baskets are different in each account. Although it is possible to associate some of the numerical references in the first feeding episode with events in Israel's early history, less convincing are the arguments associating the numbers 7, 2, and 4,000 with Gentiles in the second feeding miracle.[2] However, there is little doubt that this second event takes place in Gentile territory. After mentioning Tyre and the Decapolis in 7:24–37, chapter 8 begins, "In those days . . . ," linking this event to locations largely populated by Gentiles. Also, people "have come from a great distance"—perhaps a symbolic reference to non-Jewish nations who are "far away" from God.

Other than Jesus' care for Gentiles, there are at least three other reasons to take note of this story. First, it emphasizes anew several themes encountered in the feeding story of 6:30–44. The importance of sharing goods, the divine gift of multiplying the loaves and fishes, and the disciples' role in distributing God's gifts to others are repeatedly named in the second story. Second, because this is not the first time the disciples have witnessed Jesus' extraordinary power to multiply loaves and fishes, it is all the more striking that they do not comprehend what is happening (see 8:14–21). The Gospel heightens the tension between teacher and disciples, and those of us who hear this story are compelled to ask whether we have eyes to see, ears to hear, and hearts that are open to receive the gospel in whatever ways it is given to us by God. Finally, Jesus' compassion for those who are hungry provides the impetus for this event, and Jesus takes the initiative in addressing the crowd's need (cf. 6:35–36). God's compassion extends to all people, and God's generosity surpasses our own. The story of Jesus' feeding four thousand Jews and Gentiles reveals the eschatological **power** of God unleashed by Christ, who proves that compassion and power are welcome companions when placed in loving service to others.

Pharisees Ask for a Sign (8:10–13)

Immediately after Jesus feeds the four thousand, he departs on a journey by boat to Dalmanutha, a place that is unknown to biblical scholars and archaeologists. Although the disciples are active participants in the scenes preceding and following this episode, they are strangely absent during Jesus' encounter with the Pharisees. He has left the supportive atmosphere of the crowds and, in a more isolated location, is confronted by antagonists.

The Pharisees' request for a sign from heaven is both confusing and ironic. On the one hand, their desire to validate Jesus' authority and divine call is entirely understandable. Jewish faith is greatly concerned about false prophets, and Hebrew Scripture insists that prophetic messages and activities must be confirmed by divine signs (see Deut. 18:15–22; 2 Kgs. 20:8–9; Ezek. 12:11). It was even considered arrogant to refuse a divinely ordained sign (Isa. 7:10–17). On the other hand, it is ironic that immediately following the miracle of feeding the four thousand the Pharisees are in need of a heavenly sign. In the aftermath of this and other amazing events, they seem entirely oblivious to Jesus' authority and divine appointment. When they ask for a sign from heaven, he flatly refuses—not because he is incapable of performing signs and miracles but because the Pharisees' lack of faith renders them unable to see the **reign of God** already present among them. Jesus has given them every earthly reason to believe in the reign of God embodied in his words and deeds.[1]

The meaning or purpose of signs also varies greatly from one portion of Scripture to another. In Mark 13 when the disciples ask Jesus for a sign to note the end times, his followers are not concerned with confirming the truth of Jesus' words or validating his authority but with anticipating the eschatological timetable. Also, in contrast to John's Gospel, the Gospel of Mark does not portray Jesus as one who leads others to faith through the enactment of divine signs and miracles. Instead, Jesus' miraculous activities in Mark reveal the power of God to those who have eyes to see, ears to hear, and hearts that are receptive to the reign of God. The greatest challenge for members of "this generation" (Mark's as well as our own) is to have faith in God's activity among us and to follow the good news of God's reign revealed in the ministry of Jesus Christ. As the next episode reveals, even his closest followers fail to meet this challenge. They, like us, are susceptible to blindness and continue to need the power of Jesus' love to transform their hardened hearts.

Disciples Don't Yet Understand (8:14–21)

Leaving the Pharisees behind, Jesus enters the boat with his **disciples** and once again crosses over to the other side of the sea. This is the third of Jesus' episodes with his disciples on water, and it provides an unsettling ending to the first major section of the Gospel. When they crossed the water together in 4:35–41, Jesus calmed the storm, and his followers were filled with awe as they wondered, "Who is this?" When he walked on the sea to meet them after feeding the five thousand in 6:47–52, they were terrified and astounded because "they did not understand about the loaves, but their hearts were hardened." Now, following the second feeding miracle, they travel together for the third time across the sea. With mounting frustration, Jesus realizes that they still do not understand what has been unfolding before their eyes, and he hurls a series of questions at his obtuse followers.

The troublesome exchange between Jesus and his disciples may be divided into two sections. The first part of this episode is particularly confusing and relates the disciples' comments about bread to Jesus' warning about leaven or yeast (8:14–16). The disciples have forgotten to pack a full basket and have brought only one loaf of bread in the boat. In a seemingly unrelated comment, Jesus warns them to watch out for the leaven of the Pharisees and Herod. Given his recent encounter with the Pharisees (8:10–13), it is not surprising that Jesus is concerned his disciples will be influenced by the Pharisees' stubbornness. The obduracy shown by these religious leaders is insidious and, like leaven, is powerful enough to infect the disciples' spirits. Elsewhere in Scripture, leaven is synonymous with corruption (1 Cor. 5:6–8), false teaching (Matt. 16:12), and hypocrisy (Luke 12:1). Jesus' reference to it here recalls the Pharisees who were threatened by his ministry and teaching (see 3:6; 7:1–23), and Herod, who abused his political power by executing John the Baptist (6:17–29). Jesus' brief warning alerts his followers to the pervasive power of evil and its influence on others, including his disciples.

But his followers misinterpret Jesus' words as a criticism of their not having brought enough bread for the journey. In the second part of the story (8:17–21), Jesus becomes aware of their comments and is outraged by their preoccupation with insufficient bread. The disciples have witnessed him healing the blind and deaf, yet they do not see and hear what he is doing. They stubbornly focus on their own needs and desires. The disciples are every bit as susceptible to hardness of heart as the religious and political leaders who are threatened by Jesus' power and authority. Like them, the greatest threat comes not from without but from within their own spirits. Jesus wants them to know that he himself is the bread of life, able to feed both Jews and Gentiles. It is their own inclination to interpret literally and selfishly Jesus' words about loaves and leaven that threatens to blind them to God's reign and God's purpose of sharing the bread of life with all people.

In the span of five verses, Jesus flings nine questions at his followers. Returning to the image of bread, he prods the disciples to recall the specific details of the two feeding miracles in order to reach beyond mere numbers to recognize the extraordinary nature of God's gifts for Jews and Gentiles. His reference to hardness of heart is also of great importance. It represents the most damning spiritual condition, since hardness of heart violates God's compassion for others (see 3:5; 6:52; cf. 6:34; 8:2). Similarly, images of blind eyes and deaf ears recall key moments when Israel refused to see and hear God's presence (e.g., Isa. 6:9–10; Jer. 5:1; Ezek. 12:2). The Deuteronomic theme of remembrance (e.g., Deut. 32:7) also rises to the surface of Jesus' concern (Mark 8:18b). Jesus wants the disciples to recall the feeding miracles even as he anticipates the bread of communion he will share with his followers later in the Gospel and in the world to come (14:22–25). Finally, this encounter between Jesus and his disciples culminates in a closing question: "Do you not yet understand?" For all they have seen and heard, Jesus' companions do not yet perceive the presence and power of God's reign among them. His question is filled with anger and frustration, but there is also a hint of something more. The "not yet" spoken of by Jesus holds out hope that his disciples may yet understand and follow. As the twofold healing of the blind man in the following story reveals, we too may receive new sight thanks to the grace and power of Jesus Christ.

Preaching and teaching the Word

The three episodes at the beginning of the eighth chapter provide important indicators of what is most important in Jesus' ministry. Bread and leaven, ministry to Gentiles as well as Jews, continued disbelief among religious leaders, and spiritual blindness among Jesus' disciples all culminate in a flurry of questions that are as relevant today as they were to the early church. None of these stories appear in the RCL, yet all of them develop important themes that pervade Mark's account. Parallel texts may provide interesting points of similarity and difference in appreciating the events of 8:1–21.[1] Together, these episodes relate the importance of Jesus' compassion for others and his resolute determination to guide his followers toward faith in God's reign.

At least two facets of the feeding miracle in 8:1–9 are unique to this text. First, *Jesus' compassionate hospitality* toward others is highlighted. His first words to the disciples are words of concern for strangers who have traveled great distances. Without hesitation, Jesus takes the initiative and shows his followers the way to care for those around them. Congregations who are interested in practicing biblical hospitality toward newcomers and visitors would do well to remember that most of the people to whom Jesus ministered were strangers.[2] In his book *Welcoming the Stranger*, Patrick Keifert contends that providing "hospitality to the stranger is full of dynamic conflict. It requires a decentering of our self-centered lives that is most disturbing."[3] It means being willing to step outside of our individualistic concerns and our well-intended patterns of caregiving to see what others need and desire. We are all strangers to God and one another, yet God is generous beyond measure and takes initiative in meeting our needs. In the film *Babette's Feast*, the lead character wins the lottery and decides to spend all her money to prepare a lavish feast to thank two sisters who have provided her a home and to honor their deceased father. Babette's sumptuous meal utterly transforms the bitterness and bickering of the aging congregation whose members are invited to the meal. By the end of the evening, old grievances are resolved and thanksgiving is restored as an earthly table becomes a place of heavenly communion. It is the very nature of God to be moved by love to serve others with generosity and joy. We too may participate in the transforming power of God by recognizing the needs of those around us and serving others, body and soul, with the bread of Christ's love and compassion.

Second, *Jesus' ministry to Gentiles* urges us to consider the ways we too may cross boundaries of race and ethnicity that continue to divide neighbors, congregations, and nations. We sometimes overlook the radical nature of Jesus' eating with Gentiles. Jews were forbidden to share food with persons who did not observe their religious rituals and traditions. Food that was handled by Gentiles was considered unclean and unacceptable by Jesus' critics. But when Jesus is the host, Jews and Gentiles share the same meal. His actions declare that we are all God's children, even if we divide ourselves in myriad ways. In the Pulitzer Prize–winning novel *To Kill a Mockingbird*, Jem and Scout are two white children whose father is the defense attorney for a wrongly accused black man. Amid the contentious trial, they struggle to understand race relations and the people they have come to know. After disputing the similarities and differences between various families, clans, and "colored folks," Scout declares, "Naw, Jem, I think there's just one kind of folks. Folks." Her brother replies, "If there's just one kind of folks, why can't they get along with each other? If they're all alike, why do they go out of their way to despise each other?"[4] We are all God's children, yet we continue to forget or deny it. A sermon exploring the ways we violate this basic reality could name specific instances when we have not acted as if "there's just one kind of folks."

The Pharisees' request for *a sign from heaven* in 8:10–13 may also be of interest to us. Many people ask God for signs to show the way forward or to confirm important decisions. Later in Mark's Gospel, Jesus' disciples ask him for signs to confirm the end of time so that they may know what to look for (13:4). But most of us long for something quite different from what the Pharisees are seeking. After the scribes and Pharisees witnessed his many miracles, several of them accused Jesus of being possessed by Satan (3:22–27). Now, following the feeding of the multitudes and many other miraculous deeds, they want a sign from heaven to validate Jesus' ministry and prove his divine identity. Proof has already been given to them, but they are unable to see and hear it because their hearts are hardened and their minds are unwilling to accept what God is doing. They cannot see what they refuse to believe in.

What do we refuse to believe? Is peace on earth not possible? Do we ignore suggestions and ideas that could help alleviate suffering even now?[5] The Pharisees' request for a sign makes us wonder what it would take for us to believe in the power and presence of God today. People who genuinely long to glimpse God's reign will see the gospel of peace among persons who find alternatives to violence in addressing international crises; they will witness the gospel of love among those who refuse to draw boundary lines between ethnic groups and will condemn expressions of racism among us; they will know the gospel of justice among those who seek to eradicate "stupid poverty"[6] as we narrow the widening gap between rich and poor. If we want to have eyes to see, ears to hear, and hearts that are open to receive the gospel, we must look, listen, and receive Jesus' compassionate direction for our lives and world.

PART TWO

Teaching about Discipleship, Servanthood, and the Way of the Cross

8:22–10:52

Preliminary Remarks

Chapters 8–10 mark a turning point in Mark's Gospel as Jesus begins his journey to Jerusalem. He continues to proclaim the good news and share the power of God, but the focus shifts from his miraculous deeds to teaching his **disciples** about servanthood, the cross, and new life to come. Jesus foretells his suffering, death, and resurrection three times (8:31; 9:30–31; 10:32–34) and immediately after each of these his disciples are unable to understand or unwilling to accept what Jesus is saying. Even when Peter has the right answer, he is moving in the wrong direction (8:32–33). Yet despite their obduracy, Jesus continues to point the way ahead for his disciples to continue the journey of faith and discipleship (8:34–38; 9:35–50; 10:42–45). He is offering something beyond catechesis or a private seminar on theological orthodoxy. Jesus is issuing a call to the cross and the promise of resurrection.

This section is also punctuated by encounters with evil spirits, Pharisaic challengers, and desperate strangers. All of these characters provide opportunities for Jesus' followers to reflect anew on God's reign. In case we do not see the point of what Jesus is doing, two miracle stories about recovery of sight to the blind serve to open and close this pivotal section of Mark's Gospel. The first story relates the twofold healing of a blind man in Bethsaida (8:22–26). The second follows James and John's request for places of honor beside Jesus and describes Jesus' opening the eyes of blind Bartimaeus (10:46–52). However ignorant, arrogant, or blind his followers may be, hope is found in the power of God to give sight to the physically and spiritually blind.

Healing the Blind Man
of Bethsaida–Twice

Mark 8:22–26

Exploring the text

Following Jesus' frustrations with his disciples earlier in the Gospel and culminating in the question, "Do you not yet understand?" (8:21), the healing of the blind man of Bethsaida comes as a welcome relief. Just when we were beginning to wonder if anyone fully recognizes who Jesus is or what he is doing, we catch a glimpse of a man whose eyes are opened by the grace and power of God.

Jesus and his disciples arrive at Bethsaida on the northeast corner of the Sea of Galilee (8:22) after they were blown off course (6:45–53). Their circuitous journey included Tyre, Sidon, and the region of the Decapolis (7:24, 31), and this northern detour afforded many opportunities for Jesus to minister among Gentiles. Like the blind man of Bethsaida, it may take more than one attempt for Jesus' disciples to reach their destination, but with his help they will find their way.

In many ways, this story is similar to Jesus' healing of the deaf mute in 7:31–37. Both men are brought to Jesus by their friends, both suffer from communicative disorders, both are healed apart from the crowds, Jesus uses spittle and physical touch to facilitate both men's healing, and both are instructed to say nothing about what has happened.[1] The healing of the blind man in 8:22–26 also bears striking similarities to the healing of blind Bartimaeus in 10:46–52. Although there are differences (see "Exploring the text" of 10:46–52), the two stories serve to frame the second part of Mark's Gospel and highlight the theme of bringing sight to the blind. Through Jesus' miraculous power, we glimpse the fulfillment of Isaiah's vision of the eyes of the blind being opened and the ears of the deaf unstopped (Isa. 35:5–6).

However, two features distinguish the story of 8:22–26 from all others. First, this is the only instance in the Gospels when Jesus asks if his efforts at healing have taken effect (8:23). His question may make us wonder if Jesus is beginning to doubt his abilities or if his power is beginning to

146

weaken. However, given Jesus' miracles later in Mark's account, it does not seem likely that the narrative intends to communicate a diminishment of his abilities (e.g., 8:14–29; 10:46–52). Instead, the context of this passage marks a shift in Mark's emphasis, from Jesus' mighty deeds and words to his teaching about servanthood and discipleship. The focus of this story is not Jesus' ability as a healer but the man's prolonged experience of blindness and his repeated need for healing. When Jesus asks if the man is healed, he is not questioning his own abilities but whether the man is able to fully receive the gifts of God to see again. Whatever it takes and however long it takes, Jesus' question reveals his determination to heal those who are blind.

Second, this is also the only instance in Scripture when it takes two efforts on Jesus' part to fully heal someone. To understand the deeper significance of this twofold event we need to consider once again the context of this passage.[2] Jesus has just reprimanded the **disciples** for not yet understanding what he has been doing (8:21), and Peter is about to confess that Jesus is the Christ but does not yet know what this means (8:33). Peter and the other disciples have glimpsed God's presence and power among them, but they do not comprehend what it means to follow Jesus (e.g., 9:33–37; 10:35–40). The two-step process of recognizing Jesus as the Christ and also needing further enlightenment to understand what this means mirrors the blind man's twofold healing. In case Mark's listeners are wondering if full recovery of sight is possible, the text emphasizes the complete restoration of the blind man's vision by using three expressions in rapid succession: "he looked intently and his sight was restored, and he saw everything clearly" (8:25). Blindness is not easy to overcome, but "Jesus will finish what he began."[3]

The story closes with Jesus sending the man home and urging him not to go into the nearby village. Here as elsewhere, Jesus does not want this miracle to be advertised (see **messianic secret**). He is not eager for people to see the immediate results of the blind man's healing without knowing more of what it means to follow the one who healed him.

Preaching and teaching the Word

When preaching or teaching about this amazing event, it is important to recall its context in Mark's narrative. It not only serves as a hinge between two important sections of the Gospel but opens the way for us to reflect on various physical, spiritual, and social facets of the journey of faith.

For example, when the disciples finally arrive at Bethsaida in 8:22 it is only after having been *blown off course* (6:45). Their circuitous travels to the north took them through Gentile regions (Tyre, Sidon, and the

Decapolis), where Jesus ministered to the Syrophoenician woman, the deaf mute, and the hungry crowd of four thousand (7:24–8:10). God seems to delight in guiding us to unexpected people and places. Each year I enjoy asking incoming students about their journey to seminary and what led them to this place at this time. More often than not, they shake their heads in amazement as they recount the strange and roundabout ways God has nudged them forward, surprising them along the journey of faith. Many of them never imagined coming to seminary, but the wisest among them realize that from the time of their baptism, God has led them on a more interesting (and often more complicated) path than they could ever have imagined. Most of us are blown off-course at some point or other in our lives, and whether the storm is caused by God or other powerful forces, the journey before us holds the potential of opening up new vistas, new relationships, new visions of ministry we would never have imagined otherwise.

The story of Jesus' twofold healing of the blind man also reveals that the journey of faith and God's vision for our lives are impossible to comprehend without *the power and presence of God.* This is not only a story about one man's struggle to see; it is a story about God's determination to heal him. Thanks to Jesus' insistence on his full recovery, new sight is given to the blind man and insight is given to Jesus' disciples. Blindness can be both a physical and spiritual affliction, and this story reminds us that God longs for both to be fully restored. Jesus has a passion for pursuing us through every blind alley and for healing every ailment we suffer.

The twofold nature of the blind man's healing also reminds us that *healing is not always immediate and that faith sometimes progresses in stages.* However dramatic his healing may have been, it was not without complications. Similarly, the gift of insight may come to us gradually, and we may need Jesus' repeated help along the way. In this way, the man's story is not unlike that of other disciples who know something about God but realize that there is much more to learn. That is why the questions Jesus' disciples raise are so very important: his followers may be distinguished from Jesus' opponents not because they have the right answers but because they ask the right questions. Whereas the Pharisees ask for a sign from heaven to confirm Jesus' authority (8:11), the disciples ask, "Who then is this?" (4:41) and follow him on the road to Jerusalem.[4] The journey of faith includes many steps. In her book *Pilgrim at Tinker Creek,* Annie Dillard recounts the experiences of eye surgeon Marius von Senden, who performed the first cataract operations for persons who were blind since birth.[5] After surgery, von Senden witnessed the awe and bewilderment of his newly sighted patients, who were often baffled by the perception of distance and the darkness of shadows. Many closed their eyes, unable or unwilling to take in everything before them. It was only over a period of time that people were able to understand what they were seeing. Similarly, as the disciples travel toward Jerusalem, there is much more for them to see and learn.

Jesus' First Prediction of Suffering, Death, and Resurrection and Teaching about Discipleship

Mark 8:27–9:1

If the story of the blind man's healing offers hope that we too may see God anew, the following verses help us to know what we are looking for. "Who do you say that I am?" Jesus asks his disciples, and with this pivotal question he takes a decisive turn toward Jerusalem and challenges his disciples to follow him on the way. The verses that follow provide the first of three instances when Jesus predicts his suffering, death, and resurrection, the disciples fail to understand him, and Jesus teaches his followers about the meaning of discipleship while linking their fate to his own (8:31–9:1; 9:30–49; 10:32–45). The pattern of prediction, incomprehension, and teaching about discipleship dominates 8:22–10:52, with each of the three predictions building on and intensifying the others.

Exploring the text

The first of these sequences (8:27–9:1) is the most startling of all. En route to the villages of Caesarea Philippi, Jesus initiates a conversation with his **disciples** about who he is and what he will encounter in the time to come. It is remarkable that the setting for Peter's confession is the capital of Philip's tetrarchy, a former center of pagan worship and a Hellenistic city featuring a magnificent temple in honor of the emperor. It is also significant that this exchange takes place while they are traveling "on the way," since all three predictions include references to the journey Jesus shares with his disciples as they move toward Jerusalem (8:27: 9:33; 10:32). During the next two chapters, they will travel from Caesarea Philippi in the north to Capernaum beside the Sea of Galilee (9:33), then south to Judea, the Transjordan (10:1), and Jericho (10:46) before ending their travels outside Jerusalem (11:1). Physically and spiritually, they have considerable ground to cover.

As they begin their journey together, Jesus raises the question that remains foremost throughout Mark's Gospel: "Who do people say that I am?" The disciples' response is nearly identical to what was said about

John the Baptist in 6:14–15. In that context, Herod had heard differing reports of John's having been raised from the dead, or that Jesus was Elijah or one of the other prophets. Here in 8:28, the disciples report that the people are saying the same things about Jesus. Jesus is indeed "one of the prophets," following the tradition of Moses and Elijah (e.g., Deut. 18; 1 Kgs. 17). To underscore this point, the following story of the transfiguration places him in the company of these great prophetic figures (Mark 9:2–8). Yet Jesus is more than a prophet. Their evaluation of him is not wrong, but neither is it adequate. Jesus presses his disciples further and asks a question that urges them to stake their own claim in the events to come: "Who do *you* say that I am?"

Speaking on behalf of the twelve, Peter confesses that Jesus is the Messiah, God's anointed one (see **messianic titles**). It is the first time the word "Messiah" or "Christ" has been used to speak of Jesus since the opening of Mark's Gospel (1:1). But it will not be the last, including one occasion when Jesus identifies himself as the Messiah during his trial before the Jewish Sanhedrin (14:61; see also 9:41; 12:35; 13:21–22; 15:32, 39). The title conjures up images of a mighty leader of royal lineage. During the first century CE, Jews anticipated the arrival of David's successor, who would lead God's people to overthrow their oppressors and establish a reign of peace and prosperity for Israel.[1] Peter recognizes that Jesus' authority and **power** are divinely ordained. But since Jesus has done nothing to suggest that his way of establishing God's reign will involve the violent overthrow of Rome or Jerusalem, his practice of messianic leadership is utterly foreign to those who await divine intervention by force. Even if some of his followers did not expect a military coup, they certainly believed he was destined to put down Israel's oppressors by supernatural power (see Isa. 11:4), and they did not envision his suffering and death.[2] They cannot yet fathom Jesus' way of self-giving love for others, therefore he urges his followers not to tell anyone about him. They have not yet traveled the distance to the cross and have not yet witnessed what God will do to fulfill the promise of new life through Jesus' death and resurrection. He has much more to teach his disciples and, just as importantly, much more to show them. Who Jesus Christ is cannot be understood apart from what he does and what God does through him.

Verses 31–33 turn immediately to Jesus' prediction of suffering, rejection, execution, and resurrection. No explanation is given as to why he must experience these things, but the inevitability of his death and resurrection is stressed through Jesus' assertion that the Son of Man *must* (*dei*) undergo this sequence of events. By criticizing various Sabbath traditions, the debt code, and patterns of eating and cleanliness, Jesus is sure to incur the wrath of religious and political authorities. As the one who came "not to be served but to serve, and to give his life a ransom for many" (10:45), Jesus' death and resurrection manifest both the reality of human sin and the certainty of divine love. God will not allow death to have the last word, and therefore Jesus' resurrection is also inevitable.

In contrast to his earlier admonition to silence (8:30), Jesus speaks all of this quite openly (8:32). Before his followers confess faith in him, Jesus wants them to know that God's purposes include the healing of others as well as his own suffering, popularity among the crowds as well as rejection by religious leaders, the willingness to be killed rather than to kill others, the reality of death as well as the assurance of God's resurrection power. Who he is (the Messiah of God) and what he will experience (suffering, death, and resurrection) compose a seamless reality about which the disciples seem hopelessly unaware. In fact, Peter pulls Jesus aside and tries to rebuke him. He cannot bear the idea that Jesus, the Christ, will suffer and die. But Jesus turns to all the disciples as he rebukes Peter in the most strident terms possible, ordering him, "Get behind me, Satan!" He will not have Peter tempt him to turn away from his calling. As Susan Garrett has argued, "The severity of Jesus' rebuke of Peter in Mark 8:33 corresponds to the magnitude of Jesus' temptation here: the rebuke is sharp because the temptation is profound. Although Jesus knows where God's path for him leads–through suffering, rejection, death, and resurrection . . . he is sorely tempted to follow Peter in departing from this path."[3] To set his mind on human fears and anxieties would be to reject God's life-giving purposes and deny the power of God to overcome the forces of evil.

In the next section, 8:34–9:1, Jesus speaks not only to the twelve disciples but to the crowd as a whole. He issues a call to discipleship that bears striking parallels to what he has just described of his own fate in 8:31–33. The cross that will be carried by his followers recalls the death he will suffer in Jerusalem. Similar to Jesus' experience of the cross and resurrection, "those who lose their life" in order to gain new life will follow his path. If verses 31–33 link Jesus' fate to ours, verses 34–38 link our fate to his.

According to these verses, the call to discipleship involves three imperatives. Those who would become disciples of Jesus Christ must deny themselves, take up their cross, and follow him. In the context of Mark's Gospel, to deny ourselves involves more than giving up chocolate for Lent or belittling ourselves before others. Rather, it is a call to radically reorient our lives so that we do not seek our own priorities but those of Jesus Christ. Even more stunning is Jesus' imperative to take up the cross. The cross was not a metaphor for personal anguish or a religious icon fashioned into jewelry. Rather, it was a means of political and military execution involving public humiliation and torture.[4] For Jesus' followers, it represented a costly political choice as they engaged in the subversive activities of God's reign. Finally, Jesus' call to discipleship includes following him on the journey to Jerusalem. Physically and spiritually, it was a difficult road to travel and would most certainly lead the disciples in dangerous directions. But Jesus promises new life to those who give of themselves for the sake of the gospel. According to Hooker, the high standards of discipleship outlined by Jesus remind us that "the crucial divide is not between those who acknowledge Jesus as the Messiah and those who do not, but between those disciples who are prepared to follow him on the way of suffering and those who are not."[5]

The cost of discipleship is accentuated by Jesus' use of economic terms in verses 36–37. There is no real profit if one gains the world and loses one's life; such forfeiture reveals a bad investment. But if we are willing to stake our lives on the gospel, that is, the good news of God's reign proclaimed by Jesus Christ, then our investment will prove priceless. Jesus' use of commercial language relates the realm of material life to spiritual reality and heightens our appreciation of both. The next saying, in verse 38, conjures up images of the courtroom where those who are ashamed of Christ and his words will be denied by him when the Son of Man returns in glory. The eschatological tone continues in 9:1 as Jesus announces that some who are present to hear his words will not taste death before they see God's kingdom "come with power." This phrase is one of the most contested passages in Mark's Gospel. Some argue that Jesus mistakenly predicted God's kingdom would be fully manifest before some of his disciples had died, others insist that these verses refer to Jesus' transfiguration reported in the next several verses, and still others explore different interpretations of what it might mean for Jesus' disciples to "taste death" before Jesus' imminent return. In light of what Jesus has just said about his imminent death and resurrection and his focus on the call to discipleship, the context of 8:27–9:1 suggests that God's power must be understood in light of the cross and resurrection. The kingdom of God will indeed come with power, but it will come in the most unexpected way possible: through the death and resurrection of the Messiah. We cannot understand God's reign apart from the way Jesus lived, the way he died, and the way he was resurrected from the dead.

It is important to recognize and carefully interpret the many **apocalyptic** images that permeate Jesus' first prediction of suffering, death, and resurrection. In referring to himself as the **Son of Man** (8:31, 38), Jesus recalls Daniel 7, which views the present age in light of the age to come and envisions the Son of Man as God's "Human One" who reigns forever over all peoples and nations. Like Daniel, Jesus urges his hearers to view their current situation from God's perspective, but he does so neither to escape the reality of persecution at the hands of oppressors nor to argue that these experiences are the will of God.[6] Jesus does not propose escapism, fatalism, or a superior vindication of those who take up their cross and follow him. Rather, he wants his disciples to view the inevitability of their fate in light of his own. Just as importantly, he wants them to view their lives in light of his own. The kingdom will "come with power," but Jesus has already announced its presence (1:15) and has continually displayed God's power through his mighty deeds and words while calling his disciples to continue the same ministry of divine power (6:7–13).[7] Jesus does not speak of being vindicated or of glorious enthronement (cf. Matt. 25). Instead, he directs his disciples to go back to Galilee after his resurrection and continue the project of Israel's renewal. As the Gospel unfolds, there can be no doubt that the life, death, and resurrection of Jesus Christ not only embody God's life-giving intentions for humanity but are the basis of our own resurrection hope.

Preaching and teaching the Word

Preaching and teaching about this portion of Mark's Gospel challenges us to consider anew who Jesus is and what difference this makes to our lives and the world around us. Since his fate is closely linked to ours, it is important to consider our response to his call to take up our cross and follow him. This text is included among the lectionary readings for the Fifteenth Sunday after Pentecost as well as the Second Sunday of Lent in Year B, with the latter offering an opportunity to substitute 9:2–9 (the account of Jesus' transfiguration) for 8:31–38. Although the season of Lent is certainly an appropriate time to consider the cross of Jesus Christ, a sermon or lesson related to 8:27–9:1 may also offer new opportunities for reflecting on Jesus' identity and ministry during the long stretch of Ordinary Time. At least three approaches to preaching and teaching are suggested by this rich and multifaceted text.

Focusing on *the confession of Jesus as the Christ*, we are humbled and perhaps startled that Peter's confession is quickly unmasked as woefully inadequate. He has perceived Jesus' true nature and identity, but when Jesus describes the terms of his messianic calling and Peter refuses to accept them, Jesus sternly rebukes him. Peter's blindness and that of the other disciples makes us wonder if any of us will ever fully recognize who Jesus is and what he is about.

Yet there is also a strange comfort to be found in the inadequacy of Peter's confession. After all, are not all human confessions of Jesus Christ inadequate? Do any of us fully comprehend the mystery of his divinity and humanity, his calling to take up the cross, or his promise of the resurrection to come? When my congregation recently gathered at the water's edge to celebrate the baptism of two young men, an opportunity was given for each of them to share what led up to this moment of commitment to Christ and the church. Each expressed having had some level of familiarity with the church over the last thirty years, yet each had reached a pivotal moment of knowing that Jesus Christ and his church were more than they had ever imagined. Being a Christian connects worship with ministries of justice and peacemaking; it connects us to others who both support and challenge us along the way of Christian discipleship. It was very important for these men to publicly confess their faith in Jesus Christ, but it was just as important to confess that their journey of faith is incomplete. Whether we are baptized as infants, youths, or adults, members of the body of Christ acknowledge that we have much more to learn as we continue the journey of faith.

The cross and resurrection of Jesus Christ provide another important focal point for preaching and teaching about this passage. Given the myriad misunderstandings that surround the cross (not only the one Jesus suffered but the cross he calls his followers to assume), it may be just as important to clarify what the cross *is not* as to explore what it *is*. The cruel reality of Christ's suffering and death must not be reduced to trivial experiences that do not bear the political and religious implications of Jesus' death. The cross is not a minor illness, the imposition of an unwanted relative, or adherence to ascetic practices. It is more closely related to losing one's job, going to prison, or being abandoned by loved ones. As a form of public execution imposed on criminals and others who were considered a threat to Rome, crucifixion may be likened to current forms of state execution by lethal injection–although lethal injection takes significantly less time and is viewed by a limited number of witnesses. Neither is it wise for us to develop a strange fascination with the brutality of Jesus' death. If all that claims our attention is the violence of the cross, we lose sight of the loving power of God throughout Jesus' life and resurrection.

The inevitability of the cross and resurrection is also easily misunderstood. What kind of God would require the violent death of Jesus in order to redeem humanity? How can we call God loving if God procures salvation through brutality and violence? Such questions must be viewed in light of the entire gospel. We have no reason to believe that Jesus wanted to suffer; rather, he foresaw the inevitability of his suffering because he was rejected by religious and political power-holders. Of course, he was willing to suffer (14:36). As Witherington explains, "In the end of Mark 8, Jesus tells his disciples that there are not merely many things worth living for, but some things worth dying for."[8] Nowhere in any of the Gospels does Jesus declare or suggest that some things are worth killing for. It is our own will to destroy those who threaten us that rendered Jesus' death inevitable. The one who came "to serve, and to give his life a ransom for many" (10:45) chose to respond nonviolently to his enemies in showing us the way to newness of life.

Yet a third approach to this remarkable passage centers around *the call to discipleship.* Jesus uses three imperatives: deny oneself, take up the cross, and follow him. It is tempting to think we understand self-denial and cross bearing whenever we encounter difficult situations—as if an annoying neighbor or delayed paycheck is "my cross to bear." Just as problematic are the ways in which self-denial has been imposed on women and others who are expected to repress their needs, gifts, and desires as others exert power over them. Neither of these is what Jesus intends. To *deny oneself* is to place Jesus' priorities, purposes, and path ahead of our own; to *take up the cross* is to be willing to suffer the consequences of faithful living; to *follow him* is to travel to unknown destinations that promise to be both dangerous and life-giving. The all-encompassing nature of this call is both frightening and demanding. No wonder we would rather withhold some part of ourselves. Thomas Troeger's hymn expresses well our ambivalence: "If all you want, Lord, is my heart, my heart is yours alone—providing I may set apart my mind to be my own."[9]

In his resistance to political and religious oppressors Dietrich Bonhoeffer insisted, "The cross is not the terrible end to an otherwise god-fearing and happy life, but it meets us at the beginning of our communion with Christ. When Christ calls a man [or woman], he bids him [or her] come and die."[10] Few of us, thank God, are called to Bonhoeffer's fate. But many of us struggle with what it means to recognize our cross and take it up daily. Without diminishing the costliness or peril of cross bearing, it is possible to understand that it extends beyond martyrdom to other acts of self-giving love that risk rejection and other losses. As one member of our Markan Bible study put it, "The central struggle described here in 8:36 is to weigh what's important. Is it money? Fame? Other kinds of achievement? It is hard enough to weigh such decisions well, but if we do, then Jesus tells us we'll get the cross."[11]

The challenge and blessing of Jesus' all-encompassing call insists on a radical reorientation of our lives that draws us into a closer relationship with him—a relationship of love, peace, and newness of life. In knowing Christ, we do his will; in doing Christ's will, we know him more deeply.

In this way, we assume his life, cross, and resurrection power. In the words of Hans Denk, a sixteenth-century Anabaptist, "no one can truly know [Christ] unless he [or she] follow him in life, and no one may follow him unless he [or she] has first known him."[12] We will know what to set aside when we know whom to embrace. When Jesus calls us away from something (e.g., a stressful career, dependence on drugs), he also calls us toward something (e.g., new friendships, care of creation). One young member of our Markan Bible study put it this way: "It's not just a matter of putting stuff down–like our worries, our need to be right, spending time on the computer instead of talking to others–but taking something up. We put stuff down, but I think Jesus is saying we need to take up Jesus and his cross."[13]

The Transfiguration of Jesus

The account of Jesus' transfiguration occurs immediately after the first prediction of his suffering, death, and resurrection and references these pivotal themes. As the disciples accompany Jesus on his way to Jerusalem, the bewildering vision of Jesus, Moses, and Elijah evokes equal portions of awe and confusion.

Exploring the text

What exactly is being revealed through this miraculous event? The word "transfiguration" is based on the Latin translation of the Greek verb *metamorphothe,* from which we derive the word "metamorphosis." It implies a change in Jesus' form (*morphē*) but not a change in his basic character or identity; Jesus' divine status as God's beloved son was revealed long before this event (see 1:11). Through his transfiguration the disciples are given an outward glimpse of Jesus' inner glory that is awaiting full disclosure.

Some have argued that this is a postresurrection scene Mark has imported into Jesus' earlier ministry, others focus on the ways in which it anticipates Jesus' resurrection, and still others see allusions to the parousia in this event. Whatever the origins or implications of this account, Mark has placed it amid Jesus' predictions of his impending suffering, death, and resurrection so that we would associate the fullness of Christ's glory with his death and resurrection. Perhaps that is why Jesus' radiance does not linger (see 9:14). Mark gives us glimpses of Christ's transfigured glory to encourage our hope in the fullness of his glory yet to come.

Beginning with the words "six days later," 9:2 links this remarkable event with the preceding verses (8:31–9:1) recounting Jesus' prediction of death and resurrection. The reference to six days, Jesus' movement up the mountain, and the glorious change in his appearance also connect Jesus' experience with that of Moses at Mount Sinai (Exod. 24:16ff.). Peter, James, and John are invited by Jesus to join him as they do elsewhere in the gospel (e.g., 5:37; 14:33). Also, Peter acts as their spokesperson here as elsewhere (e.g., 8:29).

The description of Jesus' appearance in 9:3 emphasizes his heavenly glory. No amount of detergent, bleach, or dry cleaning can account for the dazzling whiteness of his clothes. His stunning appearance recalls Daniel's vision of the Ancient One who serves as agent of divine justice (Dan. 7:9–10). Standing beside him are Elijah and Moses, two of the most important figures in Israel's history. Both men are regarded as prophets, with Elijah serving as forerunner of the Messiah and Moses the bearer of God's commandments. Their presence also signals an eschatological dimension to this event. Elijah is reported to have escaped earthly death by ascending to heaven in a whirlwind (2 Kgs. 2:11), and Moses' death and burial (Deut. 34:6) were surrounded by sufficient mystery so as to inspire speculation of his assumption into heaven.

The text does not tell us what they were talking about with Jesus. Instead, Mark focuses our attention on Peter and his reaction to what he witnesses. He interrupts their conversation to say to his teacher, "It is good for us to be here" (9:5). It is a strange statement given the apparent terror he and his companions felt in witnessing this extraordinary sight (9:6). Peter then proposes building three booths or tents in honor of Jesus, Elijah, and Moses. The word "booth" recalls the temporary structures made of branches during the autumn Festival of Booths, which commemorates the lodgings Jews occupied during the wilderness wandering (see Lev. 23:42). However, the disciples cannot prolong this glorious experience by building tents or tabernacles. More importantly, they still do not understand that Jesus is more than a prophet of Israel; he is also the long-awaited Messiah, more deserving of a throne than a tent.[1] According to Hooker, "Peter's real mistake, therefore, is that he thinks of the three figures as being on a par: thinking to honour Jesus by ranking him with Moses and Elijah, he is still far from recognizing his master's true status."[2]

Another radical shift occurs when the scene is suddenly overshadowed by a heavenly cloud representing the divine presence, or Shekinah. From within the cloud, God's voice speaks directly to Peter and his companions: "This is my Son, the Beloved; listen to him!" (9:7). There is no mistaking the parallels to the divine disclosure made at Jesus' baptism (1:11), but this occasion may be distinguished from that earlier announcement by two important features. First, the words are not directed to Jesus but to his disciples, who have yet to comprehend his true nature and mission; and second, the heavenly voice commands the disciples to listen to Jesus. The command to listen is not only among the most basic tenets of Jewish faith (Deut. 6:4), but it also includes the admonition to obey what is heard (see

"Exploring the text" on 7:31–37). As suddenly as the cloud appears, it disappears along with Elijah and Moses so that the disciples can focus their gaze on Jesus alone (9:8).

Jesus, in turn, bids them not to discuss what they have seen until after his death and resurrection (v. 9). It is important that they do not speak of his glory apart from his suffering and rising from the dead (see **messianic secret**). However, the disciples do not understand what he means and discuss his comments about the resurrection among themselves (v. 10). Given that first-century Jews anticipated a general resurrection of the dead at the end of time but not the raising of a particular individual in the midst of history, their confusion is understandable.[3] The question they raise with Jesus, however, relates to the return of Elijah, whom they have just seen (v. 11). In his response, Jesus asserts that Elijah, the forerunner of the Messiah, has already come (vv. 12–13). The allusion to John is clear. The rejection and death of the prophet foreshadow Jesus' own demise.

Jesus' transfiguration may have been a private event, but it was clearly intended to be shared with others in the aftermath of Christ's death and resurrection. Although the disciples repeatedly misunderstand what they are witnessing, the divine voice speaks directly to them, ordering them to listen and, by implication, to obey God's beloved Son. This is not only a story about God's hidden glory but humanity's most difficult calling: to follow him whose glory fully emerges only after suffering and death.

Preaching and teaching the Word

In his graphic novel *Marked*, Steve Ross depicts this scene in black-and-white, comic book format, with Peter attempting to take a photo of Jesus and his holy companions. But the camera explodes in his hands as Jesus comments, "My friend, there are some things you just can't freeze in time. Nothing lasts forever. Everything changes. Everything dies. The question is simply whether you want that to be the end of the story."[4]

Clearly, this is not the end of Mark's story. But as preachers and teachers of the gospel, we are left to wonder what this strange event means for Jesus Christ and his ministry among us. Why is this glimpse of divine glory given to us? What does it have to do with us? We may approach this enigmatic text from at least two different perspectives.

We may *focus on Jesus Christ,* whose very nature radiates divine glory. He is the Ancient One, the Human One, the Son of Man, who is fully human yet fully divine (see **messianic titles**). Here we see Jesus as the heavenly Christ, outshining even Elijah and Moses. In this brief yet resplendent episode, his followers catch a glimpse of his extraordinary "otherness," but Jesus bids them to say nothing about it until he has risen from the dead. In fact, Jesus insists that his transfigured glory must not be spoken of apart from his impending death and resurrection. There is no divine glory apart from his fate, no life apart from death, no claiming his throne or taking his place amid the divine court apart from his earthly mission to serve humanity and be rejected by them while serving the purposes of God. Through suffering, rejection, and desolation, the power of God is present among us, awaiting eyes and ears to witness the fulfillment of God's glory. Until then, glimpses of resurrection power may arise in the most unlikely places: when the playground bully has you pinned to the fence and a friend stands between you and your enemy; when a drunk driver smashes into your car and you somehow find the courage to look that stranger in the eye; when estranged family members hold hands in a circle of prayer around the hospital bed of a loved one. It is often at moments like these that flashes of divine light break upon us, often unbidden and always impossible to hold.

We may also *focus on **discipleship*** and the words spoken to Jesus' followers. His three closest disciples are not only witnesses to Jesus' transfiguration, but the divine voice speaks directly to them, calling them to listen to God's beloved Son. The Gospel of Mark uses this event "to exhort readers to a truer discipleship."[5] The disciples are not simply witnesses to a christological event; they are given a glimpse of God's glory so that they may have a foretaste of the power that calls forth life from the tomb. After his death and resurrection they could speak of Jesus' transfigured glory to encourage one another on the path of discipleship that moves through suffering and death to resurrection. Similarly, we need to recall moments when God's beauty and glory have been made known to us so that we may be inspired to continue on the way of discipleship. Many high school youth who attend the Church of the Brethren's National Youth Conference speak of this weeklong event as a "mountaintop" experience. But the real witness to this event occurs in the weeks and years to follow when young people are inspired to engage in a year of volunteer service, or participate in summer work camps, or challenge their home congregations to deepen and widen the reach of Christ's love for others. Like Peter, James, and John, we are sometimes gifted with moments of God's glory that inspire us to continue the journey of discipleship with others.

Jesus Heals the Possessed Boy

Mark 9:14–29

Whereas the first eight chapters of Mark's Gospel include many stories of Jesus' powerful and miraculous deeds, the second major section of the Gospel (8:27–10:52) includes the last two healing miracles recorded by Mark (9:14–29 and 10:46–52).

Exploring the text

Immediately following the glorious experience of Jesus' transfiguration, Peter, James, and John descend the mountain with Jesus and witness their colleagues arguing with scribes and failing to heal a possessed boy. This episode is crowded with characters. Jesus, Peter, James, and John approach a mob of people surrounding the **disciples** and a group of scribes. At his arrival, everyone's attention quickly shifts to Jesus. The crowd rushes toward him, amazed and agitated (the verb *exethambēthēsan* is also used in 14:33 and 16:5). When Jesus asks what they are arguing about, a man tells him that his son is possessed and that Jesus' disciples are unable to help. While the boy writhes in their midst, the disciples are deeply embroiled in an argument with the scribes. The story begins and ends with references to Jesus' disciples, their failed faith, and God's saving mercy.

The cosmic and eschatological dimensions of this event are inescapable. An evil spirit has taken hold of the boy, convulsing him when he sees Jesus (9:20) and repeatedly threatening his life (v. 22).[1] Although some have associated the boy's symptoms with epilepsy, it is evident that he not only needs to be healed of disease but exorcised of the forces of evil within him (cf. Matt. 17:15). The power of death can only be overcome by the power of life, and the disciples apparently are not strong enough to be of help (v. 18). Jesus not only bemoans their impotence but also their faithlessness (v. 19; see also Num. 14:11).

This cosmic struggle also has an intensely personal dimension. After the father describes the long-term nature of his son's affliction, he begs Jesus to help, "if you are able to do anything" (v. 22). Jesus reacts to the man's plea

162

with one of the most perplexing promises in Scripture: "All things can be done for the one who believes" (v. 23). The father's immediate response resonates with other believers: "I believe; help my unbelief!" (v. 24). Carrying the awful burden of his son's illness, he wants to believe in his healing and does–to a certain extent. The disciples' failure to help the possessed boy and their preoccupation with scribal debate hardly inspire his faith. Yet love for his son opens the man to other possibilities and prods him to believe that new life is possible. After rebuking the evil spirit and commanding it never to return, Jesus takes the boy by the hand and, in a gesture reminiscent of other resurrectionlike moments, lifts him up (see also 1:31; 5:41).

The story concludes by drawing our attention once again to the disciples, who ask Jesus in private why they were unable to cast out the demon (9:28). He points them to prayer as the only possible means of overcoming this kind of evil (v. 29). They must not rely on their own abilities or previous successes but continually turn to God as the source of transforming **power** among them. In this way, the father's honest prayer, "I believe; help my unbelief!" reveals an awareness of his own limitations and a heartfelt longing for God to do what he cannot.

At least three theological themes are interwoven in this passage, and all three are of vital and ongoing concern to Jesus' disciples: faith and belief, the power of God, and prayer as a way of relating to God's power among us. There is no doubt that Jesus calls us to have faith in the power of God's love (v. 23), and there is no doubt that his disciples repeatedly lack faith (v. 18). Jesus links their faithlessness to the disciples' failure to heal (v. 19), just as the faithlessness of the people at Nazareth impacted Jesus' healing power in his hometown (6:6). By contrast, the boy's father confesses his faith as well as his lack of faith. His simple prayer reflects both his belief in Jesus' healing power and his hope that "Jesus will compensate for whatever is lacking in that faith."[2] The father's plea reminds us that our desire for God's help is at the very heart of prayer and is one of the most powerful means of opening the way for God to move and work among us.

Preaching and teaching the Word

Mark's account of Jesus' healing of the possessed boy is much more elaborate than that of Luke (9:37–42) or Matthew (17:14–21). It also includes rich allusions to the theological themes noted above and highlights Jesus' teaching his disciples what it means to be faithful.

Perhaps the most challenging aspect of this story arises in Jesus' statement to the boy's father: "All things can be done for the one who believes" (9:23). Believes what, exactly? Believes hard enough or long enough or correctly enough? Faithful people have long tormented themselves over not having sufficient faith to aid the healing of loved ones. However, this text does not indicate that God desires a certain kind of belief or quantity of faith, and preachers must be careful not to encourage a focus on right belief or sufficient faith as a guarantee of salvation and well-being. At the same time, we would be wise to acknowledge that belief is much more difficult than we may want to admit to ourselves or to others. There is so much cruelty, suffering, and injustice in the world we inhabit that we often find it hard to believe that things will ever really change. Jesus draws our attention to prayer because it alerts us to God's possibilities among us. Through prayer, we invoke God's power and love in the midst of hopelessness and despair. Without this, faith is unbearable and transformation impossible.

The disciples, however, prefer arguing to believing or praying. Like many of us, their faith is fickle and their prayer inconstant. It seems that one of humanity's favorite distractions is to enter into holy disputes with other members of the family of faith, rather than enter into the struggles of humanity that await us outside the sanctuary doors. We would rather form a committee than take a walk around the neighborhood, listening to the voices of children and parents who would tell us their needs and fears. We would rather argue about the style of music we sing in worship than recognize persons who endure injustice on a daily basis. Local congregations that suffer from a contentious spirit and internal strife can find no better remedy than to look outside themselves–to God in prayer and to their neighbors in service.

The story of the possessed boy also reminds us that although we cannot do everything, we can open the way for God to do something *when we pray.* When the mountains are insurmountable, the task impossible, and our faith fails us, discussions and arguments will not suffice. The evil forces at work in our world cannot be exorcised without prayer. We need to invoke the power of God already present among us and offer whatever measure of faith we have in service to others. There is hardly a congregation of people who do not need to be reminded regularly that faith in the power of God is more than faith in our own abilities and powers. It means standing close to God in prayer–so close that we can hear God's direction and discern God's possibilities.

Finally, a word must be said about demonic possession and human illness. On the one hand, we must beware of reducing the boy's symptoms to epilepsy or some other physical illness alone, as if there were no evil spirit involved in his malady. On the other hand, we must also beware of equating all physical or mental illness with demonic possession, as if we ourselves did not sometimes contribute to our own demise (e.g., through smoking). Not all affliction is caused by Satan or given to us as a punishment for sin. In preaching or teaching about this story, we need to confess our need for divine help and human compassion toward others.

Jesus' Second Prediction and Lessons on Discipleship

Mark 9:30–50

For the second time, Jesus foretells his death and resurrection, the disciples do not comprehend his teaching, and he offers them further instruction. It is the shortest of his three predictions, and it is followed by the longest of all three teaching sections (cf. 8:31–9:1; 10:32–45). Through words, gestures, metaphors, and imagery, Jesus teaches his followers to serve others and be at peace with one another.

Exploring the text

JESUS' SECOND PREDICTION
AND THE DISCIPLES' RESPONSE (9:30–32)

Jesus continues his journey to Jerusalem by passing through the region of Galilee. It is the setting for his earlier ministry (1:14–4:34) and later postresurrection meeting with the disciples (14:28; 16:7). Before he enters Judea (10:1), Jesus focuses his attention on his followers, repeats the prediction of his death and resurrection, and teaches them about servanthood. He does not want the crowds to know of their presence as he gives his full attention to the **disciples**.

Jesus' second prediction is notable for several reasons. It is not only the shortest of the three, but Jesus' teachings on servanthood (9:33–37) take on a greater sense of urgency when spoken in the context of his impending death and resurrection. Jesus uses the word "betrayed" (*paradidotai*) for the first time when referring to his fate, a term that recurs with greater frequency as the Gospel continues (e.g., 10:33; 13:9–12; 14:10, 21, 41–44; 15:1, 10, 15). The verb may also be translated as "delivered" or "handed over," with the possibility that Jesus is not just referring to Judas, the religious leaders, or Pilate (none of whom is named here), but that God is also involved in directing Jesus' fate, since it is God who has delivered Jesus into the realm of human history. Isaiah's image of the suffering servant

165

(Isa. 53) also comes to mind as we hear of Jesus being given over to human authorities, and Daniel's vision of "one like a son of man" (Dan. 7) is glimpsed in Jesus' description of the **Son of Man**.

Immediately following Jesus' prediction we learn that the disciples do not understand what he is talking about but know enough to be afraid (9:32). Fear is a frequent response of those who follow Jesus, and by the end of Mark's account, fear confounds and overwhelms Jesus' followers as they flee from the tomb (16:8). Yet as the next few verses reveal, Jesus is determined to confront their misunderstandings and to guide them beyond fear to faith.

ARGUMENTS ABOUT GREATNESS AND A LESSON ABOUT SERVANTHOOD (9:33–37)

Immediately after their arrival in Capernaum, Jesus asks his **disciples** what they have been arguing about "on the way." This expression is used twice in 9:33–34, evoking images of Jesus making his way to the cross and his followers making their way to Jerusalem and beyond. The topic of their argument, however, reveals that they have a long way to go before they understand Jesus' teaching and mission among them. While Jesus speaks of being handed over to others, the disciples seek the upper hand over one another; while Jesus anticipates being delivered over to powers and principalities, his disciples jockey for positions of power. There is a glimmer of hope, however. Their silent response to his question reveals at least some measure of embarrassment over their selfish ambitions. Yet it is clear they do not comprehend the meaning and implications of Jesus' prediction. His disciples are more concerned with comparing themselves to one another than viewing their lives in light of his teaching.

Jesus responds by sitting down (the posture of a teacher) and gathering the twelve around him. He delivers a lesson in two parts. First, he shares with his disciples a saying: "Whoever wants to be first must be last of all and servant of all." Next, he offers them an object lesson: Jesus draws a child into their midst, and while embracing the child he teaches his disciples that to be a servant means practicing hospitality with these little ones, the least members of society. At the very heart of his lesson is this simple yet difficult message: discipleship means welcoming and caring for those who are of least concern to others. Ministry in the name of Christ means giving priority to those who are without power, prestige, and possessions— in other words, those who cannot advance our professional standing, contribute to our social status, or reciprocate our material support. With no rights or status of their own, children are often the most vulnerable members of society (both ancient and modern), and Jesus' admonition to welcome them in his name no doubt shocked his followers (see also 10:13–16). More than this, he insists that welcoming one such child in his name is tantamount to welcoming the one who sent him. His reference to "my name" is also one of the few occasions when Jesus speaks of himself as he also speaks of God, "the one who sent me." Those who offer hospitality in his name to the least members of society will not only discover his presence among them but will realize that these little ones are the locus of God's concern.

FURTHER LESSONS IN DISCIPLESHIP: POWER, FIRE, AND SALT (9:38–50)

This extended series of lessons includes three teaching moments that address the theme of discipleship and what it means to serve others (9:38–41; 42–48; 49–50). There are interesting word links between these lessons and other passages of Scripture.

In verses 38–41 John informs Jesus that the disciples witnessed someone casting out demons in his name (cf. references to Christ's name in vv. 37 and 41). Widespread belief in the power of names may have incited the disciples' concern that the exorcist did not really believe in Jesus but simply invoked his name to perform the act of exorcism. Yet John's words also reveal a partisan spirit. The disciples tried to stop the unnamed exorcist because "he was not following *us*." They say nothing about the exorcist not following Jesus. Whether the competition originated with the first disciples or other members of Mark's community, a spirit of rivalry appears to have seeped into the fellowship of the early church. Jesus will have none of this. He teaches his followers that those who perform deeds of **power** in his name cannot possibly renounce the one whose name empowers them.

This brief episode also recalls Moses' experience with Joshua, Eldad, and Medad in Numbers 11:26–29. During Israel's sojourn in the wilderness, God's Spirit was given not only to the seventy elders who were sent outside the camp but also to Eldad and Medad, who remained within it. When Joshua voiced his objection to their prophesying within the camp, Moses asked him, "Are you jealous for my sake? Would that all the LORD's people were prophets, and that the LORD would put his spirit on them!" (Num. 11:29). Like Joshua, John also thinks he knows the boundaries of divine power. His arrogance not only betrays a partisan spirit but denies the radical freedom of God's Spirit to move and work as God wills. Jesus urges his followers not to draw dividing lines between themselves and others. Instead, he insists that anyone offering a cup to those who bear his name will be rewarded for their good deed.

The next series of sayings, in verses 42–48, moves abruptly from rewards to punishments. Jesus warns his disciples not to put a stumbling block before "these little ones," who may include not only children (see verses 36–37) but any others who consider themselves the least of his followers. To do so would be like hanging a giant millstone around their necks and being thrown into the sea. The image is reminiscent of the enormous stones pulled by donkeys while grinding grain. Anyone strapped to such a stone and hurled into the water would surely drown, and the dead body could not be retrieved for proper burial.

Jesus then teaches his disciples to avoid sin at all costs, even if it means the loss of a hand, foot, or eye. If any of these things causes a follower to "stumble" (the verb *skandalizō* is used three times and forms the basis for our word "scandal"), Jesus insists that it is better to amputate it than to lose one's life, enter Gehenna, and forfeit a place in God's reign (v. 47). The references to these three body parts are remarkably similar to Job's concern for purity of eye, foot, and hand (Job 31:1, 5, 7).[1] They may also reflect ancient punishments for adultery or theft, posing a merciful alternative to the death penalty.[2] Gehenna was a familiar reference point for Jesus' hearers as well. After the time of Josiah's reform (2 Kgs. 23:10), Gehenna (located south of Jerusalem) was used as a city dump where garbage was burned, maggots fed on animal entrails, and flames perpetually smoldered (see Isa. 66:24). As Hooker notes, Gehenna is not depicted as a place of eternal punishment but of utter annihilation.[3] More importantly, it is set in direct opposition to the **kingdom of God**, the intended dwelling place for God's people.

In 9:49–50, Jesus again speaks of fire but adds to it the image of salt. Although fire is often associated with punishment and sacrifice (9:43–47), both fire and salt are connected with rites of purification and ritual offerings (1 Kgs. 18:38; Lev. 2:13). Salt has the additional sense of acting as a seasoning and preservative (2 Kgs. 2:19–22). In speaking of those who are salted with fire, Jesus is most likely referring to his followers, who will be purified, refined, and strengthened by persecution of various kinds (13:9–13; see also Rom. 5:3–5). The saying seems to suggest that the distinct flavor and potency of **discipleship** is derived from disciples' encounters with opposition and difficulties. These closing words bring his teaching full circle, recalling Jesus' comments in 9:33–37 and 39 urging his disciples to stop competing and start serving one another and those around them.

Preaching and teaching the Word

Jesus' second prediction and subsequent teaching appear among the RCL readings for the Twenty-Fifth and Twenty-Sixth Sundays of Ordinary Time in Year B. When addressing contemporary hearers, it is important to acknowledge that there is an edge to Jesus' words that offends our modern sensibilities—especially in the series of punishments recounted in 9:42–48. This is more than hyperbole, and Jesus wants his disciples to imagine how terrible life is apart from God's reign so that they may realize the consequences of human sin and choose to live as God's followers. It is also important to recognize that these lessons are prefaced by Jesus' prediction of impending death and resurrection, neither of which his followers are able to comprehend. They are afraid and baffled by his talk of these things, yet both his death and resurrection are essential to the journey of faith. Like his followers today, Jesus' first disciples struggle to understand how radically different God's ways are from human ways of doing things (8:33). Bearing these concerns in mind, the following aspects of Jesus' teaching can focus our attention and concern.

With *Jesus' first intimation of betrayal,* a sinister shadow is cast over the remaining chapters of Mark's Gospel. Who exactly is responsible for handing over Jesus to death? Is it the Roman authorities who acquiesce to popular opinion (15:6–15)? Is it members of his religious tradition who were threatened by Jesus' authority (3:6; 14:55–58)? Is it his own followers who run from his side and deny knowing him (14:50, 66–72)? Is God also implicated in Jesus' death, since Jesus' fate is bound up with the will of God (14:36)? Although the theme of betrayal will be taken up in greater detail later when we encounter Jesus' trials in Mark 14–15, this early intimation of betrayal triggers an awareness of its presence among us. Whether it is a spouse who violates bonds of intimacy, a friend or coworker who whispers our secret to others, a professed Christian who misappropriates church funds, a church leader who violates professional boundaries to satisfy sexual desires, a president who leads a nation to war under false pretenses, or a corporate executive who denies contributing to global warming, everyone has been betrayed and everyone has somehow betrayed others. In whatever ways we have experienced betrayal or violated the trust of others, this text prompts us to set these betrayals within the context of Christ's betrayal and God's redemptive purposes.

The *centerpiece of Jesus' teaching is servanthood.* If we cherish the priesthood of all believers, Jesus proposes something far more radical: the servanthood of all believers. Christ insists that it is not important to be recognized by others but to recognize others, especially those who are most often overlooked, such as children. Selfless service is more difficult than we care to admit. My colleague and friend Donald E. Miller has told me, "You can accomplish anything you want—and anything Christ wants you to do—with only one condition: you cannot seek credit for what you are doing." At first glimpse, this seems grossly unfair and quite unnecessary: if we are organizing an effective outreach ministry to the homeless, is there any reason we should not be recognized for our good work? Yet the impulse to receive recognition or reward is so great that it often corrupts our best intentions and blinds us to the needs and accomplishments of others. In fact, we are sometimes surprised to discover examples of servanthood among us. Whether it is one who faithfully prepares casseroles for the bereaved, one who quietly finds ways of providing material support for strangers, or the person in the pew who warmly welcomes a newcomer, we need to encourage one another to serve as Christ serves us. In doing so, Christ promises that we will not only discover him among us but the one who sent him (9:37).

To serve as Christ serves means *recognizing and caring for those who are the focus of Christ's care and concern.* Jesus' example of drawing a child into the disciples' innermost circle is especially poignant because children are still the most likely victims of abuse, slave labor, and neglect. In contrast to the way many upper- and middle-class families in America lavish vast amounts of time and money on their own children, their hobbies, activities, and desires, Jesus reminds us to be concerned for the well-being of the "least of these," who have no one to advocate on their behalf. The fact that the Gospel mentions a second encounter between Jesus and young children in 10:13–16 also reveals the importance he places on them just as he reaches out to many other surprising characters (e.g., tax collectors, persons with various diseases, women, sinners). By his example, Jesus draws the "least of these" into his circle of concern and ours.

Jesus is also concerned about *a spirit of rivalry or partisanship among his followers.* Religious differences are highlighted and common interests are ignored when local churches fall prey to in-house rivalries, and different religious groups are prone to claim their superiority over one another. Sermons, Sunday school classes, and Bible study groups provide excellent opportunities to study Scripture and invoke God's help in understanding what it means to work with others in the name of Christ—both congregationally and as we explore ecumenical relationships and interfaith dialogue with people across religious and ethnic divides. Mark 9:33–41 challenges us to reconsider our view of others as competitors or rivals in the reign of God. It also provides a scriptural context for inviting to worship or Sunday school someone from another congregation or faith tradition to speak of outreach ministries we may share with others.

Finally, *images of salty disciples and refining fires* compel us to consider anew what is distinctive and enduring about Christian faith. Even with low-salt diets and microwave ovens, no one doubts the essential value of salt and fire for sustaining life. As one member of our Markan Bible study reflected, "Salt and fire are both good and necessary gifts. Salt refers to the enduring quality of faith and service. Fire can refer not only to the fire of hell but the fire of heaven when God stirs within us a passion for serving others."[4] God longs for us to live and love differently than others, to engage the feverish struggles of our time with passion and commitment to God's loving reign among us. Jesus' manner of speaking is meant to stir our own imaginative juices to encourage new images of Christian discipleship today.

Family Matters

As Jesus continues to teach his followers about the meaning of discipleship, the scene shifts from private instruction at the end of chapter 9 to public teaching at the beginning of chapter 10.

The focus of this section is on family life and includes teachings on marriage, divorce, remarriage, and children. It is a theme Jesus pursues elsewhere in the Gospel, including his radical redefinition of family as those who do the will of God (3:35) and his declaration that siblings, parents, and children will be divided against one another "because of my name" (13:12–13). It is no wonder that, according to Juel, "the major criticism aimed at Christians in the Roman world–and the reason for later persecutions–was that they were antisocial, threatening bonds that held together the human community from the family to the state."[1] The larger purpose of Jesus' radical approach to familial relationships, however, was not destructive but constructive: he sought the transformation of all human relationships (personal, familial, social, and political) through a radically different relationship with God and the reign of God he proclaimed.

Exploring the text

MARRIAGE, DIVORCE, AND REMARRIAGE (10:1–12)

The brief allusion to Jesus' travels through "the region of Judea and beyond the Jordan" in 10:1 describes a southward journey as Jesus makes his way from Capernaum to Jerusalem. While Jesus is on the move, crowds gather near to hear him preach and teach. Several Pharisees are also present, and Mark tells us from the outset that they have come to test Jesus, hoping to entrap him in a controversial discussion over what is permitted and not permitted in divorce (cf. 8:11; 12:15). They begin their encounter by asking a question for which they already know the answer: "Is it lawful for a man to divorce his wife?" According to Deuteronomy

24:1, a man is indeed allowed to divorce his wife. When Jesus asks them what Moses commanded, they correctly cite this passage and recall the practice of issuing a certificate of divorce. A divorce certificate provided a woman with legal proof that her marriage had ended, severing the man's economic and familial obligations and allowing her to marry someone else. Although Roman law permitted wives to initiate divorce proceedings, the Torah did not. Instead, Jewish religious leaders debated the circumstances under which a man could justify divorcing his wife.[1]

Jesus, however, turns the conversation in an entirely different direction. He focuses our attention on marriage rather than divorce and moves away from discussing legal loopholes to pursuing God's intention for the union of two people.[2] Jesus insists that it is only "because of your hardness of heart" (cf. 3:5; 6:52) that Moses wrote this commandment, and he appeals to Genesis 1:27 and 2:24 to explain God's vision of marital union as "the two shall become one flesh." The climax of the passage occurs in 10:9 as Jesus asserts his authority: "Therefore, what God has joined together, let no one separate." His declaration not only serves as a proclamation of divine intention but is meant to thwart the Pharisees' preoccupation with what is permissible in divorce. In this passage, Jesus is not interested in discussing under which circumstances divorce is allowed, whether divorced persons should be allowed positions of religious authority, or how we are to minister to persons experiencing marital turmoil. Instead, he challenges the Pharisees and all others who seek ways of diminishing the value and permanency of marriage to remember the sacred union of two who become one by the presence and power of God.

However, marital separation and divorce is a reality with which people of faith must also contend. This is no doubt the reason why Jesus' followers pursued the subject when they addressed him in private (10:10–12). However harsh his response may seem, Jesus' words remind us that marital ties endure beyond the formality of signing divorce decrees. Anyone who has experienced the painfulness of a broken relationship knows that the bonds of marriage are not easily severed and do not quickly dissolve. Because of this, Jesus does not prohibit divorce but speaks plainly of its impact. Most remarkably, Jesus' comments reflect concern for both women and men. In a patriarchal society that assumed wives to be the property of their husbands, it was extraordinary for Jesus to suggest that a woman could also be the victim of spousal infidelity (the unfaithful husband is said to commit adultery "against her") and that a woman may divorce her husband and choose to marry another. His words suggest that equitable relations and mutual responsibility are foundational to all enduring relationships.

BLESSING CHILDREN AND RECEIVING
THE REIGN OF GOD (10:13–16)

From marriage to children, Jesus continues his interest in family matters. Mark reports that people brought their children to Jesus hoping he would touch them. No wonder: his hands had fed thousands, healed the diseased, and raised the dead. But his **disciples** were shooing them away. They were expert at crowd management and accepted the social norms that devalue children and give priority to adults. When Jesus witnessed them speaking sternly to the children and those who brought them, he was indignant (cf. Matt. 19:13–15; Luke 18:15–17). They seem to have entirely forgotten his earlier teaching in 9:36–37 when Jesus drew children into their midst and offered the disciples a lesson in humility. Here Jesus not only teaches his disciples to receive little children, but he insists that they will never enter the **reign of God** unless they receive God's reign "as a little child." Whereas Matthew suggests that we must become more childlike (18:3), Mark's account emphasizes that we are to receive God's reign in the same way that little children receive God's blessing–as a gracious gift awaiting our reception.

Gathering the children in his arms, Jesus lays his hands on them in a gesture of blessing. Although this text has sometimes been used to support the practice of infant baptism, it does not refer here to baptism but emphasizes that the gift of God's loving embrace is available to all people, even and especially the least members of society. Also, this text does not romanticize children or provide us with lessons on the virtues of childhood. Instead, we are given a glimpse of God's reign open wide to those who seek divine blessing and strength.

Preaching and teaching the Word

The RCL includes these verses among the readings for the Twenty-Seventh Sunday of Ordinary Time in Year B. Although many people advocate "family values," it is wise to remember that *Jesus' teachings about marital relationships and children are far more complicated* than we may want to recognize. When 10:1–16 is taken alongside 3:31–35 and 13:12–13 we quickly realize that Jesus does not present us with simple rules for family life. Instead, he envisions all relationships according to God's loving intentions rather than our own notions of socially acceptable behavior. Like the Pharisees, it is all too easy to become preoccupied with what is permitted or not permitted in marriage, family, and other relationships. The Greek word for hardness of heart that Jesus uses to describe this condition, *sklerokardia*, sounds like a disease, which it is. Marriage, children, and family life in general call for compassion and insight on the part of preachers and teachers who address these personal and socially relevant relationships. There is hardly a marriage that has not been tested in one way or another, and all marriages have fallen short of God's vision of the sacred union of two who become one. Jesus turns us away from our preoccupation with what is permissible or impermissible and recalls God's intimate involvement in the union of two people. At the social or public level, more attention is sometimes given to prenuptial agreements than the fulfillment of wedding vows. At a more personal level, more than one marriage partner has been eager to decry the infidelity of his or her partner (whether sexual, emotional, or another form of betrayal) while resisting the difficult work of exploring each of their needs, gifts, and failings. Complicating matters further, we may become so entangled in fulfilling particular role or gender expectations in marriage that we do not open ourselves to new ways of relating to one another in Christ.

Also, 10:13–16 invites us to *Christ's blessing of children.* Jesus turns us away from cultural norms that ignore children's well-being, whether by refusing to care for the basic needs of children who are poor or overindulging wealthy children. He urges us to look at children anew, as persons who receive God's reign by entrusting themselves to God's grace. In laying his hands on children, he extends a gesture of tenderness and blessing. By word and deed, Jesus embodies respect and compassion for them. In ancient and modern societies, children are often the first victims of disease, neglect, sexual abuse, and slave labor.[1] His abiding care for "the least of these" stands as a sharp indictment of the ways we have chosen to ignore the millions of children who do not receive adequate health care, food, and education. Whereas we tend to neglect, victimize, or overindulge our children, Jesus fully recognizes their presence, vulnerability, and needs.

In addition, Jesus teaches his disciples that we will never enter God's reign except if we receive it as little children. It is their openness to receiving from God what they cannot procure on their own that he highlights in these verses. Children are far more attentive and alert to the world around them than most grown-ups. They are also more willing to recognize and receive God's gifts. One has only to spend ten minutes in the woods with a five-year-old to discover anthills and arrowheads, groundhog holes and snakeskins–all of which go unnoticed or unappreciated by most adults. Perhaps it is this ability to perceive the world around them that prepares children so well to receive the world to come. Christ is eager to share the blessing of God's reign with these little ones and with each of us as well.

Poverty, Wealth,
and the Reign of God

Mark 10:17–31

Jesus' longest sustained discussion of any one issue in Mark's Gospel focuses on wealth and material well-being. Within the larger context of teaching his followers about **discipleship** (8:22–10:52), the opening story (10:17–22) and subsequent exchanges between Jesus and his disciples (10:23–31) are permeated with the language of inheritance, money, poverty, treasure, possessions, wealth, land, and other precious goods and relationships. Jesus' demand that the rich man sell his possessions and give the money to the poor is as startling as his announcement that it is all but impossible for those who are wealthy to enter the **reign of God**. Yet these verses also proclaim **good news**: God makes possible what is otherwise impossible for us to accomplish on our own (v. 27). Jesus also promises those who have given up their most beloved possessions for the sake of the gospel that they will receive far more in return than they ever imagined (vv. 29–30). God continues to surprise us, to reverse our expectations and upset our careful calculation of what is good and valuable, what is first and last (v. 31).

Exploring the text

THE RICH MAN WHOM JESUS LOVED (10:17–22)

The opening words of this story tell us that Jesus is "setting out on a journey" when he is confronted by a stranger. The roadside setting is a reminder that Jesus is heading for Jerusalem, where he will be put to death for fulfilling God's will and proclaiming God's reign. The third and final prediction of his death and resurrection follows in 10:32–34, lending greater urgency to his teaching.

As he proceeds, a man rushes toward him, kneels at his feet, and addresses him as "Good Teacher." The man's actions and greeting are unusual and reveal genuine respect for Jesus. He does not ask how to

176

receive eternal life or how to *enter* the **kingdom of heaven** but what he *must do to inherit* eternal life. He uses the language of property and economic privilege and also assumes that eternal life is given in exchange for good behavior or in fulfillment of certain conditions. The man's plea stands in stark contrast to Jesus' teaching in the previous episode that his followers must receive God's kingdom as little children, trusting and depending upon God's help and mercy (v. 15).

In response to the man's plea, Jesus offers a swift and surprising rebuff by refuting the title "Good Teacher" (v. 18). This puzzling and harsh response may lead us to wonder if Jesus is somehow offended by the man's inquiry or if this is his way of turning the man's attention toward God as Jesus asserts his divinity.[1] Jesus then recalls several of the Ten Commandments and reminds the man of his responsibility toward others. Significantly, Jesus omits the first four commandments having to do with our relationship with God. Although the man has successfully fulfilled the latter six commandments, perhaps he has completed many good deeds without particular awareness of God's ultimate authority or claim on his life (the focus of the first four commandments). It is also interesting to note that Jesus replaces the command "You shall not covet" with "You shall not defraud." As Myers notes, the new reference makes explicit the sin of economic exploitation: "With this deft bit of editing, Jesus reveals that he is more interested in how this man became so affluent than in his pious claims."[2] Whether or not he has coveted his neighbors' goods, Jesus presses him to consider how he has taken advantage of others and broken the bonds of neighborly love that God commands us to uphold (see 12:28–34).

When the man assures Jesus that he has kept these commands since his youth, Jesus responds with unprecedented affection. He does not refute the man's testimony or his ability to fulfill God's requirements. Instead, Jesus loves the man. This is the only occasion in Mark's Gospel when we are told of Jesus' love for a particular person. Because of his love for him, Jesus challenges the man to a new understanding of love for others, including both God and neighbors. He looks intently at him and sees what the man cannot, urging him to sell what he owns, give the money to the poor, and follow him (10:21). Five imperatives ("go," "sell," "give," "come," and "follow") challenge the man to reach beyond the Decalogue and reorient his life anew. In the midst of these five commands is the promise of treasure in heaven. Contrary to the man's expectations, eternal life is not inherited but freely given to us by God, who calls us to freely give of ourselves to others. In other words, the good news of God's reign and the promise of eternal life have everything to do with giving ourselves, including our possessions, in service to others.[3]

The man feels the full impact of Jesus' words and is deeply grieved. As he turns away from Jesus, we learn that he has many possessions (v. 22), and it is the fear of losing them that keeps him from seeing what he has yet to gain. To give away all his possessions would mean the loss of financial resources and security; it would render him vulnerable to poverty and deprive him of the much-coveted opportunity to serve as a benefactor to others, garnering the attention and respect of his peers. He realizes that Jesus is proposing something far more challenging than a system of welfare management and that the personal consequences of Jesus' call are far too costly. Like so many others whom Jesus cares for, this man is possessed– but it is not by Satan's minions but by his own spirit of possessiveness, the most tenacious demon of all. He is the only person in Mark's Gospel to refuse Jesus' invitation to follow. The rich man's refusal is the impetus for Jesus' further discussion with his disciples on the dangers of wealth.

HARD TEACHINGS FOR THE RICH,
GOOD NEWS FOR EVERYONE (10:23–27)

While the rich man walks away, Jesus turns to his **disciples** to continue teaching about wealth. He issues two very similar warnings. The first is that it is all but impossible for those who have wealth to enter the **kingdom of God** (10:23). He has moved the conversation from "inheriting eternal life" to "entering God's reign," and with this change in terms Jesus once again makes the kingdom of God the primary reference point of his teaching. His followers are amazed and confused at what he is saying. Although several of the psalms and much of Jesus' own teaching identify the poor as genuinely faithful and pious people (e.g., Ps. 70:5; Mark 12:41–44; Luke 16:19–31), the common assumption is that riches are a sign of God's favor and poverty an indication of divine judgment (see Deut. 28:1–14). Before the disciples can voice their shock, Jesus issues his second warning. He addresses the disciples as "children" (10:24), warns them again about the dangers of wealth, then uses a creative hyperbole: it is easier for a camel to walk through the eye of a needle than for a rich person to enter heaven (v. 25). Although some commentators have attempted to dilute the impact of Jesus' statement by suggesting that the eye of a needle refers to a gateway in the city of Jerusalem (a nonexistent passageway), it seems more likely that Jesus wanted his followers to understand the impossibility of earning their place in God's reign by their own effort.

Like the rich man, the disciples are astounded by what Jesus is saying. If there is no way to ensure our place in heaven, they wonder, "then who can be saved?" (v. 26). Their question goes right to the heart of the **gospel**.

Once again, Jesus looks intently at his followers (cf. vv. 21, 23). He announces the good news that for God all things are possible (v. 27). The love and tenderness Jesus felt toward the rich man extends to his disciples as he assures them that salvation is a gift of God. There is no earthly sign of success, no reward or accomplishment that ensures our place in heaven. Instead, Jesus announces a new economy of divine grace that makes possible our place in God's reign. The promise of God's power makes possible what we cannot accomplish or procure on our own—eternal life as children of God.

LEAVING EVERYTHING,
RECEIVING EVERYTHING (10:28–31)

Jesus has scarcely finished speaking when Peter insists that Jesus recognize what he and others have given up in order to follow him (10:28). Whether he is anxious or boastful, there is an unspoken question behind Peter's statement: what will happen to me if I give up everything I cherish in service to God and neighbor? Jesus assures his followers that those who have left everything for the sake of the gospel will gain far more than they ever imagined in this age and the age to come. God will provide for their every need.

There are four facets of Jesus' teaching in 10:29–30 worth noting. First, his reference to the **gospel** as the reason for giving up everything underscores its importance as the focal point of Christ's proclamation (see 1:1, 14, 15; 8:35; 13:10; 14:9). Second, the multiplication of resources and relationships spoken of here is particularly poignant when we remember that home, land, and familial relationships were the most valued components of ancient (and perhaps contemporary) life. Third, the mention of persecution introduces a sobering note and provides "a brilliant reminder of the mystery of the cross in the midst of a list of the positive benefits of discipleship."[1] Finally, drawing on Jewish apocalypticism, Jesus speaks of both the present and future reality of **God's reign**. Amid persecution, loneliness, and loss, Christ's followers are promised God's help now and in the age to come.

Jesus' discourse ends with a brief saying that summarizes much of what he has been teaching his followers throughout the Gospel: the first will be last and the last first. Just when we think we have it all figured out, God reverses our expectations and upsets our careful calculations. Jesus is not only announcing a reversal of values but a reversal of fortunes. Only one thing is certain: to save our lives we must lose them, and to gain the world we must give up everything.

Preaching and teaching the Word

No other topic occupies Jesus' preaching and teaching more than wealth and material resources. Of the thirty-eight parables in the New Testament, seventeen pertain to possessions and giving. Over 2,100 verses touch on the subject, far more than the 272 on believing/believers or 371 on prayer.[2] More than right beliefs, Christ is concerned with the right use of resources as we learn to care for the needs of neighbors near and far. In North America, where unprecedented levels of wealth are enjoyed by a privileged few while the gap between rich and poor continues to widen around the world, there is hardly a topic that needs our attention and understanding more than the material well-being of all people. Thankfully, Mark 10:17–31 is included among the readings for the Twenty-Eighth Sunday of Ordinary Time in Year B.

We may begin to address these provocative verses by admitting *how difficult it is for us to hear Jesus' command to the rich man.* Does Jesus expect all of us to sell our possessions and give the money to the poor? Is he speaking symbolically when he commands us to give away our resources, or is Jesus issuing a deeper call that encompasses a new understanding of how we are to relate to money and other material resources? Like the rich man, most of us would rather walk away from this discussion than pursue its implications for our lives. Yet the rich man's reaction confirms that there are few things more difficult to overcome than our preoccupation with wealth and material goods. Possessions have a way of possessing us when all we have is what we own. In his book *Consuming Religion: Christian Faith and Practice in a Consumer Culture,* Vincent Miller argues that the Christian desire for the kingdom of God has been seduced or misplaced in North American culture by the insatiable desire for commodities that never satisfy. The "constant search for gratification, which in the end proves to be more gratifying still," fully preoccupies us.[3] It is all too easy to place great value on things of little worth.

There is good news even in the midst of this impossible calling. Nothing shakes our resolve so quickly as the prospect of losing our home, giving up our IRAs, or handing over our children's college funds—especially if we think that hardship and ridicule will follow. Amid our worst fears, Jesus promises that God will bless us beyond our wildest imagination. Jesus commands the rich man to sell all that he has and promises him treasure in heaven. When his disciples are convinced that it is impossible to fulfill God's commands, Jesus tells them nothing is impossible for God. When they wonder if it is worth giving up everything, Jesus assures them they will receive more than they ever imagined. In the movie *Pay It Forward,* twelve-year-old Trevor accepts his teacher's challenge to come up with an idea that will change the world and then put that idea into action. Trevor decides to do something for three other people that they cannot do for themselves—something that is very, very difficult. His plan is for each of the three people he helps to do something for three others, so that each person "pays it forward." By the end of the film, even though Trevor cannot see it, his gifts to others have changed countless lives in amazing ways. Whenever we freely give ourselves and our resources in service to others, God widens and blesses the circle of giving in ways we could never have anticipated.

It is also important to *recognize what is and what is not proposed by Jesus.* He is not advocating a government-sponsored policy of economic reform, an overhaul of the welfare system or a particular approach to economics (e.g., capitalist, communist, socialist). But he is proposing something far more difficult: Jesus calls us to reform our lives, including our use and misuse of resources, in accordance with his proclamation of God's just and loving reign. Of course, this also has political implications, as Christians work with others to develop compassionate social policies for those in need. Jesus proposes that to love God fully we must place all of our possessions at God's disposal, and this means giving all of what we have in loving service to our neighbors (10:21; see 12:28–31).

Neither does Jesus propose a double standard where some people give and others do not. All of Jesus' followers are called to give their best and most precious gifts in service to God and neighbors. For some, this means choosing to receive a low salary in order to live beneath the taxable income level. In this way, persons do not contribute to taxes that are used to support the military, while bearing witness to a sustainable lifestyle that cares for all of creation. For some, it means struggling amid the reality of daily compromises, educating ourselves and neighbors about goods that are produced without adequate compensation to workers, opening the family table and our homes to those who need a meal and a place to stay. For some, it means planning carefully how our financial resources may be used in service to others through church and other charitable organizations. For everyone, the call of Christ is to fully give our heart, soul, mind, and possessions in loving service to God and neighbors.

Finally, this text opens the way for us to explore *financial stewardship and charitable giving.* Many Christians are embarrassed or afraid to discuss what we put in the offering plate, which nonprofit organizations we support, and whether or not we tithe our income. Also, many preachers avoid speaking about money altogether—a deplorable omission, since many congregants long to hear their pastors address the ways Scripture speaks to the wise use of resources entrusted to us by God.[4] Mark 10:17–31 reminds us that Jesus does not hesitate to speak with strangers and friends about the difficulties and challenges of material wealth. He places his consideration of wealth in the context of God's reign and reveals God's passion for the poor as the essential reference point for our deliberations over what we give and to whom we give. In his "Eight Degrees of Charity," the thirteenth-century Jewish philosopher Maimonides teaches that the highest level of righteousness is to give a present, loan, or job or to establish a partnership for someone who is poor so that he or she is no longer materially vulnerable.[5] Based on Deuteronomy 15:7–8 and Leviticus 25:35, this teaching is applied not only to Jews but to strangers and sojourners as well. Beyond our careful calculations of who is worthy and what is worthwhile, Maimonides urges us to "strengthen the hand" of others, thereby fulfilling God's righteousness on earth as it is in heaven.

Jesus' Third Prediction and Lessons on Servant Leadership

Mark 10:32–45

The pattern of prediction, incomprehension, and teaching about discipleship continues with this third and final exchange between Jesus and his disciples before they enter Jerusalem. Compared to his earlier predictions, this is the most extensive and detailed. The urgency of the moment inspires some of Jesus' most powerful teachings about the significance of his death and the nature of discipleship.

Exploring the text

JESUS' THIRD PREDICTION BEFORE ENTERING JERUSALEM (10:32–34)

Once again, Mark tells us that Jesus and his followers are "on the road" to Jerusalem. The expression denotes more than physical movement, since it is also a metaphor for "the way" of **discipleship** (see 8:27; 9:33; 10:17). The reference is a reminder that they are nearing the city of Jerusalem, where Jesus anticipates suffering, death, and resurrection. Jesus is ahead of his followers as they walk along the road, resolutely stepping toward his fate while those who follow are both amazed and fearful.

Jesus takes the twelve away from the crowd to share his final prediction (10:32). Referring to himself as the **Son of Man**, he describes his impending suffering, death, and resurrection in greater detail than we hear in his earlier accounts. Whereas the first prediction speaks of his death at the hands of Jewish authorities (8:31) and the second of his betrayal into "human hands" in general (9:31), the third represents the culmination of Jesus' predictions and implicates both Jews and Gentiles. Religious and political figures are among the mix of responsible persons; indeed, as Lamar Williamson Jr. notes, "Every reader can identify with some party to the death of Jesus."[1] Interestingly, neither here nor in his earlier predictions does Jesus speak of being crucified. The cruel nature

183

of his execution, the full impact of his death, and the political implications of Jesus' messianic role come to a climax later in the narrative (see 14:53–16:8).

COMPETING FOR GLORY (10:35–40)

Jesus has scarcely finished speaking about his death when James and John step forward to ask for places of honor beside him when he takes his place in glory. The seats they covet are places of honor at the messianic banquet or thrones adjacent to Jesus when he takes his place in the messianic kingdom. Either way, it seems incredible that they have misunderstood what Jesus was saying about his suffering, ignominy, and death, for they have been with him since the very beginning of his ministry (1:19–20). Yet perhaps they have understood some part of what he is saying, since they anticipate he will someday rule in glory. What they do not understand is that his crown will be made of thorns, his throne will be a cross, and those who occupy his left and right sides will be bandits hanging on adjacent crosses.[1]

Their request is both outrageously selfish and utterly human. The sons of Zebedee ask that Jesus "do for us whatever we ask of you." In response, Jesus asks the same question of them that he asks blind Bartimaeus in the story that follows: "What do you want me to do for you?" (10:36; cf. v. 51). Whereas Bartimaeus knows what he needs, James and John do not. They only know what they want, and they do not want to lead Vacation Bible School or clean dishes at the next potluck. They seek privilege, recognition, power, and glory when Jesus is enthroned.

Jesus responds to their request by telling them they do not know what they are asking: "Are you able to drink the cup that I drink, or be baptized with the baptism that I am baptized with?" The images of the cup and baptism are rich in meaning. Although the cup may refer to the cup of God's blessing (Ps. 23:5), in the context of Jesus' impending death it more likely refers to the cup of bitterness and suffering (Isa. 51:17, 22; Lam. 4:21). Jesus himself prefers to forgo this cup yet accepts it as necessary to fulfill God's will (Mark. 14:36). The water of baptism is also a dangerous image for those who suffer God's wrath (Isa. 42:2; Gen. 7:17–24; cf. 1 Pet. 3:18–22). It recalls the harsh beginning of Jesus' ministry (see 1:9–13) and anticipates his death and the death of others who will suffer the baptism of blood when they give their lives for the sake of the gospel. The church's practices of communion and baptism are associated with Christ's suffering, death, and resurrection.

James and John naively announce that they are able to drink the cup of Christ and to be baptized as he is baptized. However, in a few days they will fall asleep during his hour of need (14:32–42) and desert him in his time of trial (14:50). Even so, Jesus promises they will one day share his cup and baptism (10:39). He also insists that it is not his to say who will sit at his right hand or left. That decision is not appointed by executive order. Instead, as the following verses reveal, "it is achieved only through an apprenticeship of the cross (10:39f)."[2]

THE SERVANTHOOD OF ALL BELIEVERS (10:41–45)

Here we find Jesus' most pointed and profound lesson on the meaning of **discipleship** and how it relates to his own ministry. Just before entering Jerusalem, Jesus tells the disciples that true greatness resides in being a slave of all. These powerful and empowering words are the culmination of this entire section on discipleship (8:22–10:52).

In 10:41 we learn that the ten disciples are angry at James and John for trying to maneuver their way into positions of privilege and power. As is often the case, dissension and division are the result of internal strife rather than external pressures. Hearing their dispute, Jesus sets before his disciples the negative example of Gentile rulers who "lord it over others" as tyrants. These "great ones" exercise power through a combination of physical force, political intimidation, and a system of patronage that seeks unquestioning loyalty.[1] Jesus calls for an entirely different kind of leadership. He teaches that "whoever wishes to become great among you must be your servant, and whoever wishes to be first among you must be slave of all" (vv. 43–44). Most remarkable is the notion that in following one Lord, we are now bound in servitude to all people.

Jesus makes it clear that the basis for the disciples' servant-ministry is his own ministry. Just as he came to serve, so are we to serve. Of equal importance, Jesus completely overturns all earthly perceptions of **power**, since he does not base his authority on lording it over others but on serving others. In a series of paradoxical statements, Jesus redefines the nature of leadership not in terms of patronage but servanthood, not according to privilege but slavery, not seeking economic advantage over others but offering his life as payment to secure the release of others. Verse 45 not only links his own life of service to the vocation of his disciples as described in verses 43–44, but this saying is also the first time Mark gives any indication of the purpose of Jesus' death: to give his life as "a ransom for many."[2] The term "ransom" refers to purchasing a slave or prisoner in order to grant him or her freedom and redemption. Jesus' words suggest that humanity is held captive by powers from which we need deliverance and that his death provides the means for our freedom and redemption.[3] We also glimpse Isaiah's vision of the suffering servant who bears the sins of others and "poured out himself to death" (Isa. 53:12).[4] Although Herod and Pilate may appear to be free to exert power over others, in Mark's narrative they are coerced by the power structures they support to do what they do not want to do (see 6:26–27; 15:6–15).[5] By contrast, Jesus and his disciples are truly free to exercise power for the sake of others, not to be served but to serve.

Preaching and teaching the Word

Unfortunately, the RCL does not include verses 32–34 when it lists 10:35–45 as the Gospel reading for the Twenty-Ninth Sunday of Ordinary Time in Year B. These first few verses include several details not noted elsewhere, including both Jews and Gentiles who are implicated in Jesus' death and his being mocked, spat upon, and flogged—important points of contrast to the glory that James and John seek in verses 35–40. These details also help us appreciate the gravity of Jesus' call to serve others in verses 41–45. Several themes are highlighted in this portion of the Gospel.

First and foremost, *to be a disciple of Jesus Christ is to serve others as Christ serves us.* Jesus insists that true greatness arises when we offer ourselves in loving service to others, not when we seek privilege, prestige, or our own advancement. All such claims to power are not only corrupt but ineffectual, resulting in our downfall and the resentment of others. These verses teach us that Christology and discipleship are necessarily and vitally related to one another. As Christ is, so are we to be; as we serve, so will others know the One who guides and empowers us. Whether it means providing child care in the church nursery, picking up food and medicine for shut-ins, leaving a paid position to participate in volunteer service, or suffering alienation from those who resent our ministry to AIDS patients, true greatness and real power is not realized through seeking our own advantage but the good of others. There never seems to be a shortage of opportunities for pursuing this kind of greatness.

Underlying Jesus' lessons about servanthood is *a radically new understanding of power.* He does not disparage the importance or necessity of power, but he radically redefines it. He is realistic in his appraisal of those who abuse power by "lording it over others." Jesus' teaching about servanthood avoids two common misunderstandings of power. The first is that all power is evil and we must therefore set ourselves in subservience to others because it is better to be victims of abuse than it is to abuse others. The second is that some areas of power and authority (e.g., political governance, business management, pastoral leadership) are better than others because they are inherently more important or effectual than others. Instead, Jesus teaches his followers that whatever our job, status, or profession, we are called to serve others by participating in the power of God's reign among us. The "servanthood of all believers" that Jesus proposes (see "Preaching and teaching the Word" for 9:38–50, p. 169) is based on his own ministry, death, and resurrection, and by the power of his Spirit we participate in God's service to others. As Christ's followers, we are able to do what we could not accomplish by human effort alone. During times of war, for example, we are given steadfast love and wisdom to respond to our enemies; likewise, by the power of Christ we are given patience, endurance, and financial means to provide leadership in ministry and service to persons suffering from drug addiction. When we are willing to serve, the power of Jesus Christ reorients our priorities, making true greatness possible.

It is also remarkable to note *how Jesus relates to his disciples* throughout this section. Despite their self-centeredness and persistent misunderstanding, he continues to teach them what it means to be his disciples. He responds to James and John without condescension, yet he corrects their errors. Their faults are real, yet he never rejects them. Perhaps that is why they continue to follow him, even when they are blind to his meaning or fearful of the journey ahead. Jesus' tenderness and forbearance toward his disciples is good news for those of us today who hear his words yet do not fully understand what he means, or who struggle to relinquish our own plans for success.

The *cup and baptism* Jesus mentions in these verses provide wonderful images for us to explore. As ordinances or sacraments of the church, communion and baptism are regularly included in public worship, yet not often with reference to Jesus' predictions. A sermon focusing on Jesus' allusion to baptism in this passage may connect it more intentionally to his own suffering, death, and resurrection.[6] Similarly, Jesus' allusion to communion in this passage focuses our attention on the cup of sorrow and his blood poured out as a ransom for many (10:45). In his book *Can You Drink the Cup?*, Henri Nouwen reflects on the experience of holding, lifting, and drinking the cup of Christ, which contains both sorrow and joy. As sorrow, the cup includes not only Jesus' suffering but that of the whole human race, so that we must sometimes look carefully to discover the joy hidden within it: "When we are crushed like grapes, we cannot think of the wine we will become."[7] Yet the promise of Christ is that his cup is also our cup. As we drink it and savor the sorrow and joy within it, we will taste his gift of freedom and salvation, in this world as in the world to come.

Blind Bartimaeus Sees and Follows

Exploring the text

Part 2 of Mark's Gospel ends as it began, that is, with an account of Jesus healing a blind man (cf. 8:22–26). Both stories serve to "frame" this second major portion of the Gospel, which includes Christ's three predictions of suffering, death, and resurrection as well as subsequent lessons about **discipleship** and servanthood. Despite Jesus' teaching and miraculous activity, his followers are still blind to what awaits them in Jerusalem. Ironically, blind Bartimaeus sees Jesus for who he is and eagerly follows him.

Just before Jesus and his disciples arrive in Jerusalem, they make one last stop at Jericho, located fifteen miles northeast of their final destination (10:46). As they are leaving town, a blind beggar sitting by the roadside hears that Jesus of Nazareth is passing by, and he calls out to him, "Jesus, Son of David, have mercy on me!" (10:47). Bartimaeus is blind, but through the eyes of faith he is able to see what others do not, namely, that Jesus is the **Son of David** whose mission is one of mercy for God's people. "Son of David" was a familiar designation for the messianic king of Israel and with his declaration, Bartimaeus is the only person other than Peter to correctly identify Jesus as the Christ (8:29). Bartimaeus also calls on Jesus to fulfill the expectation of Israel's messiah, to have mercy and deliver him from blindness (Isa. 29:18; 55:7). The people try to silence him, but Bartimaeus shouts all the more loudly (10:48).

After hearing Bartimaeus, Jesus stops in his tracks and issues his own call for the blind man to join him. The crowd now changes its tune. They encourage Bartimaeus to step forward, perhaps curious to see what will happen. The cloak he stretched on the ground around his feet to catch a few coins is hurled aside as Bartimaeus rushes toward Jesus. Before he has a chance to repeat his plea, Jesus asks him the same question he asked James and John in the previous episode: "What do you want me to do for you?" (10:36, 51). Without hesitation, Bartimaeus asks to be freed from his affliction. Whereas James and John sought positions of privilege and power, Bartimaeus seeks the restoration of his sight. The clear-sightedness of the blind man who recognizes Jesus stands in stark contrast to the blind ambition of the brothers of Zebedee. Jesus commands Bartimaeus to go; his faith has made him well (v. 52). He is immediately restored to health because of his faith (see also 5:34). He follows Jesus to Jerusalem without hesitation.

If we compare Bartimaeus's story with that of the blind man of Bethsaida in 8:22–26, it is easy to identify several differences. The earlier healing required two attempts, Jesus used spittle and touch, it occurred in private, and Jesus sent the man home instead of allowing him to enter the local village. Between his healing and that of Bartimaeus, Jesus' many lessons in discipleship and servanthood have been largely ignored or misunderstood by his followers. As they are about to enter Jerusalem, Bartimaeus provides an ironic counterpoint to James, John, and the other disciples. We may also compare his story to that of the rich man who walked sadly away from Jesus when he heard the call to give up all he had to follow him (10:22). Bartimaeus gave up his beggar's cloak and whatever coins lay scattered by the roadside to receive the gift of sight and follow Christ. The rich man's wealth becomes a burden, whereas the poor man's losses become an opportunity for gain. As Geddert notes, "Rich or poor are asked to give up only one thing, *everything.*"[1] Bartimaeus gives eagerly and without reservation because he knows in whom he places his trust.

The story of Bartimaeus provides us with the last healing miracle in Mark's Gospel yet it is as much a call narrative as a healing story. To be sure, Bartimaeus is cured of physical blindness, but it is the combination of cure and call that claims our attention. The blind man calls out to Jesus twice. Jesus also issues a call. When Bartimaeus responds with energy and enthusiasm, he not only demonstrates that he knows who Jesus is, but he is willing to follow him as his disciple. It is this combination of knowing and doing, of clarity of faith and the conviction to follow, that marks him as a disciple of Jesus Christ.

Preaching and teaching the Word

The healing of Bartimaeus is among the most well-known and beloved stories of Scripture. The blind man is able to see what others do not and to follow where others will not.

Although we may certainly focus our attention on Jesus and how he demonstrates his power and authority through this event, there are *many reasons to look closely at Bartimaeus* instead. There are several qualities in him that we can admire: he recognizes Jesus as God's messiah who brings mercy to his people, he is willing to risk ridicule, he is persistent in seeking what he wants even when others try to discourage him, and he is genuinely willing to follow Jesus. These are all remarkable qualities of faith. At the close of this section of the Gospel, which focuses so intently on the meaning of discipleship, there are at least two lessons Bartimaeus can teach us.

First, Bartimaeus teaches us *the importance of choosing carefully what we want in life.* The rich man wanted to inherit eternal life. James and John wanted places of honor. But when Jesus asked Bartimaeus what he wanted, the blind man knew what he longed for: the gift of sight. It is amazing how easy it is to lose sight of what is most important and valuable. We continually need to remember what is worth pursuing. As a pastor, when I led couples through marital counseling during times when they no longer knew what they wanted, I would have each partner sit directly across from the other with knees touching. The first person would look into the eyes of the second and ask, "What do you want?" The second was free to respond until she or he could think of nothing further to say. Then the question was repeated by the first person until the second named more deeply, completely, or honestly what it was he or she wanted. Then they changed roles so that the first person had a chance to name his or her deepest desires. Invariably, each person was not only impressed by what their partner said but what they themselves wanted. Whether we need to reevaluate our hearts' desires or to entrust our desires to God like Bartimaeus, God longs for us to choose carefully what it is we want in life.

Second, Bartimaeus not only teaches us to choose carefully what we want but *to pursue the desires of our hearts with great passion.* With more than stubbornness and determination, Bartimaeus wholeheartedly pursued Jesus by the only means available to him—his voice. His was the loudest prayer Jesus had ever heard. Bartimaeus's voice soared above the crowd, called Jesus by name, identified him as Messiah and implored him to fulfill God's promise of mercy. He was willing to risk ridicule and rejection to pursue the gift of life. If only our own prayers (both private and public) would reveal such stamina, passion, and will. Sometimes we can hear this combination of faith and passion in the unrehearsed prayers of children. Sometimes we hear it when a woman who has repeatedly been discouraged from pastoral ministry decides to step forward and claim the call of Christ. Sometimes we can hear it when someone whose son has served two tours of duty in Iraq prays for the end of the war. Perhaps Bartimaeus is not the last person to see and follow the desires of his heart. Perhaps he is but one in a long line of ordinary beggars who display this extraordinary gift of faithful passion.

PART THREE

The Cross of Christ, the Power of God

11:1–15:47

Preliminary Remarks

The cross is everywhere present in the Gospel of Mark, casting its shadow and illuminating the way ahead for Jesus and his followers. But nowhere is its presence more powerfully felt than in the final chapters. The cross is more than a means of Jesus' execution, although it is certainly that, and the resurrection is more than a vindication of Christ's divine authority, although it is also that. The death and resurrection of Jesus Christ reveal God's way of overcoming evil, of participating in human suffering and, above all, of transforming sin and death to newness of life by the **power** of divine love. In Mark's portrayal of the passion of Jesus Christ, God's love is greater than the power of human sin, systemic evil, satanic forces, and even death itself.

Whereas parts 1 and 2 of Mark's narrative focus on Jesus' powerful words, deeds, and his teaching the disciples, part 3 brings us to the city of Jerusalem and the events leading up to Christ's death. Over one-third of Mark's Gospel is devoted to the last week of Jesus' life. We hear of his entry into Jerusalem, disruption of the Temple, confrontations with various religious leaders, predictions of the Temple's destruction, last supper with the disciples, and their betrayal and desertion of him. Following Jesus' trial before Jewish leaders and Pilate's interrogation, Jesus is crucified and laid in a tomb. When women come to anoint his body, a messenger tells them Jesus has been raised from the dead. They flee the scene in terror and amazement (16:8). This strange and disturbing ending was later emended to include additional verses describing Jesus' postresurrection appearances to his disciples (16:9–20). Yet the original ending provokes our response and holds the promise of God's resurrection power at work among those who continue to **proclaim** the **good news** of Jesus Christ.

Jesus' Arrival in Jerusalem and Actions in the Temple

Mark 11:1–26

W e could hardly have received a more dramatic account of Jesus' entry into Jerusalem and the Temple if a journalist had been present to record these events. In fact, Mark gives us something better than an eyewitness report–a theologically rich and complex account of some of Jesus' most controversial activities. His procession into the city and overturning the tables in the Temple are prophetic actions that signal a decisive turning point in the Gospel of Mark. They lead to Jesus' confrontation with various religious and political leaders (11:27–12:44) and ultimately result in his rejection, trial, and crucifixion.

JESUS' ENTRY INTO JERUSALEM (11:1–11)

Exploring the text

As Jesus and his disciples approach Jerusalem, they pass Bethphage, located on the Mount of Olives, and Bethany, approximately two miles east of the city (11:1).[1] The latter will serve as Jesus' home away from home during the final week of his life (11:11, 12; 14:3). Jesus will return to the Mount of Olives on two other occasions: when he foretells the destruction of the Temple (13:3) and shares a last supper with his disciples (14:26).

In 11:2–6, a surprising amount of attention is given to the preparations for Jesus' entry into the city. Jesus instructs two of his disciples to enter the neighboring village (probably Bethphage), locate a colt that has never been ridden, untie it, and bring it to him (v. 2). It is not entirely clear whether previous arrangements for the animal have been made, or if Jesus is exercising predictive powers by telling his disciples what they will encounter. If anyone inquires after the disciples' activity, they are to affirm, "The Lord needs it and will send it back here immediately" (v. 3). The unusual reference to "the Lord" probably refers to Jesus, who is exercising his kingly authority to requisition the animal for his own use.[2] Also, the fact that the colt has never been ridden may suggest greater honor for the one who rides it (see Zech. 9:9 LXX). Because it needs to be untied, scholars have associated these verses with Jacob's oracle regarding Judah in Genesis 49:10–12.[3] As Mark's narrative continues, everything unfolds according to plan (vv. 4–6). The disciples faithfully carry out all of Jesus' commands, and each detail of his prediction is fulfilled. The preparations for Jesus' entry take place in public, as do his procession into the city and later confrontation at the Temple (vv. 15–18).

When the disciples bring the colt to Jesus, they throw their cloaks on top of it for him to sit upon (v. 7). A crowd soon materializes, casting garments and leafy branches along the roadway in a gesture of homage (v. 8; cf. 2 Kgs. 9:13). The waving of green branches also recalls Simon Maccabaeus's triumphal entry into Jerusalem (1 Macc. 13:51).[4] Perhaps most importantly, we must not take for granted the sudden appearance of the crowd. If they are there in preparation for the Passover festival (14:1–2), they have arrived quite early for an event that takes place later in the week. Some scholars suggest that waving green branches and reciting the Hallel of Psalm 113–18 is reminiscent of the autumn Feast of Tabernacles. Others suggest that this scene may reflect the influence of the Feast of Hanukkah, commemorating the cleansing of the Temple by Judas Maccabaeus in 165 BCE.[5] Two things are certain. First, Mark 14 clearly links Jesus' week in Jerusalem with the commemoration of Passover. Second, Passover celebrates both the religious and sociopolitical liberation of God's people. Jesus' grand entry into the city in anticipation of Passover signals his liberative mission amid the powerful forces of human sin and institutional corruption.[6]

Shouts of "Hosanna" (meaning, "Save, I pray") serve to frame 11:9–10. Quoting from Psalm 118 (celebrating Israel's deliverance in battle), the crowd extols Jesus as "the one who comes in the name of the Lord" to deliver his people (see **messianic titles**). These verses resonate with Bartimaeus's earlier cry to Jesus as the Son of David (10:47–48) and also recall 2 Samuel 14:4 and 2 Kings 6:26, where "Hosanna" signifies a form of kingly address. According to Witherington, Hosanna is "a standard praise word (as it still is today) used in glorifying God."[7] Yet here, as in 12:10–11, there is an ironic twist: the cry for God to save is shouted at Jesus, who is stepping closer to death. As the story unfolds, he will be delivered into the hands of religious and political authorities who will condemn him before he serves as "a ransom for many" (10:45). The one who comes in God's name will soon be crucified as "King of the Jews" (15:26).

Further irony arises in the antimilitary tone of these proceedings: Jesus chooses to ride a colt rather than a steed, and his entry does not include a military entourage but a band of fishermen, tax collectors, and laborers. Nevertheless, Jesus' royal dignity is indisputable. The people who go ahead of him and those who follow (perhaps a subtle allusion to the prophets who precede Jesus and the disciples who follow) shout "Hosanna" in grand anticipation of God's reign.

Jesus' first act upon entering the city is to visit the Temple (11:11). Initially, it may appear that this stop is of little consequence and serves only as a brief act of reconnaissance before he returns the next day.[8] But Jesus takes his time and inspects everything. He witnesses firsthand all that is happening before retreating with the twelve to Bethany for the night. This seemingly inconsequential verse communicates two things. First, Jesus' first priority in Jerusalem is the Temple—the cultic, political, and economic center of Jewish faith and life. Second, in light of this earlier visit, it is clear that Jesus' decisive, prophetic action in the Temple during his second visit is not simply a rash or impulsive reaction to what he sees but a purposeful response to what he encounters there.

Preaching and teaching the Word

Jesus' entry into the city of Jerusalem is at once elaborate, purposeful, enigmatic, and holy. Many of us are so familiar with this scene that we do not recognize the mix of irony, pathos, and mystery present in it. One of the greatest challenges in preaching and teaching this text is that it is often recounted on Palm Sunday to people who will not hear the Scripture texts of Maundy Thursday or Good Friday. Without hearing the tragic events leading up to Jesus' death on a cross, it is all but impossible to appreciate the implicit ironies of Jesus' entry into the city or the events of Easter Sunday. If the Sunday before Easter does not include elements of Christ's passion, it is all the more important for preachers and teachers to highlight the pathos intimated in Mark 11:1–11 and all that it portends for Jesus' impending death and resurrection.

A sermon related to Jesus' entry into Jerusalem may *explore the many ironies* inherent in the text as the events of Holy Week unfold. In Mark's carefully detailed account, Jesus enters the holy city amid the accolades of the crowd, which later turns against him and demands his crucifixion. He is greeted as a king yet rides a humble colt. He is acclaimed with "Hosanna" yet does not act to save himself when he has the opportunity to do so. The crowd recognizes that his presence in Jerusalem signals "the coming kingdom of our ancestor David," yet in the final chapters of Mark his sovereignty is unrecognized by nearly everyone he encounters. These turns in the text suggest several truths: things are not always what they seem at first glance, we have a way of fooling ourselves into seeing what we want to see, that which claims our attention is sometimes least deserving of it, divine sovereignty is not determined by popular appeal, those who work for peace are often the victims of violent reprisals, and the poor are often the last to receive our attention and support. Amid the fanfare and processions that claim our attention, are we able to recognize God's strange, surprising, and subversive power at work among us?

Another approach to this text is to focus on Jesus' messianic identity as we ask, *What kind of Messiah is Jesus Christ?* He was not an elected official who won by a landslide or a simple majority, the wealthiest members of ancient society did not bankroll his campaign, he was not published, he never earned a Purple Heart or staged a successful military coup. In the last week of his life, it is clear that religious and political authorities were sufficiently threatened by him to plot his death. If not a military dictator or political hero, what kind of leader was he?

Some did have eyes to recognize Jesus for who he was, including blind Bartimaeus. In the verses immediately preceding Christ's entry into Jerusalem (10:46–52), it was Bartimaeus who called out, "Jesus, Son of David, have mercy on me!" Bartimaeus knew that at the heart of Jesus' **power** and authority is God's mercy and compassion. Jesus healed the sick, exorcised demons, fed the hungry, and welcomed strangers. Before entering Jerusalem, Jesus' many acts of mercy revealed that the **kingdom of God** had drawn near (see 1:15). If we really want to know what kind of Messiah he is, we must look past the crowds, the parade, and the accolades to see one who loved the outcast, cared for the despised, and led his followers to a cross. When we seek saviors for our nation, our churches, our schools, our children, ourselves, and our world, we would do well to remember that God's reign has less to do with military victories and political campaigns than with the will to love and serve others with compassion.

Although his power does not reside in military might or political parties, Jesus' entry into Jerusalem and his arrival at the Temple reflect both the *religious and political implications of his messianic identity.* As Messiah, his liberative mission takes on cultic and political dimensions both in the way he enters the city and what he chooses to do upon entering. According to Mark, Jesus' one and only visit to Jerusalem (cf. John's Gospel) takes place near the time of the Passover, when pilgrims to Israel remember their liberation from political oppression and celebrate their faith in God's redeeming purposes. There is no severing of religious concern from political action, since God wills the transformation of all institutions and individual lives. A change in political parties is not enough. Neither does our hope reside in religious piety or fervor alone. Jesus does not inaugurate a new system of government or establish a new religious denomination. His entry reminds us that all religious and political institutions are in need of God's transforming power as we anticipate the fullness of God's reign among us.

JESUS CURSES THE FIG TREE AND DISRUPTS THE TEMPLE (11:12–26)

Exploring the text

The day after his entry into Jerusalem, Jesus continues his messianic mission through two dramatic events. The cursing of the fig tree provides a disturbing object lesson for Jesus' confused disciples, and the disruption in the Temple signals God's will to overturn the center of Israel's religious establishment. These two prophetic actions proclaim God's judgment through Jesus' initiative. By sandwiching one event inside the other, Mark signals that the fate of the fig tree anticipates the Temple's impending demise (13:2). This technique of intercalation is prevalent throughout the Gospel (e.g., 1:21–28; 2:1–12; 5:21–43). In the eleventh chapter, Hooker recognizes a further "sandwiching" of events in the two paragraphs dealing with Jesus' identity and authority that surround the incidents of the tree and Temple (11:1–10, 27–33).[1] This additional layer links the pronouncement against the fig tree and the disruption of the Temple in 11:12–26 with Israel's failure to understand or grant authority to Jesus as the Messiah. As a whole, this section reflects increased opposition between Jesus and the religious authorities in Jerusalem as he proclaims God's reign in the Holy City.

The opening incident involving the fig tree in 11:12–14 is particularly confusing for Jesus' followers, both past and present. The Passover season in Palestine is not the time of year to expect fully ripened figs. Why would Jesus demand that the fig tree bear fruit out of season? Since he was able to provide loaves and fishes for the multitudes on other occasions, why was Jesus so frustrated with the barren fig tree? As the only negative miracle in Mark's Gospel, this startling event is troubling. Jesus appears to be unfair in his expectations and intemperate in his use of power.

One way to approach this incident is to explore other Hebrew texts with which it resonates. In Judges 9:10–11, for example, Jotham speaks parabolically of the fig tree that refuses to reign over other trees, providing a symbolic contrast to Jotham's brother, who became king and then was killed because of his unjust reign over others. The Hebrew prophets also associate figs with God's blessing and the demise of fig trees with God's judgment (e.g., Hos. 9:10; Jer. 8:13; Mic. 7:1). In the messianic age, explains Hooker, the presence of fig trees signifies peace and prosperity:

"Hope for the future is expressed in terms of sitting in security under one's vine and one's fig tree (e.g., Mic. 4.4; Zech. 3.10) and gathering fruit from them (Hag. 2.19)."[2] Mark's earliest readers would have understood that the fruitful tree was a symbol of God's abundant grace while the withered tree was a sign of God's judgment.

However, the larger significance of the cursed fig tree becomes evident in the verses immediately following. In 11:15–17, Jesus overturns the tables in the Temple and pronounces judgment on those who have turned God's house of prayer into a cave of robbers. Jesus hungered for figs on the tree but discovered it was fruitless; he longed for the fulfillment of God's reign but found corruption in the Temple. The fact that Jesus expected figs when it was not their season underscores the symbolic significance of the tree: the fig tree did not bear fruit just as the Temple did not provide holy sustenance for God's people. Jesus' curse of one implies judgment on the other.

Given the many positive demonstrations of Jesus' **power** elsewhere in Mark's Gospel, these destructive acts command our attention. What in particular provoked his anger? The narrative describes Jesus' driving out those who were selling and buying in the Temple courts, overturning the tables of moneychangers and the seats of those who sold doves. Since doves were an offering that poor people could afford and were also purchased for the purification of women and the cleansing of lepers, Jesus' actions suggest his contempt for those who are taking advantage of the poor and the least honored members of the community.[3]

Two other points are unique to Mark's account and suggest that Jesus is undertaking something far more comprehensive than simply cleansing or purifying the Temple (cf. Matt. 21:12–13; Luke 13:6–9; John 2:13–17). First, Mark alone speaks of Jesus' not allowing anyone to carry goods (a general term that may refer to vessels, cultic objects, and even weapons) through the Temple. His disruption of commerce and cultic activity cuts to the core of Temple life and indicates the depth of Jesus' intention to discontinue business as usual. Second, Mark is the only Gospel to record Jesus' speaking of God's house as a house of prayer *for all the nations* (Isa. 56:7, echoing Ps. 67). The deliberate inclusion of non-Jews is consistent with Jesus' other ministries to Gentiles in Mark's account (e.g., 5:1–20; 7:24–37). The Temple has become a den of robbers (or cave of bandits)[4] who have stolen what belongs to others while securing their own safety. According to Blount, "The house of Jewish prayer must become a house of prayer for all the nations. This is the eschatological fruit the temple-tree must bear. If it does not, if it *will* not, it will, like the fig tree, experience destruction."[5] No wonder the chief priests and scribes are threatened by

Jesus (11:18). He has denounced the Temple and caught the attention of the crowds, who are spellbound by his teaching. For the second time in Mark's account, religious leaders plot Jesus' death (cf. 3:6). At the end of their long day, Jesus and his followers leave the city (11:19).

The next morning, the fate of the fig tree is taken up again when the disciples see that it has withered away to the roots (vv. 20–21). Peter directs Jesus' attention to it, inviting his comment. In his response (vv. 22–27), Jesus does not mention the fig tree in particular but appears to focus his attention on prayer. Myers suggests that the mountain Jesus speaks of in verse 23 is a further reference to the Temple that, like the fig tree, will be destroyed.[6] But Jesus' words also point to the power of God alive among us. In speaking of prayer, faith, asking, believing, and forgiving, he connects the spiritual dispositions and disciplines of his followers with God's power available to us. It is a power that longs to engage human beings in the holy work of God's will; a power that seeks to integrate our will, our faith, and our prayerful communion with God; a power that aligns our will to forgive with God's reconciling intentions for humanity; a power that bids us to participate in God's reign through prayer and mercy toward those who offend us.

The brief portion of the Lord's Prayer that appears in verse 25 (cf. Luke 11:2–4) calls us to remember that divine forgiveness is necessarily bound up with forgiving one another. At first glance, it may seem strange that Jesus speaks of forgiveness immediately after cursing the fig tree and overturning the Temple tables. Yet these deeds and words belong together: Jesus' anger bends toward forgiveness. His most strident acts of protest are accompanied by a call to repentance and the promise of divine forgiveness. It is the simple yet supremely difficult act of forgiving those who offend us that opens the way for God's forgiveness of us. As we love those who sin against us, we make a way for God's mercy to move freely through our lives. The Temple will soon be destroyed, but God's love and mercy are available to all who participate in Christ's reign through their reconciliation with others. It is a suitable word to hear before Jesus encounters those who repeatedly challenge his authority in the next several episodes.[7]

Preaching and teaching the Word

Mark's stories of cursing the fig tree and disrupting the Temple are not included in the RCL. Instead, during the Third Sunday of Lent in Year C, we hear Luke's account of the parable of the fig tree, which concludes with an additional year's time being given to the tree so that it may bear fruit (Luke 13:1–9). John's story of Jesus overturning the tables in the Temple is listed among the readings for the Third Sunday of Lent in Year B, but it does not mention the fig tree and moves immediately to Jesus' assertion that the Temple will be destroyed in three days (John 2:13–17). Only Mark places the stories of the fig tree and Temple alongside one another, followed by his teaching on the power of God available to us in prayer.

In exploring these episodes as a complete unit, the preacher or teacher may focus on the reality of *fruitlessness and corruption among God's people.* There is a word of warning here for all religious persons, because one does not have to be a religious leader or extremist to wreak havoc on others; good, well-intentioned people of faith easily lose sight of God's purposes and are susceptible to corruption and negligence. We are capable of doing great damage to ourselves, others, and the world around us by insisting we are the only ones who know God's will. In or out of season, we are empowered by God to bear fruit and share it with others. By overturning the tables in the Temple courts, Jesus demonstrates God's frustration over the monopoly of economic privilege we claim for ourselves and our stinginess toward others. In the words of one Bible study member, the Temple leaders insisted "that doves and other offerings had to be bought at their concession stand."[8] An offertory prayer in the ministers' manual of the Church of the Brethren reads, "The fruit tree gives of its fruit, and we know it is alive. When it refuses to give, we know real life has gone out of it. The heart that hoards the blessings of God is no longer alive with spiritual power."[9] Do church budgets consume more of our congregational concern than efforts to welcome all people to worship? The sin of privileging some at the expense of others is more insidious than we realize.

Another approach to this text is to focus on *Jesus' anger.* Many of us find his behavior in these verses disturbing and enigmatic. Jesus' cursing the fig tree and Temple offends our image of Christ the gentle shepherd. However, he is revealing more than impatience or personal grief. Jesus' actions invoke God's presence and power at a place and time it was most desperately needed. These incidents urge us to consider more deeply the reasons for Jesus' outrage so that we may more fully identify those circumstances and conditions when our own anger is not only justified but necessary to disrupt business as usual. As noted above, Jesus is most concerned about matters of economic exploitation and the exclusion of persons outside our own clan, ethnic group, or economic circle. Are his concerns our concerns? What is it that we are most angry about, as individuals and communities of faith? How do we give voice and expression to our anger? What prophetic actions may rouse the attention of others and also invite God's presence and power into our midst?

Jesus *disrupts the old order and introduces a new order* of God's grace, generosity, and care for others. In calling on the fig tree to bear fruit out of season, Jesus alerts us to a state of readiness that is accountable first and foremost to God rather than our own sense of right timing or acceptability. Jesus' prophetic actions demonstrate that God calls for a new orientation to life that flies in the face of what seems right or timely to others. Thus, African Americans have sung of divine freedom and release in the midst of slavery and oppression; women preach when the Spirit calls them to do so, whether or not religious institutions ordain them; churches in poor urban contexts begin bold ministries of outreach to their neighbors. God's reign is often recognized in the startling disruption of old patterns and the inauguration of new ways of love among us.

Jesus' prophetic acts are accompanied by his teaching on the *power of God in prayer*. These verses provide an intriguing setting for exploring the meaning of prayer as both a personal and corporate practice. Theologically, we need to remind ourselves that Jesus does not call us to believe in the power of prayer but to believe in the power of God. Prayer is not a test of faith—as if the fulfillment of our prayers is an indication of the sincerity or depth of our faith. Rather, it is a way of participating in God's transforming power among us. Just as importantly, Jesus' call to prayer is a call to reconciliation. Indeed, the only condition Jesus places on our prayer is that we learn to forgive one another. What might our prayers sound like if they regularly began with our efforts to honestly forgive one another? Such vulnerability and hope is only possible when we look beyond ourselves and trust that God is the source of everyone's well-being. When we turn to God again and again in prayer, we continually open a way to receive and extend divine power, grace, and forgiveness among us.

Opposition to Jesus' Authority and His Challenge to Religious Leaders

Mark 11:27–12:44

Following Jesus' dramatic entry into Jerusalem and prophetic actions in the Temple, a series of controversial dialogues takes place between Jesus and religious leaders who challenge his authority. Similar to the cycle of controversies in 2:1–3:6, these verses communicate a sense of impending danger and the escalation of opposition to Jesus. This time, however, all of the exchanges take place within the Temple precincts. Jesus assumes a more commanding tone as he refutes chief priests, scribes, elders, Pharisees, Herodians, and Sadducees, condemning their greed and hypocrisy. By the close of chapter 12, he has defied their attempts to entrap him but fortified their resolve to destroy him.

QUESTIONS ABOUT JESUS' AUTHORITY (11:27–33)

Exploring the text

Jesus enters Jerusalem for the third day in a row. Once again he walks through the Temple (11:27) where he is approached by various Jewish leaders. It is the first in a series of five controversial exchanges in 11:27–12:44 that concern Jesus' authority. This first encounter comes the day after he overturned the tables in the Temple and just before the parable of the vineyard, both of which reveal Jesus' indictment of the Temple and its leaders. The chief priests, scribes, and elders named in these verses represent three groups that comprise the leadership of the Sanhedrin, the Jewish supreme court (see **Jewish religious leaders**). Jesus named the same three groups in 8:31, and they appear again near the close of the narrative when they are instrumental in Jesus' arrest, trial, and condemnation (14:43, 53; 15:1).

The questions raised by the priests, scribes, and elders are concerned with the authority by which Jesus speaks and acts (11:28). Having witnessed his disruption of the Temple, they feel threatened because Jesus seeks neither their approval nor their authorization. They are also aware of his popularity among the crowds who, as early as the first chapter, marvel at the extraordinary authority of Jesus' teaching (1:27; see also 2:10). It is the same authority he grants his disciples (3:15; 6:7; 13:34).

In contrast to the religious leaders who are concerned with human sources of authority, Jesus' response directs us toward the divine source of his authority (11:29–30). In good rabbinic fashion, he counters their questions with another question. By invoking the memory of John and his call to repentance and baptism, Jesus once again aligns himself with the prophetic ministry of the Baptist, whose fate foreshadowed his own (6:14–29). Just as John's authority was not recognized by religious or political leaders, so does the Sanhedrin refuse to acknowledge the source of Jesus' divine authority. Because the people supported John, the religious leaders are afraid to challenge Jesus. For all their power and authority, they are vulnerable to popular opinion.

The text allows us to overhear the chief priests, scribes, and elders arguing among themselves (11:31–32). They do not raise questions or agonize over God's authorization of Jesus' ministry. Rather, they are afraid of contradicting popular opinion. In trying to trap Jesus, they are ensnared by their own fears and need for others' approval. Jesus, however, asserts his divine authority by refusing to answer their questions. He has aligned himself with John's prophetic ministry and revealed the petty maneuverings of his opponents. More than rhetorical quickstep, Jesus confronts those who refuse to acknowledge God's presence and power at work among them.

Preaching and teaching the Word

Who or what validates our call to serve and lead others? Given the current leadership shortage in many denominations and local congregations, it may be meaningful to explore the *human and divine sources of authority* alluded to in this passage. Whether we are ordained, exploring a call to ministry, serving on a church board, recently baptized, considering what it means to be baptized, or proposing a new outreach ministry, questions of authority arise whenever we offer ourselves in service and leadership. In alluding to the baptism of John, Jesus introduces the theme of baptism into the question of authority, reminding us that there can be no more powerful sign of God's authorization of our call to Christian ministry than our baptism into the body of Jesus Christ.

Some of us err on the side of claiming too much personal authority while ignoring God's initiative in calling others. When Jesus questioned the religious leaders, he spoke a word of warning to all who question the possibility of divine authority at work among others because it differs from our own perception of God's will. Others of us err on the side of refusing to claim God's authority at work within us. We may be reticent to accept God's call because we know that others will reject us, or because doing so will upset the plans we have already made for our lives. In his book *As One with Authority: Reflective Leadership in Ministry*, Jackson Carroll describes four concepts of authority in ministry: sacramental/priestly (i.e., the office of ordination), personal piety (i.e., one's spiritual presence, prayer), certified competence (i.e., training, education) and demonstrated competence (i.e., gifts for ministry).[1] Although we may judge the value of these sources of authority differently, both divine and human sources of authorization are needed to fulfill God's call to leadership.

THE PARABLE OF VINTNERS AND VIOLENCE (12:1–12)

Exploring the text

In this disturbing and provocative parable, Jesus takes the initiative in confronting his detractors. It is the second of five confrontational exchanges recorded in 11:27–12:34 and the only one in which he uses a parable to communicate judgment against his hearers. In chapter 4 Jesus used parables while teaching the crowds about the reign of God, noting the mysterious and confounding nature of parabolic speech (4:12). On this occasion, however, Jesus' meaning is painfully clear. His opponents hear his words as judgment against them. In first-century Palestine, absentee landlords required their tenants to deliver to them shares of goods that were often difficult to transport or impossible to produce. Debts accumulated quickly among tenants who had to feed themselves, their families, and other workers while the distant landowners prospered.[1] In killing the landowner's slaves and son, the tenants not only hoped to thwart the owner's collection of goods but to eliminate his heir, since undisputed property fell to the current landholders as the rightful owners.

The parable begins with Jesus' description of a wealthy landowner who creates a new vineyard and leases it to knowledgeable vintners (12:1). The scene recalls Isaiah 5:1–6, "The Song of the Vineyard," which also mentions a fence, wine press, and tower set amid the vines. In Isaiah, the vineyard represents the people of Israel, who commit the sin of bloodshed against others and build many houses that become desolate (5:7–10). In Jesus' parable, it is not the vineyard but its caregivers who are guilty of violence and greed. The shift in focus from vines (Isa. 5) to vintners (Mark 12) suggests Jesus' indictment of laborers who have violated God's people and wrongfully laid claim to what is not theirs.

The most striking feature of the parable is the escalating violence with which the vintners respond to the landowner's representatives. The first is beaten and sent away empty-handed (12:3), the second is beaten over the head and insulted (the verb in v. 4 may also be translated "raped"), and the third is killed along with many others who are similarly abused and/or murdered (v. 5). The violence culminates in the murder of the landowner's beloved son (cf. 1:11), who suffers the greatest offense when his body is thrown out of the vineyard and denied burial (12:6–8). Just as disturbing, the violence of the tenants is fully matched by the retribution of the landlord. Jesus says the owner will return to destroy the tenants and give the vineyard to others (v. 9).

The landowner in Jesus' parable has often been understood to represent God, yet the violent response of this character stands in stark contrast to Jewish teaching and God's command of forgiveness and cancellation of debts (Lev. 25; Isa. 58; Neh. 10:31). The landowner's behavior also opposes Jesus' teaching elsewhere, including another of his parables that compares God to a creditor who forgives debts (Luke 7:41–43).[2] Thus, we must be careful not to overallegorize this parable and associate each element with only one interpretive meaning. Its larger focus is on the escalation of violence inflicted by the tenants, who were themselves victims of exploitation. Residents of first-century Palestine who heard this story would have understood the behavior of the tenants to reflect the desperate, sometimes violent, and ultimately futile attempts of the largely agrarian local population to rebel against their foreign oppressors. The Jewish leaders who heard this story clearly identified themselves with those who wrongfully claimed ownership of what was not theirs and understood the tenants' rejection of the landowner's son as referring to their rejection of Jesus (12:12). In both cases, Jesus condemns the escalation of violence perpetuated by victims and oppressors. Jesus' hearers are able to relate to the parable from varied perspectives, yet his indictment of those who perpetuate violence and claim rights over what is not theirs is evident to all who have ears to hear.

Current hearers need to be aware of the church's history of having misinterpreted and misused this text to condemn Jews and justify Gentiles as the true inheritors of God's vineyard (the "others" to whom the landowner entrusts his property in 12:29). However, this misses entirely Jesus' word of judgment against those who perpetrate violence against God's people. The quotation from Psalm 118:22–23 in Mark 12:10–11 may help us appreciate Jesus' larger frame of reference, since this psalm offers hope for the people of Israel who suffered rejection by others yet were welcomed by God. In its present context, whether the stone that is rejected refers to Jesus or God's people (or both), the reference to Psalm 118 recalls the power of God to transform despair to hope, disgrace to glory, death to life.

Preaching and teaching the Word

Jesus' parable urges us to ask, *Who is the owner of the vineyard?* Is it the tenants who have labored long and hard over its fruits? Those who provide daily oversight of its upkeep and care? A distant landowner whose initial investment called it into being? A sermon on this text could associate the vineyard in Jesus' parable with the church of today and urge us to remember that the body of Christ is not ours to possess or control. No one holds proprietary rights to the church and its ministries—no deacon, Sunday school supervisor, choir director, pastor, elder, district leader, or denominational executive. Like the religious leaders who first heard Jesus' parable, we are too easily inclined to claim ownership of what is not ours. Although we are responsible for the care of the church, we must remember that it belongs to God. No matter how many years we labor, how lightly or significantly we toil, the church is not ours to possess or relinquish but to care for and entrust to others.

Similarly, a sermon on this text could associate the vineyard with the whole of creation and urge us to reconsider *our role as stewards of God's earth.* Many of us act as though the world belongs to us or that we have authority to take from it what we will without considering the consequences. The result has been an inequitable distribution of resources and the abuse of land, water, air, and wildlife around the globe. Jesus' parable calls us to something other than this. More than tenants, we are stewards, caregivers, and farmers of what has been entrusted to us by God. In his story "A River Runs through It," Norman Maclean recounts the words of his father, a Presbyterian minister: "To him, all good things—trout as well as eternal salvation—come by grace and grace comes by art and art does not come easy."[3] As we learn to care for God's gift of creation, we will discover the difficult and beautiful art of restoring the atmosphere, forests, and endangered species with whom we share this beloved world.

This parable also speaks powerfully of *the danger of perpetuating violence.* Whether we seek vengeance against those who have wronged us, or use force to acquire what is not ours to possess, Jesus' parable teaches us that inflicting violence on others incites a never-ending cycle of cruelty. No matter how well justified our actions may seem, when neighbors seek revenge against neighbors, gang members strike back against rivals, and nations invade other nations, the result is the same: violence begets violence. There is only one way to end it, and that is to stop responding violently to others, just as Jesus Christ sought nonviolent means of engaging his enemies.

Rick Polhamus, a pastor, has served in Hebron as a member of the Christian Peacemaker Teams and was threatened at gunpoint by an Israeli soldier while trying to escort a group of Palestinian children home from school. When his cell phone rang unexpectedly in the midst of their confrontation, Rick answered it, then held the phone out to the soldier and said, "It's your mother–she wants to know what you're doing." It took the soldier a few moments to realize that it was not his mother on the line, but in the meantime Rick used the opportunity to ask the young man what he would tell his mother if she were there at that moment. The soldier released Rick so he could walk the children back to their homes.[4] Christ's way of enemy love calls us to continually explore new ways of peacemaking.

A QUESTION OF TAXES (12:13–17)

Exploring the text

Jesus' authority is put to the test once again when he is asked about paying taxes to Caesar, the third in a series of five controversies between him and **religious leaders**.[1] Having just incited the anger of the Sanhedrin with his parable of the violent vintners (12:1–12), Jesus' opponents seek to entrap him over the issue of taxation (v. 13). The poll tax was imposed by Rome in 6 CE on the residents of Judea, Samaria, and Idumea and was bitterly opposed by the population at large. The Pharisees and Herodians know that if Jesus openly opposes the tax he can be charged with sedition and arrested; if he supports the tax he will lose the approval of the crowds who have been instrumental in his survival (11:32; 12:12). It is the only occasion when the word "entrap" is used in the New Testament. At this point we have a clear sense that Jesus is a "hunted man," to use Myers's description.[2]

The Pharisees and Herodians act as interrogators, partnering with one another as they did earlier in the Gospel to plot Jesus' demise (3:6). The Pharisees resisted Roman rule and were therefore reluctant to support payment of taxes to the emperor. The Herodians were known to be loyal to the occupying regime and at least tacitly accepted the imposition of imperial taxes. Their joint efforts to ensnare Jesus reveal something of the widespread resentment against him. They begin by approaching Jesus with what appears to be a compliment, commending him for his fairness and impartiality in speaking God's truth (v. 14). However, their cordiality masks a deeper hypocrisy, which Jesus immediately recognizes (v. 15). In asking them to bring him a denarius, Jesus reveals that he does not carry Roman coins yet they presumably do. His action is not evasive but disclosive: those who are concerned with the commerce of Caesar carry his image and inscription with them while Jesus does not. When Jesus points out Caesar's image on the coin (v. 16), his hearers recall the superiority of the divine image above all others. When he draws attention to the coin's inscription "August and Divine Son," the hearers of Mark's Gospel anticipate another inscription from the time of Jesus' crucifixion–"King of the Jews" (15:26). Both the image and inscription of Caesar on the imperial coin would have been highly offensive to Jews. Jesus' questions challenge our allegiance to governments and economic systems that lay claim to our lives and loyalties.

Jesus' teaching in 12:17 forms the climax of this exchange and inspires the amazement of his hearers. His words have been interpreted in a variety of ways. Some believe that his instruction to "give [or render] to the emperor the things that are the emperor's" acknowledges the necessity of offering support to the state with our finances and other human resources. Others hear Jesus' concluding words, "and to God the things that are God's" as an admonition to remember God's ultimate claim on our lives, which overrides all other allegiances. The word "render" is used only once in Mark, but Myers convincingly argues that its appearance elsewhere in the New Testament refers to the payment of debt or recompense and is best understood as "repayment."[3] Accordingly, Jesus is urging his hearers to repay the one to whom they are indebted, and he sets before them two opposing allegiances–to the government and to God. In Mark's apocalyptic narrative, human sources of authority and power are at odds with the reign of God, and Jesus urges our allegiance to God above all other authorities.

Preaching and teaching the Word

In the complex negotiation of church-state relations, this passage affords preachers and teachers the opportunity to explore the *tensions we experience as followers of Jesus Christ and citizens of our nation.*

One way of approaching this is by *looking at the larger context of Jesus' life and ministry.* Jesus' words in 12:17 and his interactions throughout the Gospel challenge us to remember that the **reign of God** is often at odds with earthly authorities, yet we are to pursue God's will before all others. When his ministries of healing and outreach offend religious leaders, Jesus repeatedly calls God's people to give priority to God's purposes (e.g., 3:6, 33–35; 7:6–8). When his authority becomes a threat to civil rulers, Jesus refuses to deny his messianic identity and calling (15:2–5). In the series of conflicts between Jesus and various opponents in 11:27–12:44, he teaches that love of God and neighbor is the greatest commandment of all, and he clearly associates this commandment with the kingdom of God

(12:28–34). Throughout the Gospel, Jesus intends for us to place the things that are God's before the things that are Caesar's.

Another way to explore this issue is to consider the occasions when our government's policies and practices are in violation of Christ's most basic teachings. In particular, this text urges us to relate our assessment of state activities to *the question of whether or not it is lawful to pay taxes*. For example, many Christians believe that the United States has wrongfully used its economic and military power in opposing enemies around the world, and some have decided to withhold a portion of their taxes in protest. Elizabeth Boardman, a sixty-five-year-old Quaker who lives in San Francisco and opposes the U.S. wars in Iraq and Afghanistan, withheld 41 percent of her taxes in 2007, a percentage she estimates the government to be spending on the military from its total budget.[4] Ralph Dull, an Ohio farmer and member of the Church of the Brethren, was so disturbed by U. S. support of the contras in Central America that on April 15, 1982, he drove a farm truck heaped with 333 bushels of bright yellow corn to the IRS office in Dayton. He and his family have worked for generations to feed people and not finance their deaths, so Ralph offered the load of corn to the IRS commissioner in lieu of the portion of his taxes he determined would be used to fund the military. When the commissioner politely refused, Ralph sold the corn to a country elevator and had the check made out to a Food for Poland project sponsored by the National Farmers' Organization.[5] These and other acts of war tax resistance encourage us to consider anew what we owe to Caesar and what we owe to God.

A QUESTION ABOUT RESURRECTION (12:18–27)

Exploring the text

The fourth in a series of five controversies between Jesus and various **religious leaders** is instigated by a group of Sadducees who want to challenge Jesus' understanding of life after death. Unlike the Pharisees and Herodians (12:13–17), the Sadducees were members of wealthy and privileged families whose popularity was waning among the people. They were also religiously conservative, rejecting the oral traditions of the Pharisees and insisting that only the five books of Moses were authoritative. As the text plainly states, they did not believe in resurrection (v. 18).

The question they raise with Jesus is set within the context of a hypothetical situation that is absurd as well as revealing (vv. 18–23). The Sadducees recount Moses' teaching on levirate marriage in Deuteronomy 25:5–6, which outlines a man's responsibility to marry the wife of his deceased brother and raise up children with her in his brother's name. In their example, a succession of brothers die, each leaving childless the same widow. In the resurrection, the Sadducees ask, whose wife will she be (v. 23)? The scenario they sketch for Jesus is woefully revealing. They not only mock resurrection from the dead but also accept without question the notion of patriarchal authority to preserve a man's name and perpetuate inheritance among male family members. The Sadducees show no concern for the woman, who is passed along from brother to brother. With no rights or privileges of her own she also experiences the shame of barrenness.[1] They further objectify the widow by wondering who she will "belong to" in the resurrection to come.

In the most strident terms possible, Jesus refutes the scenario the Sadducees set before him. He begins and ends his refutation by declaring they are wrong (vv. 24, 27) and insists they neither know the Scriptures nor the power of God. As for knowing Scripture, Jesus quotes a phrase that is used three times in the book of Exodus to speak of God as "the God of Abraham, the God of Isaac, and the God of Jacob" (Exod. 3:6, 15, 16), who has an ongoing relationship with those who are deceased. He uses a passage from the Torah, the only Scriptures the Sadducees believed to be authoritative, to challenge their disbelief in the resurrection.[2] As for knowing the **power** of God, Jesus insists that the Sadducees are utterly ignorant. They have failed to recognize the power of God who is able to cast out demons, feed the multitudes, forgive sin, cure disease and, ultimately, overcome death itself. Indeed, God's power is such an essential part of God's being that later in the Gospel Jesus will speak of God as "the Power" beside whom the Son of Man will be seated (14:62). Because God is "God not of the dead, but of the living" (12:27), there are myriad other ways God moves, speaks, and works among us.

Thus, Jesus confronts the Sadducees by addressing their arrogance and ignorance. Their hermeneutical arrogance has led them to believe that they fully understand the teachings of Moses with no need to engage with others in the work of scriptural interpretation. At the same time, they are ignorant of God's power at work among them and blind to the ideological biases they hold in treating women as commodities. The Sadducees are more committed to the notion of patriarchal succession than they are willing to acknowledge God's power to overturn the forces of sin and death. With divine authority, Jesus challenges their ideological biases and unmasks their hermeneutical arrogance.

Preaching and teaching the Word

We may discover within this contentious encounter something strikingly familiar to our own religious quarrels. There are at least two ways to explore the relevance of this text for today.

Focusing on the Sadducees, we may find their *arrogance and ignorance more familiar than we care to admit.* The Sadducees not only assume they believe the right things, but their question to Jesus betrays a level of self-righteousness and arrogance that leaves no room for discussion. In refusing to engage respectfully with others while ignorant of their own biases, the Sadducees are uncomfortably close to our own tendencies toward arrogance and ignorance. Their behavior reminds us of the disturbing tendency among Christians to pass judgment on one another, to pit one political party against another, to draw lines of social demarcation between people while ignoring the presence and power of Christ among us. Recently, one of my students was interviewed for a pastoral position and was asked by a member of the search committee if he would describe himself as conservative, liberal, or evangelical. He wisely replied that such categories do not help us to really understand one another, and he hoped they would enter instead into genuine conversation that would open the way for them to seek the mind of Christ together. In our search for the living God, it is best not to confine ourselves to tight spaces or to back one another into corners.

Focusing on Jesus' response to the Sadducees, when Jesus declares that God is *"God not of the dead but of the living"* (12:27), we hear the good news at the heart of the gospel. Many people do not believe in resurrection from the dead, and fewer still are persuaded by biblical proof-texting or logical arguments. Yet Jesus associates God's power with Scripture as a living source of renewal and spiritual understanding. He not only refutes the scenario of patriarchal succession but rejects the Sadducees' narrow construal of the age to come. Amid the most obstinate arguments of his opponents, Jesus preaches a hopeful word that creates a bridge from this world to the next: the ancestors of our faith dwell in our midst, and God thrives among the living in unexpected and powerful ways. Like the paintings of Marc Chagall, Jesus' vision is of two worlds abiding in one colorful canvas; like the stories of Yiddish writer I. L. Peretz, Jesus' words bridge the chasm between good and evil, death and redemption. Our preaching and teaching may continue this proclamation of God alive among us.

A QUESTION OF FIRST IMPORTANCE (12:28–34)

Exploring the text

Similar to the previous two encounters, the exchange between Jesus and the scribe begins with a question. However, on this occasion the questioner does not seek to entrap Jesus and, unlike the parallel accounts in Matt. 22:34–40 and Luke 10:25–28, he does not intend to test Jesus.

Rather, the scribe raises his question in a spirit of respect and receptivity. This episode marks an important break in the series of five controversies recounted in Mark 11:27–12:44 because it is the only exchange not marked by hostility, yet it continues to assert Jesus' authority among **religious leaders**.

The scribe watched and listened carefully to the previous episode (12:28) and now raises a question that was common among the rabbis: Which of the 613 commandments of the Torah (248 positive commands and 365 prohibitions) is first and foremost? If, as Daube suggests, there is a parallel between the four questions of the Passover Haggadah and the four questions Jesus addresses in verses 14, 23, 28, and 35, then this third question raised by the scribe reflects that of the pious son who genuinely seeks understanding (see note 1 for 12:13–17, p. 283). Whether he is asking which commandment is of interpretive priority in helping us to understand all others or which is most important to fulfill before all others, the scribe's question goes to the very heart of religious faith.

Jesus' answer to the scribe's question is direct and succinct (vv. 29–31). He begins by quoting Deuteronomy 6:4–5, then recites a second command from Leviticus 19:18. His response is remarkable for several reasons. First, unlike the parallel versions in Matthew and Luke, Jesus does not turn the question back on the questioner but answers it himself. In Mark's Gospel, it is Jesus Christ who proclaims the great commandment to love God and neighbor (12:34). Second, also in contrast to Matthew and Luke, Jesus includes the opening verse of the Shema (Deut. 6:4), which announces that God is one.[1] Mark would have his hearers remember that because God is one, we are to love God with the whole of our lives. Third, we may note that Jesus not only speaks of loving God with all our heart, soul, and strength (in accordance with Deut. 6:5) but that he adds the injunction to love God with all our minds, a possible reflection of the Hellenistic value on "things of the mind."[2] Finally and perhaps most importantly, in citing Deuteronomy 6 and Leviticus 19 side by side, Jesus treats these two commands as a singular concern.[3] To be sure, he first names the command to love God, but he refuses to do so apart from the command to love our neighbors. Each command is distinct, and one cannot be reduced to or be a substitute for the other. Together they comprise the heart of faithfulness, so that religion is a matter of divine and human relationships, of personal devotion and public consequence.

The scribe agrees with Jesus and affirms his teaching (12:32–33). He addresses Jesus as "Teacher" and repeats what he has said with two subtle changes: the scribe does not mention loving God with all one's soul, and he replaces Jesus' word for "mind" (*dianoia*) with "understanding" (*suneseo*), a possible reflection of his intention to not only know God's will but to understand it as well. After this, he repeats the command to love one's neighbor as oneself. The most surprising aspect of the scribe's remark is his insistence that the twofold command to love God and neighbor is "more important than all whole burnt offerings and sacrifices" (v. 33). This is an extraordinary assertion to make so near the Temple precincts. For members of Mark's community who did not offer sacrifices according to Jewish law, writes Hooker, "the story would have been of great value, encouraging them in the belief that the real demands of God lay elsewhere."[4]

The exchange ends with Jesus' declaration that the scribe is "not far from the **kingdom of God**" (v. 34). On the one hand, he recognizes the scribe's wisdom and his search for understanding. Jesus affirms the scribe's nearness to God and does not close the door to the possibility of his fully entering God's reign. On the other hand, Jesus indicates that the scribe is not yet there. He may recognize God's truth and acknowledge Jesus' authority, but he is not yet a disciple who follows Christ's teaching and participates in God's reign. To love God and neighbor means more than believing or even understanding the right thing. It means offering the whole of our lives in service to others, as God in Christ loves us. In this way, we enter the reign of God that has already drawn near to us through the presence and power of Jesus Christ (1:15). With divine authority, Jesus proclaimed what is central to the gospel and silenced for a time those who challenged his ministry (v. 34).

Preaching and teaching the Word

The command to love God and neighbor is so important to the gospel of Jesus Christ that it is included in all three years of the RCL (the Thirtieth Sunday of Ordinary Time for Year A, the Thirty-Second Sunday of Ordinary Time for Year B, and the Fifteenth Sunday of Ordinary Time for Year C). There are several theological and practical reasons for preachers and teachers to address this passage of Scripture.

The exchange between Jesus and the scribe declares in no uncertain terms that *love is at the center of the **gospel***. It is God's first command and, according to Augustine, the key to understanding the entire biblical witness: "Whoever, therefore, thinks that he [or she] understands the divine Scriptures or any part of them so that it does not build the double love of God and of our neighbor does not understand it at all."[5] When Rabbi Hillel (first century CE) was approached by a potential convert to Judaism, the Gentile insisted that Hillel teach him the whole Torah in the time that he could stand on one foot. Hillel replied, "What is hateful to you, do not do to your neighbor. That is the whole Torah; the rest is commentary. Go and study it."[6]

Yet few of us do. We know less about love than we think. We wrongly assume we know what love means or how to express love without help from God and the biblical witness. With love as the focus of a sermon or lesson, we may explore *our misunderstandings of love* and how we often confuse love with romantic feelings, unconscious regard for others, or sexual attraction. We may even find it offensive that God commands love, because we generally consider love to be an unconscious response over which we have little or no control. But Jesus reminds us that love is a matter of conviction, reflection, and behavior. To love God with all our heart, soul, mind, and strength is to love as Christ loves: we are to consciously commit our wills (the biblical understanding of the heart), our ultimate concerns and being (soul), our thoughts (including questions and intellectual pursuits), and our strength (both physical activity and other material resources) to God even as we give ourselves in loving service to neighbors.

With love at the center of the gospel, we may also speak of *the priority of love in our daily living.* When Jesus repeats the love command, he does not highlight the extraordinary nature of love but calls us to infuse every ordinary facet of our lives with love. It is tempting (and perhaps easier) to recognize extraordinary examples of love embodied by such heroes of faith as Martin Luther King Jr. or Mother Teresa. Yet these persons understood the necessity of the seemingly minor or insignificant acts of service that contribute to God's greater good among us. That is what Mother Teresa meant when she said, "It is not how much we do but how much love we put in the doing—a lifelong sharing of love with others" that matters.[7] In this way, by keeping love at the heart of every conversation with our children, every purchase we make, every dish we wash, every piece of garbage we recycle, every song we sing, every gathering we attend, every message we compose, every meal we partake, and every worship service we attend, we fulfill God's first command by embodying God's love in every facet of our lives.

We may also preach and teach about *love as it relates to the nearness of God's reign.* Whenever we love God and neighbor, we are near God's reign, and where there is love, there is the reign of God. Jesus proclaimed the nearness of God's kingdom immediately after his baptism and testing in the wilderness (1:15). Now in the twelfth chapter he speaks again of the nearness of God's reign but at a very different place in his ministry—just before his death on a cross. His words are filled with the authority of one who has inaugurated a new era and whose life bears witness to the fullness of love for God and neighbor. As for the scribe, he is near to God's reign but has not yet fully entered it because it is not enough to know, acknowledge, or understand God's will. We must also participate in the reign of God by living as Christ lived and loving as Christ loved, with our whole being.

JESUS' QUESTION ABOUT THE MESSIAH (12:35–37)

Exploring the text

After silencing those who oppose him (12:34), Jesus now poses a question about messianic leadership to the crowd. It is the last in a series of controversies and questions that reveal his authority as God's son while highlighting particularly Jewish concerns. Like all the other episodes in this section, it takes place in the Temple precincts (v. 35).

Jesus begins with what appears to be an academic question, and in good rabbinic fashion he points to an apparent contradiction in Scripture. Since the Messiah must be David's son (that is, his biological descendant), how can David also call him "my Lord" (see Ps. 110:1)? Jesus' argument was perhaps clearer to first-century hearers. At that time, **Messiah** (literally, "anointed one") was a designation for the coming Davidic king, and **Son of David** was a designation for the much-anticipated offspring of David who would resume his reign and sit on his throne. In the aftermath of Jesus' resurrection, Mark's community would have understood that the exalted Lord refers to Jesus Christ, who is of Davidic lineage and also sits at the right hand of God. Later in the Gospel Jesus speaks of sitting at God's right hand when he addresses the high priest (14:62) and is subsequently crucified as "King of the Jews" (15:26). The implication is that through his crucifixion and resurrection, the exalted Lord Jesus Christ reigns over heaven and earth.

Jesus closes with a question that challenges his listeners to consider the nature of messianic leadership (12:37). It is not ancestral honor, ethnic purity, or political maneuvering that ensures a place on the royal throne, but divine command. By the inspiration of the Holy Spirit (v. 36), David declared the lordship of one who would be called forth by God to assume messianic authority. By the power of the Holy Spirit, Jesus Christ was raised from the dead so that his enemies, the powers of sin and death, were vanquished through him. Although this passage does not openly name Jesus' messianic identity, it anticipates his lordship in the events to come. The large crowd marvels at his teaching, undoubtedly aggravating the religious leaders who fear Jesus' popularity.

Preaching and teaching the Word

This brief passage inspires reflection on two key themes in Mark's Gospel. First, we hear in these verses an implicit *assertion of the lordship of*

Jesus Christ. Throughout his ministry, Jesus has proclaimed God's reign, refuted his opponents, displayed God's power, and taught his followers the way of discipleship. As he nears crucifixion, he boldly addresses the question of messianic leadership, based not only upon Davidic lineage but divine command. "The Lord" alone determines who will be exalted to the right hand of God, since human considerations of Davidic progeny and political popularity will not suffice.[1] Jesus is the Christ because he is God's beloved son, and the powers of sin and death are overcome through his death and resurrection.[2]

Second, the designation "Lord" carries with it *political overtones*. The term *kurios* suggests not only divine sovereignty but was used as a title for the emperor.[3] Thus, to proclaim Jesus as Lord is to suggest that the emperor does not hold ultimate authority or power. Jesus is not proposing theocracy or imperialistic visions. In fact, says Myers, Jesus' argument "attacks the popular assumption that messianic politics necessarily affirms the myth of a restored Davidic kingdom."[4] The questions he raises urge us to raise a few questions of our own about political authority and its claim on our lives: To whom do we pledge our allegiance? How does obedience to God's rule compete or conflict with the claims of our nation and its governing authorities? Those who follow the crucified and risen Christ not only acknowledge his sovereignty but continually seek to participate in his transforming work amid the principalities and powers of this world.

TEACHING ABOUT SCRIBES AND WIDOWS (12:38–44)

Exploring the text

Two character "types" are set in opposition to one another in these verses. The scribes are portrayed as ostentatious and self-serving, while the widow moves quietly through the Temple to deposit her meager but generous offering in the treasury. Both character types are spoken of in Hebrew Scriptures that condemn the superficial piety of **religious leaders** (Isa. 3:13–15; 29:13–14, cited by Jesus in Mark 7:6–7; Mic. 6) and advocate care for widows and orphans (Isa. 1:17; Jer. 7:6; Zech. 7:10; Mal. 3:5). They are intentionally laid side by side in purposeful contrast.

Their placement in the larger sequence of Mark's narrative is also significant. Following Jesus' teaching about loving God and neighbor and his implicit assertion of messianic authority in 12:28–37, and immediately before he predicts the Temple's downfall in 13:1–2, his teaching about the scribes and the widow provides a critique of two of the Temple's most egregious offenses: religious hypocrisy and economic exploitation of the poor. In particular, 12:38–40 cites several specific sins of the scribes: they walk around in ornate apparel and pray at length in public so that they may draw attention to themselves, they seek greetings of respect in the marketplace, they long for the best seats in the synagogues and places of honor at banquets. The latter two offenses appear to have been socially approved, since scribes were given seats in front of the Torah box in the synagogue and, writes Witherington, "it was considered good form to have such persons at one's banquets."[1] The overall impression we have is that the scribes sought out situations of social deference and privilege without regard for the well-being of those around them (cf. Sir. 38:34–39:11). The peculiar phrase "they devour widows' houses" (12:40) may refer to their serving as trustees or guardians of widows' estates and taking more than their share as payment for their services.[2]

The widow differs from the scribes in two essential ways. First, while they seek recognition and respect, she goes about largely unnoticed by others. Jesus must point her out to his disciples (12:43–44). Since widows were not allowed to manage the estate of their deceased husbands, they were wholly dependent on either the support of their children or the charity of others. Second, she is described as poor yet gives fully of her meager resources to the Temple. She deposits two *leptos*, valued at less than a penny. The contrast between her giving and that of wealthy persons is noted twice in Mark's account (vv. 42 and 43–44). In verse 44, the widow's circumstance is underscored by three parallel statements recounting "her poverty," giving "everything" she had, and "all she had to live on."

Many have characterized the widow as a model of Christian charity and beneficence. However, the context of these verses suggests another interpretation. Jesus' condemnation of the Temple throughout chapter 12 and his prophecy of its destruction in 13:1–2 suggest a critical view of the Temple and the toll it has exacted on the poor. Elsewhere in Mark's account, Jesus has demonstrated concern for the poor and issued warnings to the rich (e.g., 10:17–27), but nowhere more forcefully than here. In the harshest terms possible, he condemns persons whose piety and practices render them dangerously unaware of and unresponsive to the plight of others.

Preaching and teaching the Word

Jesus' teaching about the scribes and widow appears in the RCL during the Thirty-Second Sunday of Ordinary Time in Year B. Jesus employs some of his most passionate rhetoric in condemning religious leaders and institutionalized practices that contribute to the widow's poverty.

A sermon on *religious hypocrisy and economic exploitation* may be more challenging to compose than we might at first imagine. The scribal sins outlined in 12:38–40 do not necessarily translate easily into our own time and place (e.g., long religious robes are not generally worn in public today). Yet most of us are painfully aware of the public downfall of several well-known Christian leaders. Closer to home, there are subtle and insidious forms of insincerity and exploitation that infiltrate our lives and congregations as well. For example, rather than making a show of our prestige and formality as the scribes did, our Sunday morning worship services may make a show of our *informality* in worship style and portray this as a sign of our particular closeness and familiarity with God. In his book *Welcoming the Stranger*, Patrick Keifert critiques the culture of intimacy that has arisen across North America. When worship leaders become performers who coerce a sense of false familiarity with God and their congregants, they risk ignoring the sacred "otherness" of God and neighbor.[3]

Economic oppression also arises in our attitudes and institutional behaviors. Congregations are easily preoccupied with building funds and readily neglect the support of outreach ministries. We tend to be more welcoming of rich and middle-class persons than others who visit our churches. Often without realizing it, we condone and promulgate economic exploitation through our negative appraisal of the poor. For example, in his book *Do No Harm: Social Sin and Christian Responsibility*, Stephen Ray argues that by participating in discourse that depicts some members of society as "welfare queens" (caricatured as lazy and sexually irresponsible), we distract "the larger society from the reality of enforced localization of poverty and long-term, systemic economic exclusion and social marginalization."[4] The lure of power, prestige, and possessions is great, not only in the world around us but also within us and the religious communities we inhabit.

Finally, we need to make note of *Jesus' admiration and respect for the widow amid the exploitative forces* that surround her. Here as elsewhere we detect Jesus' reverence for women, of his affirming their gifts while being aware of the forces that oppress them (e.g., 5:12–43; 14:3–9). The widow deserves our respect—not because she is poor or even because she is generous but because Jesus notices her. He recognizes her poverty as well as her generosity but does not excuse the one for the sake of the other. Her dignity and generosity mitigate against a portrait of victimization. Jesus honors her even as he criticizes the Temple and its leaders who contributed to the worsening of the widow's condition.

Jesus' Discourse on the End of the Age: Keep Alert and Awake

Mark 13:1–37

Preaching and teaching from the thirteenth chapter of Mark is not for the faint of heart. There are enough end-time catastrophes, global disasters, public trials, familial betrayals, warnings of persecution and darkened heavens to make even the sturdiest soul quiver. Yet these disturbing images and peculiar pictures seep into our imaginations until we are every bit as fascinated as we are fearful of Jesus' **apocalyptic** discourse.

Mark 13 includes many of the themes and images recurrent in ancient Judean apocalyptic literature: Jesus foretells important events, he envisions the end of the world (the *eschaton*) amid cosmic catastrophe, and he speaks of divine intervention in resolving the crisis of oppressive imperial rule. However, chapter 13 also differs from conventional understandings of apocalyptic literature on several counts: the one who sees into the future is not a hero of the past who is told to keep the vision secret "until the time of the end" (cf. Dan. 12:4); Jesus' discourse is not offered at the close of the Gospel but before the account of his trials and crucifixion; and most importantly, this chapter does not simply describe future events but promises the fulfillment of events already underway. The sayings and parables included in Mark 13 were likely compiled during or near the time of the siege of Jerusalem (66–70 CE), revealing God's decisive activity in the midst of horrendous circumstances. Adding to the drama are some apparent contradictions in this chapter, such as Jesus' describing events that indicate the coming of the **Son of Man** and then his insistence that the time of his arrival will be entirely unexpected. In light of Jesus' impending death in chapters 14–15, chapter 13 anticipates that the empty tomb does not mark the close of Jesus' ministry but heralds the beginning of a new ministry among his followers.[1] This extended discourse alerts us to a state of watchfulness and wakefulness in anticipation of the coming Son of Man.

BEWARE! (13:1–23)

Exploring the text

We encounter some of Jesus' most disturbing announcements in the opening verses of chapter 13. In the preceding chapters, Jesus has several confrontations with various religious leaders in the Temple (11:27–12:40), and he issues an indictment against those who exploit impoverished widows (12:41–44). The Temple has been at the center of Jesus' attention since his arrival in Jerusalem in chapter 11, and his indictment of it comes to a head at the beginning of chapter 13.

In departing the Temple precincts, one of his disciples remarks on the size of the stones and buildings (13:1). This comment is not surprising since, according to the first-century historian Josephus, the Temple was a magnificent structure whose enormous white stones were as large as 25 by 8 by 12 cubits.[1] More surprising is Jesus' prediction of its destruction (v. 2). One would not expect the Temple to be destroyed quickly, yet in 70 CE Roman legions attacked its underlying supports in such a way that the entire structure collapsed and many of its stones were crushed. Later in the Gospel, we hear Jesus' opponents falsely accuse him of saying he would destroy the Temple himself and in three days "build another, not made with human hands" (14:58).

After his prophetic announcement, we hear that Jesus is seated on the Mount of Olives located opposite the Temple and east of Jerusalem (13:3). This geographical detail bears theological significance, as we can envision Jesus positioning himself in opposition to the structures of power he has come to transform. While seated there, Jesus speaks to his disciples of events that bear significant implications for the people of Israel and their oppressors, the Romans.[2] Only Peter, James, John, and Andrew are named (cf. 1:16–20), and their questions in 13:4 provide the impetus for Jesus' extended comments. They want to know *what signs* will accompany the destruction of the Temple foretold by Jesus in 13:2 and *when* this will occur.

Jesus' lengthy response to their questions is neither simple nor direct (see **apocalyptic**). Remembering his abrupt dismissal of the Pharisees when they asked for a sign from heaven in 8:11–12, we should not be surprised by his response here. In the three segments of his extended discourse (13:5–8, 9–13, 14–23), Jesus relates what is known and unknown about future events and alerts his disciples to a state of watchfulness for the coming of the Son of Man.

In verses 5–8, Jesus names the first item of concern for his followers: those who will come in his name to lead them astray. The phrase "to lead astray" echoes warnings against false prophets in Deuteronomy 13. Although many will say, "I am he," they will be false messiahs. This phrase (*egō eimi*) also occurs in Jesus' claim to messianic status in 14:62. False prophets and messiahs are mentioned again in 13:21–22 when Jesus repeats his warning to be on the lookout for pretenders. Verses 5, 9, 23, and 33 repeat the imperatives "beware" or "be alert" as Jesus admonishes the disciples to keep their eyes open at all times.

Next, Jesus lists a series of calamities that are sure to arise in the time to come (vv. 7–8). The appearance of these does not necessarily guarantee the imminent end of the world, but he insists that wars and rumors of wars will persist–as they have throughout the centuries. Although Jesus says these things "must take place," we have no reason to believe that Jesus is saying war is due to a divine plan more than human greed, pride, or caprice, since these have certainly led people to war more often than a supposed divine decree. War "must" occur only because humankind has determined that it be so and has succumbed to evil forces and violent urges. Jesus does not want his followers to be surprised by war and its interminable violence, and neither does he want them to get caught up in believing that armed combat will ultimately put an end to oppression or injustice. God alone determines when the end will be (vv. 32–33).

Jesus also foretells earthquakes and famines. Although famines are often caused by the ravages of war, they may also be due to drought and other natural causes. Similarly, earthquakes are due to conditions over which we have little or no control. Yet these natural disasters can prove every bit as deadly as war. According to Jesus, events like these signal the beginning of "birthpangs," suggesting that the wars and disasters we experience are signs that something new is about to emerge among us.[3]

In verses 9–13 Jesus moves from global events to interpersonal ones. Three themes are interwoven throughout these verses: persecution, preaching, and the promises of God. He begins with the expectation that his followers will be handed over (*paradosousin*) to local Jewish councils where they will stand trial. Those who are found guilty can expect beatings in the synagogues (see 2 Cor. 11:24). The fact that Jesus begins by mentioning interreligious disputes before civil ones is not incidental, since in-house differences can be more difficult for the accused than the condemnation they receive from outsiders. However, his disciples' problems do not end with synagogue officials. They will also be handed over to governors and kings, civil and political legates who will hear their testimony and render their judgment. In verse 12 Jesus warns that their own family members will hand them over to religious and civil authorities. Like Jesus, many of his followers will be betrayed by loved ones, handed over for trial, bear public testimony, endure much suffering, and be put to death.

In the midst of persecution and betrayal, Jesus teaches that the trials the disciples endure will provide opportunities for them to testify before others. The legal term "testimony" in verse 9 (*marturion*) is the basis for our word "martyr," or "witness." In addition to providing testimonial implications, these verses also affirm the evangelistic mission of Jesus' followers. Three times in verse 11 Jesus refers to the disciples' speaking to others and assures them that the Holy Spirit will give them the words they need at the opportune moment. Although verse 10 feels like an interruption between verses 9 and 11, it highlights the theme of **proclaiming** the good news in the midst of persecution.[4] This verse has often been interpreted to mean that the end of time will be delayed until the good news has been preached to all people. However, Juel hears embedded in verse 10 a promise: "The gospel *will* be preached. Persecutions will not silence the preachers. . . . This is not a command but a declaration of what God will make possible."[5] Amid the gruesome reality of persecution and hardship, Jesus promises that the gospel will be preached to all, the Holy Spirit will give us words to speak in the midst of tribulation, and our endurance will be blessed with the gift of salvation.

In verses 14–23 Mark issues some of the Gospel's most alarming words of warning to those who endure suffering. Three points are worth noting. First, the "desolating sacrilege" mentioned in verse 14 (spoken of in Dan. 12:11) most likely refers to Titus, the Roman general who stood in the Holy of Holies when the Temple was captured by imperial forces in the war of 66–70 CE.[6] The parenthetical comment, "let the reader understand," suggests that this reference is already understood by Mark's listeners or is capable of being decoded by them. Second, Mark's advice to flee the city speaks of the extreme conditions described in these verses. Normally, cities were places of refuge in times of battle. Similarly, Jews looked to the Temple as God's dwelling place and a sanctuary in times of trouble. But that is not the case during the reign of terror described here. As Horsley notes, the images and motifs used throughout this section—wars, famines, "desolating sacrilege," fleeing to the mountains without retrieving necessary provisions, brutal military violence against women and children, false messiahs and prophets—"pertain to the Roman imperial military practices in the conquest and terrorizing intimidation of subject peoples, or the response of the subject peoples in popular resistance and renewal movements."[7] These conditions were painfully familiar to a people forcibly dominated by the Romans.

Finally, amid these apocalyptic references, the emphasis in Mark's narrative is on the powerful manifestations of **God's reign** already present.

From Jesus' opening declaration (1:15) to his binding the powers of Satan (e.g., 1:25; 5:1–20) and showing God's healing and reconciling purposes among all people (e.g., 7:24–30; 8:1–10), "Mark portrays vindication as already accomplished in Jesus."[8] God has already judged the powers and principalities as corrupt and evil, and the renewal of God's people is occurring even now. Our task, according to Jesus, is to remember what he has already told us and keep alert to the power of God among us (13:23).

Preaching and teaching the Word

The RCL separates the end of chapter 12 and the beginning of chapter 13 between the Thirty-Second and Thirty-Third Sundays of Ordinary Time in Year B. Yet in Mark's narrative arrangement, the events of chapter 12 are closely related to Jesus' announcement at the beginning of chapter 13. God judges both individuals and religious institutions that ignore the needs of others while seeking their own social and economic advantage.

The sense of urgency and the terrifying conditions described in 13:1–23 suggest several different approaches to these verses. First, confronted with Jesus' predictions of war and suffering, we may preach and teach about the *differences between the destructive powers of Rome and the transformative* **power** *of God.* Rome dominated the Mediterranean world, often subjecting indigenous and dislocated people to military occupation, unfair levels of taxation, religious censure, and social oppression. Rome is also representative of countless other imperial and religious regimes through the centuries who have sought power over others. In his book *The Word before the Powers,* Charles Campbell argues that the powers and principalities spoken of in the New Testament are corrupted by sin and evil, seeking to dominate others by controlling them. "Both the powers' need to survive and their quest for domination find their ultimate expression in *violence,* which takes systemic as well as interpersonal forms and involves psychological and spiritual, as well as physical, dimensions."[9] When Jesus positioned himself across from the Temple on the Mount of Olives, his opposition to the Temple complex was evident in the location he occupied—just as Martin Luther King Jr. positioned himself on the steps of the Lincoln Memorial, across from the U.S. Capitol, when he delivered his speech "I Have a Dream." Both men knew the powers they opposed and called others to participate in God's transforming work among them.

Following the bloodiest century in recorded history, we need more than ever to distinguish between the powers that drive us toward domination and destruction, and God's power that seeks the well-being of all creation. The various expressions of violence Jesus foretells in 13:5–23 are not ordained by God but are the consequence of human sin and our submission to evil forces that seek to advance their own material gain, political agenda, and/or sphere of influence. In contrast to this, the power of Jesus Christ reveals God's reconciling intentions for humanity: his presence seeks to empower God's people to care for those in need, and his cross and resurrection assure us of God's redemptive purposes beyond the violent tactics of oppressive regimes. The gospel urges us not to excuse cruelty as a necessary means of accomplishing some higher good. For example, during World War II, the residents of the rural community of Le Chambon in southern France decided to provide sanctuary for a few thousand Jewish refugees despite great personal risk to themselves. "Following their consciences meant refusing to hate or kill any human being," writes Philip Hallie, "and in this lies their deepest difference from the other aspects of World War II. Human life was too precious to them to be taken for any reason, glorious and vast though that reason might be."[10]

Second, we may approach this text by focusing on verses 9–13 and *the importance of testifying to our faith in Jesus Christ*. Mark uses several words for the verbal expression of faith, including *testimony, proclamation, speaking,* and *witnessing.* However, the context of these verses is quite specific. Jesus describes a courtroom where Christians must testify to their faith under fierce scrutiny and the threat of punishment and/or death. For some Christians, their witness to Christ occurs in courts of law and their practice of faith leads to hardship and oppression.[11] Christians who are visited by IRS agents and asked to defend the basis of their war tax resistance know what it means to speak of their faith while under scrutiny or duress. So do Christian youth who are conscientious objectors to war and must respond to zealous military recruiters at their local high school.

However, for most North American Christians, the greatest resistance we encounter is within ourselves. We are intimidated, embarrassed, or not quite sure how to speak of our faith. Mark 13:9–13 can help us remember the source of our hope: Jesus promises that the Spirit will be present to guide our speech amid difficult circumstances. These verses also recall the reality of faith's costliness: we will meet resistance from family members, friends, neighbors, religious leaders, and political institutions. Whatever our circumstances, Jesus urges us to speak the truth of our faith to one another. In his book *Testimony: Talking Ourselves into Being Christian,* Long recognizes that Christians speak about their faith not simply to evangelize others but because "Christians believe we cannot tell the truth, not the whole truth, without talking about God, and if we cannot tell the whole truth, we cannot be fully alive as human beings."[12]

Third, we may preach about the *parallels between what Jesus foretells of his disciples' experiences and what he himself will encounter in the next two chapters.*

His disciples will be betrayed, handed over to the authorities and bear testimony, just as Jesus will be betrayed, handed over to the Sanhedrin and Pontius Pilate, and will proclaim his lordship (14:62). The disciples will suffer persecution and death; Jesus will be beaten and crucified. Those who endure will be saved; Jesus is obedient unto death and resurrected by God. This entire section as well as 16:1–8 propel us beyond the ending of Jesus' story to anticipate the church's future ministry. Birthpangs and suffering will arise, but they are precursors to new life in the reign of God.

Finally, a fourth approach to these verses is to focus on the several instances when *Jesus commands his followers to "beware" or "be alert."* This imperative appears three times in verses 13:5, 9, and 23, and once again in verse 33, when it is accompanied by the command to "keep awake" (also repeated in vv. 35 and 37). Jesus calls his followers to a level of alertness and anticipation not practiced by others, and his prophecies and promises are evident to those who watch carefully and keep alert to what is happening around them. Before going out on a date, my grandmother would warn, "Keep your eyes wide open." When I asked her what I should be looking for, she simply shook her head and said, "You'll know when you see it." Jesus never fully answered his disciples' opening questions about when the Temple would be destroyed and what would happen at that time. But he was confident that what he had already told them would guide their way in the time to come (v. 23).

BE AWAKE! (13:24–37)

Exploring the text

In the second half of chapter 13, Jesus' discourse moves from earthly catastrophes to cosmic events. At the end of the age, the skies will darken, heaven will be shaken, and the **Son of Man** will come in **power** and glory (vv. 24–27). These dramatic images are followed by two parables that alert us to the nearness of God's reign (vv. 28–31) and the need to keep watch as we await the return of the Son of Man (vv. 32–37). Jesus urges the disciples to remain awake so they do not miss the events unfolding before them.

In verses 24–27 Jesus draws on the poetry of Israel's prophets to describe cosmic events of terrible beauty. Images of darkened sun, moon, and stars signal the end of the age (Isa. 13:10; Ezek. 32:7–8; Joel 2:10, 31; 3:15). The order of the cosmos is disrupted, and human history will no longer mark its progress by the turn of seasons and the moon's cycles. What could be more terrifying than the demise of the sun, the disappearance of the moon, and the scattering of stars like quickened fireworks? Yet the passing of these lights signals the rise of a far greater light. The Son of Man will appear in the clouds, radiating the power and glory of God (Dan. 7:13). The one who is known in the Celtic tradition as both "Son of the sun" and "Son of the moon" will bring light to all creation.[1]

Remarkably, Mark does not associate the coming of the Son of Man with God's vengeance. Following natural disasters, persecution, familial betrayals, and the horrors of imperial violence (13:5–23), the coming of the Son of Man heralds a new era of redemption that extends to the farthest reaches of the world. The Gospel emphasizes "the positive effects of Jesus' return" as the Son of Man sends forth messengers to traverse heaven and earth, gathering God's elect and redeeming God's people.[2] In Mark's context, the Son of Man is none other than Jesus Christ (see 2:10, 28; 8:31, 38; 9:9, 31; 10:33, 45; 14:21, 41).[3] The strong man who bound Satan (3:27) and cast out his legions (5:1–20) is the one who will descend from the throne of the Power (14:62). Before they decipher the events to come, the disciples need to know the one they are looking for, who will come in power and glory to redeem God's people.

Jesus' description of the Son of Man is immediately followed by two **parables**. In 13:28–31 he describes a fig tree as he teaches his followers about the nearness of **God's reign**. In 11:12–21, he cursed a fig tree for its fruitlessness, symbolizing the corruption of the Temple and its impending destruction. Here the tree exemplifies the promise of new life; it puts forth leaves and signals the season of fruitfulness. It is less clear what Jesus may be referring to when he insists that the green tree reminds us "that *he* is near, at the very gates." The Greek verb is not accompanied by a subject, and the phrase may be translated equally well as "*it* is near."[4] Jesus could be speaking here of the Son of Man, or he could be referring to the Temple and its destruction, a topic of great concern in chapters 11–13. However, given Mark's interest in the reign of God throughout Jesus' ministry, he is likely to be speaking of God's reign (see 1:15) or of God's reign accompanied by the coming Son of Man who will herald its fulfillment upon his return. The resemblance to 9:1 in 13:30–31 further supports this possibility.

More problematic is Jesus' assertion that "this generation will not pass away until all these things have taken place" (13:30). Which things? Did Jesus mistakenly believe that the end of the world was imminent, as Schweitzer and others have argued? If indeed Jesus expected God's reign to be fully manifest in his lifetime, then he and his followers have great reason to despair. But Jesus' words reach beyond the present age in expectation for the age to come. He often told the disciples that his death and resurrection were quite near and that they would soon bear witness to these things (8:31; 9:31; 10:33–34). But he also prepared them for a future in which they would be confident in the fulfillment of God's purposes as they continued his ministry and anticipated the culmination of his death-defeating power on earth. Until that time, they could trust his words would not pass away but were more enduring than heaven and earth itself (13:31).

The second parable in 13:32–37 provides a surprising contrast to the first. Whereas the previous parable suggests we may discern the time of Christ's coming as clearly as we recognize the arrival of spring, the second insists we cannot know the day or hour when the Son of Man will return. Jesus' words provide a powerful corrective to our efforts to calculate God's timing or presume God's will: if divine messengers and the Son of Man do not know the time when he will return, who are we to claim special insight or knowledge? Although Jesus does not disparage the disciples' desire to know the timetable of final events (13:4ff.), in this closing parable he redirects their zeal and calls them to "keep awake."

This striking admonition, "keep awake," is repeated by Jesus no less than three times (vv. 33, 35, 37). It is easy to understand Jesus' urging his followers to beware of false leaders (v. 22), to remain faithful and endure suffering for the sake of the gospel (vv. 9–13). But why tell them to keep awake? This final parable in Mark's Gospel shifts our attention away from the problem of endurance to one of vigilance. Here the challenge is not enemies from without but complacency within. According to Juel, "The disciples' problem is not that they are discouraged or unable to endure in the face of pressure but that they are utterly unprepared. . . . The risk is not that they will lose heart in the face of persecution but that they will drift off, oblivious to the dangers and possibilities that lie ahead."[5] Having heard them argue over places of privilege and power, Jesus knows the disciples have no idea what is expected of them (10:35–40), and he urges them to remain alert and awake for what is to come.

It is also striking that the setting of Jesus' final parable is a household whose master has gone on a journey, leaving the slaves in charge (cf. 3:23–27; 10:28–31; 12:1–11). The household depicted here is remarkably stable and well ordered, presided over by capable servants who are given particular but unspecified tasks. Only one is identified; the doorkeeper. The keeper must be loyal, steadfast, and perceptive—or at least awake enough to recognize who is coming at any hour of the day or night. Hooker notes that the four watches mentioned in 13:35 are suggestive of upcoming events: evening (the Last Supper), midnight (the garden and Jesus' arrest), cockcrow (Peter's denial), and early morning (meeting the Sanhedrin and the trial before Pilate).[6] In the next chapter Jesus' follow-

ers fail miserably at the task of staying awake; while Jesus prays at Gethsemane, Peter, James, and John fall fast asleep not once but three times
(14:32–42). Yet our sympathy may well be roused when we remember our
own sluggishness in responding to Christ's teaching. What Jesus said to
his first disciples he intends for all: "Keep awake" (13:37).

Preaching and teaching the Word

Mark 13:24–37 is listed as the Gospel reading for the First Sunday of
Advent in Year B of the RCL. The lectionary assumes *an alignment between
the birth of Jesus Christ and the coming Son of Man* prophesied in verses 24–27.
Although the two events are separated by time, the same person fulfills
them as the church anticipates Christ's return in the age to come.
Throughout the Gospel of Mark, Jesus is portrayed as the Son of Man so
that we **proclaim** the one who came to announce the good news of God's
reign (1:15) as the one who will see to its fulfillment (13:27). What may be
more surprising to many Sunday morning worshipers is the noticeably
brief description of the Son of Man's return. Mark is not interested in the
manner or time of his arrival, but the whole of the Gospel draws our attention to Jesus' ministry, his proclamation of God's reign in word and deed,
and the cross that leads to newness of life. Also, Mark's vision of the coming Son of Man is not one of wrath and judgment. Instead, Christ's coming is overwhelmingly good news. Jesus states clearly and succinctly the
twofold promise of the Son of Man's coming in power and glory (13:26).
Because of his divine power, the universe will be reordered according to
God's purposes. Because of his divine glory, all of heaven and earth will
make way for his presence. If as one member of our Bible study noted,
"Mark 13 is the movie trailer for the big apocalypse to come,"[7] then verses
24–27 assure us of the end of human suffering and God's determination
to gather together those who have been scattered abroad.

The images of darkened sun and moon in 13:24–27 also provide an
opportunity to explore *the differences between the cosmic changes foretold in
13:24–27 and environmental disasters caused by human greed and abuse.* These
verses describe a radical reordering of the cosmos; they are a vivid
reminder that the entire universe belongs to God and even the laws of
physics are subject to a power greater than their own. The symbolism of
darkened sun and moon highlights the unparalleled brilliance of the coming Son of Man. Through him, all humankind, its institutions, and the
world will be utterly transformed. At the same time, the disruptions foretold in Mark 13 remind us of the vulnerability of our own corner of the cosmos. The earth and its resources may appear fiercely resilient, but they are
also frighteningly vulnerable. In recent decades, the documented rise of
carbon dioxide levels due to human-generated pollution has contributed

greatly to global warming as well as the increased number of hurricanes and tornadoes around the world.[8] The melting of polar ice caps and the clear-cutting of rain forests have also resulted in the extinction of countless plants and animals. The fate of nature is indissolubly linked to our own, and Jesus' love of nature, its fig trees, seeds, and stars encourages our own care for these gifts of life.

Most obvious of all, this text admonishes us to *look out for the coming of God's reign* (see "Preaching and teaching the Word" for 13:1–23, p. 224). As one Bible study member observed, "This whole chapter jars you awake!"[9] Through prophetic images and poetic artistry, Jesus disrupts our benign indifference to the fate of the world, awakening us to both the perils and possibilities of the future. He addresses those who have become lethargic, who take the gospel for granted, or who no longer expect the fulfillment of God's just and loving reign.

For many people in the pews, apocalyptic literature strains credibility. It also stretches our imaginations to see what we would otherwise ignore. The escalation of violence at home and around the world has rendered us numb to the cruel realities of which we are a part; the material success we have attained has dulled our perception of others' needs. But Jesus' parable of the doorkeeper commands our attention and alerts us to the sorrow and joy of awaiting God's reign. In his Pulitzer Prize–winning play *Death of a Salesman,* Arthur Miller portrays the last twenty-four hours of Willy Loman's life and the conflict he endures between his personal needs and the American Dream. In witnessing his demise, we realize that Willy's fate is every bit as important as that of other, more acclaimed persons; his struggle to attain professional success and familial respect amid an ever changing world is somehow bound up with our own. As Linda Loman says of her troubled and beloved husband, "Attention must be paid to such a person." Attention must be paid. Keep awake. Look out. We are nearing the cross and the empty tomb.

Trials and Crucifixion

Although time slows down in the final chapters of Mark's Gospel, events race toward their inevitable conclusion. Within three days, Jesus is anointed by an unnamed woman, betrayed by Judas, shares a last supper with his disciples, prays in agony at Gethsemane, faces trial before the Sanhedrin, and is denied by Peter, tried by Pilate, humiliated, and crucified. Scholars have debated the exact timetable of Mark's account (i.e., whether the events described take place over a two- or three-day period), but the narrative makes clear that Jesus' ordeal takes place during the time of Passover—a time of commemoration and anticipation of freedom. Many betray him and nearly all abandon him, but in contrast to these are stories of women who come to anoint him in recognition of his death (14:3–9; 16:1–4). Their acts of devotion provide a striking contrast to the disciples and various power-holders who forsake Christ and conspire to kill him.

The RCL includes significant portions of chapters 14 and 15 as a single reading for the Sixth Sunday of Lent in Year B. Mark's passion narrative is, as Myers and his coauthors insist, "an intensely political drama, filled with conspiratorial back-room deals and covert actions, judicial manipulation and prisoner exchanges, torture and summary execution."[1] The theme of betrayal permeates these verses, as do many instances of abandonment, false testimony, fear and faithlessness. Yet there is also a profound sense of purposefulness to Jesus' actions. He moves steadfastly toward the cross, proving that God's power manifests itself in the divine will to fulfill the law of charity for all people despite the costliness of self-giving.

ACTS OF DEVOTION AND BETRAYAL (14:1–11)

Exploring the text

In 14:1 we hear that the events to follow take place during the time of preparation for the Passover and the Feast of Unleavened Bread. These

231

two religious holidays were combined into one event as vast numbers of Jewish pilgrims traveled to Jerusalem to celebrate Israel's freedom from bondage in Egypt and to anticipate a time of redemption yet to come. The political and religious implications of the season are unmistakable: just as God empowered Moses to lead the people through slavery to freedom, so did Israel anticipate God's anointed one to lead them to victory over the forces of evil.

The chapter begins by focusing our attention on the plot to kill Jesus by leaders of his own religious community. The **chief priests** and **scribes** resent Jesus' popularity among the people and, fearing the reaction of the crowd, conspire to kill him at a time other than the festival. It is the fourth instance in the Gospel when we hear of such a plot (see also 3:6; 11:18; 12:12). But on this occasion Judas joins the coalition, determined to betray Jesus into the hands of his enemies (14:10–11). He arranges to hand over Jesus by stealth, under cover of darkness and away from public view, so that even during the festival the crowds will not oppose them (vv. 43–45). The religious leaders are undoubtedly pleased to have one of Jesus' closest followers participate in his arrest, and they promise to give him money in exchange for his assistance (v. 11).

The story of subterfuge and betrayal on the part of the chief priests, scribes, and Judas is abruptly interrupted by a very different story of devotion on the part of an unnamed woman (vv. 3–9). While Jesus is reclining at dinner in the home of Simon the leper (who is presumably healed of his affliction), a woman enters and anoints him with expensive nard. Her intrusion into the company of men is shocking as she breaks open a jar of ointment valued at a year's wages and pours it on Jesus' head.[1] Her gesture appears both extravagant and absurd. In breaking open the jar, she signals her intention of lavishing all of its contents on Jesus; in pouring it on his head, she functions as a prophet ordained by God for the task of anointing God's chosen one—a role not thought to belong to a woman (see 1 Sam. 10:1; 16:1–13).

Several in attendance complain to one another and scold the woman for giving to Jesus what could have been given to the poor (14:4–5). But Jesus rebukes their miserly spirits. In a verse that is often misunderstood and misapplied (v. 7), Jesus explains they will have ample opportunity to give to the poor and that her good and beautiful service to him is entirely appropriate. She recognizes his impending death and anoints him for burial, whereas they neither recognize his messianic purposes nor the imperative of long-term ministry to the poor they are called to fulfill. Myers and his coauthors suggest that Jesus' comment in verse 7 is not a statement about the inevitability of poverty but of the social location of the discipleship church called to ministry among the poor: "You will always be among the poor and can do the right thing for them at any time."[2]

Although the ritual of anointing may signify any number of meanings (e.g., healing, welcoming an honored guest, kingship, messianic status), Jesus gives the definitive interpretation of the woman's behavior: she has prepared him for burial (v. 8). She alone recognizes his impending death and responds with compassion. Unlike Judas, her actions are performed openly, she does not gain financially but gives generously to Jesus, and her behavior reveals genuine devotion in contrast to the duplicity of Judas's kiss (v. 44). Above all, her actions proclaim his death and presage the good news to come. Jesus honors her by calling us to remember her and to proclaim the good news of what she has done (v. 11).

Preaching and teaching the Word

On its own or as part of an extended reading (14:1–15:47 is designated for Passion Sunday of Year B in the RCL), 14:1–11 reveals some of Mark's most powerful themes.

The stories of Judas's betrayal and the woman's devotion compel us to ask *what it means to be faithful to God and one another.* What is it that constitutes betrayal of God? How do we best demonstrate our devotion? We do not know why Judas betrayed Jesus; the Gospel does not specify his motivations but directs our attention to how he betrayed him and the terrible consequences of his actions. Intuitively, we know that the worst betrayals are caused by those who know us and love us: colleagues, lovers, family members, and friends. A sermon related to the themes of betrayal and devotion may explore the differences between Judas and the unnamed woman, including his acts of subterfuge and her willingness to risk rejection and humiliation from others (experiences that Jesus himself suffers). Complicating our understanding of betrayal, women who hear this story may recognize that Judas is not the only betrayer depicted in these verses: the woman who anointed Jesus was a traitor in the eyes of those who scorned her. She had forsaken their expectations and standards, choosing to offer her prophetic witness and pastoral ministrations while they rejected her gifts and presence. Later, Jesus will also experience rejection when religious leaders believe he proved himself a traitor to their agenda and befriended those whom they despised (see "Preaching and teaching the Word" for 14:53–15:20, p. 246). Just as Jesus is the messiah others do not want to see, the woman is faithful in ways others cannot recognize.

Women are both powerful and empowering in Mark's portrayal of the good news. A sermon that names the unspoken but essential role of women in the ongoing ministry of Jesus Christ will proclaim the **power** of the **gospel** through these vital witnesses of faith. The story of Judas is probably more widely known and more frequently recounted than that of the woman who anointed Christ. Yet like Jesus, there are many women who empower those who are powerless and care for those who are rejected. Just as the woman who anointed Jesus with oil proclaimed his death and embodied the gospel, myriad women around the world have confronted the hardships before them with hope, thoughtfulness, and energy. It is not entirely surprising that the misunderstanding shown toward the woman in this story arises alongside *Jesus' comment about the poor, which is also frequently misunderstood* and in need of careful attention, as we have seen. In his collection of photographs and brief profiles of ordinary women in developing countries–Afghanistan, Bangladesh, Ecuador, and Ethiopia among others–Phil Borges portrays women who have broken through barriers of oppression and convention to help transform the communities of which they are a part, often at great risk and cost to themselves.[3] We do not often hear their voices, but like the woman who anoints Jesus, their stories await our telling. And their persistence in overcoming obstacles of poverty in a world of plenty provides a sobering reminder of the church's ongoing need to position itself among the poor. The woman who anointed Jesus did what she could. What can we do?

A SACRED SUPPER (14:12–25)

Exploring the text

The story of Jesus' last supper is one of the most meaningful and, as the church's history has proven, most divisive texts in all of Scripture. During the Passover meal, surrounded by his closest friends, Jesus is aware that one of his disciples will betray him, yet he proclaims new life in God's kingdom. Jesus' suffering has already begun as he shares his last meal with **disciples** who still do not recognize his messianic mission among them.

All three Synoptic Gospels record Jesus' final meal on the eve of Passover, whereas John depicts the Last Supper on the day before Passover (when the lamb is slaughtered). However, Mark's chronology in 14:12 is particularly confusing, since "the first day of Unleavened Bread" is the fifteenth of Nissan (when the Passover meal is eaten) and the day "when the Passover lamb is slaughtered" is the fourteenth.[1] Whatever way we account for the timing of these events, it is clear that Jesus' last supper with his disciples occurred in the context of the Passover meal. As Blount argues, "The Passover was first and foremost a commemoration of the Exodus intervention" of God.[2] During the first century, "the Passover sacrifice did not have an expiatory significance. As its traditional origins directed, the meal commemorates the redemption of the people from socio-historical slavery rather than sin."[3] Similarly, Jesus' last supper both commemorates and anticipates liberation from hostile authorities and evil powers. The context of the Passover season urges us to set our consideration of redemption and forgiveness within the context of God's sociopolitical liberation and Christ's passion for those who suffer unjustly.

In 14:13–16 Jesus is prescient in describing what his disciples will encounter as they prepare the Passover meal. These verses closely parallel 11:2–7 in which Jesus sends forth two disciples to prepare his entry into the city of Jerusalem. On both occasions, Jesus' prophetic powers reveal a remarkable capacity to foresee the future while embracing the fate that awaits him. Several details pique our curiosity: it is odd that a man is seen carrying a jar of water, since men carried water in leather bottles and women more often used jars; the size of the room and the fact that it was furnished (literally "strewn," perhaps with lounging pillows) suggest that the accommodations were conceived for the purposes of this very gathering.

During the meal in 14:17–21, the text focuses on Jesus' prediction that one of his closest followers will betray him. Given his detailed knowledge of upcoming events in verses 13–16, it seems likely that Jesus knows which of the twelve will hand him over, yet he neither identifies nor expels the sinner from their midst. His disciples, however, appear surprised and distressed at Jesus' announcement. Their question ("Surely, not I?") anticipates a negative response yet reveals considerable self-doubt and recrimination. It is hardly surprising when less than a day later all of them betray or abandon him. Highlighting the pathos of his betrayal, Jesus notes in verse 20 that one with whom he shares the bread (a gesture of friendship and intimacy) will hand him over (see Ps. 41:9). Jesus' statement in verse 21 is also quite startling. Although his betrayer will fulfill what has been predicted, this in no way exonerates his behavior. God's radical freedom to transform evil to good and to determine the course of mercy does not mean that we are no longer responsible for our thoughts, words, and deeds. Human freedom must never be exercised at the expense of others, and Judas will suffer the consequences of his betrayal.

Verses 22–25 mark a decisive turn in the conversation. While they are still eating, Jesus pauses to take bread and wine in hand, speaking words of blessing as he offers these gifts to his disciples. His actions recall the Passover Seder when unleavened bread and several cups of wine are shared in commemoration of the exodus. The fourfold action of taking, blessing, breaking, and giving informs the manner in which Christians participate in the Lord's Supper. Most extraordinary, however, is what Jesus chooses not to say. As Witherington notes, Jesus does not focus on the traditional elements of lamb or bitter herbs but chooses instead to reinterpret the elements of bread and wine in terms of his own body and blood.[4] He reimagines God's covenant through his own life and death. Whereas Luke describes participation in the meal as an act of remembrance (22:19) and Matthew speaks of the forgiveness of sins (26:20), Mark says nothing of these. Instead, we are compelled to listen anew to previous references to bread and cups throughout Mark's narrative. In particular, the bread Jesus gives to Jews and Gentiles earlier in the Gospel demonstrates Christ's boundary-breaking ministry to all people (6:34–44 and 8:1–9); his references to the cup associate it with his suffering (14:36) and that of his disciples (10:39). Those who proclaim **God's reign** and reach out in compassion to all people will suffer betrayal, rejection, and abuse. But Jesus promises that the cup of sorrow will not be the last we drink. A new cup awaits us in the kingdom of God.

Preaching and teaching the Word

There is a very real sense in which every meal is sacred: every time we gather with loved ones and guests to break bread and sip wine, there is reason to thank God. Yet the last meal Jesus shared with his closest followers is different. It anticipates his death while intimating new life in the kingdom of God. The elements of bread and wine invite us to participate in Christ's suffering, death, and newness of life.

Obviously, this text lends itself well to a service of *worship that includes the rite of communion.* Yet we must be careful what we say about this event. Terrible misunderstandings and divisions have arisen in the church because of differing interpretations of this key moment in Christ's ministry. Ironically and tragically, a meal that was intended to challenge, comfort, unify and define the followers of Jesus Christ has become a source of contention and division among us. A sermon that focuses on Mark 14:12–25 may *respect the multiplicity of meanings attributed to this event (e.g., remembrance, forgiveness of sins, servanthood, messianic banquet) while delving more deeply into Mark's passion account.* In particular, Christ's suffering and death, the brokenness of his body, and the cup of sorrow he shares with his disciples anticipate the newness of life promised to us in God's kingdom. Two worlds collide in the bread and cup. Those who proclaim the good news of God's boundary-breaking power are sure to encounter suffering, betrayal, and even death. (For ideas related to the theme of betrayal, see "Preaching and teaching the Word" for 14:1–11, p. 233.) But the liberating power of God is at work amid human suffering and injustice to overcome evil and transform death to life.

Another approach to this text is to explore the bread and cup as a means of **proclaiming** *the* **gospel** *to a world that hungers for that which satis-*

fies and thirsts for that which is true. Many in the world hunger and thirst for a well-balanced meal. Our celebration of the Lord's Supper must never forget this reality as we prepare loaves and cups to share beyond our churchly tables. Others have tasted the hard bread of affliction and the bitter water of adversity and need to know God's justice in this moment, in this world (Isa. 30:20; 49:25–26). Still others have eaten plenty but discovered that they have spent money for that which is not bread and have labored for that which does not satisfy (Isa. 55:1–2). It is Jesus Christ who is needed above all else. The second verse of John B. Foley's hymn "O Let All Who Thirst" speaks to this deepest need: "And let all who seek, let them come to the water. And let all who have nothing, let them come to the Lord: without money, without strife; why should you spend your life, except for the Lord?"[5] How can we, like the Lord we love and serve, be the bread of his body and the blood of his covenant for others? How can we, remembering the way Jesus included even Judas at the Last Supper, open wide the arms of the church to share the table with all who need Christ's forgiveness and freedom?

FALLING AWAY, FALLING ASLEEP, AND JESUS' ARREST (14:26–52)

Exploring the text

In 14:26, the Passover meal draws to a close with the traditional singing of hymns (probably the Hallel psalms of praise and thanksgiving, Ps. 114/115–118). Immediately following this, Jesus and his disciples go out to the Mount of Olives, located on the east side of Jerusalem and opposite the Temple (see 13:3). Three scenes follow in swift succession: Jesus predicts his followers' desertion and denial (14:27–31), he asks them to stay awake with him during his agony at Gethsemane (vv. 32–42), and he is arrested in the middle of the night (vv. 43–52). The plot leading to his death unfolds with alarming predictability.

In the first scene, verses 27–31, Jesus confronts the twelve with predictions of betrayal. He begins by saying they will become "deserters" (literally, "you will become scandalized"). The Greek word (based on the verb *skandalizō*) implies more complex and weighty motives than cowardice. It may be translated "you will fall away" (NIV) or "you will all lose faith" (REB), and it also occurs in the parable of the sower, seeds, and soil (4:17), when Jesus' neighbors take offense at him (6:3), and when he warns his followers not to cause "one of these little ones to stumble" (9:42–47). The quote from Zechariah 13:7 fortifies our sense of the inevitability of what is to happen and reveals Jesus' awareness that God's purposes are realized through these events (see also 14:49, "in fulfillment of the scriptures"). It also resonates with Ezekiel's shepherd parable that promises a regathering of the scattered sheep (Ezek. 34:11–16, 23–24).[1]

In the midst of Jesus' predictions of desertion there is a word of hope (14:28). Jesus insists that he will be raised from the dead and go before his disciples to Galilee. Although some scholars have argued that this verse is a later interpolation by the narrator, it is certainly consistent with earlier predictions of Jesus' death and resurrection (8:31; 9:31; 10:33–34). More importantly, there can be no doubt of the significance of this promise for the whole of Mark's Gospel. Jesus will be raised from the dead and go ahead of his disciples to Galilee, the place where his ministry began, where most of his teaching, miracles, and other deeds of compassion occurred and where the messenger at the empty tomb directs the disciples to go in fulfillment of what Jesus told them (16:7).

Peter, however, does not respond to Jesus' promise of hope but focuses instead on the prediction of betrayal. He insists that even if all others desert Jesus, he will not (14:29). In response, Jesus shares another prediction: before the cock crows twice, Peter will not only desert him but deny him (v. 30)–an even greater act of treachery that involves witnessing falsely against him (vv. 66–72). Like Peter, the others insist they would rather die than deny Jesus (see **disciples**). The pathos of the situation is acute, since his followers have become increasingly quarrelsome, often ignoring and misunderstanding Jesus' impending death (e.g., 10:32–45). Peter will not only deny him three times but fall asleep three times while Jesus prays in agony at Gethsemane. Others bear false testimony against Jesus (14:56), but the betrayal and desertion of his closest friends is surely a far greater blow.

A second scene commences in verse 32 when Jesus leads his disciples to Gethsemane (meaning "oil press"), probably an olive orchard on the Mount of Olives. He asks them to keep vigil for him while he prays. On two other occasions Jesus sought a place of solitude to pray (1:35; 6:46), and all three prayerful interludes occur during the night. Now as he nears death, Jesus leaves the group behind and takes with him Peter, James, and John. These three are given special notice elsewhere in the Gospel and represent the core of Jesus' followers (5:37; 9:2), with Peter as their frequent spokesman (8:29, 32–33; 9:5; 10:28; 11:21; 14:29). In great agitation and distress, Jesus tells the three that he is deeply grieved, even to death. It is an extraordinary expression of vulnerability and angst as Jesus admits his fear to his disciples and friends. On the eve of his death, we glimpse Jesus trembling as the cruelty of his fate and the inevitability of suffering bear down upon him. All that he asks is that his closest companions stay awake with him in his time of need.

Going ahead of the three, Jesus throws himself on the ground and prays that the hour might pass from him and his cup be removed (14:35). He knows that the hour of his death is drawing near (cf. 13:32) and that he is about to drink from the cup of suffering (see 10:35–40; 14:23–25). When he addresses God as "Abba" ("Daddy" or "Papa"), Jesus expresses great intimacy. But the most remarkable profession he makes is his faith in the **power** of God: "for you, all things are possible" (14:36). Jesus confesses God's radical freedom to exercise divine power as God wills. Unlike his followers, he fully submits to God and prays, "Not what I want, but what you want." He resolves to be obedient to God, even unto death.

His disciples are not as faithful. Jesus returns from prayer to find Peter, James, and John asleep, having failed in their ministry of presence to him (v. 37). Jesus admonishes Peter for not staying awake even one hour (literally, "Were you not *strong* enough?")[2] and urges the three to pray that they not come to the time of trial (vv. 37–38). The phrase is reminiscent of the Lord's Prayer, as is the form of address Jesus uses (Abba/Father) and his petition that God's will be done (see Matt. 6:9–13; Luke 11:2–4). Witherington argues that the saying about the spirit being willing but the flesh being weak refers not to the human spirit but the Holy Spirit, who is literally eager and ready (see Isa. 31:3; Ps. 51:11–12).[3] The second time Jesus catches them sleeping, Peter, James, and John do not know how to respond (14:40). Three times Jesus asks them to stay awake, and three times they fail him, paralleling the three times he speaks of staying awake in 13:32–37. His frustration is palpable when he commands the disciples to get up and get going since his betrayer is at hand (14:42).

While Jesus is still speaking, the third scene commences as Judas arrives with an armed crowd sent by the Sanhedrin (v. 43). He is again identified as "one of the twelve," signaling his place among Jesus' closest followers (see v. 10). Judas's betrayal takes a particularly perverse turn when we hear he has conspired to identify Jesus with a kiss. Although it was customary for students to greet rabbis in this manner, there is bitter irony in Judas's greeting. An expression of friendship and respect is used to betray one who is faithful and loving to the end. The fact that Jesus needs to be singled out implies that he was not known by the mob that came to arrest him.

The crowd brandishes swords and wooden clubs for their late night ambush, inspiring violence in an unidentified bystander (v. 47). The man cuts off the ear of the high priest's slave but Jesus does not comment on the actions of the attacker (cf. Luke 22:51; Matt. 26:52–54). Instead, he openly condemns the entire operation that provoked this act of violence (14:48–49). As Myers notes, the whole scene "reeks of the overkill so typical of covert state action against civilian dissidents. The secret signal, the surprise attack at night, and of course the heavily armed contingent all imply that the authorities expected armed resistance."[4] Earlier Jesus spoke of the authorities turning the Temple into a den of bandits (11:17); now it appears they are treating him as a bandit even though he is unarmed and they could have approached him during the day while he was teaching in the Temple. Jesus interprets their actions in accordance with Scripture (14:49; also vv. 21, 27).

Amid the flurry of activity, the disciples run away (v. 50). Despite their earlier pledge of loyalty, they flee in the presence of the armed mob. More surprising is "a certain young man" who is neither identified by Mark nor mentioned in the other Gospels (vv. 51–52). Wearing only a linen cloth, he is apprehended by the crowd but manages to slip away while they cling to his meager covering. This enigmatic tale is so peculiar as to appear comic: why would Mark include such a strange story? Myers suggests that two words appearing only here and later in the Gospel provide us with clues: a linen cloth (*sindona*) is again spoken of when Joseph of Arimathea wraps Jesus in a burial shroud (15:46) and a young man (*neaniskos*) also appears at the tomb to speak with the women (16:5).[5] In other words, 14:51–52 offers subtle intimations of events to come—of the shame of nakedness and desertion redeemed by one who wears a linen burial cloth and of a young messenger at the empty tomb who bears the good news of Christ's resurrection. Amid the hopelessness of his arrest, we may recall Jesus' promise and challenge to the disciples to meet him in Galilee (14:28; 16:7).

Preaching and teaching the Word

The *theme of betrayal* weaves its way through the closing chapters of Mark's Gospel with ever greater urgency. The "Preaching and teaching the Word" sections throughout 14:1–15:47 explore several different facets of betrayal. Here, a consideration of 14:26–52 focuses on the role of Peter, the disciples, and Judas in particular. As we have seen, the word "deserters" is based on the verb *skandalizō*, or "scandalize," which carries more complex and weighty connotations than cowardice alone. It is remarkable that the same night Jesus' disciples pledge their undying loyalty to him, they flee him—demonstrating the human capacity and, indeed, proclivity to fall short of what love requires of us. The particular betrayals of Peter and Judas confirm what we already know: we are able to hurt most intensely and be hurt most severely by those we love most dearly. There is no greater vulnerability than loving one another. Although Mark says nothing about Judas's motivations, his willful initiative in betraying Jesus is particularly contemptible. As one member of our Markan Bible study observed, in Dante's *Inferno* the worst punishment in hell is reserved for

Judas.[6] Along with Brutus and Cassius, Satan feasts continually on these three, who proved traitors to those whom they had promised to serve.

Judas's kiss also provides us with a provocative symbol for one of Scripture's most intriguing and disturbing moments. It represents the worst possible hypocrisy—closer to the "kiss of death" than a public gesture of respect and friendship. The early church adopted the holy kiss as a ritual means of greeting one another (e.g., Rom. 16:16; 1 Pet. 5:14), but recent scandals of sexual abuse by priests and pastors have perverted this most tender gesture of affection. Contrary to the lyrics of "As Time Goes By," a kiss is never just a kiss. It may be a universal practice, but it is always particular in its meaning. What are the ways we signify our loyalty to God and one another? What signs of hypocrisy do we recognize or perpetuate?

Jesus' time at Gethsemane also inspires us to consider anew *the nature of prayer.* In the context of Jesus' agony, prayer is a matter of *lament.* Jesus is openly agitated, literally throwing himself before God and giving voice to his deepest fears. His prayer is offered in the spirit of the psalms, nearly two-thirds of which are laments that express pain and overcome the isolation of the one who brings his or her suffering to God. Prayer is a matter of *staying awake.* Jesus intends for his followers to be alert and pay attention to God. The wakefulness that he calls for is not frenetic or anxious; it is anticipatory, God-directed, peaceful, and alert. In the final stanza of his poem "A Ritual to Read to Each Other," William Stafford writes, "For it is important that awake people be awake, or a breaking line may discourage them back to sleep; the signals we give—yes or no, or maybe—should be clear; the darkness around us is deep."[7] In this way, prayer is also a means of *accompanying others.* In prayer, we keep vigil, watch diligently, and hold carefully the needs of friends and neighbors, strangers and enemies.

Jesus' way of prayer also *recalls the **power** of God and inclines us toward the will of God.* His prayer is God-centered, not self-oriented. Jesus' request that the cup of suffering pass from him is prefaced by an affirmation of God's power and followed by an acknowledgment of God's freedom to do as God will.[8] Jesus' time at Gethsemane serves to *fortify and empower* him to be faithful to God. Hare writes, "By staying awake and praying, Jesus has been prepared for his hour of trial. By sleeping, Peter has lost the opportunity of securing God's help at his time of testing."[9]

TRIALS AND TORMENT (14:53–15:20)

Exploring the text

The two trials Jesus endures, first before the Sanhedrin and then Pilate, bear strong resemblance to one another while highlighting several key themes in Mark's Gospel (betrayal, testimony, and the identity of Jesus Christ). Whether they are trials in the sense of "due process," however, strains our credulity since Mark underscores the gross miscarriage of justice at several points along the way. Sandwiched between these two accounts is the story of Peter's threefold denial. This wrenching tale is also depicted in a trial-like manner, with Peter interrogated by servants and avoiding indictment by denying any association with Jesus.

The first trial, in 14:53–65, unfolds in several stages. In verses 53–54, Jesus is led by armed escort to the high priest and the assembly of **priests, elders,** and **scribes** who comprise the Sanhedrin. We also hear that Peter hovers at a distance, making one last courageous effort to follow Jesus. As he warms himself by the fire, Peter's presence in the courtyard of the high priest suggests that the questioning he undergoes is simultaneous with Jesus' interrogation. Judging from first-century Jewish judicial procedures (as noted in the Mishnah, codified in the middle of the second century CE), Mark's account of Jesus' trial before the Sanhedrin challenges our confidence in its authenticity for several reasons: (1) it takes place during a Jewish holiday (when the court should not be in session), (2) the trial is held at night with sentencing immediately following (whereas a full night is supposed to pass between the time of trial and sentencing), and (3) the proceedings do not begin with testimony for the defense but statements by Jesus' accusers. These historical implausibilities, however, are countered by Mark's consistent portrayal of Jesus' opponents. They are more than willing to circumvent fair procedures in their zeal to condemn him.

In verses 55–59 we learn that members of the council were looking for persons to bear testimony against Jesus but could find none. Before the trial began, the council had already decided he was guilty and wanted to put him to death. The proceedings are a sham from the outset. The few testimonies the council could muster contradicted one another and were therefore inadmissible, since at least two witnesses must agree to sustain charges against the accused (Deut. 19:15). The word "testimony" (*marturia*) arises five times in these verses and recalls Jesus' teaching about bearing testimony in court when his disciples are handed over to the authorities (13:9). It also draws our attention to a central theme announced at the outset of Jesus' ministry–**proclaiming** the **reign of God** (1:14–15). It is because of his proclamation of God's reign in word and deed that religious leaders opposed Jesus' earlier ministry and ultimately forced him to stand trial before them (e.g., 3:1–6, 22; 7:1–7; 8:11). The only false charge recorded by Mark is a misquotation of Jesus by his accusers: "I will destroy this Temple that is made with hands, and in three days I will build another, not made with hands" (14:58). Jesus did not claim he would tear down the Temple himself (see 13:2), yet ironically, the council is correct in perceiving him a threat. According to Witherington, Jesus will indeed replace the Temple "with his own resurrection body and the fellowship united to it, a building made without human hands."[1]

In verses 60–64 we sense the mounting frustration of the high priest as he confronts Jesus with a series of questions: "Have you no answer? What is it that they testify against you?" Jesus is silent, forcing the high priest to spell out the accusation against him. The high priest's next question is not only a direct challenge but forms the basis of the church's later confession that Jesus is the **Messiah,** the **Son of God**/the Blessed One.[2] Although the high priest avoids speaking the word "God" by using the ascription "Blessed One" (thus scrupulously avoiding the appearance of blasphemy), ironically, he has rightly identified Jesus–just as Pilate will in the next chapter (15:2).

Jesus' response amounts to nothing less than a declaration of his lordship (14:62). Quoting a combination of Psalm 110:1 and Daniel 7:13, he announces that they will see the **Son of Man** seated at the right hand of **Power** and coming with the clouds of heaven (cf. 13:26). Jesus' words are a direct challenge to the high priest and an announcement of God's indictment of him. The Power whose reign is manifest through preaching good news, exorcising demons, teaching compassion, feeding multitudes, and healing diseases inhabits the throne of grace and judgment. When the high priest hears this assertion of divine authority, he tears his clothes (a gesture of judicial outrage specified in the Mishnah) and accuses Jesus of blasphemy. Yet another irony is that Jesus has declared blasphemous anyone who denies God's Spirit (3:29), and the high priest has by implication denied the Spirit's working in Jesus.[3] When the high priest invites others to join in his judgment, the entire council condemns Jesus to death.[4]

Finally, verse 65 rounds off Mark's account of the trial with a harrowing description of Jesus' torment at the hands of his accusers. Some who are present beat and spit on him, just as the soldiers do after Jesus' second trial (15:16–20; see also Isa. 53:3–12). He is also blindfolded and asked to prophesy and identify his tormentors–a cruel test of Jesus' divine powers. Ironically, one of Jesus' prophecies is coming to pass in the courtyard below.

Mark recounts the story of Peter's betrayal in 14:66–72 between the two accounts of Jesus' trials. As noted above, this episode has something of a trial-like atmosphere, as Peter is questioned twice by a servant girl then once more by several bystanders. That we are meant to consider the interrogation of Peter alongside that of Jesus is evident in verse 54 when we hear that Peter followed Jesus at a distance and waited in the courtyard while Jesus faced his accusers inside. Although the servant girl and bystanders appear much less threatening than the high priest and Sanhedrin, her persistent questions and menacing glare prove every bit as indicting and penetrating.

The tension mounts with each exchange as Peter twice denies any knowledge of Jesus. Then, when the bystanders detect his northern accent and accuse him of being one of Jesus' Galilean followers, Peter curses and swears an oath that he does not know what they are talking about. Immediately, the cock crows for the second time and Jesus' prediction is fulfilled (v. 30). The contrast between the two men is acute. Whereas Jesus proves faithful to the end and is obedient to God's will, Peter refuses to even acknowledge Jesus and is so fearful of what will happen that he reneges on his promise to him. It's little wonder that Peter's despair is devastating. As the scene closes, Peter throws himself on the ground and weeps. But all is not lost: we hear of Peter once more in the Gospel when the messenger at the empty tomb names him among Jesus' disciples who are to meet the risen Christ in Galilee (16:7).

The second trial, in 15:1–20, picks up immediately where the first trial left off. Whether Mark is describing a new meeting of the Sanhedrin or the continuation of the old, we hear that they are gathered at dawn to continue their plot against Jesus. Having determined that he is a criminal, they bind him, lead him away, and hand him over to Pilate. The verb "hand over" (*paradidomi*) occurs nineteen times in Mark and three times in this passage alone (vv. 1, 10, 15). In nearly all these instances it refers to "a turning over that leads to suffering" and is most often translated "betrayal."[5] The one whose hands brought healing and blessing to others suffers cruelly at the hands of his betrayers.

Whereas the chief priest accuses Jesus of sedition and blasphemy, Pilate accuses him of treason. Normally, the Romans were not interested in religious disputes and messianic claimants unless they asserted dominion over some portion of the Roman Empire. In asking Jesus if he is "King of the Jews," Pilate recognizes the political implications of Jesus' rule and questions him about a possible capital offense. Yet the pitiful man who stands before him appears without supporters or weapons of any kind. Jesus responds to Pilate's question by pointing back to the title just attributed to him–King of the Jews. Like the chief priest, Pilate has unwittingly named Jesus' rightful identity. In yet another demonstration of Markan irony, those who do not believe in Christ's rule bear testimony to it (see also vv. 9, 18, 26, and 32). Whatever other charges the religious authorities level against him (v. 3), none surpass Jesus' being identified as the Messiah and King of Israel.

There are several parallels between Jesus' two trials, as noted by Myers.[6] Both the high priest and Pilate ask questions about Jesus' identity, both unwittingly call him by his rightful titles, Jesus is silent or refuses to reply at least once when each of his interrogators presses him, and at the end of each session Jesus' accusers stand ready to hand him over for execution. The high priest asks the council for a verdict (14:64); Pilate consults the crowd for their direction (15:6–15). There is no doubt that both the high priest and Pilate are complicit in his death.

The long-standing history of "blaming the Jews" for Jesus' death is simply not sustained by the text. Not only is Jesus found guilty by both religious and political authorities, but all his disciples and the crowds abandon him as well. We have no reason to believe that Pilate's attempt to make Jesus defend himself is an indication of fairness or favor; his actions are in keeping with judicial protocol for a public hearing, and his questions are pro forma and succinct. Similarly, when Pilate raises the possibility of Jesus' release with the crowd, it is entirely possible that he does so only to infuriate the Jews, whom he perceives are jealous of Jesus' popularity. The writings of Philo and Josephus testify to Pilate's ruthless, violent, and inflexible governance, and Mark gives us no reason to doubt this assessment of the Roman procurator.[7] Most importantly, Pilate's complicity in Jesus' death is fully realized in the torturous outcome of his interrogation: it is Pilate who ultimately hands Jesus over to be crucified.

The crowd's role in the proceedings is also significant (15:6–14). Although there is scant extracanonical evidence that civil magistrates regularly offered the release of prisoners during holy days, it may well have enhanced their popularity among the masses to do so. Ironically, the crowd is not interested in releasing Jesus, who is falsely accused of sedition, but Barabbas, who is a known insurrectionist in league with murderers. They call for Barabbas's release and twice shout for Jesus to be crucified. Throughout Mark's Gospel the crowds have proven fickle. They greeted Jesus with accolades when he entered Jerusalem, but a few days later call for his death. The crowd is easily manipulated by those who benefit from Jesus' demise and does not ask questions or pause to consider the consequences of what they are doing. Instead, the miscarriage of justice committed by religious and political leaders is compounded by the crowd, who acts as an accomplice to Jesus' execution. As standard procedure in capital cases, Jesus was likely flogged with a leather whip studded with bits of bone and metal (v. 15).[8] This was an excruciating experience that sometimes resulted in the prisoner's death and perhaps contributed to Jesus' relatively quick death on the cross.

Following this, Jesus is led into the governor's courtyard to be tortured and humiliated, just as he was after his trial with the Sanhedrin. All the soldiers on duty witness and contribute to Jesus' suffering as he is spat upon and beaten. In addition, several symbolic acts bear testimony to what Myers calls "the irreconcilable hostility between Jesus and the Roman *imperium*."[9] Yet, ironically, these reflect something of Jesus' true identity: he is given a purple cloak (the color of a king's robe) and a crown of thorns; after being struck on the head with a reed (akin to a makeshift scepter or sword), he is hailed as King of the Jews and given homage by those who kneel before him. Throughout these torturous proceedings Jesus is stripped twice, doubling his shame. It is a strange and terrible coronation ceremony that links Jesus Christ with all others who suffer unjustly and inhumanely.

Preaching and teaching the Word

Given the history of Christian anti-Semitism, it is extremely important that preachers and teachers of this text publicly recognize the culpability of all who contribute to Jesus' death, not only the Jewish authorities. His own disciples abandon and deny him, and the crowd demands his crucifixion, but it is both the civil and religious authorities who place Jesus on trial and condemn him to death. Mark offers clear parallels between Jesus' trials before the high priest and Pilate, but it is ultimately the Roman procurator who issues the order for his crucifixion and Roman soldiers who carry it out.[10]

The *theme of betrayal* comes to a climax in this section of Mark's Gospel as we witness Jesus being repeatedly "handed over" in personal, public, religious, and political settings. Everyone he encounters is complicit in his death—friends, coreligionists, magistrates, and the populace in general. Peter's betrayal strikes us as particularly painful given that he is among Jesus' closest companions and genuinely intended to follow Christ to the end. His denial prompts us to consider the ways we are untrue to Jesus today, since it is far easier to deny Christ's call to take up the cross than it is to deny our need for personal safety and financial security. We live in a culture of denial, refusing to acknowledge death, the grace of aging, responsibility for wrongdoing, and our shared culpability in the many environmental and political crises of our time. Among other things, Peter's story warns us that we are more inclined to deny what we know of God than admit what we do not know about ourselves.

The *crowd's role* in Jesus' death is also chilling. In response to Pilate's question, they are easily manipulated by Jesus' enemies and refuse to ask questions, pursue justice, or explore alternative possibilities. The scene is more like a lynching than a trial, recalling other savage instances of mob rule. "Strange Fruit," a song first sung by Billie Holiday in 1939, describes what many Americans would rather forget—the bodies of lynched black men swaying from southern trees, representing the bitter fruit of prejudice and mob rule.[11] Unquestioning acquiescence to the fearful prerogatives of others necessarily results in the violation of justice.

Pilate's role before the crowd is also disturbing. As representative of the ruling regime, he would rather kill a nonviolent preacher than release a known insurrectionist who collaborated in murder. Pilate's presence and that of the soldiers who delight in torturing Jesus reveal what veteran war correspondent Chris Hedges calls "the capacity for evil that lurks not far below the surface of all of us."[12] As much as we would like to believe ourselves incapable of such behavior, images from Iraq's Abu Ghraib prison and the perpetuation of violence against enemies and terrorists bear unwanted testimony to the evil we inflict on others in the name of national good and civil order.

The *Sanhedrin's role* in handing Jesus over to the Romans also compels us to think carefully about the ways religiously motivated people can wrongly denounce those with whom they disagree. The religious leaders are so zealous to protect their own understanding and practice of religion that they accuse Jesus of sedition (claiming he threatened to destroy the Temple) and blasphemy (for profaning God's name and asserting his lordship). These accusations mask a deeper sense of betrayal on the part of Jesus' coreligionists. They believe he betrayed their understanding of faith, befriended those whom they despise, and proved himself a traitor to their agenda (see "Preaching and teaching the Word" for 14:1–11, p. 233, and 26–52, p. 240). We may have different versions of identity politics and religious zeal, but people of faith today are every bit as susceptible to false idols and shallow pursuits as our religious forebears. Whenever the church is divided over who is allowed at the communion table and who is not, we reenact the prejudices that deny God's grace among us.

Another way to think of betrayal in light of this text is to explore how *Jesus himself betrayed the expectations of others to be faithful* to God's purposes. What does it mean for people of faith to be traitors to religious standards, social expectations, and political agendas? Jesus' story and those of countless other outsiders urge us to consider the possibility that, as James Logan states, "rebellion is a form that holiness takes."[13] There are indeed times when faithful people must betray common opinion and risk being called traitors for the sake of God's reign. The woman who anointed Jesus' feet in 14:3–9 was certainly a rebel and traitor in the eyes of those who scorned her. She forsook their expectations and standards, choosing to offer her prophetic witness and pastoral ministrations while they rejected her gifts and presence. In describing his childhood experience of befriending an

English officer during the British occupation of Palestine in the 1940s, Jewish author Amos Oz recounts the bitter rejection he endured from his friends who put him on trial for his seditious behavior. When Amos (known as "Proffy" by his friends) asked the prosecution what he had done to earn the charge of treason, the judge (his best friend) replied, "It's because you love the enemy, Proffy. Loving the enemy, Proffy, is worse than betraying secrets. Worse than betraying fighters . . . [it] is the height of treachery."[14] Because Jesus loved those whom others despised, he too was subject to their harshest condemnation.

The *many ironies* that infuse this section of the narrative *point to Jesus' messianic identity and kingly authority.* Most remarkably, divine truth is revealed through human injustice and cruelty: Jesus' detractors seek persons to testify against him, yet the one false testimony that is given (that he would destroy and replace the Temple in three days) ultimately comes to pass when he and his followers constitute a temple not made with human hands. The members of the Sanhedrin condemn Jesus to death for blasphemy, yet they are the ones to commit the unforgivable sin of denying the Spirit in him (see 3:28–30). Peter tells bystanders in the courtyard that he does not know Jesus, yet his lack of faith and loyalty suggests that he still has not grasped the truth of his earlier confession in 8:29–33. Pilate and his cohort repeatedly mock Jesus, yet all the while they proclaim the truth of his identity. Jesus' person and work undermine all human notions of messianic status and kingly authority. As Thomas Merton has rightly observed, "The great question in the trial and condemnation of Christ was precisely the denial of God and the denial of [God's] holiness. So God [in Christ] was put to death on the cross because [God] did not measure up to [humanity's] conception of [Divine] Holiness."[15]

THE CRUCIFIXION, DEATH, AND BURIAL OF JESUS CHRIST (15:21–47)

Exploring the text

The gruesome outcome of Jesus' trials is recounted in the description of his crucifixion. Mark's spare yet powerful account does not expand on the awful details of torn flesh and splattered blood but chooses instead to emphasize Jesus' utter abandonment by others. As he endures the agony of crucifixion, Jesus does not know the support of companions, disciples, crowds, civil servants, coreligionists, or even God. Instead, he experiences the betrayal of all whom he has loved and served. Yet for all his isolation, the text is crowded with characters who briefly pass in and out of Christ's ordeal. In addition, Mark makes regular use of the historic present tense throughout this section to draw hearers and readers of the Gospel into the circle of participants who bear witness to Jesus' derision, suffering, and death.

After torturing and taunting him, Pilate's soldiers lead Jesus out of the courtyard and beyond the city gates, where crucifixions routinely took place (15:21). As Myers notes, the procession of condemned criminals was a public spectacle meant to demonstrate imperial triumph and to deter potential rebels.[1] Along the way, they encounter Simon of Cyrene (part of modern-day Libya) coming into the city from the country, and they force him to carry Jesus' cross. Although condemned criminals were expected to carry their own horizontal cross beam, Jesus' flogging and torment was apparently extensive enough to warrant his needing assistance from others. (His relatively swift death in six hours also testifies to his weakened condition.) There is irony in Simon's presence: he shares the same name as Jesus' closest follower, who was urged to take up his cross and follow Jesus but ended up abandoning him in his hour of need (8:31–9:1; 14:32–42, 66–72). Because Simon of Cyrene is likely to have been a Jewish visitor to the city during the season of Passover, he probably knew very little of Jesus, if anything at all. However, the mention of his sons Alexander and Rufus suggests these persons were known to Mark's community.

The soldiers offer Jesus wine mixed with myrrh as a mild narcotic to help ease his pain (15:23). Their humanitarian gesture recalls Proverbs 31:6. But Jesus will have none of it, perhaps intending to keep his vow not to drink wine until he drinks it new in the kingdom of God (14:25). He chooses instead to accept the fullness of his suffering without relief. As described in Psalm 22:18, Jesus' clothes are divided among the soldiers, who cast lots to decide what each will take. This psalm also speaks of enduring derision from enemies (22:8) and recounts the anguished cry of one who is abandoned by God (22:1). Thus, Mark's account of Jesus' crucifixion, death, and burial alludes to Hebrew Scripture in subtle yet significant ways, contributing to our sense that even the details of Jesus' crucifixion are in accordance with God's will.

At nine in the morning the soldiers complete their torturous task.[2] Mark's account moves past the terrifying details of Jesus' crucifixion and directs our attention to the charge against him, **"King of the Jews"** (15:26). In plain sight of all who bear witness to these events, the inscription announces the reason for his conviction: As King of the Jews, he is "being executed for presuming to challenge the authority of Rome."[3] For those who recognize Jesus as the Messiah, the inscription proclaims his true identity; for those who reject and mock him, the inscription recognizes that Jesus proclaims an alternative dominion that threatens the order and security of their own (see 15:2, 9, 18, 32, and "Exploring the text" and "Preaching and teaching the Word" for 14:53–15:20, p. 241).

Three sets of people are present to deride Jesus. First, the crowds shake their heads and shout their derisions (15:29–30; see Lam. 2:15; Ps. 22:77). The verb *eblasphaemoun* is stronger than mere mockery. It speaks of their blaspheming Jesus who, ironically, was earlier accused of blaspheming God and warned others not to blaspheme the Holy Spirit (2:7; 3:29; 14:64). The crowd also recalls the charge of sedition leveled against Jesus in his trial before the Sanhedrin (14:58). In calling for Jesus to save himself and come down from the cross, it is possible that some were curious to see if he would perform one more miracle. However, given that Mark reports no miracles performed by Jesus in Jerusalem, it seems unlikely that the people expected such a display of power now.

The second group to deride him include the **chief priests** and **scribes** (15:31–32). Along with the **elders**, they have actively sought Jesus' demise (11:18; 14:1, 55; 15:1, 11). Their comments are less public than those of the crowd, as they speak to one another about how Jesus saved others but "cannot save himself." They also mock him and recall the titles "**Messiah**" and "King of Israel," a more Hebraic or "insider" way of expressing Pilate's inscription, "King of the Jews." We may be tempted to interpret their final words to him in 15:32 as an indication of ambivalence or a deeper desire for Jesus to rise above these awful circumstances and slay his Roman oppressors, but this seems unlikely. Their contempt for Jesus remains unyielding. Jesus has betrayed their messianic expectations and violated their sense of God's rule (see 2:7; 3:22; 7:5). Finally, the third group to deride Jesus includes two bandits who hang on his right and left (cf. Luke 23:39–43). The fact that he is surrounded by insurgents (not mere thieves) further confirms that Jesus was mistaken for a rebel despite clear indications that he did not associate with violent movements (see 14:48 and the reference to bandits/[*lēstas*], whom Jesus repudiates in 11:17). Remembering the request of James and John to sit on the right and left of Jesus in glory (10:37), it is ironic that he is surrounded in death by those who, according to Myers, "undergo the 'baptism' of death at the hands of the state,"[4] a fate many of his followers will share for their non-violent witness, also.

The darkness covering the entire land from noon to three o'clock reveals the cosmic and **apocalyptic** significance of Christ's suffering and death (15:33). Echoing Jesus' prophetic vision in 13:24 (see also Amos 8:9–10), heaven and earth participate in Christ's suffering and anticipate his coming glory. His last recorded words convey the worst possible agony for Jesus to endure: having fully committed himself to fulfilling God's will and proclaiming God's reign, Jesus feels utterly forsaken and abandoned by God (Ps. 22:1). Those who hear his cry believe he is calling for the prophet Elijah (15:35), but this is yet another instance of Jesus' being misunderstood. For Mark's hearers, the reference is a reminder of the prophetic witness of Elijah, who appeared at Jesus' transfiguration (9:2–8), and John the Baptist, who was sometimes mistaken for Elijah and whose death presaged that of Jesus (6:14–29). We do not know whether the bystanders who offer Jesus a sponge soaked with sour wine (a common drink among soldiers) are hoping for a last-minute reprieve or are simply curious to see what will happen next. But their efforts are to no avail. Jesus cries out one last time and breathes his last (15:37). The Messiah, the King of Israel, is dead. It appears that the powers of death have conspired with imperial and religious forces to secure Jesus' defeat.

Immediately afterward, two peculiar events take place. First, the curtain of the Temple is torn in two (15:38), just as the heavens themselves were torn asunder at the time of Jesus' baptism (1:10). The curtain that once separated the Holy of Holies from the rest of the sanctuary is ripped apart so that God's people are no longer distanced from the source of divine judgment and saving grace. The fierce and holy **power** of God is on the loose, no longer confined by Temple walls. God incarnate has entered the realm of the dead for the sake of the living and opened the way for those who follow him to enter life anew. The second event is just as peculiar. The centurion who has supervised Jesus' crucifixion and witnessed his death stands opposite him and declares, "Truly this man was God's Son"–or "a son of God" (15:39). The lack of a definite article suggests grammatical ambiguity: the Gentile officer may have testified that Jesus was "*a* son of God" (a general Hellenistic statement of respect) rather than "*the* Son of God." As Juel argues, interpreters have generally presupposed that this Gentile sees what Jews cannot and have assumed that the statement of the centurion is the first "Christian" confession of faith.[5] However, this is hardly consistent with Mark's portrayal of others who confess Jesus' identity throughout the Gospel and do not know who he is. It is only the demons who are fully aware of Christ's identity, authority, and power (see 1:23–26). The high priest, Pilate, the soldiers, chief priests, and scribes unknowingly ascribe to Jesus the correct titles. Like these unknowing witnesses, the centurion was probably not confessing his faith in Jesus Christ as the Son of God but nevertheless bore testimony to more than he realized. There is no mistaking the genuine significance of his utterance at the foot of the cross: it is through Jesus' crucifixion and death that God reveals Jesus' identity as Messiah and King.

Other witnesses are present at the cross also (15:40–41). Mark names several women who stood at a distance observing all that happened, including the two Marys and Salome. Their presence is remarkable not only because they will be the only ones to return to the tomb later to anoint the body of Jesus (16:1) but because they have followed Jesus (*ēkolouthoun autō*) and served him (*diēkonoun autō*), reflecting the Gospel's understanding of discipleship. Mark also notes that they are not from Jerusalem but accompanied Jesus in Galilee, where his disciples can expect to meet him again following his resurrection from the dead (14:28; 16:7). Unlike their male counterparts, the women keep vigil until the end and, in an amazing act of reversal, they are the first witnesses to testify to his death and resurrection (15:40; 16:1–8).[6] However fearful, sorrowful, or confused they may be, the women disciples are indispensable witnesses to Christ's death and resurrection.

The scene ends with Joseph of Arimathea boldly requesting that Pilate give him the body of Jesus (15:42–47). It is late in the day, and there is little time left to care for Jesus' burial before the Sabbath. Although it no doubt took courage to approach Pilate on Jesus' behalf, Joseph's motivations are not clear. The text portrays him as a respected member of the council (presumably the Sanhedrin) who waited expectantly for the **kingdom of God**. Perhaps he was fastidious in observing the commandment of Deuteronomy 21:22–23 and wanted to bury Jesus the same day as his crucifixion to avoid defilement of the land. Or perhaps he was genuinely caring toward a fellow Jew. We must be careful not to assume too much since, as a member of the Sanhedrin, Joseph would have been counted among those who condemned Jesus to death (14:64). One thing is certain: the threefold repetition of the word "dead" confirms that Jesus' life has ended. Joseph wraps Jesus in a linen cloth (the same word also appears in 14:51–52; see "Exploring the text") and lays him in a rock-hewn tomb. He then seals it with a cylindrical stone that was probably set into a groove to prevent grave robbing. When all is said and done, two women take note of where Jesus is buried. They are witnesses to these terrifying events.

Preaching and teaching the Word

The RCL includes the account of Christ's crucifixion, death, and burial among the readings for the Sixth Sunday of Lent, Year B. However, it is also one of two possible Gospel readings for the Sunday before Easter. The other, focusing on Jesus' entry into Jerusalem in 11:1–11, is often chosen instead to celebrate Palm Sunday. Consequently, many Christians approach Easter with little opportunity to reflect on Christ's passion and its theological implications. Yet this text offers myriad opportunities for critical reflection and spiritual insight.

One way to draw hearers into the reality and relevance of Jesus' crucifixion is to view it through the eyes of one or more of *the many characters who populate Mark's account.* Despite his alienation, Jesus is surrounded by an array of people who bear witness to his ordeal, with each person or group reflecting a particular facet of faith or faithlessness. It may help listeners to envision the presence of these characters if the text is read in multiple voices, with persons dressed in simple costumes taking their places before a wooden cross. Whether or not their physical presence is represented in worship, however, the sermon could describe their significance in Jesus' passion.

Simon of Cyrene is compelled to bear Christ's cross so that he becomes an unwilling participant in his death. His presence in the story reminds us of those who observe life's tragedies from a distance but are suddenly pulled into the center of human suffering. He may also be contrasted with *Simon Peter,* who professes undying loyalty to Christ yet, in the end, refuses to take up his cross and follow him. *The soldiers* appear to be unrelentingly cruel as they mock Jesus and cast lots over his clothes, but they also offer him wine mixed with myrrh, an act of comfort that suggests a glimmer of humanitarian concern. *The crowds* who mock Jesus from the foot of the cross offer little reason for hope. They feed off one another's zeal, allowing no room for dissenting voices and utterly lacking in moral leadership. As noted above, *the religious leaders* provide a cautionary example for people of faith who are eager to denounce those with whom they disagree (see "Preaching and teaching the Word" for 14:53–15:20, p. 246). *The bandits* on Jesus' right and left show neither remorse nor pity and appear to be insurgents for a lost cause (cf. Luke 23:39–43). *The centurion* at the foot of the cross professes the truth of Jesus' identity even if he does not fully understand what he is saying. His confession reminds us that the least likely people can serve as witnesses to divine truth. Our image of *Joseph of Arimathea* also deserves great care. As a member of the Sanhedrin, he shares responsibility for Christ's death, yet Mark explains that he is waiting expectantly for God's reign. It takes great courage to ask Pilate for Jesus' body, and Joseph also generously provides a shroud and tomb for Jesus' burial. Finally, after following and serving Jesus in Galilee, *the women* who keep vigil at the cross are his most faithful disciples. Unnoticed by others, their witness proves essential to the proclamation of the gospel. Through all of these characters, Mark bids us stand before the cross to encounter Christ's suffering anew.

These characters also challenge us to consider some *very difficult questions related to our own failings and faithlessness.* In particular, what is the use in trying to be faithful if we, like Jesus' first disciples, appear incapable of obedience? Given that evil persists despite our best efforts, why continue to battle against the forces of injustice among us? One response is found in the *Pirke Avot* 2:21 of the Mishnah: "It is not your duty to complete the work; neither are you free to desist from it." Even if we do not see the fulfillment of God's will among us, we are still called to participate in God's purposes. Amid our despair and complacency, Jesus calls us to **proclaim** the reign of God even as he proclaims God's life-giving purposes through his own radical obedience to God's will. Jesus' death on the cross, his sense of abandonment by God, and his resurrection from the dead testify to the power of God at work among us even when we cannot recognize it ourselves. This is the source of our hope and power: God's purposes will not be fulfilled by our own hard work and good intentions but are assured through the power of God alive among us, empowering us to fulfill God's will. Despite our faithlessness and failings, despite our desertion and denial, despite our cowardice and greed, all things are possible with God, who is determined to overcome evil, sin, and even death itself with newness of life.

Yet another theological challenge awaits us in these verses related to *the purposefulness of Jesus' suffering and death.* Why did he suffer? What is the meaning or purpose of Christ's death? Although we may argue that his death provided atonement for our sins (giving his life "as a ransom for many," see 10:45), that God would require Christ to suffer and die to satisfy a divine need for sacrifice is a horrifying notion.[7] Yet we sense the inevitability and seeming necessity of Christ's suffering as it is presented in the Gospel of Mark through numerous allusions to the fulfillment of Hebrew Scripture (e.g., the parallels between Ps. 22 and Mark 15:24, 29, 34) and earlier indications that Jesus anticipated his death and resurrection (e.g., 8:31; 9:31; 10:32–34; 14:27–28, 41). It is not surprising that Jesus is betrayed and abandoned by those he loves; the Gospel depicts these events as the fulfillment of Christ's destiny.

At one level, we may say that Jesus' death was the inevitable result of his having challenged the religious and political authorities of his time. He shares the fate of all who suffer unjustly, and Jesus' death is an act of self-identification with all who appear to be forsaken by God amid the machinations of human cruelty. At another level, however, Jesus' crucifixion reveals something powerful and empowering about God. In moving steadfastly toward the cross, Jesus proves that divine power manifests itself in the will to fulfill the law of charity toward all people, despite the costliness of self-giving. From the perspective of his entire life and ministry, Jesus does not resign himself to the powers and principalities of this world, but is determined to show the way of God's love by sharing in human suffering, confronting evil, and transforming human transgression. He loves all people and refuses to kill his enemies. Jesus is willing to suffer for the sake of participating in the transforming work of God's reign. Through him, the redeeming power of God breaks through the power of death, and his disciples are empowered to continue his work of divine love. Today we witness the ongoing power of Christ's death and resurrection whenever we care for the sick, welcome the outcast, and teach people the good news of God's reign.

Finally, Jesus' death on the cross gives us reason to *rethink the practice of capital punishment.* As the victim of a gross miscarriage of justice, Jesus experienced the injustices suffered by persons today who cannot afford adequate legal counsel and/or who are the victims of racial, economic, and other prejudices. We must also remember that Jesus never took up arms against enemies, criminals, or those who betrayed him, and he offered no reason to believe that it is God's will for us to do so. No system of justice is immune from human error, and even the most "humane" means of execution involve unforeseen and gruesome complications. God alone must act as the judge of capital cases. For these and other reasons, this text fortifies Christians to protest the practice of capital punishment.

Continuing the Gospel

The Power of God
on the Loose in the World

Mark 16:1–8

Unlike the other Gospels, Mark's original ending does not include accounts of the risen Jesus performing miraculous deeds or offering final instructions to his disciples. It suggests nothing of his ascent to heaven and, most importantly, he does not appear in his resurrected glory so that his followers may see and hear him again. Instead, three women come to anoint the body of Jesus and encounter a heavenly messenger who tells them he has been raised from the dead. The messenger commands them to go tell the disciples that they will find Jesus in Galilee. But they flee the tomb in terror and amazement, saying nothing to anyone. By 16:8 every one of Jesus' disciples has abandoned him, the women are fearful, and no one is willing to share the good news of his resurrection.

What does Mark *mean* by this ending? Or better yet, what is Mark *doing* by ending the Gospel in this way?

The close of Mark's Gospel in 16:1–8 is so strange, so dissatisfying, and so disturbing that within centuries of its completion, the church amended Mark's narrative with two substitute endings (vv. 9–20).[1] The first, designated in most Bibles as "the shorter ending of Mark," wraps up the account by insisting that the women told others what had been commanded them and that Jesus appeared to direct the disciples in their ministry. The second, "the longer ending of Mark," includes twelve verses that recount several appearances by Jesus to his disciples and a lengthy commission that introduces new vocabulary, ideas, and concerns that do not occur elsewhere in the Gospel. These additions abruptly shift the direction and momentum of Mark's account and offer a "happy ending" to the disquieting scene in 16:1–8. Since there is little doubt that the Gospel originally ended at verse 8, why did Mark choose to close the narrative in this way?

Exploring the text

Three women (Mary Magdalene, Mary the mother of James, and Salome) prepare to anoint the body of Jesus as soon as the Sabbath has ended. Their names are listed differently in 16:1 than in 15:40, but Mark gives the distinct impression that the women who go to anoint Jesus' body two days after his burial are among those who stood vigil at the cross. Two of them are likely to have also observed the place where Joseph of Arimathea laid him in a tomb (15:47). In the final verses of Mark's Gospel, it is "the women who provide the continuity between the story of Jesus' death and burial and the story of Easter morning."[2]

As soon as they are able, they purchase spices for anointing and head toward the tomb by early sunlight. Their work is a labor of love, since anointing the deceased was intended to cover the stench of decaying flesh. Along the way they wonder how they will remove the large stone that blocks the entry (16:2–3). Since it seems odd for them not to have accounted for this problem before they set out, it is likely that Mark has inserted this thought to heighten our appreciation for the miraculous nature of what they will soon encounter.

Their eyes are cast downward, but when they arrive at the tomb they look up to see that the stone has been rolled away (v. 4). Mark notes the size of the stone to again enhance our sense of the extraordinary nature of what has occurred. Upon entering the darkened tomb, the women are alarmed to see a young man dressed in a white robe and sitting on the right (v. 5). Both of these details indicate his heavenly authority: his radiant apparel is appropriate for divine messengers (see also Jesus' transfiguration, 9:3), while his place on the right is the position coveted by Jesus' disciples (10:37) and the seat of power spoken of by Jesus in 14:62. The young messenger also recalls the unnamed disciple who flees the scene of Jesus' arrest (15:51) and is the only other character in the Gospel described as a young man. The women had not expected to see this angelic visitor when they set out to anoint Jesus' body, and they are alarmed. The verb (*ekthambeomai*) indicates fear as well as amazement, and Mark uses the same verb in 9:15 to describe the reaction of the crowd after Jesus' transfiguration and again in 14:33 when Jesus prays at Gethsemane. To allay their fears, the messenger urges the women not to be alarmed (repeating the same verb) and tells them that Jesus cannot be found in the tomb. It is interesting to note that the messenger not only refers to Jesus by his hometown ("of Nazareth") but speaks of Jesus as the one "who was crucified." When announcing the resurrection, the Gospel will not have us forget Jesus' human origins and the manner of his death.

In keeping with the whole of Mark's narration, the messenger's announcement is brief yet power packed. He tells the women that Jesus has been raised (the aorist passive indicates divine activity) and is no longer in the tomb (see 5:1–20). As Witherington notes, the women are both eyewitnesses of the empty tomb and "earwitnesses" of the Easter message.[3] The powers of sin and death have been utterly defeated, and the women are the first to hear this amazing message. The heavenly messenger then charges them to "go tell his disciples and Peter that he is going ahead of you to Galilee" (16:7). The separate references to the disciples in general and Peter in particular signify the twofold abandonment of Jesus—first by the entire group of disciples at his arrest (14:50) and then by Peter during Jesus' trial (14:66–72). Peter's role among the twelve is reinstated. Indeed, the commission to Jesus' disciples indicates something of great importance to the entire Gospel: his followers are forgiven for their abandonment and betrayal of him. Without their having spoken to him, Jesus forgives them, granting them the gift of renewed relationship before they ask. It is the gracious will of the crucified and risen Lord to redeem from sin and sorrow those who have turned away from him.

The messenger also reminds them of what Jesus said earlier in 14:28—that he is going ahead of them and will meet them in Galilee. It is the place where Jesus first proclaimed the gospel of God's reign (1:14–15). It is also the place where his disciples were called to follow him and where they began their own ministries of preaching, healing, and exorcism (6:12). Far from the Temple and the seat of political power in Jerusalem (cf. Lk. 24:47), the turn to Galilee represents a renewal of the work that was begun earlier and is in need of continued labor. Two other facets of the messenger's charge are remarkable. First, in concluding his remarks to the women with the words "as he told you," the messenger recalls many other instances in the narrative when Jesus made promises and predictions that came to pass. Just as his prophecies concerning the disciples' abandonment and Peter's denial came to pass (14:27–30), so would other promises he made concerning God's resurrection power (13:26–27; 14: 62). As Juel contends, "Promises that are fulfilled provide a basis for confidence that others will be."[4]

Second, three women are commissioned to proclaim the resurrection of Jesus Christ. Throughout Mark's Gospel women have been faithful disciples (1:31), willing to speak the whole truth of what has happened to them (5:25–34) and serving as prophetic ministers despite the condemnation of men (14:3–9). Here at the scene of Jesus' burial and resurrection, they are called to be the first witnesses to Christ's resurrected glory. Earlier Jesus commanded his followers to keep **silent** when they wanted to share the good news of what he had done for them (e.g., 1:40–45; 7:31–37; 8:22–26). Here they are commanded to remind others what Jesus said and to **proclaim** that he has been raised from the dead. But when the women hear the call to preach, they flee the scene in terror and amazement, intending to say nothing to anyone. The Gospel ends with fear and silence. Even the most faithful of Jesus' disciples, those who kept vigil while others fled, abandon their calling.

What does Mark *mean* by this ending? Or better yet, what is Mark *doing* by ending the narrative in this way?

We know that the story does not end here; there would be no Gospel narrative if the women had followed their first impulse. In a very real sense, the end of Mark's Gospel does not record the end of the gospel. Indeed, it never intended to do so. The many allusions to Jesus' earlier ministry and promises in 16:1–8 draw us back into the story, provoking the hearers to respond to what we have heard and pick up where the women left off. As Myers insists, "The power of Mark's Gospel ultimately lies not in what it tells the disciples/readers, but what it asks of them."[5] Similarly, Blount argues that Mark "has shown Jesus' kingdom preaching and the transformative effect it can have. He has shown that the disciples have the power to emulate that transformative preaching. And he has demonstrated the promise of this transformative preaching that comes from the historical transformation that Jesus' ministry accomplishes. . . . He challenges them to Go Preach!"[6]

Mark 16:1–8 does not bring closure to the gospel but opens wide the doorway of the tomb, beckoning Jesus' followers to take another look inside, then to go out to proclaim what they have seen and heard of the resurrected Lord. By the power of the Holy Spirit, he is already out ahead of us, leading the way. By the power of the Holy Spirit, we will proclaim Christ's life-giving message in word and deed. The Gospel of Mark begins and ends with the proclamation of good news and the invitation to participate in God's reign alive among us (1:14–15; 16:7). But between these words and beyond them are the myriad words of Christ's witnesses, who continue his ministry and anticipate the fullness of God's reign. For those who preach, teach, listen, learn, minister, and serve beyond boundaries of our own making, the good news does not end with fearful disciples. The power of God continues to be proclaimed throughout the world (13:10).

Preaching and teaching the Word

It takes five chapters to record the final week of Jesus' life but just a few short verses to unleash the mystery of his resurrection among us. As one of two possible Gospel readings for Easter Sunday of Year B, these provocative verses urge the listener to respond to the **gospel** by proclaiming **God's reign**. The good news of this text arises in several ways.

Jesus Christ is risen from the dead and is going ahead of you. Amid the fear and confusion of the women's encounter with the angel, we must not miss his twofold message. First, Jesus Christ has overcome the power of death.

Human sin, satanic power, sociopolitical systems, and even death itself are subject to God's life-giving purposes. Through his life, death, and resurrection, Jesus Christ reveals that nothing is stronger than the **power** of God's love. Despite the appearance of powerlessness, the misperceptions of others, and at great costliness to himself, Jesus shows that the radical freedom of God is always in service to God's life-giving purposes—and as with the women at the tomb, it often catches us by surprise. What does the power of God's love look like, sound like, feel like? In "O Tell Me the Truth about Love," W. H. Auden asks, "When it comes, will it come without warning / Just as I'm picking my nose? / Will it knock on my door in the morning, / Or tread in the bus on my toes? / . . . O tell me the truth about love."[7] However we experience Christ's resurrection power among us, it is likely to take us by surprise as it did the women at the tomb.

Second, Christ is going on ahead of us. The message of the angel inspires hope not only because we hear that Jesus is alive but because he shows us the way ahead. We are not without direction or purpose as long as we seek Christ's way in the world. The angel points the disciples toward Galilee, and Mark's audience is compelled to look anew at the pages of Mark's Gospel where Jesus' ministry first began. But we see with new eyes and hear with new ears, guided by the Spirit of Christ, who urges us forward. If Scripture alone would suffice, we would have no need for Christ's Spirit as our guide. But the Spirit abides among us and beyond us because we need her presence, power, and wisdom. No wonder the women were terrified. Who knows where the journey of faith will take us?

God uses unlikely and unwilling witnesses. The fate of the gospel depends on three women who run from the tomb in terror and amazement. They are among the least likely persons to be noticed or respected; in fact, they appear to have been overlooked or ignored by nearly everyone. Jesus, of course, notices women as well as other outsiders. Gentiles, tax collectors, widows, and children—none escape his attention, and he treats all of these as members of God's reign. In the final verses of Mark's Gospel, it is three women who are entrusted with the gospel message, continuing God's subversive and surprising way among us. Ancient Jewish law required two male witnesses to provide credible testimony in legal proceedings, and although Roman law recognized the testimony of women, Pilate did not summon the women, but the centurion to confirm Jesus' death (15:44). However, the women prove to be just as fearful as their male counterparts. When they see the empty tomb and hear the angel's message, they abandon God's call and flee in terror and amazement. But the gospel does not end in silence as 16:8 might lead us to expect. Someone had to tell the story, because it did not end with fearful disciples. When their knees stopped shaking and their tongues began to loosen, they looked at one another and asked what they had just witnessed. Then, empowered by the risen Christ, these unlikely and unwilling witnesses proclaimed the good news of God's reign.

*The **power** of God is on the loose in the world, calling for our response.* From the beginning of the Gospel when Jesus first proclaimed God's reign (1:14–15), to the closing verses that announce his resurrection from the dead (16:6–7), the power of God is on the loose in the world as never before. Through his preaching, teaching, healing, and boundary breaking ministry, Jesus calls others to proclaim the gospel by participating in God's reign. The close of Mark's Gospel does not include multiple descriptions of Jesus appearing to his disciples: there is no need for these. He has already told them what they need to know. Mark's story directs his hearers beyond the written page to recall what Jesus has taught them so they may continue his ministry anew.

What is the shape of that ministry? Christ has shown us what it means to participate in God's reign and has given us the power to do so. He has broken through the most impenetrable boundaries of ethnic identity, national loyalty, economic standing, and sexual differences to reach out in compassion to all people. Like the first disciples, we are called to continue the gospel where verse 8 leaves off. The extraordinary, open-ended way that Mark concludes his narrative anticipates God's continued work among us through Christ's undying love.

NOTES

INTRODUCTION

1. For further discussion of Jesus' preaching as it proclaims God's radical intervention in human affairs, see Brian K. Blount, *Go Preach! Mark's Kingdom Message and the Black Church Today* (Maryknoll, NY: Orbis Books, 1998), 91.
2. Donald H. Juel, *A Master of Surprise: Mark Interpreted* (Minneapolis: Fortress Press, 1994), 25.
3. See Eugene F. Roop, "The Interpreting Community of Faith," in *Ruth, Jonah, Esther* (Scottdale, PA: Herald Press, 2002), 267.

MARK 1:1–13

1. For a thorough treatment of the literary boundaries of Mark's prologue, see Frank J. Matera, "The Prologue as the Interpretive Key to Mark's Gospel," *The Interpretation of Mark*, 2nd ed., ed. William R. Telford (Edinburgh: T. & T. Clark, 1995), 289–306.

MARK 1:1–8

1. Although the title "Son of God" was probably not part of the original text, its presence in several reputable early manuscripts suggests that it was of importance to the early transmitters of Mark's Gospel. Other references include 9:41; 12:35; 13:21; and 15:32. See Joel Marcus, *Mark 1–8*, Anchor Bible 27 (New York: Doubleday, 2000), 141.
2. The theme of God's apocalyptic intervention in human life and history as it is proclaimed in Mark's Gospel is developed fully in Blount, *Go Preach!*, chap. 6.
3. See Ben Witherington III, *The Gospel of Mark: A Socio-Rhetorical Commentary* (Grand Rapids: Wm. B. Eerdmans Publishing Co., 2001), 72.
4. According to Marcus, during the first century CE, priests who were preparing themselves for ritual sacrifices as well as other persons who contracted some sort of ritual impurity took part in a ritual bath or immersion for cleansing. Similarly, Gentile proselytes to Judaism were purged of their pagan uncleanness through a ritual bath. Members of the community at

Qumran also practiced ritual immersion (*Mark 1–8*, 155). However, in contrast to repeated experiences of ritual purification, John's practice of baptism appears to have been a once-and-for-all event in the life of individual believers.
5. See Charles L. Campbell, *The Word before the Powers: An Ethic of Preaching* (Louisville, KY: Westminster John Knox Press, 2002).

MARK 1:9–11

1. Juel, *Master of Surprise*, 35–36.
2. Donald H. Juel, *Mark*, Augsburg Commentary on the New Testament (Minneapolis: Augsburg Press, 1990), 33.
3. The dove arises as a frequent symbol in Hebrew Scripture, suggesting personal and corporate expressions of Israel's experience; see Ps. 55:6–7; 68:13; 74:19; Hos. 7:11; 11:11.
4. Carrie Eikler, group Bible study of July 2005.
5. Marilynne Robinson, *Gilead* (New York: Farrar, Straus & Giroux, 2004), 23.

MARK 1:12–13

1. Christian Peacemaker Teams provide intensive training in nonviolence and peacemaking skills for full-time and Reserve Corps members who serve in a variety of settings, including southern Arizona; Kenora, Ontario; Colombia; and the Hebron. CPT are supported primarily by the historic peace churches (Church of the Brethren, Friends United Meeting, Mennonite Church Canada, and Mennonite Church USA), but other denominational representatives and agencies also participate.

MARK 1:14–45

1. See Brian Blount's discussion of the grammatical parallels throughout Mark 1 indicating that Jesus' ensuing activity should be interpreted in light of his central metaphorical "preaching" about God's kingdom. (*Go Preach!*, 86–92). According to Blount, "Jesus . . . speaks authoritatively with demons. He teaches with supernatural authority. He exorcises and heals. But these are not ways he represents the kingdom. *They are manifestations of his preaching.* The preaching is the way Jesus intervenes. Preaching, in Mark's narration, is what shatters boundaries" (91).
2. Ibid., 91. Blount also notes that Jesus' ministry in Mark 1 is bracketed by the verb "preach" (*kērussō*, vv. 14, 38).

MARK 1:14–15

1. Marcus, *Mark 1–8*, 172.

MARK 1:16–20

1. See Joan L. Mitchell, *Beyond Fear and Silence: A Feminist-Literary Reading of Mark* (New York: Continuum, 2001), 8–9.
2. Gardner C. Taylor, *How Shall They Preach? The Lyman Beecher Lectureship Lectures and Five Lenten Sermons* (Elgin, IL: Progressive Baptist Publishing House, 1977), 38.
3. See Marcus, *Mark 1–8*, 174–75, where he outlines parallels between Mark 1:14–15, Rom. 3:12, 1 Thess. 5:5–6, Col. 1:13, and Acts 26:18.

MARK 1:21–28

1. Ched Myers, *Binding the Strong Man: A Political Reading of Mark's Story of Jesus* (Maryknoll, NY: Orbis Books, 1990), 142.

MARK 1:29–31

1. For a thoughtful discussion of the ways in which Mark's Gospel reflects the role of women among Jesus' disciples, see Mitchell, *Beyond Fear and Silence*, 62–64, and Susan Miller, *Women in Mark's Gospel* (New York: Continuum, 2004). In contrast, Deborah Krause asserts that the woman who was healed of her fever was not freed from her traditional responsibilities but rose to resume her prescribed tasks. See "Simon Peter's Mother-in-Law– Disciple or Domestic Servant? Feminist Biblical Hermeneutics and the Interpretation of Mark 1:29–31," in *A Feminist Companion to Mark*, ed. Amy-Jill Levine with Marianne Blickenstaff (Cleveland: Pilgrim Press, 2001), 37–53.

MARK 1:32–34

1. Marcus, *Mark 1–8*, 200–201.

MARK 1:35–39

1. Thomas Merton, *Contemplative Prayer* (Garden City, NY: Doubleday, 1971), 115.

MARK 1:40–45

1. This and other stories are reported in Carl Waldman's *Atlas of the North American Indian* (New York: Facts on File, 1985).

MARK 2:1–3:6

1. Marcus, *Mark 1–8*, 214.
2. See Juel, *Mark*, 50–51.
3. See Ronald J. Allen and Clark M. Williamson, *Preaching the Gospels without Blaming the Jews: A Lectionary Commentary* (Louisville, KY: Westminster John Knox Press, 2004).

MARK 2:1–12

1. See Witherington, *Gospel of Mark*, 117–118.

MARK 2:13–17

1. Levi's relationship to the twelve disciples is a matter of interest and speculation among scholars. Jesus does not name him among his closest followers in 3:13–19, but some have wondered if James the son of Alphaeus (listed among the twelve) may be his brother or if the disciple Matthew (also identified as a tax collector in Matt. 9:9–13) is actually the same person. Perhaps Mark is purposefully ambiguous as to Levi's relationship to the twelve, drawing our attention instead to the remarkable fact that Jesus has called a tax collector to follow him.
2. Richard Gardner, group Bible study of August 2, 2005.

MARK 2:18–22

1. See Morna D. Hooker, *The Gospel according to Saint Mark*, Black's New Testament Commentary (London: Hendrickson Publishers, 1991), 100.

MARK 2:23–28

1. Allen and Williamson cite *2 Baruch* 14:18 and *Mekilta Exodus* 31:13 as examples of Jewish teachings that sympathize with Jesus' assertion that care for those in need takes priority over other Sabbath rules governing work-related activity (*Preaching the Gospels without Blaming the Jews*, 107). In contrast to Allen and Williamson, however, I do not see this passage as reflecting the early church's need to vilify Pharisaic practice. Instead, this and other controversies between Jesus and Jewish leaders may be considered within the larger context of Mark's Gospel, where no one (neither Jewish authorities nor Roman politicians nor even Jesus' closest disciples) is able to recognize God's gracious, life-giving intentions revealed in Jesus Christ.
2. According to Marcus, "This sort of reshaping of a biblical story in order to make one's point stronger is also a common feature in ancient biblical interpretation" (*Mark 1–8*, 241).
3. See Dorothy C. Bass, *Receiving the Day: Christian Practices for Opening the Gift of Time* (San Francisco: Jossey-Bass, 2001); Marva J. Dawn, *Keeping the Sabbath Wholly: Ceasing, Resting, Embracing, Feasting* (Grand Rapids: Wm. B. Eerdmans Publishing Co., 1989); and Wayne Muller, *Sabbath: Finding Rest, Renewal, and Delight in Our Busy Days* (New York: Bantam Books, 1999).
4. Witherington, *Gospel of Mark*, 128–30.

MARK 3:1–6

1. According to the Babylonian Talmud, *Yoma* 85, if someone's life is in danger, Sabbath laws must be broken to secure the well-being of the one who is threatened.

2. See Mishnah, *Sabbat* 14:3–4.
3. Robert R. Beck, *Nonviolent Story: Narrative Conflict Resolution in the Gospel of Mark* (Maryknoll, NY: Orbis Books, 1996), 73.
4. In his exploration of the possible parallel between the Pharisees and Pharaoh, Marcus writes, "Pharaoh's hardness of heart was, from one point of view, his own fault (Exod 8:11, 28; 9:34 . . .), but it was also willed by God (Exod 7:3; 9:12; 11:10; 14:4, 8, 17 . . .). There is the same curious duality in Mark's conception of hardness of heart: it is both a sin that angers Jesus (3:5; 8:17–18) and an affliction for which he grieves . . . , and elsewhere in Mark it can visit even those who are well intentioned (see 6:52; 8:17–18 . . .). Pharaoh's obduracy, moreover, ultimately led to the revelation of God's glory (see Exod 10:1–2; 14:4, 17 . . .), and Mark probably thinks that the Pharisees' hardness of heart has a similarly salvific effect: it causes them to plot Jesus' death, but that death becomes the occasion for God's self-disclosure (cf. 15:37–39)" (*Mark 1–8*, 253).
5. Barack Obama (D.-IL), speaking on ABC's *This Week* in September 2005 about the Hurricane Katrina response. Quoted by the Associated Press in *Messenger*, November 2005, 7.
6. Marcus, *Mark 1–8*, 252.
7. We may wonder about the emotions of the man with the withered hand as Jesus called him forward that day. Was he excited, anxious, fearful, embarrassed, relieved? What were his reactions to this event? Mark tells us little about him and chooses instead to highlight Jesus' role.
8. The Church of the Brethren manual for ministers offers prayers and services of anointing for times of surgery, reconciliation, after a broken relationship, during grief, and when facing physical illness. See *For All Who Minister: A Worship Manual for the Church of the Brethren* (Elgin, IL: Brethren Press, 1993), 253–69.

MARK 3:7–12

1. After realizing the murderous plot against him (see 3:6), in 3:7–19a, Jesus enlists the help of others to continue his mission—just as in 1:14–20, following the announcement of John's imprisonment, Jesus begins his public proclamation of the gospel and calls forth others to join with him in ministry.
2. Brian K. Blount and Gary W. Charles, *Preaching Mark in Two Voices* (Louisville, KY: Westminster John Knox Press, 2002), 43.

MARK 3:13–19a

1. Myers, *Binding the Strong Man*, 164.
2. See Marcus, *Mark 1–8*, 267.
3. Donahue argues that the relationship between the twelve and the disciples in general is unclear in Mark's Gospel and that the responsibilities of the

twelve are shared by others: "Though the narratives of the call and commissioning of the Twelve are important in the structure of Mark, their main
function seems to be to symbolize the nature of discipleship (see 3:13–15)
rather than to perform the actions confined to a particular group" (John R.
Donahue, SJ, and Daniel J. Harrington, SJ, *The Gospel of Mark*, Sacra Pagina, ed. Daniel J. Harrington, SJ (Collegeville, MN: Liturgical Press, 2002),
126–27.

4. Don Postema, *Space for God: The Study and Practice of Prayer and Spirituality*
(Grand Rapids: Bible Way, 1983), 157.

5. Nan Erbaugh, group Bible study of August 2, 2005.

MARK 3:19b–35

1. The word "Beelzebul" combines the name of the Canaanite storm god,
Baal, with the epithet *zeboul*, meaning "house."

2. According to Donahue and Harrington, in terms of the political context of
Jesus' first hearers and Mark's readers, "both the kingdom and household
of Herod the Great were divided after his death in 4 BCE and 'came to an
end.' Also when Herod Antipas divorced the daughter of the Nabatean
king Aretas and married Herodias (see 6:17–19), Aretas defeated Herod
Antipas' armies, which led to the downfall of Herod Antipas." These internal divisions contributed to the defeat of the Jews in the Jewish War and to
the strife in Rome attending the death of Nero and its aftermath, which
included the reigns of three emperors in the year 68–69 CE (*Gospel of Mark*,
130–31).

3. Myers, *Binding the Strong Man*, 164–67.

4. Juan Luis Segundo, "Capitalism versus Socialism: Crux Theologica," in
Frontiers of Theology in Latin America, ed. R. Gibellini (Maryknoll, NY: Orbis
Books, 1979), 240.

5. Myers, *Binding the Strong Man*, 164–68.

6. Richard Gardner, group Bible study of August 2, 2005.

7. Truman Capote, *A Christmas Memory, One Christmas, and The Thanksgiving
Visitor* (New York: Modern Library, 1996), 104.

8. Katharine Rhodes Henderson, *God's Troublemakers: How Women of Faith Are
Changing the World* (New York: Continuum, 2006), 108–9.

MARK 4:1–34

1. Luise Schottroff, *The Parables of Jesus*, trans. Linda M. Maloney (Minneapolis: Fortress Press, 2006), 67.

2. Brian Blount (*Go Preach!*, 113) argues that the Gospel of Mark uses the term
"parable" outside of chapter four only in times of conflict (7:17; 12:1, 12;
13:28). However, if one considers the breadth of parabolic literature
recorded in the Synoptic Gospels, it is evident that Jesus drew on parabolic

speech not only as a means of subverting his opponents but also to teach his followers the essential nature of discipleship and their relationship to God's reign as citizens of the kingdom. See, for example, Luke 10:25–37 and 12:13–21.

MARK 4:1–20

1. The Shema, which is foundational to Jewish faith and worship, is one of the few selections of Hebrew Scripture that all of the Synoptic Gospels record having been recited by Jesus. This, along with the teaching to love one's neighbor as oneself, is the undisputed centerpiece of Jesus' understanding and practice of faith. The Shema summarizes Deut. 6:4–9, 11:13–21, and Num. 15:37–41.
2. Ched Myers, Marie Dennis, Joseph Nangle, OFM, Cynthia Moe-Lobeda, and Stuart Taylor, *"Say to This Mountain": Mark's Story of Discipleship* (Maryknoll, NY: Orbis Books, 1997), 40.
3. The Hebrew prophets often drew upon images of fruitfulness as they anticipated the divine harvest of God's reign on earth (e.g., Jer. 31:12; Joel 2:19, 21–24; Zech. 8:12).
4. Myers et al., *"Say to This Mountain,"* 41.
5. Marcus argues that the sharp dualism portrayed in 4:10–12 reflects the Markan community's painful experiences of powerlessness and persecution so that "a theology of apocalyptic determinism functions to assure the hard-pressed faithful that their suffering does not signal a loss of divine control." He also notes that this passage does not end in resignation. For Mark, as for Isaiah, a new age of reversal is sure to come (*Mark 1–8*, 307).

MARK 4:13–20

1. Schottroff, *Parables of Jesus*, 71.
2. Juel insists that "soil" is a passive image (*Mark*, 73). Although I agree that the power to resist the threats outlined in 4:15–19 does not lie with the soil but with God, the overall context of this parable (amid conflict and resistance to Jesus) suggests a scene of apocalyptic urgency that provides hope for the oppressed and a wake-up call for others.
3. Helen Lester, *Listen Buddy!* (New York: Houghton Mifflin, 1995).
4. Martin Luther, "A Mighty Fortress Is Our God," in *Hymnal: A Worship Book* (Elgin, IL: Brethren Press, 1992), no. 165.

MARK 4:21–25

1. Blount, *Go Preach!*, 119.
2. Marcus, *Mark 1–8*, 319.

MARK 4:26–34

1. Marcus, *Mark 1–8,* 325.
2. Schottroff recognizes that despite the hope-filled imagery of this passage, images of "harvest" and "sickle" cannot be separated from God's judgment of the nations. However, she urges readers to consider 4:29 in conjunction with 13:26 and 14:62, which proclaim Jesus' return to the nations who may yet repent and recognize his dominion (*Parables of Jesus,* 119–22).
3. Amy Gall Ritchie, group Bible study of August 22, 2005.
4. C. Clifton Black, *The Rhetoric of the Gospel: Theological Artistry in the Gospels and Acts* (St. Louis: Chalice Press, 2001), 137.
5. For a practical and insightful exploration of how to create new parables, see Ryan Ahlgrim, *Not as the Scribes: Jesus as a Model for Prophetic Preaching* (Scottdale, PA: Herald Press, 2002).

MARK 4:35–41

1. Hooker, *Mark,* 139.
2. O. Lamar Cope, *Matthew: A Scribe Trained for the Kingdom of Heaven* (Washington, DC: Catholic Biblical Association of America, 1976), 96–97.
3. Marcus, *Mark 1–8,* 338.

MARK 5:1–20

1. Marcus, *Mark 1–8,* 348–49.
2. Some have suggested that the unclean spirit planned to enter the pigs and intended their subsequent death in order to incite resentment toward Jesus from the townspeople who would suffer economic hardship. But this explanation contradicts the demons' wish to remain in the land of the Gerasenes, and when they are destroyed the demons are entirely unable to reassert their power over the healed man and his townsfolk. See Marcus, *Mark 1–8,* 345.
3. Myers et al., *"Say to This Mountain,"* 59.
4. Marcus suspects that the townspeople, like the scribes in 3:22–30, interpret Jesus' exorcism as the work of the devil (*Mark 1–8,* 346). However, given the stark contrast between Jesus' presence and the very positive, healthful influence on the man who has now come to his senses, it seems more likely that the witnesses to this event are overcome with fear of the unknown power that Jesus commands.
5. In response, the American Bible Society produced a video, *Out of the Tombs–ABS Multimedia Translation of Mark 5:1–20,* in 1991.

MARK 5:21–43

1. Marcus, *Mark 1–8,* 357.
2. See Spencer's summary of the work of Shaye Cohen, Ross Kraemer, Amy-

Jill Levine, and Paula Fredriksen in F. Scott Spencer, *Dancing Girls, Loose Ladies, and Women of the Cloth: The Women in Jesus' Life* (New York: Continuum, 2004), 59–60.

3. In the first century CE (and among Orthodox Jewish communities today) women were not counted when determining the minimum number of ten participants (*minyan*, or quorum) required for various liturgical services.

4. Marcus, *Mark 1–8*, 370.

5. After the exile, Aramaic, the language of Syria, came into common usage among Jews in Palestine and was the language most often spoken by Jesus.

6. Mitchell, *Beyond Fear and Silence*, chap. 7.

7. Ibid., 80 and 82.

8. Miller, *Women in Mark's Gospel*, 64.

9. Given the ways women's power and presence in Scripture has often been interpreted negatively throughout the church's history (e.g., the one-sided interpretation of Eve's role in the story of "the fall" of humanity), the compassion shown in Mark's portrayal of these two women urges us to look more deeply at their experiences, including what they receive and call forth in their interactions with Jesus Christ. For an insightful interpretation of various portrayals of women in the Synoptic Gospels, see Spencer, *Dancing Girls*.

10. Wendy Farley, *The Wounding and Healing of Desire: Weaving Heaven and Earth* (Louisville, KY: Westminster John Knox Press, 2005), 101.

11. Godana's story is included in a pictorial collection of photos and journalistic summaries in Phil Borges, *Women Empowered: Inspiring Change in the Emerging World* (New York: Rizzoli, 2007), 73.

12. Wendy Cotter, CSJ, "Mark's Hero of the Twelfth-Year Miracles: The Healing of the Woman with the Hemorrhage and the Raising of Jairus's Daughter (Mark 5:21–43)," in Levine, ed., *Feminist Companion to Mark*, 59–60.

13. These statistics are from the Children's Defense Fund and can be found at http://www.childrensdefense.org/site/PageServer?pagename=research _child_health.

MARK 6:1–6a

1. Witherington, *Gospel of Mark*, 195.

MARK 6:6b–13

1. The willingness to accept care and sustenance in exchange for one's service is evident in other texts of the early church, such as Acts 16:15, 40; 18:1–3; and Phil. 4:14–15.

2. Marcus provides a detailed comparison between Mark 6, Luke 10, the Cynics, and the exodus story. He contends that if the parallels between Mark and the exodus are indeed deliberate, "Mark probably wishes to

imply that the disciples' missionary journey will be a participation in the new exodus inaugurated by Jesus" (*Mark 1–8*, 389).

MARK 6:14–29

1. Witherington, *Gospel of Mark*, 214.
2. Marcus provides a detailed comparison of the two sources, Mark and Josephus, in *Mark 1–8*, 399–400. He also suspects that Mark's repeated use of the title "king" when referring to Herod is not simply a mistake but "an example of the evangelist's irony. . . . We see that this supposed 'king' is not even in control of himself, much less of his subjects" (398).
3. Myers et al., *"Say to This Mountain,"* 72–73.
4. Spencer, *Dancing Girls*, 54.
5. Isaac Ottoni Wilhelm, group Bible study of September 8, 2005.
6. In her helpful exploration of Herodias and Salome's roles in the death of John the Baptist, Janice Capel Anderson notes the tendency among scholars to lay the blame for John's demise on Herod's wife and daughter, as well as the frequent artistic depictions of Salome as seductress at her father's banquet. Capel Anderson alerts readers to be aware of those who "project upon woman what they fear or do not like in themselves, their own desire and violence." Janice Capel Anderson, "Feminist Criticism: The Dancing Daughter," in *Mark and Method: New Approaches in Biblical Studies*, ed., Janice Capel Anderson and Stephen D. Moore (Minneapolis: Fortress Press, 1992), 126.
7. The Church of the Brethren decided to adopt the following description of its mission and ministry based in part on its understanding of discipleship in relation to the teaching and example of Jesus Christ: "Another Way of Living: Continuing the Work of Jesus. Peacefully. Simply. Together."
8. John Howard Yoder, *The Politics of Jesus* (Grand Rapids: Wm. B. Eerdmans Publishing Co., 1972), 62–63. Yoder explores John's prophetic ministry and its political consequences as it relates to that of Jesus in chapter 2.

MARK 6:30–56

1. Amy Gall Ritchie, group Bible study of September 8, 2005.

MARK 6:30–44

1. It seems incredible to imagine people outrunning a boat as it makes its way across the sea. But if, as Guelich suggests, Jesus and his companions are moving from one cove to another along the relatively secluded shoreline between Tiberius and Bethsaida, then this is entirely possible. See Robert A. Guelich, *Mark 1–8:26*, Word Biblical Commentary, 34A (Dallas: Word Books, 1989), 340.

2. Marcus, *Mark 1–8*, 406 and 417.
3. Since a typical day's wage for a laborer was a denarius, two hundred denarii would have represented an enormous sum for the disciples to procure, especially since Jesus had recently instructed them to take "no bread, no bag, no money" for their missionary journey (6:8).

MARK 6:45–52

1. Marcus, *Mark 1–8*, 423.
2. Ibid., 426.
3. Donahue and Harrington note that the traditional translation "it is I" does not do justice to the rich connotations of the Greek phrase *egō eimi* and "can obscure the echo of the powerful OT divine revelational formula, 'I am' used in the context of God's saving presence (Exod. 3:14; Isa. 41:4; 43:10–11)" (*Gospel of Mark*, 213).

MARK 6:53–56

1. The words of this simple poem are recorded in Doris Janzen Longacre, *More-with-Less Cookbook* (Scottdale, PA: Herald Press, 1976), 59. Another verse reads, "Let it not lie uncared for, unwanted. So often bread is taken for granted."
2. Jeffrey D. Sachs, *The End of Poverty: Economic Possibilities for Our Time* (New York: Penguin Press, 2005), 1–3.
3. Desmond Tutu, *An African Prayer Book* (New York: Doubleday, 1995), 117.
4. Many Jewish organizations were involved in the March on Washington on April 29, 2006, to advocate for U.S. intervention in Darfur.

MARK 7:1–23

1. For a fuller exploration of the many complex and controversial source- and form-critical approaches to Mark 7:1–23, see Guelich, *Mark 1–8:26*, 360–62, and Donahue and Harrington, *Gospel of Mark*, 226–28.

MARK 7:1–8

1. See Witherington, *Gospel of Mark*, 224. By the end of the second century CE, numerous oral traditions (including those related to handwashing) were recorded and edited by Judah the Prince, head of the rabbinic academy, and became known as the Mishnah.
2. According to Hooker, "The tradition of the elders was the oral law, handed on from rabbi to pupil; the tradition was meant to protect the Torah, but grew so complex that in time it tended to conceal the Law's real intent" (*Mark*, 174).
3. Marcus, *Mark 1–8*, 441. Although it is highly unlikely that the ritual of handwashing before meals was universally practiced by all Jews as 7:3

reports, it is nonetheless likely that rituals of purification and other practices served to identify persons of Jewish faith.

MARK 7:9–13

1. Witherington, *Gospel of Mark*, 226, cites the work of J. D. M. Derrett to demonstrate that the term "honor" in such passages as Prov. 28:24 was taken to mean providing financial support for parents.
2. Myers et al., *"Say to This Mountain,"* 80.

MARK 7:14–23

1. Marcus, *Mark 1–8*, 457.
2. As Donahue and Harrington note, if Jesus had indeed spoken words that clearly announced the acceptability of all foods, then Paul and others would no doubt have invoked his teaching when the early church wrestled over questions of food laws and other Jewish practices (*Gospel of Mark*, 227).
3. Juel, *Mark*, 106.
4. Witherington, *Gospel of Mark*, 230–31.
5. See, e.g., the volumes in the Practices of Faith Series, Dorothy Bass, series editor (San Francisco: Jossey-Bass), and Miroslav Volf and Dorothy C. Bass, eds., *Practicing Theology: Beliefs and Practices in Christian Life* (Grand Rapids: Wm. B. Eerdmans Publishing Co., 2002). Richard Foster has also encouraged the practice of various Christian disciplines. See *Celebration of Discipline: The Path to Spiritual Growth,* 25th anniversary ed. (San Francisco: HarperSanFrancisco, 1998).
6. Mark Ottoni Wilhelm, group Bible study of September 22, 2005.

MARK 7:24–30

1. The socioeconomic context of this passage is fully depicted in Gerd Theissen, *The Gospels in Context: Social and Political History in the Synoptic Tradition,* trans. Linda M. Maloney (Philadelphia: Fortress Press, 1991), 65–77.
2. See Sharon H. Ringe, "A Gentile Woman's Story, Revisited: Rereading Mark 7:24–31," in *A Feminist Companion to Mark*, ed. Amy-Jill Levine with Marianne Blickenstaff (Cleveland: Pilgrim Press, 2001), 86.
3. As Marcus points out, although the term for dog used here is diminutive (*kunariois*), "it does not necessarily mean that Jesus is referring affectionately to the woman and her daughter as 'little dogs' or 'pups,'" since the term "can be employed with no diminutive force at all" (*Mark 1–8*, 463).
4. Ibid., 462.
5. To further explore the similarities, differences, and distinct contributions of various women characters in the Gospel of Mark, see Levine and Blickenstaff, eds., *Feminist Companion to Mark*; Spencer, *Dancing Girls*; and Carol A. Newsom and Sharon H. Ringe, eds., *The Women's Bible Commentary* (Louisville, KY: Westminster/John Knox Press, 1992).

6. This and other stories are recorded in Donald E. Miller, Lon Fendall, Dean Johnson, and Scott Holland, eds., *Seeking Peace in Africa: Stories from African Peacemakers* (Telford, PA: Cascadia Publishing House; Scottdale, PA: Herald Press, 2007).

MARK 7:31–37

1. Hooker, *Mark*, 185.
2. Juel, *Mark*, 110.
3. Marcus, *Mark 1–8*, 480.
4. Richard Lischer, *The End of Words: The Language of Reconciliation in a Culture of Violence* (Grand Rapids: Wm. B. Eerdmans Publishing Co., 2005), 11–13.

MARK 8:1–9

1. Whereas the word *kophinōn* in 6:43 appears elsewhere with reference to small baskets used by Jews, *spuridas* is used in 8:8 and refers to larger baskets used by Gentiles.
2. Marcus contends that the number 7, for example, does not have any more connection with Gentiles than with Jews and may simply reflect the fullness of what has transpired in the abundance of leftover food. Similarly, the number 4,000 occurs several times in Jewish sources and appears to be a round number signifying a large group of people (*Mark 1–8*, 488–90).

MARK 8:10–13

1. Myers contends that Jesus rejects the Pharisees' request for "theological proof" because "the sole significance of messianic ministry lies in its concrete, historical commitment to justice and compassion." Myers provides a much needed corrective to theologies that would ignore the significance of Jesus' ministry to the poor and outcast (*Binding the Strong Man*, 224).

MARK 8:14–21

1. It may be illuminating to explore parallel accounts of the feeding miracle (6:30–44), Jesus' disputes with religious leaders (2:1–3:6; 3:22–30; 7:1–13), and other journeys at sea with his disciples (4:35–41; 6:45–53).
2. See, e.g., Fred Bernhard and Steve Clapp, *Widening the Welcome of Your Church: Biblical Hospitality and the Vital Congregation* (Elgin, IL: Brethren Press, 2004).
3. Patrick R. Keifert, *Welcoming the Stranger: A Public Theology of Worship and Evangelism* (Minneapolis: Fortress Press, 1992), 59.
4. Harper Lee, *To Kill a Mockingbird* (Philadelphia: J. B. Lippincott Co., 1960), 240.
5. See John Paul Lederach, *The Moral Imagination: The Art and Soul of Building Peace* (New York: Oxford University Press, 2005), chap. 2.
6. In the foreword to Sachs's *End of Poverty*, Bono writes, "we could be the

first generation to outlaw the kind of extreme, stupid poverty that sees a child die of hunger in a world of plenty, or of a disease preventable by a twenty-cent inoculation."

MARK 8:22–26

1. See Elizabeth Struthers Malbon, "Narrative Criticism: How Does the Story Mean?" in Capel Anderson and Moore, eds., *Mark and Method*, 47.
2. According to Ernest Best, the Gospels of Matthew and Luke omit this story from their accounts because their narrative purposes are different than Mark's: "In Matthew's Gospel the confession of Peter is a true confession, . . . and the confession itself is attributed to God's revelation. In Luke's Gospel the failure of Peter to understand Jesus' prediction of his passion disappears. In neither case is there any reason for preserving a story which rejects immediate complete understanding on the part of Peter" (*Following Jesus: Discipleship in the Gospel of Mark,* Journal for the Study of the New Testament, Supplement Series 4 [Sheffield, England: JSOT Press, 1981], 136–37).
3. Juel, *Mark,* 117.
4. Malbon, "Narrative Criticism," 46.
5. Annie Dillard, *Pilgrim at Tinker Creek* (New York: Harper & Row, 1974), 25–31.

MARK 8:27–9:1

1. Douglas R. A. Hare, *Mark,* Westminster Bible Companion (Louisville, KY: Westminster John Knox Press, 1996), 99.
2. Ibid.
3. Susan R. Garrett, *The Temptations of Jesus in Mark's Gospel* (Grand Rapids: Wm. B. Eerdmans Publishing Co., 1998), 82.
4. Myers, *Binding the Strong Man,* 245–46.
5. Hooker, *Gospel according to Mark,* 208.
6. According to Myers, Jesus is establishing "a new apocalyptic landscape" that rejects all notions of fatalistic abandon to the powers that be: "According to the understanding of Peter, 'Messiah' *necessarily* means royal triumph and the restoration of Israel's collective honor. Against this, Jesus argues that 'Human One' [Son of Man] *necessarily* means suffering" (*Binding the Strong Man,* 244).
7. According to Donahue and Harrington, "the term *dynamis* is used by Mark with reference to Jesus' miracles (6:2, 5, 14; 9:39), to God (12:24; 14:62), and to the heavenly 'powers' and to the coming of the Son of Man (13:25–26). Its appearance here (*en dynamei*) contributes to the eschatological mood of the episode that follows" (*Gospel of Mark,* 268).
8. Witherington, *Gospel of Mark,* 254.
9. This hymn, "If All You Want, Lord," is based on Deut. 6:4 (the "first com-

mand" of Jesus, Mark 12:29–30) and can be found in *Hymnal: A Worship Book* (Elgin, IL: Brethren Press, 1992), no. 512.

10. Dietrich Bonhoeffer, *The Cost of Discipleship* (New York: Macmillan, 1979), 99.
11. Mark Ottoni Wilhelm, group Bible study of October 10, 2005.
12. Cited in Thomas N. Finger, *Christian Theology: An Eschatological Approach,* vol. 2 (Scottdale, PA: Herald Press, 1989), 206.
13. Isaac Ottoni Wilhelm, group Bible study of October 10, 2005.

MARK 9:2–13

1. See Witherington, *Gospel of Mark,* 260.
2. Hooker, *Mark,* 217.
3. Witherington, *Gospel of Mark,* 264.
4. Steve Ross, *Marked* (New York: Seabury Books, 2005), 97.
5. Best, *Following Jesus,* 58.

MARK 9:14–29

1. Myers points out that this event alludes to at least one element of each of the previous healings/exorcisms in Mark's Gospel: the "unclean spirit" of 1:26–27; the presence of scribes and the crowd in 2:1, 6; signs of demon possession in 5:3–6; the issue of faith in 5:34; deafness and speech impediments in 7:31–37 (*Binding the Strong Man,* 254).
2. Juel, *Mark,* 132.

MARK 9:38–50

1. Hooker, *Mark,* 232; Witherington, *Gospel of Mark,* 272.
2. Hooker cites the work of Duncan Derrett, who notes that although the Torah does not specify such customs, other nations did practice mutilation or amputation of limbs as punishments for adultery or theft (*Mark,* 232).
3. Ibid.
4. Torin Eikler, group Bible study of October 10, 2005.

MARK 10:1–16

1. Juel, *Mark,* 137.

MARK 10:1–12

1. According to the Mishnah, two very different approaches were taken, one by the followers of Shammai (who argued that divorce is only permitted in cases of adultery) and the other by the followers of Hillel (who permitted men to divorce their wives for a variety of reasons). According to Witherington, "There is some evidence that some Jewish women in Palestine could both write out a bill of divorce and even pronounce the divorce

formula. Some Jewish women of high rank such as Herodias did divorce their husbands [as allowed by Roman law], but this could be seen as the exception which proves the general rule." This raises "the possibility that 10:12 is Jesus' own comment on the famous case of Herodias" (Witherington, *Gospel of Mark*, 278).

2. Mark's version of Jesus' teaching concerning divorce differs from that of Matthew, which allows for the possibility of divorce when one of the marriage partners has commited adultery (Matt. 5:32; 19:9). Mark heightens the eschatological ideal of marriage, portraying Jesus as one who urges his followers to focus on God's real and enduring presence in the bond of marriage.

MARK 10:13–16

1. The Gospel of Mark is especially attuned to the victimization of children. As Myers points out, every time we meet a child in Mark's Gospel "it is in situations of sickness or oppression: the synagogue ruler's daughter (5:21ff), the Syrophoenician's daughter (7:24ff), the deaf and dumb son (9:14ff)" (Myers, *Binding the Strong Man*, 268).

MARK 10:17–22

1. Hooker suggests that this saying is likely to be authentic precisely because of its difficulty and because "it fits in well with the emphasis in the rest of Jesus' teaching on the Kingdom of God: Jesus makes no claims to independent authority—he calls on men and women to respond to the claims of God" (*Mark*, 241).

2. Myers et al., *"Say to This Mountain,"* 125.

3. In the command to love God with all your might (Deut. 6:5), the Hebrew word *me'od* not only refers to physical strength but material possessions. God's command includes not only physical service but giving of one's wealth as well.

MARK 10:28–31

1. Donahue and Harrington, *Gospel of Mark*, 306.

2. Wesley K. Willmer, "Stewardship: A Key Link to Commitment and Ministry," address given at the Talbot School of Theology Chapel, LaMiranda, CA, April 5, 1994, *Journal of Stewardship: Learning from Research*, Vol. 48 (Ecumenical Center for Stewardship Studies, 1996), 27.

3. Vincent J. Miller, *Consuming Religion: Christian Faith and Practice in a Consumer Culture* (New York: Continuum, 2005), 199.

4. In a study of twenty-eight Christian congregations representing a variety of denominations, sizes, settings, and ethnic groups, persons who regularly listen to sermons voiced a strong desire to hear their pastors preach about

financial matters and the use of material resources. See Mary Alice Mulligan, Diane Turner-Sharazz, Dawn Ottoni Wilhelm, and Ronald J. Allen, *Believing in Preaching: What Listeners Hear in Sermons* (St. Louis: Chalice Press, 2005), 97, 103.

5. In order from the greatest to the least, Maimonides teaches (1) strengthening the name and well-being of one who is in need by giving a present, loan, or partnership, (2) giving without knowing to whom we give and without the recipient knowing the benefactor, (3) giving to one we know without the recipient knowing the benefactor, (4) giving without knowing to whom we give while the recipient knows the benefactor, (5) giving to the poor without being asked, (6) giving to the poor after being asked, (7) giving to the poor gladly and with a smile, and (8) giving to the poor unwillingly.

MARK 10:32-34

1. Lamar Williamson Jr., *Mark*, Interpretation: A Bible Commentary for Teaching and Preaching (Louisville, KY: John Knox Press, 1983), 194.

MARK 10:35-40

1. Williamson, *Mark*, 192.
2. Myers et al., *"Say to This Mountain,"* 132-33.

MARK 10:41-45

1. Donahue and Harrington, *Mark*, 316.
2. As Hooker argues, the reference to "many" here does not indicate that Jesus came to ransom "many but not all." Rather, according to Semitic thought, "the emphasis is more likely to be inclusive: the contrast is not between the many who are saved and others who are not, but between the many and the one who acts on their behalf. It is this contrast we find in Isa. 53.11f." (*Mark*, 249).
3. Witherington interprets Jesus' death as a ransom in this way: "Jesus came to set people free from the wrong sort of servitude so that, like himself, they might become free servants of God, exchanging all false masters for a true one" (*Gospel of Mark*, 290).
4. It seems likely that Isa. 53:12 stands in the background of Mark 10:45. The two texts not only share a common servant language and make reference to "giving his life," but the contrast between the one who suffers and the many for whom the servant suffers is also highlighted by both texts. See Witherington, *Gospel of Mark*, 288-90.
5. See the discussion of Herod and Pilate as rulers who appear to be free to govern within their own jurisdictions yet are coerced by the power structures they allegedly command to act contrary to their own wills in

Alberto de Mingo Kaminouchi, *But It Is Not So among You: Echoes of Power in Mark 10:32–45* (London: T. & T. Clark, 2003).

6. This is one of five significations of baptism named in WCC paper no. 111, "Baptism, Eucharist and Ministry" (Geneva, Switzerland: World Council of Churches, 1982). The others are conversion, pardoning and cleansing, the gift of the Spirit, incorporation into the body of Christ, and the sign of the kingdom.

7. Henri J. M. Nouwen, *Can You Drink the Cup?* (Notre Dame, IN: Ave Maria Press, 1996), 49.

MARK 10:46–52

1. Timothy Geddert, *Mark,* Believers Church Bible Commentary (Scottdale, PA: Herald Press, 2001), 256.

MARK 11:1–11

1. Bethphage, meaning "house of unripe figs," is an interesting namesake given Jesus' impending curse of the fig tree in 11:14 (Donahue and Harrington, *Gospel of Mark,* 321).

2. Robert H. Gundry, *Mark: A Commentary on His Apology for the Cross,* vol. 2 (Grand Rapids: Wm. B. Eerdmans Publishing Co., 1993), 624.

3. Jacob's oracle was "understood messianically in Jewish circles both before and after the Christian era" (Juel, *Mark,* 153).

4. According to Witherington, there were no palm trees around or in Jerusalem in this era, so leafy green branches had to be gathered from the fields to cushion the pathway (*Gospel of Mark,* 309).

5. Hooker offers a careful comparison of these events, noting that elements of each festival may be identified with Jesus' entry into Jerusalem. However, she also recognizes that "John, who knows of earlier visits by Jesus to Jerusalem, agrees with Mark in placing not only the triumphal entry but the cleansing of the temple at Passover (John 12.12; 2.13)" (*Mark,* 256).

6. According to Blount, the Gospel of Mark provides a critical alignment between Jesus' entry into the city and the celebration of Passover: "Passover was celebrated as a remembrance of socio-political liberation. Jesus' entrance personifies the extension of God's kingdom power into the holy city at the time when the people were celebrating the historical extension of God's liberative power through the Exodus event" (*Go Preach!,* 144).

7. Witherington, *Gospel of Mark,* 309.

8. Ibid., 311.

MARK 11:12–26

1. Hooker, *Mark,* 261.

2. Ibid., 262.
3. Witherington, *Gospel of Mark*, 314.
4. In his explication of the term "cave of bandits" (*spēlaion lēstōn*), Blount notes that the same Greek phrase is used by Josephus when he describes the caves where Zealot bandits hid during the initial periods of the revolt. It is entirely possible that Jesus is reacting against using the Temple as a staging ground for revolutionary activity rather than a place of international prayer (*Go Preach!*, 152–55).
5. Ibid., 151.
6. Myers, *Binding the Strong Man*, 305. In this interpretation, Jesus appears to be saying that if even the Temple can be destroyed, then it is possible for other centers of political power to be overthrown as well.
7. Some ancient manuscripts include v. 26, which is most likely an editorial addition: "But if you do not forgive, neither will your Father in heaven forgive your trespasses."
8. Nan Erbaugh, group Bible study of November 10, 2005.
9. This prayer, composed by Earle Fike, concludes with the words "To give is to live." See *For All Who Minister* (Elgin, IL: Brethren Press, 1993), 120.

MARK 11:27–33

1. Jackson W. Carroll, *As One with Authority: Reflective Leadership in Ministry* (Louisville, KY: Westminster/John Knox Press, 1991).

MARK 12:1–12

1. According to Schottroff, the inability to pay off debts was "*the* burning social conflict of the time. The violence of the tenants reflects the economic hopelessness of the increasingly poor agrarian population and their hatred for their new masters" (*Parables of Jesus*, 17).
2. Schottroff argues, "The owner of the vineyard acts like an opponent of God: he does the opposite of what the God of the Torah and the Lord's Prayer desires and does" (ibid).
3. Norman Maclean, *A River Runs through It and Other Stories*, twenty-fifth anniversary ed. (Chicago: University of Chicago Press, 1976), 4.
4. Lani Wright and Susanna Farahat, *Shalom: Christ's Way of Peace* (New Windsor, MD: On Earth Peace Assembly, 2006), 3.

MARK 12:13–17

1. David Daube notes that the question raised by the Pharisees and Herodians is the first in a series of four questions in Mark 12 that parallel the questions attributed to the four sons in the Passover Haggadah service. The first question is raised by a wise son (vv. 13–17), the second by a wicked son (vv. 18–27), the third by a pious son (vv. 28–34), and the fourth by the youngest

who does not know what to ask but whose father instructs him (vv. 35–37) (*The New Testament and Rabbinic Judaism* [New York: Arno Press, 1973], 158–69, as discussed by Hooker in *Mark*, 278–79).

2. Myers, *Binding the Strong Man*, 310.

3. Ibid., 311–12.

4. Boardman argues that this percentage excludes what the government pays out to war veterans. See Pia Sarkar, "The Tax Bucks Stop Here: Resisters Withhold Payment in Protest of U.S. Sending Troops to Iraq," *San Francisco Chronicle*, April 3, 2007, http://www.sfgate.com/cgi=bin/article?f =c/a/2007/04/03/BUGOOP09VL1.DTL.

5. See Ralph Dull, *Nonviolence Is Not for Wimps: Musings of an Ohio Farmer* (Xlibris, 2004), 167–68.

MARK 12:18–27

1. Elisabeth Schüssler Fiorenza, *In Memory of Her: A Feminist Theological Reconstruction of Christian Origins* (New York: Crossroad, 1985), 144.

2. As Hooker states, Jesus' mode of argumentation here appears artificial to most modern readers but it was an acceptable method of exegesis at the time. The verses from Exodus 3 that he cites do not "depend on the use of the present tense, *I am*, since there is no verb, either in the Greek here or in the Hebrew of Ex. 3:6; rather it depends on the belief that God would not have described [Godself] as the God of dead heroes" (*Mark*, 285).

MARK 12:28–34

1. See also the discussion of Jesus' command to hear the gospel in "Exploring the text" of 4:1–20.

2. Donahue and Harrington, *Gospel of Mark*, 355.

3. Witherington notes that other rabbis had combined Deut. 6:5 and Lev. 19:18 in response to similar questions and discussions regarding the greatest commandment of the Torah: *Testament of Issachar* 5:2, *Testament of Dan* 5:3, and *Testament of Reuben* 6:9 (*Gospel of Mark*, 330–31).

4. Hooker, *Mark*, 289.

5. Saint Augustine, *On Christian Doctrine*, trans. D. W. Robertson Jr. (Upper Saddle River, NJ: Prentice-Hall, 1958), 36.30. In section 35, Augustine describes the priority of the love command: "The sum of all we have said since we began to speak of things thus comes to this: it is to be understood that the plenitude and the end of the Law and of all the sacred Scriptures is the love of a Being which is to be enjoyed and of a being that can share that enjoyment with us, since there is no need for a precept that anyone should love himself [or herself] . . . so that we love those things by which we are carried along for the sake of that toward which we are carried."

6. In the full account of *b. Shabbat* 31a, R. Shammai is first approached by the

same Gentile, but Shammai chases him away with a stick. A current edition of this and other rabbinic stories is found in Nina Jaffe, Steve Zeitlin, and John Segal, *While Standing on One Foot* (New York: Henry Holt & Co., 1993).

7. Mother Teresa, *Words to Love by* . . . (Notre Dame, IN: Ave Maria Press, 1983), 75.

MARK 12:35–37

1. According to Witherington, "It is best to say that Jesus is repudiating the adequacy, not the accuracy, of assessing the Messiah by means of his Davidic descent. The point is that in Jesus' view the Messiah is more than, not other than, Son of David" (*Gospel of Mark*, 333).
2. Donahue and Harrington, *Gospel of Mark*, 359.
3. Ibid., 361.
4. Myers, *Binding the Strong Man*, 319.

MARK 12:38–44

1. Witherington, *Gospel of Mark*, 334.
2. See Hooker's description of Duncan Derrett's analysis (*Mark*, 295). Myers also notes parallels between this passage and 7:9–13, where Jesus objects to the practice of Corban, which often resulted in the impoverishment of elderly parents (*Binding the Strong Man*, 320).
3. Keifert, *Welcoming the Stranger*, 15–26. Keifert contends that many congregations "pursue personal identity but not social interchange or mutual activity with strangers" (21) and that pastors and "other performers on Sunday morning are required to expose their deepest feelings in an attempt to create the intimate community" (23). These personal, self-disclosures have the effect of focusing more attention on ourselves than God and, like the scribes criticized by Jesus, render us unresponsive to the particular needs and sacred identities of those around us.
4. Ray critiques social and theological constructions of reality that promote the one-dimensionality and supposedly homogenous nature of women's poverty. It is "a discourse of stereotypes and decontextualized behaviors" that perpetuates the very social marginalization we seek to dismantle (Stephen G. Ray Jr., *Do No Harm: Social Sin and Christian Responsibility* [Minneapolis: Fortress Press, 2003], 7–12).

MARK 13:1–37

1. Juel suggests further that in addition to projecting beyond the empty tomb at the end of Mark's Gospel, chapter 13 teaches that "our concern should be how the immediate 'tribulations' of Jesus and his band are to be understood against the backdrop of the future—and how the tribulations that lie

ahead appear in view of Jesus' confrontation with the religious and political leadership" (*Mark*, 174).

MARK 13:1–23

1. A cubit equals about 18 inches.
2. In light of the history of anti-Jewish interpretations of Mark 13, it is important to recognize that Jesus does not speak of God's judgment against "the
   Jews" in these and preceding verses. As Horsley recognizes, after Jesus' initial announcement that the Temple will be destroyed, "Nothing in the
   ensuing prophecies of Mark 13 . . . has anything to do with the destruction
   of Jerusalem or the Temple. . . . The concerns of the movement Mark represents are the renewal of Israel–including here the ingathering of the dis-
   persed 'from the four winds' (13:27). . . . Mark is clearly not proclaiming
   God's judgment of 'the Jews' and their Temple because they had killed
   Jesus. Jesus' speech in Mark 13 rather focuses on his movement's struggle
   against the repressive violence of Roman rule" (Richard A. Horsley, *Hearing the Whole Story: The Politics of Plot in Mark's Gospel* [Louisville, KY: Westminster John Knox Press, 2001], 136).
3. The image of birthpangs also recalls the description of Jesus' baptism in
   1:10 when the heavens were torn apart and the Spirit came to earth, driving Jesus into the wilderness and empowering him to proclaim the nearness
   of God's reign (see "Preaching and teaching the Word" for 1:9–11, p. 11).
4. Jesus combines the words "good news" and "proclaim" at the beginning of
   his ministry in 1:14 and just before he is crucified when he affirms the
   woman who has anointed him with oil in 14:9. The term "good news," or
   "gospel," occurs in two other key contexts: 8:35 and 10:29–30.
5. Juel, *Mark*, 177.
6. In support of this interpretation is the grammatical irregularity employed
   by Mark: whereas the noun for "desolating sacrilege" is neuter, the par-
   ticiple that describes it, "standing," is masculine and thus may be understood as referring to a person. See Juel, *Mark*, 180.
7. Horsley, *Hearing the Whole Story*, 134.
8. Ibid., 127.
9. Campbell, *Word before the Powers*, 27.
10. Philip Hallie, *Lest Innocent Blood Be Shed: The Story of the Village of Le Cham-
    bon and How Goodness Happened There* (New York: Harper & Row, 1979), 10.
    See also André Trocmé, *Jesus and the Nonviolent Revolution* (Scottdale, PA:
    Herald Press, 1973). Trocmé was pastor of Le Chambon during and after
    World War II.
11. For a moving example of the power of Christian testimony during a time of
    political persecution, see the sermon by Choang-Seng Song, "Truth-Power
    and Love-Power in a Court of Testimony," in *Social Crisis Preaching*, ed., Kelly
    Miller Smith (Macon, GA: Mercer University Press, 1984), 101–16.

12. Thomas G. Long, *Testimony: Talking Ourselves into Being Christian*, Practices of Faith Series (San Francisco: Jossey-Bass, 2004), 5.

MARK 13:24–37

1. J. Philip Newell, *The Book of Creation: An Introduction to Celtic Spirituality* (New York: Paulist Press, 1999), 59.
2. Hare, *Mark*, 176.
3. Donahue and Harrington further note that Daniel's reference to "one like a human being coming with the clouds of heaven" suggests that since this human one (Son of Man) is *like* a human being, the prophet recognizes that he is something other than human—perhaps an angel (*Gospel of Mark*, 374). Also, in 14:62 when Jesus is asked by the high priest if he is the Messiah, he confesses his identity and further associates himself with the Son of Man "seated at the right hand of the Power."
4. Hooker, *Mark*, 320.
5. Juel, *Master of Surprise*, 86–88.
6. Hooker, *Mark*, 185.
7. Mark Ottoni Wilhelm, group Bible study of November 28, 2005.
8. For an overview of the conditions and consequences of global warming see Al Gore, *An Inconvenient Truth: The Planetary Emergency of Global Warming and What We Can Do about It* (New York: Rodale, 2006).
9. Carrie Eikler, group Bible study of November 28, 2005.

MARK 14:1–15:47

1. Myers et al., *"Say to This Mountain,"* 183.

MARK 14:1–11

1. Her actions are so remarkable that the story appears in all four Gospels, with each account differing somewhat from the others. In Luke 7:36–50, the woman is said to be a sinner; Matt. 26:6–13 mentions that Jesus' disciples object to the woman's behavior; in John 12:1–8, the woman is identified as Mary, the sister of Lazarus, and she uses her hair to anoint Jesus' feet.
2. Myers et al., *"Say to This Mountain,"* 184.
3. Borges, *Women Empowered*.

MARK 14:12–25

1. Hooker argues for the historicity of John's timing (the evening of the day before Passover) but proposes a possible explanation for Mark's discrepancy: if we remember that the Romans counted days as beginning at midnight and the Jews at sunset, it is possible that Mark's timetable represents a combination of the two, with the lamb being slaughtered in the afternoon while the meal was shared by Jesus and his disciples that evening (*Mark*, 334).

2. Blount bases his discussion of the liberative significance of the Passover meal on the work of Barry D. Smith, *Jesus' Last Passover Meal* (Lewiston, ME: Mellen Biblical Press, 1993). See Blount, *Go Preach!*, 162.
3. Ibid., 163.
4. Witherington, *Gospel of Mark*, 374.
5. John B. Foley, SJ, "O Let All Who Thirst" in *Hymnal: A Worship Book* (Elgin, IL: Brethren Press, 1992), no. 495.

MARK 14:26–52

1. Myers, *Binding the Gospel*, 365.
2. Donahue and Harrington see a connection between 14:37 and 1:7, where Jesus is the strong one sent by God, and 3:27, where Jesus designates Satan as the strong one (*Gospel of Mark*, 409).
3. Witherington, *Gospel of Mark*, 380.
4. Myers, *Binding the Strong Man*, 367.
5. Ibid., 369.
6. Torin Eikler, group Bible study of December 20, 2005.
7. William Stafford, "A Ritual to Read to Each Other," in *The Darkness around Us Is Deep: Selected Poems of William Stafford*, ed. Robert Bly (New York: Harper Perennial, 1993), 135–36.
8. According to Myers et al., "The first concern of prayer is not to remedy personal distress but rather to seek the One whose will is the healing of our broken history" (*Say to This Mountain*," 189).
9. Hare, *Mark*, 195.

MARK 14:53–15:20

1. Witherington, *Gospel of Mark*, 384.
2. The last time these two terms were placed side by side in Mark's Gospel was in 1:1. As Juel notes, the high priest is also the first person (other than demons and God) to use the title "Son of God" for Jesus (*Mark*, 205).
3. Witherington, *Gospel of Mark*, 385.
4. Although blasphemy was punishable by death (see Lev. 24:10–16), it is not clear that the Jewish court at that time had the right to execute persons for capital crimes. As Juel notes, Mark makes no effort to explain why Jesus is not immediately stoned to death, but he certainly was "condemned to death by the Jewish authorities" (*Mark*, 209).
5. Blount, *Go Preach!*, 166. Blount highlights Mark's use of the verb during the description of the Last Supper and Judas's plans to betray Jesus immediately before this (14:10, 11, 18, 21). Each of Jesus' three predictions of death and resurrection also mention his betrayal.
6. Myers, *Binding the Strong Man*, 370–71.
7. When we recall Herod's role in John the Baptist's death we have yet

another indication that Mark does not intend to exonerate the role of political leaders in Jesus' death.

8. Donahue and Harrington, *Gospel of Mark,* 434.
9. Myers, *Binding the Strong Man,* 380.
10. According to Myers, Mark's descriptions of the Jewish court, the Roman procurator, and the fickle masses "work together to indict the entire politico-legal process of the colonial condominium, not just the Jewish leadership. . . . The powers railroad Jesus because they know he is committed to their overthrow; in political trials, justice is subordinate to the need for conviction" (*Binding the Strong Man,* 371).
11. The lyrics were composed by Abel Meeropol, a Jewish writer sympathetic to the plight of black Americans, who wrote under the pseudonym "Lewis Allen." The first verse reads, "Southern trees bear a strange fruit, / Blood on the leaves and blood at the root, / Black body swinging in the Southern breeze, / Strange fruit hanging from the poplar trees."
12. In his book *War Is a Force That Gives Us Meaning,* Hedges describes endless examples of political genocide and torture by nations and individuals for whom the violent excesses of war can be an exhilarating and even addictive behavior. "[War] can give us purpose, meaning, a reason for living" (Chris Hedges, *War Is a Force That Gives Us Meaning* [New York: Random House, 2003], 3).
13. This helpful and provocative phrase comes from a lecture given on September 7, 2007, by Logan, assistant professor of religion and African American studies at Earlham College, describing the controversial and decisive actions of James Pennington and Nat Turner in their efforts to end slavery.
14. Amos Oz, *Panther in the Basement* (New York: Harcourt Brace, 1997), 69.
15. Thomas Merton, *New Seeds of Contemplation* (New York: New Directions, 1972), 62.

MARK 15:21–47

1. Myers, *Binding the Strong Man,* 384–85.
2. Mark's audience would have undoubtedly been familiar with Rome's practice of crucifixion. According to Hans Ruedi Weber's description of crucifixion, condemned criminals were laid on the ground so that the soldiers could nail or tie their hands or forearms to the horizontal beam, which was then raised and fitted into the vertical beam. Their feet were not supported by a footrest, as later artwork depicts, but were nailed or tied to the beam. Usually the victim "sat" on a peg that was fixed to the middle of the pole. The condemned man died slowly and painfully of asphyxiation, often taking more than a day to suffocate to death. If the victim was to be visible from afar, a high pole was chosen, but usually it measured no more

than seven feet in height. The dead body was accessible to wild animals, who would tear it apart (Weber, *The Cross: Tradition and Interpretation* [Grand Rapids: Wm. B. Eerdmans Publishing Co., 1975], 6).

3. Myers, *Binding the Strong Man,* 386.
4. Ibid., 387.
5. Juel, *Mark,* 227–28.
6. Their presence near the end of Mark's Gospel further reminds us of another woman, Peter's mother-in-law, who at the beginning of the Gospel distinguished herself as the first disciple to serve Jesus (1:31).
7. In his careful examination of atonement theories, J. Denny Weaver provides a provocative appraisal of the Christus Victor theme while offering an alternative understanding of God's saving work through our acceptance of God's call to be colaborers with Jesus in the reign of God. See Weaver, *The Nonviolent Atonement* (Grand Rapids: Wm. B. Eerdmans Publishing Co., 2001).

MARK 16:1–8

1. Not only do the two oldest Greek manuscripts conclude with 16:8, but internal evidence indicates that the vocabulary and style of vv. 9–20 are non-Markan.
2. Witherington, *Gospel of Mark,* 413.
3. Ibid., 414.
4. Donald Harrisville Juel, "A Disquieting Silence: The Matter of the Ending," in *The Ending of Mark and the Ends of God: Essays in Memory of Donald Harrisville Juel,* ed. Beverly Roberts Gaventa and Patrick D. Miller (Louisville, KY: Westminster John Knox Press, 2005), 7.
5. Myers, *Binding the Gospel,* 403.
6. Blount, *Go Preach!,* 189.
7. W. H. Auden, "O Tell Me the Truth about Love," *Ten Poems by W. H. Auden* (New York: Vintage Books, 1994), 4.

GLOSSARY

Apocalyptic. This term (from the Greek *apokalypsis*) means "revelation" and refers to events anticipated at the end of human history. In the context of first-century Judaism, the Gospel of Mark reflects an apocalyptic worldview emerging out of extreme social, political, and spiritual distress. Characteristic of this view is a longing and urgent expectation for the fulfillment of God's promises often expressed in terms of God's reign or kingdom. According to Mark, Jesus Christ not only announced the advent of God's reign (1:14–15) but also proclaimed its presence through his acts of healing, exorcism, and preaching. As a means of apocalyptic discourse, Jesus' parables reveal something of the elusive reality of the divine kingdom among us (4:10–11, 33; 13:28, 34), and Mark's Gospel is infused with prophetic images and discourse that convey a sense of urgency and expectation. The so-called "Little Apocalypse" of Mark 13 is characteristic of ancient Judean apocalyptic literature in that Jesus foretells important events, envisions the end of the world amid cosmic catastrophe, and speaks of divine intervention in resolving the crisis of oppressive imperial rule. But it also differs from conventional understandings of apocalyptic literature because the one who sees into the future is not a hero of the past who is told to keep the vision secret "until the time of the end" (cf. Dan. 12:4), and Jesus' discourse is not offered at the close of the Gospel but before the account of his trials and crucifixion. Most importantly, this chapter does not simply describe future events but promises the fulfillment of events already underway. Some of what has been known will be utterly destroyed (e.g., the Temple), but the renewal of the world is promised through the Son of Man, who will come again with great power and glory (13:26).

Disciples/discipleship. Although crowds were often attracted to Jesus and many people chose to follow him, Christ called to himself twelve disciples whose primary responsibilities included being with him (1:17) and being sent out by him to preach and exorcise demons (3:13–19; 6:7–13; *apostle* refers to one who is sent forth). Among the twelve were Peter,

291

James, and John, who accompanied Jesus at pivotal moments in his ministry (e.g., 5:37; 9:2; 14:33). Peter often served as chief spokesperson for the twelve (i.e., 8:29, 31–33; 9:5). Mark's Gospel highly values the call and responsibilities of discipleship, and in the first six chapters Jesus devotes considerable time to teaching his followers about the reign of God in word and deed; in chapters 8–10 he focuses on what it means to follow him in light of his impending suffering, death, and resurrection. Jesus' disciples share in his mission and destiny; those who take up his cross will suffer persecution and receive a hundredfold God's gifts of life (10:29–31). In contrast to the crowds, the twelve are privileged to receive private instruction (e.g., 4:34; 9:28–29), but this appears to be of no special advantage since their faults and failures persist to the end (4:13, 40; 6:51–52; 8:4, 21; 9:32, 34; 10:35–40; 14:66–72). In contrast to the twelve are several other less well known yet more faithful disciples of Jesus Christ, including the healed demoniac (5:20), blind Bartimaeus (10:52), the woman who anoints Jesus (14:3–9), and the women who follow him from Galilee to the cross (15:40–41) and tomb (16:1–8). The angel at the tomb calls the women to join with Jesus' other disciples and meet him in Galilee, just as he instructed them (14:28; 16:7), but they flee in terror. Like the rest of Christ's followers, it is only after his death and resurrection (and through his ongoing gifts of forgiveness and power) that the disciples engage his ministry anew.

Ending of Mark's Gospel. Mark is the only Gospel not to include postresurrection appearances by Jesus. As noted in most English translations of the Bible, the earliest manuscripts end at 16:8 and do not include the shorter or longer endings, which introduce new vocabulary and stylistic differences (vv. 9–20). It therefore appears likely that the early church was so disturbed by the prospect of ending the Gospel with women fleeing the tomb in fear, saying nothing to anyone, that new material was added later. However, there are literary, theological, and other compelling reasons for Mark to have ended the Gospel at verse 8. According to Donald Juel, "An ending does things. It can achieve closure, pulling together loose threads from a story, or it can resist closure, refusing to answer burning questions posed in the course of the narrative" (*Master of Surprise,* 110). At the end of chapter 16, Mark resists closure by leaving open the doorway of the tomb, signifying that Christ has risen from the dead and will fulfill his promises just as he said (16:7). According to Juel, the disciples are utterly incapable of being faithful and are terminally flawed by fear, but God is on the loose through Christ's resurrection power. Brian Blount also resists premature closure but urges us to take a different perspective, one that compels us to pick up where the Gospel leaves off: to go in search of Jesus and continue his boundary-breaking ministry. He argues that the ending of the Gospel compels the reader/hearer to actively respond to Christ's promises rather than passively wait for their fulfillment: "Mark does not expect [the reader] to succeed, to achieve; Mark only wants [the reader] to follow" ("Is the Joke on Us? Mark's Irony, Mark's God, and Mark's Ending," in Gaventa and Miller, eds., *Ending of Mark,* 28). The ending of Mark calls us to move through fear and failure with Christ's resurrection power as we search for his presence and participate in his reign.

Gospel/good news. The word *euangelion* occurs several times in Mark's Gospel but never in reference to a literary genre (1:1; 1:14, 15; 8:35; 10:29; 13:10; 14:9). Rather, it refers to Jesus Christ and/or the reign of God he proclaims in word and deed. Because "good news" was associated in ancient times with the announcement of military victory or the ascension of a new political ruler (and Jesus neither engages in combat nor establishes imperial rule), it appears that Mark reappropriates the term to describe a new understanding of divine power, success, and political rule. The good news portrayed by Mark is that of God's intervention in human history to establish divine justice, mercy, forgiveness, well-being, and peace for all people. This message is entrusted to Jesus' disciples (3:14–15), who are empowered and authorized by Christ to preach repentance, cast out demons, and minister to those in need (6:7–13).

Jewish religious leaders. Mark's Gospel includes various leaders who interact with or oppose Jesus. As Ronald J. Allen and Clark M. Williamson contend, all four of the Gospels reflect tension and animosity between early Christian communities and other Jewish groups. It is therefore important for preachers and teachers to recognize contentious themes and reflect critically on the ways in which Scripture caricatures Jewish people, practices, and institutions (*Preaching the Gospels without Blaming the Jews,* xiii). We may identify the following groups within Mark's Gospel:

> **Scribes.** Well trained in the interpretation of Jewish law (and often referred to as "lawyers"), scribes comprised the intellectual elite of Judaism and rejected the oral tradition of the elders. In the centuries before the Christian era they replaced the priests as guardians of religious tradition. Their opposition to Jesus often put them in an unlikely alliance with the Pharisees, but not all scribes resisted Jesus' teaching and authority (12:28–34).

Pharisees. A lay rather than priestly group, the Pharisees included privileged members of Jewish society who adhered to both the written law and oral tradition of the elders. They were strictly observant of religious practices, believed in the resurrection of the dead, and entered into disputes with Jesus about fasting, Sabbath practices, eating with sinners, and ritual handwashing. Otherwise at odds with the scribes, they became unlikely allies because of their shared opposition to Jesus.

Chief priests. Residing in Jerusalem, chief priests were persons of authentic priestly ancestry who were in charge of Temple worship. This group included the high priest, his living predecessors, and other priests who exercised important administrative functions. The priests, elders, and scribes comprised the Sanhedrin, the council responsible for Jesus' trial in 14:53–65.

Elders. As senior members of prominent families, elders were laymen of considerable status, wealth, or power. Functioning in Jerusalem, they reflected the Hebrew tradition of wise counselors and were members of the Sanhedrin.

Sadducees. Less is known of this group, since no Sadducean writings have been preserved. As members of the priestly aristocracy, they insisted on a literal reading of the Torah, they did not endorse Pharisaic oral law (the tradition of the elders), and according to Acts 23:8, "The Sadducees say that there is no resurrection, or angel, or spirit; but the Pharisees acknowledge all three."

Herodians. Sympathetic to Herod and likely partisans of his family, the Herodians are only mentioned twice—in 3:6 when they join the Pharisees in plotting Jesus' demise and in 12:13 when they and the Pharisees confront Jesus about the payment of taxes to Caesar.

Kingdom of God/reign of God. As the centerpiece of Jesus' preaching, the kingdom of God is good news that calls for human response (1:14–15; 12:28–34; see also **proclamation** and **parables**). Mark uses the term with reference to God's will and actions revealed in Jesus Christ, who resists evil, feeds the hungry, crosses social boundaries, heals the diseased, nonviolently confronts those who oppose him, exorcises demons, and proclaims God's mercy for sinners. Morna Hooker notes that the Aramaic phrase underlying the Greek *parabolē tou theou* is better translated as "the kingship of God," with the emphasis on God's rule or reign rather than the territory where divine rule is exercised (*Gospel according to Saint Mark,* 55). Although there has been considerable debate among biblical scholars as to what Jesus meant by the term, or when he anticipated the full manifestation of God's kingdom, his parables and ministry reveal both ethical and existential, present and future dimensions of God's reign. It is perhaps best understood as a "tensive" symbol that is able to represent or evoke a range of meanings (see Brian Blount, *Go Preach!,* 23–29). In Mark's apocalyptic framework, the kingdom of God is set in opposition to the kingdom of Satan, whose dominion will be plundered (3:23–27) and whose minions are even now being defeated (e.g., 1:23–28; 5:1–13).

Messianic secret: Silence and disclosure. On eight occasions in Mark's Gospel, Jesus admonishes demons, disciples, or healed suppliants not to tell others who he is (1:25; 1:34; 1:44; 3:12; 5:43; 7:36; 8:26; 8:30; 9:9). Early in the twentieth century, Wilhelm Wrede attempted to explain the "messianic secret" that runs throughout Mark's Gospel as a reflection of the tension between the early church's faith in Jesus as the Messiah and the surprising character of his messianic ministry. From this perspective, it is only after his death and resurrection that we may understand who he is and what his ministry signifies (see 9:9; *The Messianic Secret,* trans. J. D. G. Greig [Greenwood, SC: Attic Press, 1971]). Yet Wrede does not fully appreciate those occasions in Mark when Jesus does not impose silence and/or people cannot help but proclaim the gospel (1:45; 5:19–20; 5:33; 7:36). Both silence and disclosure are key to Mark's narrative, as Jesus is determined to proclaim God's reign and teach his disciples what it means to follow him. Joan L. Mitchell argues that when several unnamed and lesser-known characters speak freely and publicly of Jesus and his ministry in Mark's narrative, these instances of gospel proclamation by marginal characters contribute to the reversal of expectation that occurs when Jesus' closest disciples fail to speak of him when they should have (e.g., 14:66–72; 16:8, *Beyond Fear and Silence,* 80). These anonymous witnesses urge us to look beyond the pages of the text in anticipation of other unlikely persons who will proclaim the good news of Jesus Christ.

Messianic titles and other designations for Jesus. Jesus' identity is of great importance to Mark's Gospel. He is introduced as "Jesus Christ, the Son of God" at the beginning of the Gospel (1:1), he challenges Peter's messianic understanding in the middle of the Gospel (8:27–9:1), and he admits to being the Messiah during his trial near the end of the Gospel

(14:61–62). Although demons and strangers correctly identify him (e.g., 1:27; 1:38–39; 2:10; 3:23–27), his closest followers do not understand him or refuse to accept the humility and suffering essential to his messianic role (e.g., 8:31–33; 9:32; 10:35–40). The titles most frequently attributed to Jesus include:

> **Messiah/Christ.** From the Greek *christos* (meaning "anointed one") and equivalent to the Hebrew *mashiach* ("messiah"), this title most often appears in the second half of Mark and refers to the Davidic king who will arise at the end of time to deliver Israel. Jewish leaders accuse Jesus of blasphemy when he claims to be the Messiah (14:61–62); Roman leaders deride his royal status as **King of the Jews** (15:26–32). The concept of a suffering, dying Christ defies conventional expectations, and by applying it to Jesus, Mark radically reorients our understanding of messianic rule.

> **Son of Man.** The most frequent epithet for Jesus, it occurs exclusively on his lips as a self-designation (e.g., 2:10; 2:28; 8:31; 9:31; 10:33; 13:26). "Son of Man" does not necessarily denote messianic status; however, references in Daniel 7, *1 Enoch,* and *4 Ezra* describe a heavenly figure with divine honor and power.

> **Son of God.** Jesus is called God's Son by a divine voice at his baptism (1:11) and transfiguration (9:7) as well as by numerous demons (e.g., "Holy One of God" in 1:24; "Son of the Most High God" in 5:7) and the Roman centurion (15:39), all of whom confess his identity even if they do not accept or understand his authority. The term most certainly carries royal overtones.

> **Son of David.** As the earthly, national, and political title of the ruler of Israel, "Son of David" recalls 2 Samuel 7:12–16 and Psalm 89 where God promises an offspring to David who will occupy his throne and secure Israel's well-being. Blind Bartimaeus (10:47–48) and the crowds outside Jerusalem (11:11) recognize Jesus as David's rightful descendant and heir.

> **Prophet.** Jesus is frequently thought of as a prophet in Mark's account and even refers to himself as such (e.g., 6:4). He suffers the fate of God's prophets (rejection, suffering, death, vindication) and keeps company with Moses and Elijah (9:2–8). Although some confuse Jesus with Elijah (6:15; 8:28), it is John the Baptist who fulfills Elijah's role (1:2, 6; 9:13; see also 2 Kgs. 1:8).

Parables. The Greek word *parabolē* refers to something that is "thrown alongside" something else, resulting in the collision of two distinct worlds (e.g., that of God and that of humankind). Perhaps the most widely known definition is C. H. Dodd's: "At its simplest the parable is a metaphor or simile drawn from nature or common life, arresting the hearer by its vividness or strangeness, and leaving the mind in sufficient doubt about its precise application to tease it into active thought" (*The Parables of the Kingdom*, rev. ed. [New York: Charles Scribner's Sons, 1961], 5). Recognizing the history of parabolic teaching in Judaism, Luise Schottroff insists, "A parable is not to be regarded as a genre of its own, but as part of the genre of public Torah teaching and prophecy" (*The Parables of Jesus* [Minneapolis: Fortress Press, 2006], 108). Although Mark includes considerably fewer parables than the other evangelists, the fourth chapter overflows with them. They were Jesus' preferred mode of discourse ("he did not speak to them except in parables," 4:34) and several are scattered throughout the text, including numerous brief, pithy sayings (e.g., 2:21–22; 13:28; cf. 12:1–11). Jesus' parables disclose something vital about God's reign; they are not intended to describe a particular historical event but a political or social structure that invites our critical and theological reflection, as well as our application and response.

Power. The power of God permeates Mark's Gospel as Jesus battles earthly opponents and engages in a cosmic struggle with the forces of evil. He reveals God's power through miracles (6:2, 5, 14; 9:39) and associates it with God's reign (9:2) and the divine will to overcome death (12:24). Jesus describes the Son of Man, who will come "with great power and glory" (13:25–26) and be "seated at the right hand of the Power" (14:62). He not only announces God's power to bind Satan ("the strong man" of 3:23–27), but he repeatedly demonstrates power to overcome evil spirits (e.g., 1:23–28; 5:1–13; 9:14–29). When faith is present (that is, faith in God's life-giving will to act on our behalf and not faith in particular beliefs or doctrines), the power of God is accessible to those in need (e.g., 5:34; 9:14–29), but when faith is absent, so is God's power (e.g., 6:4–5; 9:14–29). Authorized by God and empowered by the Holy Spirit, Jesus exercises power differently than those who oppose him; he never uses power to coerce or control people. Even when others crucify him, he refuses to respond violently or vengefully and makes a way through death to newness of life. As Charles Campbell argues, Jesus turns "the world's notions of power and rule and authority on their heads" (*Word before the Powers*, 48). After his death, he forgives those who betray him and calls his disciples to follow him anew (16:7). Their ministry also is divinely empowered, as Jesus sends the disciples out to proclaim God's reign, exorcise demons, and serve others (6:7–13).

Proclamation. From the very beginning of his ministry, Jesus proclaims the nearness of God's reign, calling people to repent and believe the good news he inaugurates among them (1:14–15). In preaching "the good news" (e.g., 1:14; 13:10; 14:9), or more generally "the message" (e.g., 1:38–39; 3:14), Jesus' proclamation cannot be reduced to any one doctrine or event. It is related to the whole of God's reign and way of being in the world, including Christ's death and resurrection. According to Brian Blount, Jesus' proclamation not only declares God's intervention in human history but also effects it; through his words and interactions with others, Jesus enters human reality with the purpose of transforming it (*Go Preach!*, 91–92). His proclamation of God's reign includes preaching as well as other acts of divine intervention such as exorcising demons, healing the diseased, eating with outcasts, teaching disciples, and confronting those who oppose God's reign. Jesus entrusts this ministry of proclamation to his disciples, who also preach repentance, cast out demons, and heal many who are ill (6:12–13). However, by the end of the Gospel, all of Jesus' followers have denied him or fled the empty tomb in fearful silence, leaving us to wonder who will continue the gospel message. Mark leads the way for future generations of Christ's followers to go where the messenger points and to proclaim the good news to others while searching for the living Christ (16:7).

SELECT BIBLIOGRAPHY

Allen, Ronald J., and Clark M. Williamson, *Preaching the Gospels without Blaming the Jews: A Lectionary Commentary.* Louisville, KY: Westminster John Knox Pres, 2004.

Beck, Robert R. *Nonviolent Story: Narrative Conflict Resolution in the Gospel of Mark.* Maryknoll, NY: Orbis Books, 1996.

Belo, Fernando. *A Materialist Reading of the Gospel of Mark.* Trans. Matthew J. O'Connell. New York: Maryknoll Books, 1981.

Blount, Brian K. *Go Preach! Mark's Kingdom Message and the Black Church Today.* Maryknoll, NY: Orbis Books, 1998.

Blount, Brian K., and Gary W. Charles. *Preaching Mark in Two Voices.* Louisville, KY: Westminster John Knox Press, 2002.

Boring, M. Eugene. *Mark: A Commentary.* New Testament Library. Louisville, KY: Westminster John Knox Press, 2006.

Campbell, Charles L. *The Word before the Powers: An Ethic of Preaching.* Louisville, KY: Westminster John Knox Press, 2002.

Donahue, John R., SJ, and Daniel J. Harrington, SJ. *The Gospel of Mark.* Sacra Pagina. Collegeville, MN: Liturgical Press, 2002.

Gaventa, Beverly Roberts, and Patrick D. Miller, eds. *The Ending of Mark and the Ends of God: Essays in Memory of Donald Harrisville Juel.* Louisville, KY: Westminster John Knox Press, 2005.

Geddert, Timothy J. *Mark.* Believers Church Bible Commentary. Scottdale, PA: Herald Press, 2001.

Guelich, Robert A. *Mark 1–8:26.* Word Biblical Commentary, 34A. Dallas: Word Books, 1989.

Gundry, Robert H. *Mark: A Commentary on His Apology for the Cross.* 2 vols. Grand Rapids: Wm. B. Eerdmans Publishing Co., 1993.

Harrington, Daniel J., SJ. *What Are They Saying about Mark?* New York: Paulist Press, 2004.

Hooker, Morna D. *The Gospel according to Saint Mark.* Black's New Testament Commentary. London: Hendrickson Publishers, 1991.

Juel, Donald H. *Mark.* Augsburg Commentary on the New Testament. Minneapolis: Augsburg Press, 1990.

———. *A Master of Surprise: Mark Interpreted.* Minneapolis: Fortress Press, 1994.

Levine, Amy-Jill, ed. *A Feminist Companion to Mark.* With Marianne Blicken-staff. Cleveland: Pilgrim Press, 2001.

Marcus, Joel. *Mark 1–8.* Anchor Bible 27. New York: Doubleday, 2000.

Miller, Susan. *Women in Mark's Gospel.* Journal for the Study of the New Testament, Supplement Series 259. New York: Continuum, 2004.

Mitchell, Joan L. *Beyond Fear and Silence: A Feminist-Literary Reading of Mark.* New York: Continuum, 2001.

Myers, Ched. *Binding the Strong Man: A Political Reading of Mark's Story of Jesus.* Maryknoll, NY: Orbis Books, 1990.

Spencer, F. Scott. *Dancing Girls, Loose Ladies, and Women of the Cloth: The Women in Jesus' Life.* New York: Continuum, 2004.

Telford, W. R. *The Theology of the Gospel of Mark.* New Testament Theology. Cambridge: Cambridge University Press, 1999.

Witherington, Ben, III. *The Gospel of Mark: A Socio-Rhetorical Commentary.* Grand Rapids: Wm. B. Eerdmans Publishing Co., 2001.